SCOTLAND'S EVANGELIST: D.P. THOMSON

—

A new biography

Frank Bardgett

British Library Cataloguing in Publication Data:
A catalogue record for this publication
is available from the British Library

ISBN 978-1-871828-71-9

Typeset in 11 pt. Garamond
at 35 Dunbar Rd, Haddington

Printed by Thomson Litho, East Kilbride

Publication supported by the Drummond Trust,
3 Pitt Terrace, Stirling

Contents

Illustrations

* The originals from which these illustrations were taken are held in the D. P. Thomson Archive and are reproduced courtesy of the Council on Mission and Discipleship.

+ The originals from which these illustrations were taken were kindly made available for reproduction by Mr Robert Rothnie.

All other illustrations, not otherwise attributed, derive from those of DP's lantern slides gifted first to Rev. David J. Torrance and then to the author.

Front cover. From a box of slides entitled: 'Samuel Rutherford Memorial Service at Anwoth.'

ACKNOWLEDGEMENTS

Without permission to explore the D. P. Thomson Archive from the Church of Scotland's Board of National Mission and its successor, the Council on Mission and Discipleship, a research grant and their open-handed consent to my use of copyright materials, clearly this book would have been impossible. The Rev. Douglas A. O. Nicol's former Department also made available the minutes of National Mission's predecessors, the Home Mission Committee and the Home Board of the Church of Scotland. Thanks are also due to the Strathmartine Trust for a grant towards research costs and to Rev. David J. Torrance for a number of DP's lantern lecture slides, given to him at the closure of the St Ninian's Centre. Financial support towards publication from the Drummond Trust, 3 Pitt Terrace, Stirling, and the Handsel Trust, is gratefully acknowledged.

Consent for the use of copyright extracts was also kindly granted by: Rev. Dr Ian B. Doyle for the text of the chorus *Tell Scotland*; Action of Churches Together in Scotland for the *Tell Scotland* papers; New College Library: The University of Edinburgh Library, for The John White papers and The Tom Allan Papers; The William Temple Foundation for an extract from *Christian Engagement with the Secular World: The William Temple Foundation and its Origins and History*; St John's in the City Presbyterian Church, Wellington, New Zealand, for an extract from *Church Standing Tall*; The World Council of Churches for extracts from *Ecumenical Studies: Evangelism in Scotland*. Further thanks are due to the editors of *Life & Work*, and of the *Dunfermline Press*, for extracts as cited in the Endnotes; and to Mr Robert Rothnie and Mrs Marsaili Mackinnon for assisting with illustrations. I have not attempted, Wikipedia-style, to reference every assertion but sources of the more significant are mentioned in the text itself or in more detail in the Endnotes. I have certainly benefited from conversations with Rev. Sandy C. Forsyth, currently researching the Missiology of Tom Allan. The section on Sources offers a fuller list of materials that have been consulted.

I never personally met D. P. Thomson; my own route into Christian mission came through Scripture Union Scotland and the witness of Rev. Richard B. Gorrie. While in broad sympathy with DP's theological approach as it developed, I have primarily approached this project as a historical investigation, seeking to understand DP's life, faith and times on the basis of written records, whether manuscript or published. I have attempted to discuss issues rather than personalities when exploring the controversies of the period and for this reason I have not followed a wholly chronological approach to the narrative of events. Readers will discover some overlap between chapters. A timeline is offered to avert possible confusion.

As research progressed, conversations with those who did know D. P. Thomson were invaluable. Quotations from a small number of a much larger group are cited in the text. I wish particularly to thank those who made perceptive comments on pre-publication drafts and Dr John Berkeley, Rev. Dr Ian Doyle, Rev. Bob Jones, Rev. Ian and Mrs Elsie Moir, Rev. Peter Neilson, Rev. Douglas A.O. Nicol, Rev. Bill and Mrs Betsy Shannon, Rev. David W. Torrance, Miss Molly Wilkie and Douglas and Mary Wiseman for their encouragement along the way. This book would never have been published without the enabling of Rev. Jock Stein or without my wife Alison's patient support.

Remembering, too, the late Brian Burden, an elder of the Church, counsellor and friend.

Tigh an Iasgair, Boat of Garten
October 2010

Research and publication supported by:

The Church of Scotland Council on Mission and Discipleship

The Strathmartine Trust

The Drummond Trust

The Handsel Trust

D. P. Thomson's life and times: a brief guide

1896, May 17th	D. P. Thomson born, Dundee
1907, Nov. 10th	The date DP later kept as 'New birth in Jesus Christ'
1909	Thomson family moved to St Andrews
1912	Thomson family moved back to Dundee: DP left school and began work in Dundee
1913, October	DP became a communicant member of the McCheyne Memorial congregation of the U. F. Church of Scotland
1914, August	**Britain declared war on Germany**
1914, September	DP enlisted with the Seaforth Highlanders
1914, November	DP commissioned 2nd Lieutenant, Army Service Corps; training and initial postings in Scotland
1915, March	DP posted to Le Havre, France
1915, August	DP's first public sermon preached, Chapelle Evangelique Methodiste, Rue Thiers, Le Havre, France
1915, November	DP posted to Salonica, Greece: continued his 'Soldiers' Own Gospel Campaign' ministry
1916, April	DP challenged to a full evangelistic ministry
1916, June - Sept.	DP invalided first to Malta and then to Britain
1916-17	The ASC posted DP to Dunfermline; he engaged in *ad hoc* evangelistic preaching
1917, October	DP discharged from the Army as unfit; took up appointment as Scottish Organiser and Deputation Secretary for the Heart of Africa Mission; also began studies at the Bible Training Institute, Glasgow, and at the School of Study and Training run by the United Free Church College, Glasgow
1918, May	DP resigned from the Heart of Africa Mission

1918, June	DP began a series of part time appointments as Locum or Assistant at United Free congregations, first with Glasgow: Wallneuk; continued studies to obtain university access
1918, November	**End of the First World War**
1919, October	DP began M.A. degree course, Glasgow University
1921, March	DP's first evangelistic mission as solo visiting preacher at Kilmarnock: Glencairn United Free Church
1921, September	Thomson home at Hyndford Terrace, Dundee, sold
1921, December	DP's week at the Fraserburgh Revival
1922, March	The Glasgow Students' Evangelistic Union formed
1922, June	DP graduated M.A. from Glasgow University
1922, October	DP began training for the ministry of Word and Sacrament at the United Free Church College, Glasgow
1923, January	Trading company 'Thomson & Cowan' formed
1924	Thomson & Cowan published the series *Handbooks of Modern Evangelism* and other books
1924, February	DP suspended his training for the ministry
1924, autumn	'The Manhood Campaigns' with Eric Liddell
1925	DP resumed training for the ministry
1928, February	DP ordained and inducted to the Dunfermline: Gillespie congregation of the United Free Church
1929, May	Union of the United Free Church with the established Church of Scotland
1931, January	Edinburgh Colleges Evangelical Union retreat at Deepsykehead, West Lothian
1931, spring	DP's 'Oxford Group' phase at its height
1931, May	West Fife Retreat and Conference Centres opened Glassiebarns
1931, October	Glasgow Conference of the Church of Scotland 'Forward Movement'

1934, summer	St Ninian's, Lassodie acquired and refitted as a Residential Centre with DP as Warden; followed by the creation of the Lassodie Press
1934, November	DP demitted from Dunfermline: Gillespie Memorial
1934, December	DP appointed as part-time Evangelist of the Church with responsibility for Seaside Missions and Camps
1937, March	Opening of the 'Recall to Religion' campaign of the Scottish Churches
1937, December	DP's appointment with Home Board expired
1937, November to 1938, March	DP and Rev. Jack S. Malloch led a mission in Jamaica at the invitation of the Presbyterian Church
1938, September	Marriage of D. P. Thomson with Miss Mary Rothnie
1939, March	DP inducted as parish minister at Cambuslang: Trinity
1939, September	**Britain declared war on Germany**
1940, May	The Commission for the Interpretation of God's Will in the Present Crisis, chaired by the Rev. Prof. John Baillie, appointed by the General Assembly of the Church of Scotland
1940, September	DP's renewed offer of service to the Home Board rejected
1941, March	Major German bombing raids over Clydebank
1942, March	Formal creation of the Church of Scotland Fellowship in Evangelism
1944, September	The Lassodie Press and The West Fife Retreat and Conference Centres wound up
1945, May	**End of Second World War in Europe: surrender of Germany**
1945, August	**Surrender of Japan**
1945, October	DP demitted from Cambuslang: Trinity and offered his services to the Home Board
1946, January	DP appointed as the Home Board Organiser for Seaside Services and Summer Camp Work

1947, September	Mission at Glasgow: North Kelvinside: Rev. Tom Allan, minister
1949, January	DP appointed as Evangelist under the Home Board
1949, spring	Fellowship in Evangelism ceased to function
1949, December to 1950, May	Mary's solo visit to Jamaica
1950	Year of the Glasgow Churches Commando Campaign; also the first Radio Mission.
1950, March to 1951, April	The Paisley Churches Mid-Century Campaign
1951, March	'United Christian Witness' movement created by Tom Allan
1951, April	DP and Mary, and Dr Christine Thomson, moved home to Barnoak, Crieff
1951, August to 1952, March	The Dunfermline Training Schools; the West Fife and Kirkcaldy campaigns
1952, spring	Second Radio Mission
1952, October	Beginning of the *Tell Scotland* movement, initially as the third Radio Mission
1952, April to 1953, Nov.	The multi-phase Strathmore Churches Campaign
1953, July	The 'Work & Witness' movement created by DP
1953, September	Public launch of *Tell Scotland* with Tom Allan as Field Organiser
1953, December	DP's appointment as Evangelist renewed
1954, spring	*Tell Scotland* Inverness, Nairn and Caithness Training Schools
1954, May	*Tell Scotland* invites Dr Billy Graham to conduct an evangelistic Mission in Scotland
1954, August to 1955, July	DP running local campaigns in Edinburgh and leading the training for the All-Scotland Crusade events in Edinburgh

1955, Mar.-April	The All-Scotland Crusade led by Dr Billy Graham
1955, August	The *Tell Scotland* campaign in the Presbytery of Tongue
1955, autumn	Resignation of Tom Allan as *Tell Scotland* Field Organiser: appointment of Rev. I. MacTaggart (until 1958)
1955, autumn to 1956, spring	Local *Tell Scotland* visiting campaigns across Scotland
1956, spring	*Tell Scotland* campaigns in the Presbyteries of Mull and Ross
1956, July to Sept.	*Tell Scotland* campaign in Orkney
1957, May to Oct.	*Tell Scotland* campaign in Shetland
1958	The Glasgow Central Churches Campaign
1958, autumn	Training Schools in Galloway
1958, December	Service of Dedication for the St Ninian's Training Centre, Crieff; DP's appointment with the Home Board renewed and his position as Warden of St Ninian's recognised
1962	DP awarded the D.D. from the University of Glasgow
1966	DP retired from service with the Home Board and from St Ninian's
1974, March 6th and 16th	Deaths of Mary and Rev. D. P. Thomson M.A., D.D.

INTRODUCTION

D. P. Thomson and the Quest for a New Evangelism

> The Church of today is met by a demand not merely for Evangelism, but for a *New Evangelism* that will do justice to the needs and problems of the present hour.
>
> D. P. Thomson, 'Introduction' in *Evangelism in the Modern World* (1924) and also in: D. P. Thomson, *Aspects of Evangelism* (1968)

Christian churches have attempted many things besides their worship of God. They have sought to educate – to serve those in need – to challenge those in power. By nurture they have sought to bring children up in the faith and through evangelism they have tried to extend the love and grace of Christ around the world. All these activities have proved controversial at some time or another, but evangelism has been and can still be especially so. Evangelism, nevertheless, was once part of the mainstream of the life of the Scottish presbyterian churches and in the 20th century one man in particular was known as 'The Evangelist of the Church of Scotland'. The Rev. D. P. Thomson, 'DP' (as he was known), twice held the post of Evangelist from the Home Board of the Church of Scotland and led evangelistic campaigns across the nation. When in 1951 DP wrote in *The Road to Dunfermline* . . .

> To me it has been given to conduct and lead a larger number of campaigns of one kind and another, over a longer period of time, than to any other minister of the Church of Scotland.

. . . already it was no exaggeration: and his longest and most ambitious campaigns were still to come. Yet such national acceptance was relatively recent. In February 1944, Thomson had written in his diary:

> I have to watch that the iron does not enter into my soul – the church makes so little use of me – has so little place for me – and I have so very much to give. No one knows more about Evangelism than I do but they don't want me!

The next month he repeated this strong sense of rejection, of being unwanted by the leadership of the Church:

> No Assembly Committee wants me. No Assembly Commission wants me. The Home Board doesn't want me. The BBC doesn't want me. At 48 is my day done?

Views about D. P. Thomson clearly changed over time, and one purpose of this book is to see why so many came to support his sometimes controversial work.

Though DP was eventually to be acclaimed by the 1966 General Assembly of the Church of Scotland as 'one of the outstanding leaders of the Church in this generation', he was never invited to be the Moderator of the General Assembly. That other mark of acceptance then commonly given to Scottish churchmen of significance, the award of an honorary D.D. by one of the nation's four ancient universities, came to him relatively late, in 1962, 25 years after the doctorate awarded his contemporary, Rev. George F. MacLeod. Although after DP's death short appreciations were published, by Rev. W. H. Frame and Rev. Dr Ian Doyle, no full-length biography has previously drawn on his many publications and his voluminous personal archive of diaries.[1] During the 1960s the style of evangelism with which he had become so closely associated – visitation evangelism – fell out of favour. As the 20th century progressed no further such ordained evangelist with a national ministry arose within the Kirk, so that Ian Doyle's tribute to DP has seemed prophetic in a sense that was surely not intended: 'We shall not see his like again.'[2]

This book, then, is a biography of the Rev. D. P. Thomson M.A., D.D, evangelist of 20th century Scotland. Its purpose, however, is not simply to recall his life, his motivations and achievements. My intention is, by looking at DP's place within his church, also to understand more of the life of the Church of Scotland itself: to examine its quest, conducted over thirty years from 1930 to 1960, for a 'new evangelism'. We will travel the whole course of DP's life, though with more attention to his early ministry (1915-1945) and the years of his national leadership (roughly the long decade from 1946 to 1960) than to his period associated with the St Ninian's Centre, Crieff (1958-1974). For this there are two main reasons, the first of which is practical. In 1941 DP resumed (after a gap of ten years) a near-daily habit of keeping a personal Diary that had begun in 1913 and finally totalled 28 volumes, of which two are now missing. 17 volumes of The Diary of My Life, as he entitled it, were written between January

1941 and March 1959 and clearly these are significant sources for this study. The cessation of the series in 1959 means that with the ending of the 1950s we also near our terminus.

Beyond the practical there is also good reason to focus this study in the central decades of the 20th century. Those were years when the Christian churches of Scotland were growing. Scots joined congregations in increasing numbers after the Second World War, and church halls hosted much of social life. During the 1950s the *Tell Scotland* Movement flourished. This evangelistic coalition, with which DP was associated, was an ecumenical movement created by Scotland's protestant denominations and the Iona Community. It sought to inspire outreach of unprecedented extent and variety.[3] Church growth turned down after 1956, however, and has yet to resume: during the 1950s a historic opportunity to prepare for the contemporary world was missed by the Scottish churches.[4] A close look at D. P. Thomson, a figure near the centre of the missionary enterprises of the period, clarifies why the Kirk's quest for a 'new evangelism' ended in disarray. Surely it is also timely to recall the enthusiasm, the sense of urgency, the vitality, the innovative zest that DP brought to recommending outreach as the primary calling of Christ's Church.

EVANGELIST IN TRAINING

I: Dundee to Salonica: the origins of a vocation, 1896 - 1916

> Monday, 31st May [1915] I have made up my mind, subject to Mother's approval, that I will start off on my own account when the war is over – doing a twine business in Glasgow and district in winter and starting a golf ball emporium at leading seaside resorts in summer.
>
> D. P. Thomson, The Diary of My Life part 2

Enthusiasms of Youth

What brought D. P. Thomson into the presbyterian ministry? His decision to pursue this vocation was made – called into question – remade – in maturity. He was not ordained until he was nearly 32. Entering the ministry of Word and Sacrament was not his youthful ambition. As a committed Christian from a young age, however, he did believe that God was calling him to service within the Church, perhaps to the exciting and expanding sphere of foreign mission; or perhaps as a Christian businessman. DP began seriously to explore his capacity for preaching when the outbreak of war in 1914 compelled him to leave home and find his own way in the world as a junior officer serving with the British Army in France and Greece. The examples, influence and fellowship of his family were nevertheless formative for his faith, enduring lifelong, the bedrock of his life; and it is therefore with his home life that we begin his story.

DP's home and family

For those previously unacquainted with David Patrick Thomson, his own summary of his early years, taken from the second of his four main autobiographical publications, *The Road to Dunfermline: the story of a thirty-five years' quest,* may assist:

> I was born in Dundee, on Sunday, 17th May, 1896, the second son of a well-known lawyer in that city. My father, who was a graduate of St

> Andrews and Edinburgh Universities, was an active Churchman, an interested Home Mission Worker, and an occasional lay preacher. My mother, who was a woman of singular charm of personality and great beauty of character, was the daughter of Provost Pringle of Leith, a well-known elder of Broughton Place Church, Edinburgh . . . I was educated at Dundee High School and later at Madras College, St Andrews, and at the age of 16 I left school to enter business. It was while I was serving my apprenticeship in Dundee, with the firm of P. P. Fleming, Jute Merchants, that the first World War broke out, on 4th August, 1914. A month later I was in the 4th Seaforth Highlanders, a private in 'D' Company, stationed in John Bunyan's town of Bedford. In November, 1914, I received my commission in the Army Service Corps, and the following March I went to France. Eight months later we embarked for Salonica, where the story told in this book begins.

Before our present story rushes on, however, we can now take a more detailed look at DP's home. Against the background that half of the population of Scotland then lived in houses or flats of only one or two rooms, the turreted, three-story Thomson home at 1 Hyndford Terrace, Dundee, was certainly well-to-do. Besides DP's father James (a solicitor) and his mother Helena, his sister Christina (born 1893) and brothers James (born 1889) and Robert (born 1899), there were three resident servants: a nurse, a housemaid and a cook. DP himself, born 1896, as a toddler was under the jurisdiction of his nurse Mary Ann Lindsay, to whose care – professional, substitute-parental and spiritual – DP would later pay a large tribute. His parents were somewhat remote, he wrote, in his early years; as younger children, DP and Robert only saw their late-Victorian parents for a short time in the evenings. The contrast is extreme between this spacious home and that of, for example, my own wife's grandmother, Mary Anderson, a young girl living in a 'single end', working 16 hours a day in the jute mills of Dundee in the 1890s and making her own way in life from the age of 12 assisted by the minister and members of the Long Wynd Baptist Church.[1]

#1: 1 HYNDFORD TERRACE, DUNDEE, NOW KNOWN AS 2 HYNDFORD STREET

#2: JAMES AND HELENA THOMSON, DP'S PARENTS

A description has survived of James and Helena Thomson and of their home as it was in April 1894, before DP was born. John P. Green, on retiring as a Senator in the State legislature for Ohio, U.S.A., during a tour of Great Britain was invited to Dundee to inaugurate a local group of the Society for the Furtherance of the Brotherhood of Man. An African-American, Green enthused about his Dundee host:[2]

> James Thomson, Esq., LL. B., Solicitor and Notary Public – a real Scotsman – a 'right good fellow' in the fullest acceptation of the term, and as humanitarian and patriotic as any man who walks God's green earth, met me at the station, and escorted me to his handsome residence, carrying my satchel in his hand, a part of the time . . . [He] and his good wife of No. 1 Hyndford Terrace, are of the elite of Dundee, and are elegantly domiciled, in an imposing stone mansion, which contains all the modern improvements and many of the luxuries which wealth can afford. Mrs. Thomson is an earnest, conscientious, Christian lady . . . Everything that broad minds, big hearts, great souls and good breeding can suggest, is being done for me by these kind people. I can never repay them.

DP's home, then, in John Green's opinion, was 'of the elite of Dundee', 'an imposing stone mansion'. We may speculate that the senator was over-egging his published reflections a trifle. Yet when we read of the 'broad minds, big hearts, great souls' of the as-yet-unborn DP's parents it is also possible to perceive the origins of his own personality traits. James Thomson himself had been given his start in life by the success of his father, another James, who having trained as an architect, joined his wife's family business as a potato merchant. He eventually sold out to Batchelors and entered Dundee's local politics, to become the burgh's Senior Baillie.[3] His solicitor son, DP's father, was to serve as Dundee's Burgh Fiscal, or law-officer, early in his career. DP began life with an entrée into Scotland's commercial and business world.

Very little of the young David's schooldays was recorded, beyond paragraphs written to fill in pages at the end of his early diaries, and the tributes recorded in his last autobiography, *Personal Encounters* [1967] to his parents, siblings, nurse and cousin. DP's memories of 'strappings' – the punishment then common in Scottish schools of being beaten with a leather strap on the palm of the hand – and of the Boxer Rising (1900-1901), recall how much the world has changed since his childhood:

> [July 1914] It has always been my bitter and poignant regret that I did not start to keep a diary sooner and have had the pleasure of preserving such incidents as the various summer holidays, the phases of my school life, the happy times I had at Madras, the strappings from the various teachers; when I stayed with various people, with Nurse both in Dundee and at Monifieth – with Bessie at Dunkeld, with James in Edinburgh and the great adventures I had there . . . the great week at Crieff Hydro . . . Time fails me to tell too of my caddying for Johnny Burnet . . . in pouring rain when he reached the Final at Monifieth; of my taking up Rugby, of the hundreds of thrilling football and golf matches I have seen of Celtic, Rangers, Aberdeen, Dundee, St Mirren, Hibs, Hearts, Queens Park, Dumbarton etc; . . . of my marking in the Open Championship, of the Coronation, the great quincentenary of St Andrews University in all the celebrations of which I took part, of the great speech of the Earl of Rosebery, of my first sight of Andrew Carnegie. Farther back, of my governesses, of the Boxer Rising, of Cousin Bessie's Sunday Class and before that of her at school . . . of my toy soldiers, of the deaths of [*uncles and aunts and grandmother*] . . . space, time and memory forbid me to tell.

It may be observed that in this retrospect DP mentioned no friends; and, indeed, in a similar passage at the end of his Second Diary (in June 1915), he recorded that he was somewhat unpopular among his age-group during his years at Dundee High. 'At Madras,' however, 'I had great times and there made many, many friendships and one real chum: John Whiteford Stevenson of 4 Kinburn Place, St Andrews, now my greatest friend.' His upbringing at 1 Hyndford Terrace may have been somewhat isolating both socially and even geographically: the house was in a still-developing section of the outskirts of Dundee. An intense boy – and man – DP nevertheless made a number of close friendships.

We jump DP's childhood years to meet him as a young man of 17, hardly a year after leaving Madras College, a senior secondary school in St Andrews. At that stage the family had just returned to their house in Dundee from St Andrews, where they lived (without selling their Hyndford home) between 1909 and 1912. The oldest brother, James Pringle Thomson (known in the family as 'JP') had left home having graduated M.A.; he published books on Scottish History, and was working as subeditor with the influential daily newspaper *The Glasgow Herald.* Indeed, the Thomsons were an academic and literary family. Besides JP, James senior, his daughter Christina Jane (more often, Christine, Janie or 'CJ'), DP himself and (in conjunction with DP) Robert too would in due course have books published. James Thomson M.A., LL.B. was a Fellow of the Society of Antiquaries of Scotland by 1922 and in his Saturday afternoon leisure time he frequented the second-hand book barrows at Dundee's Grain Market. Back in 1912, CJ was still at home. Her 21st birthday was celebrated within a family clearly affluent:

> Saturday, 25th July [1914] This is Christine's 21st birthday and we have had great times today. Among the dear girl's presents were 1) a clock for bedroom from Nana; 2) a bottle of scent from Miss Scott; 3) a Scofield Bible from Bessie; 4) a motor drive of 50 miles from Bessie; 5) a gold wristlet watch from the family; 6) a diamond and pearl pendant from Aunt Elsie; 7) a solid silver jewel case from Mrs Soernsen; 8) £2 2/- from Aunt Mary. Assembled in the drawing room at 1 Hyndford at 8pm were Nurse, Bessie, Father, Mother, Christine, myself and Robert and we sat down to a rare spread. Salmon, ham, chickens, cheese, coffee, jellies, 'snows' trifle, birthday cake, sweets, meringues, etc etc. Afterwards we played games all evening and dear Christine presented me with the Scofield Bible which Bessie had given her in 1911.

Christine never married: perhaps her life opportunities were changed by the First World War. She graduated M.D. and Ph.D., practised – sometimes struggling against both prejudice and continuing ill-health – as a doctor, and remained close to DP all his life. DP's account of her birthday also reminds us that his was a family who, before 1914, enjoyed a good measure of prosperity; children brought up within a local elite, perhaps with that self-assurance or even self-regard that such an upbringing can inculcate.

As a young man

D. P. Thomson's The Diary of My Life part 1 [16 March 1913 to 31 July 1914] offers a picture of a young 17-18 year old who was coming to maturity in the last months before the First World War. At the back of this First Diary DP compiled an index of the people he had come across beyond his wider family and friends: a list of 56 names, of which 42 had

#3: THE THOMSON CHILDREN.
FROM THE LEFT:
ROBERT, CJ, DP, JP

the honorific 'Rev.' There was also one 'Pastor' and a number of 'Mr's who can be identified as lay preachers or evangelists. This young man was very involved with the church! He had four main pursuits in the final months of peace. Besides Christian affairs, he was an enthusiastic rugby and golf competitor, and was also interested in local and Scottish history. The love of history is plain from the carefully written pages recounting a week's holiday in July 1913 when DP set out by himself on a tour by train and on foot – he could cover 50 miles in two days – that took him down through East Lothian across the Border to Northumberland and back via the Border counties, visiting and describing castles and abbeys all the way: 'So this is England!!! Not a bad place: still I am glad that I am a Scot!!' Pages of his diary also transcribed sermons from notes or recollected word for word; further pages gave accounts of games of golf with friends at Monifieth, Carnoustie or St Andrews. Much space was given to blow-by-blow accounts of matches he played with the East of Scotland rugby club – he captained the 2nd XV – and there are hints in the First Diary that DP was a – perhaps *the* – key organiser for this small club. The name 'East of Scotland' seems excessively grand for a club to whose annual meeting only 16 came. If this was in fact an ambitiously-named structure he had created around a group of his friends, that would certainly be well in keeping with DP's later life. Tall (6' 4" in maturity) and well-built, he played second row in the scrum and enjoyed what he called a 'coarse', bruising game.

As DP was not a university candidate and left Madras College earlier than his more academic contemporaries, East of Scotland's rugby games against the Madras school XV were key fixtures. On 1st November 1913 the final score was a draw, East - 5, Madras - 5:

> Saturday, 1st November [1913] It was a rousing, tousing game. I got a black eye when crashing through on my own and just failing to score. Joe Craig got away on his own and was only stopped by my fouling him heavily, for which Madras got a free kick . . . I walked back with the Madras chaps and was complimented on the great improvement in my team. Johnnie Stevie had me to tea and we had a ripping hot bath together and a game of ping-pong, I arriving home a battered wreck.
>
> Sunday, 2nd November [1913] I missed both services on account of my 'black eye' but attended the Bible Class.

Almost no attention in his diary was given to DP's work as a jute merchant's apprentice clerk. He was to recall, in a sermon printed much later in *When Christ Calls* that he felt himself free to be himself only on evenings and at weekends:

> When I was 16 years of age . . . I began my business training, and I began it as every apprenticeship begins, on a basis of commitment. There were certain hours I had to keep. There were certain duties I had to perform. There were certain rules I had to obey. It was not for me to choose what I did at any particular hour of the working day. That was chosen for me. It was not for me to decide where I sat, or whom I worked next, or under. That was settled for me. I was there in that office from 9 to 6, five days a week, and from 9 to 1 or later on Saturdays, on a basis of commitment. I was there to do what I was told to do, and I was there to do it in the way in which I was instructed. But this, let it be realised, was not all-out commitment. It was, in point of fact, a very partial one. It governed only one's working hours. It left you completely free to do whatever you wanted to do every evening and every week-end.

Except for days when he mentioned he got away from work early, there was only one diary entry relating to work:

> Thursday, 12th June [1913] Was promoted at the office today. A. C. Jones, the new 'junior', takes over my work and I tackle the invoicing.

Commercial business, however, was part of the family background of DP's life. As a teenager DP took his own tentative steps as an entrepreneur, buying and reselling stamp collections and golf balls at a profit and less successfully trying to sell on balls of twine:

> Sunday, 10th May [1914] It has been my earnest prayer tonight that the Lord would provide all my capital (£6, I need) free of all interest and that a stock of 1d balls of Jute Twine which looked like being a heavy loss may be yet sold at a profit. 'He heareth before we call.' Oh may my faith increase, may it be even as a mustard seed.

The world was wide in 1913-14; travel was easy under the Union flag and with a British passport, if slow by jet-age standards; the 'scramble for Africa' between the European powers and the age of exploration was barely completed. Still less than one year away from school, tied down to his desk and invoices during the week, DP devoured news and lectures of Christian missions. The foreign missionary activity of the Scottish churches was truly global, with many examples of Scottish heroism and adventure to grasp youthful imaginations. His First Diary opened on Sunday 16 March 1913 ('This being observed as Livingstone Sunday in the Churches') with an account of a sermon about David Livingstone; and on the next Tuesday evening DP attended a 'great meeting in Kinnaird Hall in connection with centenary of David Livingstone'. The main speaker was the Director of the London Missionary Society, Rev. C. Silvester Horne M.A. MP, of Whitefield's Tabernacle, London. DP drank in and recorded as much as he could of what was said. In maturity he even sported a moustache very similar to Livingstone's! Missionary societies whose meetings DP attended in these months included the Japan Evangelistic Band; the work in China and East Africa of the 'Cambridge Seven' and C. T. Studd; the presbyterian Irish Mission; the Sudan United Mission; the North Africa Mission; and the Inland South America Missionary Union. DP had been drawn to the small, independent ISAMU by his 31-year old cousin and family Sunday class teacher, Bessie Scott, and she recruited him to join her in meetings and prayer as the mission's joint Local Secretary, introducing him to the ISAMU's founder, John Hay. The sheer commitment behind DP's interest in foreign mission may be detected in many entries in his diary, though only one can be cited here:

> My renewed and deeper interest in the foreign missionary enterprise of the Church of Christ on earth resulted in the idea commencing on the next page and I anticipate that this work will be a great service of blessing to me and to others.

This 'idea' was a series of 58 proposed missionary lectures. There is no indication that DP ever got round even to the research. An element of teenage fantasy may be detected and he remained a man of somewhat egotistical enthusiasms, not of all of which eventually proved practical and some of which were contradictory. He never did learn Arabic, despite recording a solemn commitment to the cause of challenging Islam in Africa, but the vision of extended service overseas stayed with him for another 30 years, until poor health forced him to abandon his youthful hopes.

D. P. Thomson was a child of the British Empire at its most confident: an inheritor of the spiritual and secular dreams, evangelistic, humanitarian, commercial, that took Scots of Queen Victoria's age across the world. Davie Thomson's Scotland was not far removed from that of Davie Crawfurd, the fictional hero of John Buchan's *Prester John*, published 1910, a youthful Scottish imperialist boys' adventure reflecting the humanitarian racism of its 'white man's burden' era. DP came to maturity at the very apex of what historical sociologists describe as 'the modern' as opposed to our own 'post-modern' world.[4]

Youthful faith

Above all, DP's devout faith dominates his diaries. As a teenager he had an active prayer life, whether alone at night or in small prayer meetings. In *Personal Encounters*, DP recalled that their home was one where 'ample provision was made both for family worship and for private prayer, and where the work of the church and the message of the pulpit were freely discussed round the table.' In a 1951 diary entry DP acknowledged his debt to his father: 'He was a man to look at twice and in how many ways, good and bad, I take after him.' Theirs was a home that regularly hosted visitors from across the world, ministers and missionaries; a home where racial prejudice was combatted. In later life DP wrote: 'I speak as one who was brought up – 60 years ago – in a home where coloured students were entertained every Sunday. How much of what I have been able to do, in contacts with men and women from more than 70 countries, over the years, do I owe to that home background?' At the age of 4, sitting on the knee of a visiting missionary, DP promised to go to see her in Jamaica: the invitation and promise were renewed during subsequent furloughs in Dundee. On 10 November 1907, when DP was 11, he and his younger brother Robert responded to a call to commitment to Christ issued during a mission at the McCheyne Memorial, and their parents invited the evangelist to tea so that the boys could question him further. A man who took anniversaries seriously, DP kept this anniversary through his life: 'Nov. 10: New birth in Jesus Christ.' In *Personal Encounters* he wrote of that day less in terms of conversion and more as affirmation – 'that boyish experience meant at least three things of immeasurable value':

First, it gave us both a sense of belonging, such as neither baptism nor the background of a Christian home and family circle had done. This helped to steady and enrich our lives until the time came for our entering upon the full communicant membership of the Church. Second, it made us conscious for the first time of standing in a personal relationship to Christ, into which we had entered of our own accord, and by which prayer became for both of us something very much more meaningful than it had been before. Third, it definitely quickened and enriched an interest, which had hitherto been mainly dormant, in the work of Christ and the Church at home and overseas, taking us to the many meetings to which we eagerly went from that time onward, and leading us into the various forms of work in which we were both actively engaged before becoming full communicants. Had there been no 10th November, 1907, I have often asked myself since, would I ever have become an evangelist? I very much doubt it.

In 1913, aged 17, DP became a full member of his family's Dundee congregation of the United Free Church of Scotland, McCheyne Memorial. After beginning communicant classes on 28 September with seven others, he made his profession of faith a month later at the Thursday night Preparatory Service for the October Communion. The questions asked were particular to the congregation, the UF Church having no set national formula:

Thursday, 23rd October [1913] Today I took the solemn step of affiliating myself with the Church of God on earth and after a short prayer of intercession I went to the Preparatory Service at 8pm in our church. The Rev. Mr Taylor of Melville Parish Church, Montrose, conducted the service and preached from Luke 18, 37: 'And they told him that Jesus of Nazareth passeth by.' Mr Taylor prayed beautifully and spoke beautifully and drove straight to one's heart. At the close of the hymn which followed the sermon, Mr Sutherland came forward and the seven elders [*named*] took their places at his side. We were then asked to stand and were asked the following questions.

1. Do you accept the Scriptures of the Old and New Testaments as the Word of God, and the supreme rule of faith and practice?

2. Do you believe in one God – the Father, the Son and the Holy Ghost?

3. Do you acknowledge yourselves to be sinners, and therefore in need of salvation, and do you believe that you can be saved only by the grace of God, the redeeming work of Christ, and the regenerating and sanctifying power of the Holy Spirit?

4. Do you believe in Jesus Christ as the only Redeemer of men? Do you accept and trust Him as your Saviour, own Him as your Lord, and engage,

> in the promised help of the Holy Spirit to obey His commands, and follow his example?
>
> 5. Do you accept the vision of truth and duty held by this Church, and the principles upon which its constitution and order are founded?
>
> 6. Do you promise to submit to the Session of this Congregation, and to the higher Courts of the Church as being over you in the Lord, to observe the ordinances of God, to contribute, according to your ability, towards the support of the Gospel and its extension both at home and abroad? And will you study to promote the welfare of this congregation, and seek by a holy life to adorn the doctrines of God, our Saviour?
>
> The pastor and elders gave us the right hand of fellowship, the former giving each a communion card and text – mine being, 'Oh that thou wouldst bless me indeed – and that thou wouldst keep me from evil.'

When he came publicly to commit himself to Christ and to a particular denomination, DP thus chose his family church. Memory of the occasion stayed with him all his life. When in 1969 he published *First Communion*, DP commented that in 1913 he had been profoundly impressed that his family's elder had called in advance of the admission service to visit him personally:

> He came to do three things – (1) To say how glad he was that I was taking this step; (2) To say a few simple but significant things about what it could mean to a boy of 17; and (3) To offer a short prayer for me. That was one of the greatest moments of my life, and the practice is one I have commended since to many hundreds of elders up and down the country in my work among them. Can a minister do less?

As well as being a child of Empire, D. P. Thomson was a child of the liberal-evangelical age. After the national union of the Free Church with the United Presbyterian Church in 1900 both the congregations to which his family belonged, Dundee: McCheyne Memorial and St Andrews: Hope Park, adhered to the new denomination, the United Free Church, while a much smaller number of more traditional congregations and ministers successfully fought to reconstitute themselves as the Free Church of Scotland. Meanwhile the UF branch of Scottish presbyterianism was moving away from Calvinism.[5] The result was what British historians have described as liberal-evangelicism: a mixture of loyalty to the evangelical practices of earlier generations with some openness to take new views about the Christian faith in the light of scientific and philosophical developments. Broadly, the older approach had understood the Bible –

throughout its length and with the authority of God – to reveal propositional truths about God and the history of his dealings with Israel and humanity. The task of theology was thus to systematise and expound doctrine underlying texts. By the late 19th century the new stream of academic thought known as 'The Higher Criticism' held that the Bible had developed over time out of a number of historical contexts, and that its books contained more types of composition than pure factual narrative. There was a deliberate concentration on the figure and teaching of Jesus, emphasising those parts of the Old Testament that appeared to prophesy or prefigure him, giving less attention to, and perhaps acknowledging less authority in, the rest. More attention was given to authenticating religious truth by inward personal experience, perhaps at the expense of the previous reliance on the external authority of revelation. The generation of ministers that led the churches in D. P. Thomson's youth thus preached less about doctrine and more about a personal relationship with Jesus Christ. One reflection of the theological debates of this period can be found in DP's First Diary. Staying the weekend at St Andrews with a former school-friend, DP:

> . . . sat out in the garden and read a book on the Higher Criticism. Ian [Macpherson] suggested playing solders, but I wasn't having any and said I should prefer to read.

. . . and some indication that what he read troubled him is suggested by a further entry:

> . . . I felt greatly strengthened by the Rev. J. Stuart Holden's utterance that he believed the Bible from cover to cover.

The young DP's faith centred on a personal experience of communion with God, to which he sought to respond by dreams of eventual service. He had a youthful habit of writing in huge letters phrases that had really impressed. The largest entry in his First Diary was made on Sunday 28 April 1913, and was the text of the day's sermon: 'Love thy neighbour as thy self.' As the preacher, a representative of the Sudan United Mission, interpreted Christ's command, 'our neighbour' was 'the black man, the yellow man, the red man, the barbarians of the islands of the seas, the pagans of Africa, the cannibals of the islands, the pygmies of the equatorial forests, these are our neighbours.' The call to foreign service that D. P. Thomson seemed to hear so clearly had many attractive notes to a young man tied to a very mundane job: the note of adventure, the note of travel, the note of a world opening up, the note of the essential response of a

Christian to the love of God. He had already begun actively to seek the conversion of his rugby-playing friends, both by prayer and by attempting person-to-person counselling. Some twenty years before, Mary Anderson had also been moved by a meeting addressed by Dundee's own Mary Slessor to dream of missionary service overseas. It must have been a common enough ambition for young Scots in the decades before 1914, perhaps brought into focus by the 1910 Edinburgh international conference on world mission.

One doctrinal issue that especially engaged the young David Patrick's attention was that of the Second Coming of Christ. The connection between this doctrine and foreign mission was strong, being based on Christ's words recorded in Matthew 24:14: 'And this gospel of the kingdom shall be preached in all the world for a witness unto all nations; and then shall the end come,' which on a literal reading taught that Christ would not return *until* the world – 'all nations' – had been evangelised. Successful and thorough foreign mission was therefore thought a precondition for the Second Coming and, as globalisation proceeded apace at the start of the 20th century, many speculated that Christ's return in judgment was near, seeking 'The evangelisation of the world in this generation'. On Sunday 8 June 1913 DP noted: 'After supper had a great discussion on the Second Coming and the Millennium' and on 15 June he was somewhat disappointed by omissions from an evening sermon on Revelation at McCheyne Memorial:

> Sunday, 15th June [1913] The evening subject was No. 666 but was only about Nero and the beasts not about the false prophet and the end of the world.

When 1914 dawned DP was aware that that year saw: 'The beginning of what the 'Millennial Dawnists' say will be the last year of the world': the name 'Millennial Dawnists' was then given to the Jehovah's Witnesses, otherwise the Watch Tower Bible and Tract Society. On Saturday 14 February 1914 he heard a charismatic exposition of the Second Coming by Mr W. R. Tredinnick at a drawing room meeting his older sister Christine attended. The speaker began, DP recorded, by saying:

> This week I have got a solemn word from God in prayer. 'Jesus Christ is even now at the door.' Yes, God has told me that the Gospel has been preached for a Witness to every nation, nothing has now to happen till Jesus comes. The Master may come tonight! Who will be taken? . . . Will everyone in this room be taken if the Master comes tonight? Taken to be with Him there, or will you be left behind?

Those filled with the Holy Spirit would be taken to be with Christ in rapture, while less spiritual Christians, Tredinnick asserted, would be 'left behind' with the unconverted for a time of 'great tribulation.' DP was greatly affected by this 'beautiful – aye – and solemn' address, that night asking himself: 'Will I be taken if He comes tonight? No!!'

DP's circle of family and friends were caught up in the interest provoked in evangelical circles by the *Scofield Reference Bible* of 1909, which first publicised such views as DP heard in February 1914, known under the technical description of dispensational pre-millennialism. Both DP and his sister owned Scofield Bibles.

Further connections can be made. Tredinnick was a representative in Scotland of the Japan Evangelistic Band, co-founded by the Rev. Barclay F. Buxton and A. Paget Wilkes at the Keswick Convention of 1903. Buxton and the JEB retained their connections to the 'holiness' spirituality promoted by the Keswick Convention: and, for its part, the annual Convention and its permanent leadership laid great stress both on the Second Coming of Christ and on foreign missions. Hudson Taylor of the China Inland Mission had been a regular speaker; Amy Carmichael, founder of the Dohnavur Fellowship in south India, conceived her vocation having heard an address by Taylor at the Convention in 1887. Keswick teaching emphasised the empowering of the Holy Spirit offered to those who fully surrendered themselves to God – as was indeed necessary to undertake the sacrifice involved in overseas missions. One particular Scottish connection to Keswick was the Faith Mission, founded by businessman John G. Govan in 1886 following accounts he had received of Keswick teaching. The China Inland Mission, the Dohnavur Fellowship, the Faith Mission were united in holding firmly to the principle that God would provide for their material needs: in contrast to the practice of the mainstream denominations, appeals for funds and similar advertising were forsworn. The circles that introduced David Thomson to the world of foreign missions also introduced him to strains of theology at some variance from the Scottish presbyterian tradition.

The young D. P. Thomson's spirituality was essentially evangelical. His father was Treasurer of the Dundee Home Mission Union, and it was in the working-class world of Mission Halls that DP met John Hay of the ISAMU. For the son of leading lawyer that was a new experience both socially and religiously:

> Monday, 15th September [1913] For the first time in my life I attended the Tent Mission in Peter Street tonight. The class of people was, if anything, a little better than I had expected, the place was no means crowded but those who were there, were just the kind who attend the meetings faithfully all through the year. Cousin Bessie introduced me to Mr John Hay Director of the Inland South America Missionary Union, and we had a chat before the meeting . . .

We have already seen DP enjoying the Keswick speaker and devotional author, J. Stuart Holden. In April 1914 he was preparing for communion with a book by the Bishop of Liverpool and evangelist J. C. Ryle, the leading evangelical of the Church of England of his day. In May 1914 he was reading the autobiography of the ground-breaking American evangelist C. J. Finney. Preachers and speakers of British and international reputations could be also heard in Dundee, as for example:

> Sunday, 16th November [1913] I went in to School Wynd UF Church this forenoon to hear Rev. Charles Inglis, the great evangelist . . . Mr Inglis is like Mr Paterson a man on fire. He put great power into his Bible readings and spoke without a note. He raised his voice frequently and drove home the message well. He was a friend of D. L. Moody's and did much work at the Moody Bible Institute. He has spoken at Northfield Convention this summer and come to Dundee direct from London where he had been taking part in Mr W. R. Lane's united campaign.

Another contact with the world of D. L. Moody came in March 1914:

> Sunday, 22nd March [1914] In the evening I went to Falcon Hall, West Port, to hear J. Charleton Steen of the Moody Bible Institute, Chicago. He is perhaps the most telling lay speaker I have ever heard. He had a perfect command of eloquent speech – and of his emotions and speaking without a note for 40 minutes on the Parable of the Good Samaritan . . . At the close a convert was baptised in the water – I had never seen an adult baptism before and was greatly interested. Falcon Hall belongs to the Plymouth Brethren. The hall was crammed to the doors.

'Speaking without a note' was clearly something that DP admired, mentioning it frequently in relation to sermons he appreciated, delivered extempore, from memory and by the Spirit. Leading preachers of the United Free Church were not neglected. In July 1914 DP first heard the Rev. Prof. W. M. Clow D.D., then of the United Free Church Theological College in Glasgow, and greatly enjoyed his offer of a 'Gospel so full and free.' As late as 1971, in *New Testament Christianity,* DP was happy to write that Clow was 'one of our great Scottish preachers'.

By 1914 DP had begun to speak at Sunday afternoon worship in his family's drawing room, taking such subjects as the parables of the sower and of the tares. Who attended 'the Hyndford Chapel', we may wonder? His younger brother Robert? His 20-year old sister Christine? His parents? Any friends of his own age? That his family encouraged his growing sense of vocation and his deepening – intense – Christian commitment is clear from the presents he was given at Christmas 1913: three gifts of cash, one blue tie, one diary and seven books, including three by F. B. Meyer, a leading Baptist evangelical, friend of D. L. Moody and regular speaker at the Keswick Convention. When in 1967 DP looked back to those who had most guided his early spiritual life, he chose to write about his nurse, his older cousin Bessie Scott, and his younger brother, Robert. As a young man, however, he had connections with trans-Atlantic revivalism, approximating to the legacy of the New School Presbyterianism in the United States. Such Christians were activists, with an emphasis on conversion and consecration and the inward working of the Holy Spirit; missionary-minded and – in line with trends following the Edinburgh missionary conference of 1910 – inter-denominational.[6] It goes without saying that DP's was an explicitly protestant faith. He was a youthful member of the Scottish Reformation Society, and shared something of the militantly anti-Roman Catholic sentiment then common among Scottish and Northern Irish protestants. In his case, however, his historical interests soon awakened appreciation of pre-reformation expressions of Christian faith, thus mitigating his sectarianism:

> Sunday, 16th March [1913] . . . Two years later St Francis died, one of the noblest and best souls that have ever adorned this frail earth of ours. I was greatly impressed by this lecture and half my bitter rancour against the Papists was melting like snow before the noonday sun.

Entries on the Second Coming from DP's diary in part demonstrate a continuing spiritual search; in part they stem from his somewhat romantic sense of history and hence of time; in part they came from his openness to emotional impression. He was stirred by vigorous preaching; he was enthused by vigorous games of rugby and the comradeship in the club house afterwards; he was roused by the sight of a Territorial Army Regiment parading:

> Sunday, 8th June [1914] The annual parade of the TA . . . took place in our own church this forenoon. They are a very fine looking regiment in their colours, especially the officers are ripping. How I wish I were an officer in the RNVR or the Territorials!

This reference to the Royal Navy's Volunteer Reserve came from his friendship with Ian Macpherson of St Andrews, who was a cadet in the pre-war RNVR. DP's political innocence and youthful optimism – which he shared with so many in 1914 – had not yet been shaken by the building international crisis. Church, work, sport and conventional middle-class respectable behaviour seem to have left DP as a young man with little time for the opposite sex, despite his emotional nature. He did note that a 15-year old cousin, Gladys Burnet, came to stay in June 1914; in 1915 they had a date together ('quite a respectable meal' and a visit to a sweet stall and a walk through the streets of Perth to see her to her train). She was perhaps the only girl out of a list of 24 friends and family to whom he promised to write with the distinction, kept for only a few, of a star against her name. Gladys was the daughter of DP's father's sister; her own father was a minister of the United Free Church, and formerly of the Free Church.

DP and the Outbreak of War

Across the lives of D. P. Thomson, his parents, sister, brothers and friends broke the First World War. DP joined up as a volunteer, with from the start a view to the officer's commission that his family's social status might expect. What he experienced changed his life, as it did that of so many others who survived that conflict. Several times the occasion of anniversaries led him to reflect: for example, on the anniversary of his brother James' death while serving as a soldier in France:[7]

> Saturday, 15th August [1953] This is the anniversary of dear JP's death – now 37 years ago. I have had all that time to live and work that were denied him . . . Who would have thought then that I, the weakling and the war casualty, would survive so long . . . It is a solemn thought! What have I done to justify it?

This reflection was simply a later, private version of what DP had made public in 1951, when *The Road to Dunfermline* was published, that when he sought – with perhaps some underlying guilt – to understand why, out of so many multitudes, he had survived, he came to believe that God had spared him for a special purpose, that he should be an evangelist. Only in this way could he make sense of what had happened: his blossoming as a preacher while abroad during the war, his survival when invalided home and expected, perhaps, to die; the further preaching opportunities that came his way and that only wartime made possible.

D. P. Thomson's reaction to the outbreak of war was a mixture of emotions. The sheer size of the event was overwhelming and he sought to understand it from within his Christian world-view. The contrast between what he expected – *both* the end of the world with the return of Christ *and* extra-hard work at the office was at first entirely unresolved!

> Wednesday, 5th August [1914] At midnight last night we declared war on Germany and the Netherlands, France, Belgium, Germany, Russia, Great Britain, Austria Hungary and Serbia are all engaged in the most bloody war that has ever been waged since the World began. By air, sea and land the rival nations are ferociously attacking one another and the thunder of the heavens this afternoon adds to the confusion. I feel that the end of the world is at hand and that Jesus Christ is very near at hand for his redeemed. David Fleming was not at the office today, having left to join his regiment and so I foresee plenty of hard work in front of me. Crowds line the streets to watch the Territorials leave and recruits are pouring in to join the Forces. Verily the end draweth nigh. A German defeat both on air and sea is reported but what can one believe in times like these.

The next days saw further entries about the war, with the contrast now between DP's own family holiday (golfing at St Andrews) and the seeming adventure begun by his 'bosom pal', John (*otherwise*, Ian):

> Thursday, 6th August [1914] The long dark night of the world has commenced, and I really have neither space nor time to enumerate all the things that are happening round about us . . .
>
> Friday, 7th August [1914] Troops drilling daily in the High School playground and garrisons in all the towns around – Wormit, Newport, Broughty etc. People being turned out of their houses to make room for the soldiers . . .
>
> Saturday 8th August [1914] . . . [*DP had travelled to St Andrews, playing golf with his brother Robert and Father*] . . . News about the war continues very exciting and interesting. News indeed – my bosom pal – Cadet John Macpherson – is on HMS Bulwark fighting in the war. Where Ian goes I must follow. I have no earthly idea how I can possibly screw up my courage to the necessary pitch or even if I could, how I could enlist?

RNVR Cadet Ian Macpherson was among the early naval fatalities of the war. His ship, HMS Bulwark, a *Formidable*-class battleship of the 5th Battle Squadron, was blown apart on 26 November 1914 while at anchor in home waters off the River Medway: only 12 of a crew of 750 survived. An accident with the ammunition, and not enemy action, was concluded to have been the cause. Later, DP was to write that he understood the sense of loss a colleague was feeling: 'Since coming here [*Glasgow*] I have learnt that at the Battle of Neuve Chapelle, Friend was killed and Clayton and Garmsey were wounded. I feel very much for the latter as he and Friend were absolutely inseparable, and I know what it was to lose Ian.' At the back of his Second Diary, which ended in June 1915, DP recorded three names under the heading 'Died'. Ian Macpherson headed the list. A long way had been travelled since Ian had 'suggested playing soldiers' at St Andrews the previous summer.

Being at St Andrews on the first Sunday of the War the family attended, in the morning, Holy Trinity Parish Church, whose preacher urged better church attendance as a response to the national emergency. DP and his father went to the St Andrews Baptist Church in the evening, however, where the preacher was more forthright:

> Sunday, 9th August [1914] . . . In the evening I went with Father to the Baptist Church, a cosy, airy delightful sanctuary with a spirit in the air – reminding one of the Upper Room. The pastor, Rev. Sam Hirst B.A., B.D., preached on Judges, 7,20: 'And the companies blew their trumpets . . . and they cried "The Sword of the Lord, and of Gideon".' It was an impressive and moving address to a crowded congregation and the preacher let himself go while the power of God was upon him . . . If the cause is just and right and true, God will be on its side and God will give the victory, no matter how great the disparity between the forces engaged. Germany had let loose the hounds of hell – their motto was 'Might is Right' but God would bring their armies to nought and this outbreak of war had already shown that the barbarism underlying modern civilization came to the front only too easily. I enjoyed his discourse greatly.

By the end of the holiday DP had decided that he, too, must enlist. No thought of any pacifist option appears to have been discussed by those Christians whose opinions he valued:

> Tuesday, 11th August [1914] . . . Great preparations are being made to resist invasion and I decided tonight after long and anxious consideration to apply for a commission in the army – 2000 special ones being offered just now.

> Saturday, 15th August [1914] This forenoon at 10.42am Mother and I entrained for home and after our safe arrival I went in to the Recruiting Office to find out about my commission in the Army but returned home for dinner without having got any information. I was to have played golf with Robert at Carnoustie but decided suddenly to go up to Perth about the commission and went down to the station to tell Robert I was not to golf but did not find him there so correctly presuming he had had a

> breakdown [*i.e. of travel arrangements*] I arrived at Perth at 3.40pm and after considerable difficulty and much walking I reached the Queen's Barracks, where I got showed in to Major-General Gordon, the commanding officer's room, and after explaining my business, was interrogated and then sent with an awfully nice young officer to the hospital to be medically and physically examined.

> Saturday, 22nd August [1914] I left for Perth this afternoon by the 2.40pm train and on arriving there made straight for the Queen's Barracks where I handed in my application for a temporary commission in H.M. Army.

Nothing immediately came of these enquiries but on Thursday 3 September he took a train to London, attempted to join the London Scottish Regiment, failed as it was then full, and – though no Highlander – was redirected to a kilt-wearing Territorial Battalion of a Highland Regiment, to the 4th Seaforth Highlanders:

> I . . . filled in my papers, took the oath, and now was Private D. P. Thomson – no. 2130. I at once wired home and to Riversdale, telling them of the step I had taken and received back a wire in reply from the latter place 'Three Cheers for the 4th Seaforth Highlanders – Bessie,' which gratified me greatly . . .

#4: CAP-BADGE, SEAFORTH HIGHLANDERS

Between 3 September 1914 and 29 March 1915, DP remained in Britain. He trained first as an infantry private with 4/Seaforth Highlanders within the 51st Highland Division at Bedford, in England's East Anglia: 'These eight weeks I spent at Bedford were among the happiest of my life and I had made many friends.' While there he organised a Battalion rugby team to take on the Bedford Grammar School 1st XV and the 5th and 6th Seaforths. On 1 November, however, 'Word came from the War Office this morning appointing me to a temporary commission in the Army Service Corps.' The Army Service Corps [ASC] had behind-front-lines functions, attending to the material supplies of the armies, both overseas and in the UK. DP was now sent back to Scotland to Bridge of Allan for officer training – this included learning to ride (but not to drive) and he was a dreadful horseman. Here things did not go so well and he narrowly avoided being returned to the ranks: only a desperate plea by phone to his father and his father's arrival at the depot to interview the Commanding Officer resulted in a moderated final report being sent to the War Office.

DP's posting at Bridge of Allan was his first extended period away from home with time on his hands. Besides the troubles of his dubious military progress, it was also a time of potential spiritual hazard. At first he shared accommodation with a man who had been some years ahead of him at Dundee High School 'in no way a gentleman'; and he noted that normal talk in the mess after dinner involved 'smutty' stories. It was, however, DP's own playful courting that brought an emotional surprise during these weeks:[8]

> Saturday, 23rd January [1915] I went home to Dundee for the day today with the 7am train. I found waiting for me in the morning before I started a passionate love letter from A. and realised at last with a shock that she was in love with me. There came back to me then memories of the evenings I had slept in their parlour with her soft cheeks resting against mine, of the hours which she had sat on my knee, while I whispered 'sweet nothings' in her ear; of the kisses I had bestowed on her, and I knew I had gone too far. The train was very late, so I had time to return to the hotel for breakfast and ran upstairs to A.'s bedroom and kissed her good morning before I left.

DP was eighteen, A., seventeen. He was temporarily billeted with her parents while attached to an ASC Depot at Stirling after his initial six weeks' officer training at Bridge of Allan. Later in 1915 he was to call again at her home, but the friendship did not continue. Whatever A. felt, DP had not been smitten: a week after receiving the letter he and a fellow young officer were off – on horseback – to visit another young lady, 'the fair Miss B.' to whom he had been given a letter of introduction.

In another way DP was pushing towards maturity during this time. Again taking the opportunity of leave, he visited Edinburgh to make the acquaintance of an uncle and aunt, one of his two uncles in the business world:

> Thursday, 24th December [1914] . . . made for the offices of the Edinburgh Roperie and Sackcloth Co. Ltd, 15a Bath Street, Leith, where I arrived just as a Directors' Meeting was breaking up. This was the first time I had even seen Uncle Pat but I took to him right away: he was very nice to me and after finishing things off at the office he secured me a taxi and spun off to 2 Rothesay Place, which I also entered for the first time. There I had afternoon tea and a pleasant chat with Aunt Jeanie and congratulated myself that the ice was at last broken in this direction and my latest aspirations were beginning to promise success at last.

In *Personal Encounters*, DP suggested that his family had had ambitions for him to succeed one or other of his uncles, both of whom appeared well-placed in the commercial world and without direct heirs; at Madras College he had done well in commercial and mental arithmetic. 'My latest aspirations' were presumably eventual management of the Edinburgh Roperie and Sackcloth Co. Ltd, once the war was over. Another opportunity was soon opened by the death of James Pringle, another cousin, who had worked with Dyster, Nalder & Co. (London, established 1770) which dealt in hides, skins and leather. Careers with either of these companies seem somewhat at odds with DP's pre-war sense of calling to the mission field.

On 3 January 1915 DP heard by telegram that his cousin Bessie Scott had died, aged 33, of rheumatic fever following a chill she had caught when visiting him at the camp at Bedford. He had visited her sickbed for a last time while on leave that Christmas. She left him £10 in her will and with the money he began a lifetime's habit of purchasing books for his library. Bessie's evangelicism became DP's evangelicism when he was a young man and it is likely that his interest in pre-millennial theology stemmed from her and her foreign missionary enthusiasms. In his memory, however, it was her living faith that he sought to honour:[9]

> For all these years I have tried to be true to what she taught me: God is real and He loves you! The Bible is a wonderful book! The Church has a world-wide mission, and it is one in which all of us can share!

In the meantime, on 5 January, DP visited Drummond's Tract Depot in Stirling, 'buying a large quantity of tracts written by the late saintly Bishop J.C. Ryle of Liverpool; also that monumental work, *Thinking Black* by Dan Crawford FRGS one of the greatest modern missionaries.' While in the area he attended (when free) Allan Park United Free Church. Yet DP was still a young man: some weekends off he spent with relatives at Dunblane, playing toy soldiers with 'the twins'. He made a special visit to Glasgow to buy sufficient stocks of toys so that they could hold large battles, with the names and ranks of imaginary commanders and regiments carefully detailed in his diary as 'The History of the Median Army'. The young officer was perhaps a somewhat immature – if large – young man, happily indulging in a fantasy world in which Mohawk and Texas Ranger Brigades served alongside the Irish Rifles and the Grenadier Guards under such commanders as Alexander the Great, Cromwell, Red Panther and Robert the Bruce.

Next, DP was posted in February 1915 to Sighthill, Glasgow, to a unit overseeing butchery and the distribution of bacon to troops throughout Scotland. At times he was to be very frustrated and perhaps embarrassed by his safe postings in the ASC – he had to be discouraged from transferring back to the infantry – but by 1967 he was able to write:

> Had it been otherwise I might not have been here today: and I would certainly not have gained the experience I did, nor enjoyed the type of command I came to exercise, and from which the later years have benefited so greatly.

DP determined to benefit spiritually from his time in Glasgow by selecting each Sunday the most interesting sermons to attend. He was fortunate. On Sunday 14 February he went in the evening to hear one of his favourite Keswick-associated authors, 'that great pillar of the faith Rev. F. B. Meyer B.A., D.D. of Regent's Park Chapel, London.' 'Dear old Dr Meyer was obviously affected by the concourse which had turned out to hear him but preached with glorious power and acceptance on Revelation 5,9.' On Sunday 14 March he went 'to hear Rev. J. D. Jones of Richmond Hill Congregational Church, Bournemouth – Bessie's favourite preacher' but was a little disappointed: Jones preached from notes. Then the same evening he went to Hillhead Baptist Church to hear 'Rev. J. W. Kemp of Charlotte Chapel, Edinburgh, conductor of *The Life of Faith* Bible Correspondence Course, who preached and prayed with great fervour.' Because his family moved to St Andrews when he was thirteen, returning to Dundee when he was sixteen, DP's connection to a home congregation was less strong than it might otherwise have been. As a teenager in Dundee DP's main written source of spiritual input, after the Bible, came from Missionary Magazines, the printed addresses from the annual Keswick Convention, and the newsletter associated with Keswick, *The Life of Faith*. Perhaps he had even undertaken J. W. Kemp's 'Bible Course'. DP's ties to the UF Church came through his family, and hence were enduring, but wartime conditions and his Sunday roving habits certainly attenuated them.

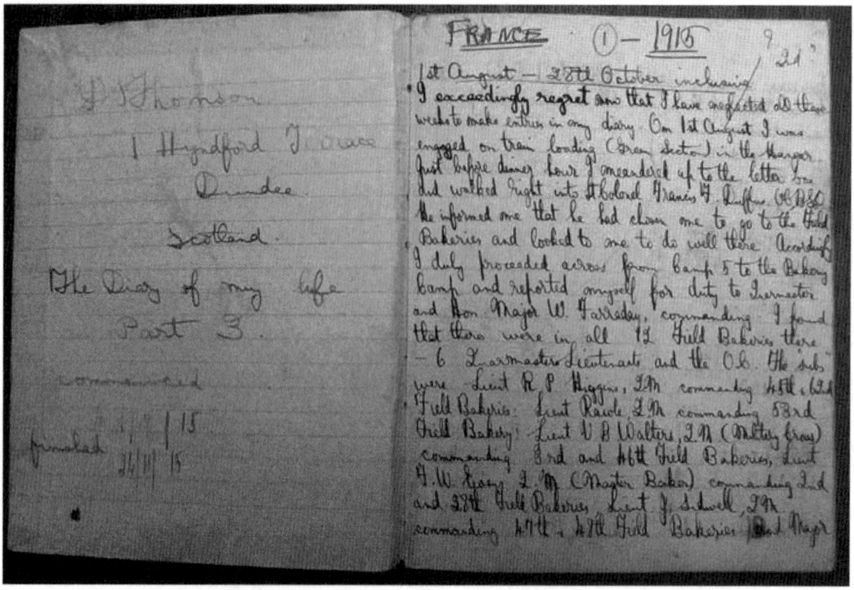

D P Thomson
1 Hyndford Terrace
Dundee
Scotland
The Diary of my Life
Part 3.
commenced [illegible] 15
finished 24/11/15

FRANCE (1) – 1915
1st August – 28th October inclusive
I exceedingly regret now that I have neglected all these weeks to make entries in my diary. On 1st August I was engaged on train loading (Grain Section) in the Hangars. Just before dinner hour I meandered up to the letter box and walked right into Lt Colonel Francis H. Duffus, CB DSO. He informed me that he had chosen me to go to the Field Bakeries and looked to me to do well there. Accordingly I duly proceeded across from Camp 5 to the Bakery Camp and reported myself for duty to Quartermaster and Hon Major W. Farraday, commanding. I found that there were in all 12 Field Bakeries there – 6 Quartermaster Lieutenants and the O.C. The "subs" were Lieut R P Higgins, QM commanding 45th & 62nd Field Bakeries; Lieut Rawle, QM commanding 53rd Field Bakery; Lieut V B Walters, QM (Military Cross) commanding 3rd and 46th Field Bakeries; Lieut F.W. [illegible] QM (Master Baker) commanding 2nd and 22th Field Bakeries; Lieut J. [illegible], QM commanding 47th & 48th Field Bakeries [illegible] Major

5: THE DIARY OF MY LIFE PART 3, PAGE 1

In the Army: France

On Sunday 21 March 1915, DP was informed that he was being posted on foreign service. Within a week he was in London – his brother James came up from Basingstoke (where he was now stationed) to meet him – and on 29 March DP was shipped across the Channel to the ASC main Depot at the port of Le Havre, France. Men, food and supplies came in to Le Havre, and the young lieutenants of the ASC had to see to the unloading of ships and the loading of trains with frozen food, petrol, hay, oats, medical supplies etc. DP's diaries give the impression that his tasks, if time-taking, were not actually too demanding. By May he was fuming at being passed over (again) for promotion:

> Friday, 7th May [1915] Today I hear of more people being moved and of most hopeless idiots attaining to most priceless jobs. I rave with annoyance but am led to understand that I will be the next to go. I pray that it may be to a really good job, right up at the front at last.

On 2 August 1915 a new job was given him, a junior command within the ASC's Field Bakeries Section, but still at Le Havre. Though more responsible, this again was hardly demanding:

I was engaged on train boarding (Green section) in the Hanger. Just before dinner hour I meandered up to the letter box and walked right into Lt. Colonel Francis F. Duffus, O.C., ASC. He informed me that he had chosen me to go to Field Bakeries and looked to me to do well there . . . The duties at the bakeries were very light indeed, consisting chiefly of censoring letters in the morning, replying to what little correspondence there was and walking round the bakeries to see that everything was in order.

Young ASC officers clearly did not get their hands too dirty, and no doubt they relied on their non-commissioned staff, enlisted labourers and the established system to see that things got done.

His posting at Le Havre, however, perhaps *because* it left him with time on his hands, saw DP soon renewing aspects of his spiritual commitment. There was his own desire to be active in foreign missions:

Monday, 26th April [1915] Have decided, God willing, to sell the Sacred Scriptures in every land on earth before I pass home to the everlasting city of the Lord.

A list of missions that he particularly supported was drawn up – a list that is perhaps notable for its lack of presbyterian-based causes:

Thursday, 6th May [1915] I resolved today that as long as I was enabled to do so, I should lend my support to the following missions:

Egypt General Mission
LMS – Madagascar
Japan Evangelistic Band
Evangelistic Union of South America
Inland South American Missionary Union
Mission to Lepers
China Inland Mission

So far, though, DP's spiritual experience had not advanced beyond his pre-war days.

Then on Sunday 9 May 1915 he attended the Chapelle Evangelique Methodiste in Rue Thiers, Le Havre, and began a time of great consequence for his spiritual growth and, indeed, for his entire life and vocation:

Sunday, 9th May [1915] I left the Hanger with the 5.30 bus tonight and went to the Wesleyan Church, Rue Thiers, for the 6.30pm service. I had a pleasant chat with the chaplains both before and after the service. Rev. Capt. Pickard preached with great vigour and acceptance on Matthew 7, 14 'Strait is the gate and narrow is the way, which leadeth unto life, and few there be that find it.' He is a very young minister but spiritual and powerful – urging Calvary as the only way to Christ and earnestly pleading for souls. I was most agreeably surprised. I came nearer to the throne tonight than I have since I landed here and I thank God for a new vision of the life of fuller purpose.

From this point, DP's Second Diary records a real spiritual blossoming through a series of new experiences with committed Christian friends met at the Forces' evening service at Rue Thiers. He was invited to a midweek prayer meeting:

Tuesday, 11th May [1915] This evening I had a great spiritual conflict as to whether or not I should go to a prayer meeting for soldiers held in the Conferences Evangelique quite near the Hanger. Eventually God prevailed in my heart and I went. There were present myself, the chaplain (Captain Watson, Baptist) a Quartermaster Sergt. Major and a private. We had a very blessed time. We sang, then the Chaplain prayed, then expounded the Scriptures of Ezekiel, then another hymn, then the CSM prayed, then I was enabled to pray with great power, then the Private prayed. I felt great joy in Christ tonight and devout thanks for such a sweet communion with fellow pilgrims on the way. The Chaplain is a deeply spiritual man and prayed and spoke with great earnestness and power.

For some time he continued to attend the evening services taken by Forces Chaplains at the Evangelical Methodist Church:

Sunday, 23rd May [1915] . . . I caught the first available tram and just reached the little Methodist Church before the service began. We had pleasant fellowship and quite a good turn out. Rev. Captain Teale preached from Proverbs 17, 24 'The eyes of a fool are in the ends of the earth' and I felt that his words really did refer in some measure to one and my inordinate passion for the 'wanderlust'. After the service I had a long talk with Rev. H. S. Whelpton, 17bis, Rue Montgomery, Le Havre, who is English and French minister of that same church where we have the services. He is a young chap of about 23, very nice, earnest and spiritual, and has a keen desire for travel like myself.

With growing confidence in this fellowship, DP now for the first time spoke publicly about his faith:

Tuesday, 1st June [1915] This evening I attended in the Conference Evangelique a class meeting or I should better describe it as a testimony meeting conducted by Captain Teale. Sergt. Major Hughes of the RE spoke first, I next – it being the first time in my life that I had ever spoken in public and although I felt frightfully nervous when I began I mastered that feeling and was enabled to freely testify to the sanctifying power of my Redeemer and Lord. I thank God that I was thus strengthened and that thereby on future occasions I shall feel much more confidence in the guiding hand of the Holy Spirit. It was a very blessed meeting – a real foretaste of better things.

Chaplains to the Forces came and went with some rapidity, and Capt. Kendall, a Primitive Methodist, soon replaced Capt. Teale:

> Tuesday, 8th June [1915] In the evening at 7pm I attended as usual our little meeting in the Conference Evangelique – this week it took the form of a prayer meeting and was conducted by Capt. Kendall. God enabled me to pray with exceptional power; I never before felt such an outpouring or such freedom in prayer and it was a most blessed and wonderful experience for me. I afterwards chatted with my friend Quartermaster Sergt. Major Hughes R.E. and he got me to promise to attend their little Bible Study meeting . . . when the subject is to be 'The Second Coming of Christ'.

The next day he accepted an invitation to dine from a fellow ASC lieutenant and added personal testimony to his newly found confidence:

> Wednesday, 9th June [1915] . . . when we had got settled down at dinner I brought the point home by asking if he was interested in religious matters, if religion appealed to him. I found that truly God had sent me there that night with a set purpose for R. was striving after light, and reason – and morality – were the stumbling blocks. I laid bare the deepest secrets of my life and spoke with great earnestness for several hours, telling of my own temptations, of my joy in Christ and of the power of the Holy Ghost already come into my life . . . Unto one another we laid bare our hearts, our inmost secrets and strivings, and I thank God that I was able to clear away some although not all his difficulties . . . This is the first time I have spoken at such length on spiritual matters to an acquaintance and I thank God for the new power in my life He has given me.

New experiences were thus coming one after another, and more followed:

> Monday, 14th June [1915] I attended the little schoolroom in Rue Thiers attached to the Wesleyan Church for a Bible Study meeting at 8pm this evening. There were 10 present, Rev. H. Whelpton (the minister), 3 French Christians and 6 soldiers. The subject was to have been the Second Coming of Christ but we had scarcely started when we were surprised to find that Mr Whelpton who was the leader proposed to leave out Revelations from the study as he didn't believe in it as in the rest of the New Testament. For the rest of the hour a hot discussion raged round that Prophetic book, I taking the leading stand in its defence, and being well backed by the soldiers. Finally we agreed to spend 4 Mondays on the subject of the Second Coming from 1: The Gospels of Matthew, Mark and Luke; 2: John; 3: Pauline Epistles; 4: Revelation. I met at this little class one or two very earnest Christian men with whom I have not previously come into touch.

The subject of the Second Coming had been one DP had studied with his family and for his own interest back in Scotland before the war: he was able to challenge the young minister with some credibility. From this meeting came DP's acceptance as a leader among that small group of 'very earnest Christian men'. He was now asked to stand in for the Chaplain at a midweek meeting:

> Tuesday, 15th June [1915] I met R. on my way back to Camp 5. We walked slowly on together to the Conference Evangelique where our little company numbered 11 tonight. Capt Kendall . . . did not turn up so at the request of Sergt. Major Hughes I took the meeting though still retaining my seat in the body of the hall. I read from Acts, 2nd – the descent of the Holy Ghost, and then led in prayer. We had a wonderful meeting, no less than 9 praying and an ASC private spoke at the close for 10 minutes on the Second Coming of Christ. Although not experiencing tonight the power that I felt last Tuesday, I nevertheless was enabled by God's Holy Spirit to speak a few words on soul winning.

Thus within a month of that first evening service he had attended at Rue Thiers, DP became – aged 19 – an accepted Christian leader:

> Wednesday, 16th June [1915] This evening I had promised to go round to Cinder City and help Rev. Mr Hamilton of Glasgow with the prayer meeting. I prepared Hymns, Bible Reading etc but when I got round to Cinder City . . . I found out that instead of the prayer meeting I had been led to expect there was going to be a glorified religious concert and I did not go in. I returned to camp and saw West of the YMCA and stood chatting with him for a minute or two when his friend Easton came out and asked me to take the prayers. I was rather taken aback but could not refuse. I therefore stepped on to the platform at 8.20pm in the YMCA tent, feeling conscious of no spiritual power. We sang hymn 305, 'Abide with me' then I prayed, and then we joined in the Lord's Prayer and closed with the Benediction and the National Anthem. It was the first time I had ever tackled a meeting like this and there were about 100 men present. I was enabled to carry it through successfully although not with power and vigour I had hoped for. Lesson to be taken seriously to heart – I must set apart hours for private prayer and communion with Christ – must myself be bathed with the Spirit before another such occasion.

June, July and August 1915 were decisive months for D. P. Thomson. He had been thinking of a career in commerce after the war – he was still in May 1915:

> Monday, 31st May [1915] I have made up my mind, subject to Mother's approval, that I will start off on my own account when the war is over – doing a twine business in Glasgow and district in winter and starting a golf ball emporium at leading seaside resorts in summer...

In so far as he had had religiously-based goals, they had been directed towards foreign mission – and his commercial and his missionary ambitions had never harmonised: both still had a ring of fantasy about them. Being without university education he had no opening for the ordained ministry in Scotland's larger presbyterian denominations. In the Church of Scotland as in the UF Church, entrance to divinity college required a prior arts degree. Now, however, and quite outside the regular discipline of the UF Church, DP became a regular preacher at services for the forces. At it happened his Second Diary ended at this point and the Third began with an apology: 'I exceedingly regret now that I have neglected all these weeks to make entries in my diary.' The Fourth, however, though beginning *as a diary* from February 1918, was written in a volume originally headed 'My Addresses' that began on 1 August 1915, and from this a list of nine sermons given at Le Havre has survived. Despite his youthful preachings in his family's drawing room and those *ad hoc* incidents already recorded, DP dated his public ministry from 1 August 1915, his first prepared public sermon:

> 1. A sermon preached in Chapelle Evangelique Methodiste, Rue Thiers, Havre, France. Sunday evening, 1st August 1915.
> Soldiers (Wesleyan) Service, 6.30pm.
> 'The night is far spent, the day is at hand': Romans 13, 12.
> About 85 present including 2 chaplains.
> Service conducted by CQMS Hughes.

It is significant that this, with another four of these nine recorded addresses, took a text associated with Christ's Second Coming. The subject was clearly close to his heart and central to his appeal for conversion. DP's emergence as a preacher led to his small group of 'very earnest Christian men' of various ranks constituting themselves as, in effect, a brethren-style or mission hall assembly for the Forces: a 'Soldiers' Church' with its Sunday evening worship, its midweek devotional meetings, its own communion service and its recognised 'brethren'. DP wrote later that at this time he helped to create 'The Soldiers' Own Gospel Campaign', no doubt after the model of those missionary societies with which he was acquainted, to give form to these developments. Forces Chaplains were available but DP recorded that he came to be theologically suspicious of them. The 'Campaign' also sponsored evangelistic gospel meetings:

8. A sermon preached in Salvation Army Hut, Camp 13, Harfleur.
Sunday evening, October 10th
Evening Gospel Meeting, 6.30pm
'Watch and pray, that ye enter not into temptation' Mt. 26,41
Service conducted by Farrier J. Barry
About 200 present, 1 probably 2 converted at the after meeting – the most powerful prayer meeting Barry or I have ever been in – 14 Brethren led in prayer.

In his published autobiographies, D. P. Thomson, while mentioning his time at Le Havre in passing, tended to stress what came next, during his posting to Salonica later in November 1915. Yet the change between DP at Bridge of Allan / Stirling (November 1914 to February 1915) and DP during this latter period at Le Havre (August to November 1915) was considerable. Indeed in November 1915 he had a short period of leave back in Scotland and he noted: 'Aunt Jeanie remarked that I had left for France a boy and returned a man.' For this change some credit may be given to Quartermaster Sergeant-Major Hughes of the Royal Engineers and those others who recognised the young man's spiritual potential and gave him serious Christian work to do: work for which he was perhaps more fitted than he was to be an army officer, and yet it was in part his status as an officer that helped to pave his way.

During a week of leave, 29 October to 6 November 1915, DP managed to visit a large number of relatives, including his parents back in Dundee. The most significant meeting was with his older brother James, the historian and journalist, by now a Lieutenant in the Cameron Highlanders, an infantry formation that had already been in the line at the Western Front:

> . . . off to Richmond, where James is stationed. I . . . found James down meeting me at the station. I thought he was looking very much older than when we parted in March, certainly the worse for his trench experiences. We at once repaired on foot to the King's Head Hotel and quaffed a ginger pop each at my expense. JP then returned on foot to camp while I remained at the hotel, partook of a hearty supper of cold ham, bread, butter and tea and then off to bed.
>
> Sunday, 31st October [1915] [*After breakfast*] I set off for the 2 mile walk to JP's camp . . . JP welcomed me and a blazing fire greeted me in his room. All morning we sat beside it in easy chairs and chatted. He is not at all in favour of my transferring to the infantry. At one o'clock we dined at the mess of the 8th Camerons, JP being attached to them at present. It was a poor meal, the only redeeming feature being an excellent ginger pop. We sat talking for about 1 hour after lunch, then set out for Richmond

> by road. We visited the old Grey Tower and Richmond Castle, the latter a glorious pile, excelling St Andrews both in size and beauty. Then once again we meandered up to the King's Head partook of drinks and sat talking in the smoke room until 5 o'clock. We went upstairs and had a splendid high tea consisting of cold chicken and ham and boiled eggs: also a glass of milk the first I have tasted for 7 months – greatly enjoyed. My train left Richmond at 6.50pm and James came down to see me off. It was a great day with him, both fully realising that it might be the last together in this world.

The two brothers never did meet again. Lieut. James Pringle Thomson died on 15 August 1916 from wounds sustained during the battle of the Somme while serving with 6/Cameron Highlanders. He is buried in France in Plot III.D.7 in the Warloy Baillon Communal Cemetery Extension, near Amiens, among some 1,330 other Commonwealth war-graves there. In later life, DP liked to think of his own historical enterprises as being in some sense dedicated to JP: items of James' kit, sent home from France, are still retained in the D. P. Thomson Archive.

In the Army: Salonica

On return from leave DP discovered that the ASC Field Bakery units were making preparations to be shipped closer to action. By 24 November he, his 53rd Field Bakery and many other units of the 27th Division were on board HMT Alaunia, a former Cunarder, en route to Salonica in northern Greece. He enjoyed the voyage: officers dined in the First Class restaurant and he reproduced the printed menus in his Diary. Once they had landed, still well behind the lines, DP was in charge of 100 or so men providing bread for a now largely forgotten British and Commonwealth army, then ineffectively seeking to defend Serbia against Bulgaria and the Central Powers. Indulging an enduring sense of the dramatic, DP began *The Road to Dunfermline* with his call to be an evangelist, received at the ASC base for the Salonica front:

> It was on the evening of Sunday, 16th April, 1916, in the ancient city of Thessalonica, just a stone's throw from where the Apostle Paul had so often preached . . . An officer in the Army Service Corps, and a youngster of 19, I had found myself far from home, with 100 men under my command, for whom no spiritual or social provision of any kind was made other than that which I was prepared to make for them. Out on the plains of Lembet where we were, hard by the Egnatian Road, down which St Paul came on his first journey to Europe, there was no Y.M.C.A., no

> padre, no Churches Hut or Canteen, in the early winter of 1915-16, when the temperature fell to 15 degrees below zero. If anything was to be done for my men, and for the hundreds of men in the camps round about us, it would have to be done by me, a very junior officer. I knew that I owed it to these men to tell them of the power I had come to know in my own life, of the Bible on which I had been nourished in home and Sunday School, and of the Gospel I had already learned to preach while serving in France a few months before. And so it came about that in what we called the Lembet Tabernacle – a double-lined E.P. hospital marquee I had managed to procure – we held on Sunday evenings a popular evangelistic service at which a choir from the neighbouring No. 1 New Zealand Stationary Hospital led the praise.

That Sunday, 16 April 1916, one of the New Zealanders serving with the Red Cross accosted DP with the words 'Lieutenant Thomson, God wants you to be an evangelist' and DP was to take this as a call from God that went beyond preaching to the specific ministry of enabling conversion, of bringing men and women to repentance and faith in Christ.

In view of later discussions about evangelism, it is worth pausing to understand this ministry to which DP now found himself called. When Ray Price, the ANZAC Red Cross worker, spoke of evangelism he did not mean anything less than offering individuals the opportunity, there and then or later, to commit themselves to Christ: resolving difficulties in discussion, explaining if necessary how this could be done, offering prayerful support and giving teaching on the life of discipleship that would follow on from an act of commitment. The whole process was summarised in the phrase 'personal work', and went quite beyond even clear, persuasive, Scriptural preaching. An evangelist, as both Price and D. P. Thomson then understood the phrase, engaged *both* in preaching *and* in personal work: and it was such a complete ministry that DP heard himself being challenged that night in Salonica:

> It was after one of our Sunday evening services that Ray Price – a New Zealander working with the Red Cross – came into my tent to see me. 'You have no right,' he said that night, as we sat talking over my charcoal brazier, for it was the depth of winter and this was the only way to keep warm, dangerous as the fumes were, 'You have no right to preach like that unless you make it plain that you are prepared to see men individually afterwards, and you invite and expect them to come.'

Yet it is clear that even if a particular call to be an evangelist came in April 1916 while DP was baker for the army in Macedonia, he was thinking in terms of 'my ministry' well before then. The pattern that had developed in the autumn of 1915 at Le Havre was the model for the work of the Soldiers' Own Gospel Campaign that he transported to Salonica: the Sunday evening evangelistic worship, the mid-week fellowship meetings, the monthly communion for a small number of 'brethren,' with DP himself dispensing the bread and wine of the sacrament. He had indeed moved a considerable way from the practice of the United Free Church or, indeed, from any of the Scottish presbyterian denominations, none of which authorised an un-ordained man to celebrate communion. He did receive some support, however, from the local congregation of the Greek Evangelical Church.

The doctrine of the Second Coming of Christ continued to dominate DP's thinking while he was at Salonica and he preached a series of sermons that outlined the dispensational pre-millennial understanding of the future as contained in the *Scofield Reference Bible*. In a sense, delivering this series brought to a head his thinking since at least 1912. He was not always to remain of this mind about the Second Coming, but one other point can be made: those who held to such a doctrine also held firmly to a strictly literal interpretation of the Bible and had little truck with Biblical Criticism. Dispensational pre-millennialism took (and takes) the precise wording of Biblical prophecy extremely seriously, with little attention to any possible difference of literary form or changes in historical context between the book of Daniel, the Gospels and the Revelation of John. The

#6: D. P. Thomson in British Army uniform, c. 1917

pattern of thought could not be sustained under any other way of reading the Bible. D. P. Thomson, at this stage of his spiritual progress, may fairly be described as a fundamentalist as that word was used at that time, to describe those who opposed 'The Modern Outcry against the Gospel', to borrow the title of one of his sermons of this period.

DP's service in the First World War was cut short. His commission as 2nd Lieutenant in the Army Service Corps was both the beginning and the end of his army career. Like so many serving on the Salonica front, he soon fell seriously ill. Hospitalised with dysentery and then by a combination of heart and stomach trouble, he left Macedonia on a stretcher in June 1916 and was shipped, via Malta, to a hospital in Liverpool. He was still there in August when the news came of his brother James' death. For another year DP was to serve in the Army as Assistant Supply Officer for ASC units stationed in the east of Scotland. Finally he was discharged, with a pension, as 'medically unfit for further service' in the autumn of 1917, one doctor suggesting that he might have no more than six months to live: that at best he would be 'a semi-invalid all my days'.

Regardless of this prognosis, once back in Scotland DP resumed both his public ministry of evangelistic preaching and his contacts with his favourite foreign missions.

EVANGELIST IN TRAINING:

II – With the Heart of Africa Mission and the United Free Church, 1917-1921

> Sunday, 16th March [1919] . . . Today I felt definitely led to contemplate entering the recognised ministry – my friends have been urging me to this for a long time.
>
> D. P. Thomson, The Diary of My Life part 4.

After his enforced return from Greece to Scotland, D. P. Thomson was deployed by the ASC at Dunfermline as Assistant Supply Officer for West Fife and Kinross, and as a Field Bakery consultant. These were light duties, appropriate to his state of health, and they allowed him time to resume a preaching ministry, for which his uniform and overseas service helped to open doors. Discharged from the Army on 5 October 1917, the opportunity arose for him to be recognised as the Secretary for Scotland of C. T. Studd's Heart of Africa Mission – a post that involved deputation preaching to a yet-wider range of congregations.

DP also became a student – first at Glasgow's Bible Training Institute, then additionally at evening classes offered by the School of Study and Training associated with the United Free Church. Then came his M.A. degree course at Glasgow University (1919-22), followed by more study at the United Free College and a belated licensing as a minister of the UF Church in 1927. Before, during and after his formal education for the ministry he also served as a locum or as an assistant at a number of United Free congregations in western Scotland and furthered his growing experience as an evangelist whilst Organising Secretary (1922-25) for the Glasgow Students Evangelistic Union, of which he was a founding member. This semi-itinerant phase of life came to an end when on 1 February 1928 he was ordained and inducted to the Dunfermline: Gillespie United Free Church. Considerable changes can be detected in D. P. Thomson's theology and general approach to church affairs during this period of ten years. Choices were offered to him that, had he taken them, could have resulted in entirely different pathways of Christian service.

Peripatetic Evangelism

Between September 1916 and August 1917 DP continued his evangelistic ministry. He thus conformed to a pattern of behaviour not uncommon for his time, described in the acidic tones of the Joint-Head of the Home Department of the Church of Scotland, Rev. Arthur H. Dunnett:[1]

> It is to be supposed that Scotland is not unique amongst the countries of the world in that it harbours a very large number of men and women who are assured within themselves that their destiny in life is to preach. These aim at being evangelists. It matters not to them what be the purpose or constitution of the body which is prepared to employ them. Their desire in life is fulfilled if they become missionary agents somewhere, anywhere, where a building is available and a gathering of people can be encouraged to listen to them.

While holding down his day-job with the ASC and meanwhile acting as an independent, peripatetic evangelist, DP recorded some 40 separate occasions when he was asked to speak, and a somewhat smaller number of addresses: 13, of which three were given 20 times between them. If politicians have what are called 'stump addresses', DP had stump sermons, ready to be pulled out again time after time. Most of these meetings took place in Fife but already his connections were far-flung: in 1916 he addressed audiences (as he called them) in Rotherhithe and the Central YMCA in London; at a Baptist chapel in Penzance; and, during a week in July 1917, at a number of locations around Dalmellington, Ayrshire. Four addresses were delivered at the James Street Hall in Dunfermline where he was based; other congregations included Lochgelly's and West Dunfermline's Baptist Churches; the influential Charlotte Chapel Baptist congregation in Edinburgh; the Rosyth Navvy Mission, the Mission Halls at Lochore and in Cowdenbeath's Broad Street, and at the Hill of Beath. Invitations to the young ASC lieutenant also came from United Free congregations at Tarbet (Loch Lomond); Dunfermline: Townhill; Dunfermline: Gillespie; and the Kingseat Mission. Such Missions were generally directed at working class areas or vocations by congregations and voluntary societies controlled by the middle and upper classes; their Halls might be sponsored by wealthy presbyterian individuals. The James Street Hall in Dunfermline was actually owned and directed by Robert Steel, an elder of Dunfermline: Abbey United Free congregation. Steel, DP's spiritual mentor in Dunfermline, was also President of the Fifeshire

County Christian Union, which sponsored Tent Missions in the smaller mining communities. When DP was in Ayrshire in July 1917, it was to speak at the Ayrshire County Christian Union [ACU] conference and at its Patna branch; to preach at Dalmellington United Free Church and at the YMCA Hall there. Other speakers included the Dalmellington UF minister; the Pastor of the Anniesland Hall, Glasgow; and the Evangelist of the ACU.

Exposition of a Biblical passage was not what the young DP attempted when asked to speak. He sought to persuade hearers to accept Christ for themselves, and chose a text that would allow for contemporary, spiritual application. His emphasis in recording 'My Addresses' was on the title, not on the text. A rough average suggests attendance of less than a hundred at most of these meetings, though some were simply prayer meetings of less than ten, and one – at Rotherhithe Central Hall – was of a thousand. Most were Sunday afternoon or evening Gospel services, or midweek meetings: as yet DP was not entrusted with the Sunday forenoon service, but in any case it was evening services that were, by convention, evangelistic. They might include what he at this time called 'fishing'. Once his address had concluded, a notice would be given that any who wished further counselling or to decide there and then to commit themselves to Christ should stay behind or otherwise make themselves known. Conviction of sin was often a precursor to decision. During this period some 17 conversions were notified to him – 'Maggie professed decision', 'one boy converted' – including eight to ten decisions at Charlotte Chapel alone. On another occasion, 'I didn't seek to press the matter home' and earlier, in March 1917, DP recorded that he 'could have wept with chagrin' because of his inability 'for personal dealing'. He looked for 'the presence of the Spirit to be manifest', for 'impression', evidenced by an emotional response from his hearers, and the 'visible fruit' of conviction or a decision publicly made. He also measured his performance in terms of 'freedom' and 'power'. 'I was hampered by want of freedom' might be contrasted with 'great freedom', as 'great power with the Word' might contrast to 'lack of power'. Though little assistance is given in the diaries to unpack this shorthand for experiences that meant so much, DP's valuing of extempore speaking suggests that by 'freedom' he meant the ability of a speaker fluently to improvise from inner resources rather than from a script, responding to the mood of the congregation. 'Power' may well reflect DP's own emotional response to the occasion: was he just giving a prepared address, or did he *deeply* seek the spiritual good of *these* people, *now*? And did his tone of voice and whole physical delivery convey any sense of *urgency*?

This mode of Christian preaching and worship was emotional both in appeal and in response. Following the precedent of Ira Sankey's musical contribution to D. L. Moody's evangelism, both choirs and soloists featured to support speakers by creating a receptive atmosphere. Thus at Cowdenbeath's Kirkford Hall in August 1917, when some 150 people were present:

> The hall was crammed, the singing was most rousing and I spoke with freedom for nearly an hour. Mr McEwen led the praise, sang a solo, took part in a duet and led the Crossgates Quartette – great power in the meeting and a number at least touched and moved.

Much relied on the preacher's personality as Rev. Arthur Dunnett recognised: '[*these evangelists*] centre their religious organisation round their own personality.' In *The Road to Dunfermline*, D. P. Thomson's highest commendation of his avowed model as an evangelist, D. L. Moody, was that his personality was unforgettable:

> They might forget his message; they might pass beyond the scope of his activities; they might even come to repudiate his theology; but they never lost the impress his personality made upon them.

In his article 'The Conduct of Children's Meetings' [in *Winning the Children for Christ*], DP wrote that in the field of children's missions what mattered was the personality of the missioner:

> Humanly speaking, everything depends on the Missioner . . . The children's evangelist must needs be a man (or woman) of winning personality, with something of that fine combination of strength and tenderness for which the young people of both sexes will insensibly look . . . Next in importance to the personality of the speaker, are the methods adopted in the conduct of the meetings, and the form in which the message is delivered to the children.

The evangelist-preacher's calling was not simply to teach or proclaim: he was to persuade, to enable hearers to decide for Christ, and his whole being served as a vehicle for the Holy Spirit – or not. DP knew times of discouragement:

> This meeting had been well announced, 500 handbills having been distributed and larger posters put up at various places – yet the audience scarcely filled the hall. My heart had been troubling me, my voice seemed to have lost its power and altogether I had lack of freedom and lack of the Holy Spirit's presence and power in the meeting. Another seeming failure – will the Spirit of Christ show any fruit from this meeting? . . . What ails the preacher? I must a season of deep heart searching and waiting for the Lord.

In August 1917 he had a further time of doubt, brought on by continued ill-health, a realisation of a growing disjunction between his normal self and his conduct as an evangelist, and a questioning of the fruit of his ministry:

> Owing to health I have had to cancel engagements meanwhile, and various circumstances have caused me to pause and reflect on my public work for the Master. I have seriously questioned whether it would not be to the interest of My Master and His Kingdom that I should retire from public speaking, the fact having been borne home to me very forcibly that my platform voice is not my normal one, but sounds unnatural and forced, also that for the amount of energy expended, the results have been amazingly meagre. These soliloquies have induced deep heart searching and in the interval that elapses between now and the resumption of my public witnessing, I must very definitely seek the Holy Spirit's guidance on all these matters.

The Heart of Africa Mission and the Holiness movement

In fact D. P. Thomson's vocation did take a new direction at this stage. Earlier in August 1917 while on leave he had attended a missionary conference held at the Swanwick Conference Centre in England's Derbyshire, resuming connection with a Society he had supported in the pre-war days, as he recounted in *Personal Encounters*:

> The Japan Evangelistic Band, whose Annual Holiness Convention was being held there, I had known for many years. More than one of its leaders I had met and heard in Dundee. Alfred Buxton, the son of its chairman, had gone a year or two before this to Africa with C. T. Studd, the well-known Cambridge cricketer and missionary, to pioneer a new enterprise, known first as the Heart of Africa Mission; then, later, as the World Evangelisation Crusade. In this venture I had become interested, and my offer to act as local secretary while stationed in Dunfermline had been accepted by its Committee. It was in the hope of effecting closer contact with both missions - the JEB and the HAM, that I went to Swanwick; and also in the expectation of the kind of spiritual blessing which at that stage I felt I very much needed. It was at Swanwick that I came to know Mrs C. T. Studd, with whom for the next few months I was to be closely associated, and by whose magnetic personality I was at times to be so deeply influenced. It was through one of Mrs Studd's many admirers and helpers, Miss Blakeman, of Parkstone in Dorset – a Heart of Africa Mission enthusiast – that I was led to become the first Scottish Secretary of C. T. Studd's Mission.

Charles T. Studd came from a wealthy English family.[2] He and his brothers were educated at Eton and he played first class cricket for Eton, Cambridge and England: he was in the England XI that famously lost the 'Ashes' to Australia in 1882. After an intense experience of rededication, Studd was one of the 'Cambridge Seven' students who joined Hudson Taylor's China Inland Mission in 1885: he was to serve in China as an unordained missionary until 1894, marrying while there another CIM missionary, an Irish girl, Priscilla Stewart. On coming of age, Studd gave an inherited fortune away to missionary work and thereafter lived on the same principle as Hudson Taylor, by faith. Between 1900 and 1906 the Studds worked in India, and then his attention was caught by Africa. He heard Dr Karl Kumm, an experienced German missionary, speak on 'Cannibals want Missionaries' in 1908 and only his health then prevented him from travelling out with Kumm. At the 1910 Edinburgh Missionary Conference, Studd again heard Kumm speak against the growing impact of Islam on central Africa, and he was also enthused by the wider vision of evangelising the remaining non-Christian world. First joining and then separating from the Africa Inland Mission, Studd and Alfred Buxton (who became his son-in-law) created the Heart of Africa Mission [HAM] in 1914 by securing four land concessions in the then Belgian Congo. After a final visit to Britain in 1915, Studd was for the remainder of his life based in the Congo. Priscilla and a committee directed the growing movement from headquarters in Norwood, London. As DP wrote, connections between the HAM and the JEB were strong and both were closely involved with the spirituality promoted at the annual Keswick Convention. Such missions attracted Englishmen of Studd's Eton and Cambridge class. Founder of the JEB, Rev. Barclay F. Buxton, also spoke at HAM meetings at which his relative, Sir Thomas F. Victor Buxton, 4th baronet Buxton, High Sheriff of Essex, presided.

Even if he was of 'the elite of Dundee', the young Scottish ASC lieutenant that DP was in 1917 came from a world very different from the missionary leaders he met at Swanwick, people he described [in *Personal Encounters*] as 'the highest circles of the evangelically-minded aristocracy'. He was probably not aware of the various difficulties even then arising from C. T. Studd's absolute determination to follow where he believed Christ led. Perhaps because the Heart of Africa Mission was such a young organisation, so centred on its absent founder, DP's abilities and offer of support were especially welcome. While at the 1917 JEB Convention he was asked to represent the HAM on the Friday when the different missions laid out their stalls. On his discharge from the Army, DP was free to be appointed HAM's representative in Scotland under the title of 'Organising and Deputation Secretary'. Miss Blakeman, one of Mrs Studd's friends, claimed to have prayed him out of the Army in order to take up this post. Bessie Scott and his home had indeed taught DP that 'The Church has a world-wide mission'. Contact with French Evangelical Methodists, Greek evangelicals and evangelical-pacifists from New Zealand during his service abroad 1915-16 had deeply impressed him. Support for the Greek Evangelical Church for long remained an interest following its welcome to him as a novice evangelist; such support was but one aspect of his enduring commitment to the world church. Representing a small African mission at the very front line of the Faith, both geographically and spiritually, must have resonated with his youthful hopes of Christian service.

Between October 1917 and May 1918 the backing of C. T. Studd's network ensured that DP was invited to preach and speak across Scotland by a wide range of Christian bodies. In *The Road to Dunfermline* he wrote:

> Visiting great centres like Carrubbers Close Mission in Edinburgh and the Tent Hall in Glasgow and contacting at many points the Railway Mission, the Faith Mission, the County Christian Unions, and the Town and Village Missions, I saw both the strength and weakness of much of the evangelistic work of the country as it had been carried on with little variation since the days of Moody and Sankey. Preaching in churches like Belhaven and Westbourne, Rutherford and Renfield Street, Finnieston and Pollokshields West in Glasgow – and their counterparts in other cities and bigger towns – I met the finest type of elder, the man who is the strength of our Scottish Churches.

Studd himself, as one of Hudson Taylor's recruits from Cambridge to the China Inland Mission, had had highly successful missionary and evangelistic meetings in Edinburgh and Lanarkshire in 1884 and 1885. 'The Cambridge Seven' – athletic, privileged, wealthy, fêted for their comprehensive renunciation of status for the sake of taking the gospel to an un-evangelised world – had become a focus of attention in both England and Scotland which, at least in missionary circles, endured.[3] DP now found himself the Scottish representative of a missionary icon: at the age of 21 he had a national remit.

Looking at the 130 or so speaking engagements he recorded in his diaries in this eight month period, what is striking is the substantial increase in invitations that came from congregations of the United Free Church: roughly 50 in all, a considerably increased proportion from the four out of 40 as he undertook as an independent preacher not connected to a missionary society. UF engagements now were more numerous than the 41 or so delivered to an assortment of Mission Halls and Brethren Assemblies that nevertheless included the Arbroath Town Mission; the Kelty Tabernacle; the Methil Seaman's Bethel; the Brethren Gospel Hall in Carluke; the Shipwrights' Hall in Greenock; the Artisans' Gospel Hall, Kelvinhaugh, Glasgow; the Free Breakfast Mission Hall, Dundee. Three requests came from congregations of the established Church of Scotland: 'St John's Parish Church, Dumbartonshire', 'Parish Church, Cowdenbeath', 'St Michael's Parish Church, Edinburgh'. Five came from Baptist Churches and one from a Scottish Congregational Church; and he also spoke at the monthly Prayer Meeting of the National Bible Society of Scotland, and at Faith Mission and YMCA conferences and rallies. DP was now being invited not simply to preach but to conduct entire services, and not just the afternoon or evening gospel service, or the prayer meeting, but on occasion Sunday morning worship as well. He agreed to wear a ministerial robe for the first time while leading the monthly Boys Brigade and Scouts evening Church Parade for Maryhill UF congregation, Glasgow. During this period he also began to offer Lantern Lectures, talks illustrated by slides (photographic or painted) in a darkened hall. Audiences might or might not respond to this way of promoting foreign mission: at Longriggend United Free Church Hall in January 1918, he had to strain to make the Lantern Lecture on the work of HAM heard above the children's noisy chatter.

Speaking on behalf of the Heart of Africa Mission was not the same as delivering a straight evangelistic address. The objective was to arouse interest in the Mission, gather funds, recruit supporters and promote the wider objective of global evangelisation. The topic was attractive to many. DP noted that the Vice Convener of the UF General Assembly's Foreign Mission Committee was in the chair for one meeting. On another occasion the chairman, 'Mr John Scott of the Jam Factory', was a leading light in Scottish Christian Brethren circles. The Chairman of the School Board for Glasgow came to hear of the 'The New Crusade'; and at Pollokshields West UF Church, DP was accompanied to the pulpit by Very Rev. James Wells D.D. – ex Moderator of the General Assembly of the UF Church of Scotland in his robes of office. His work also included organising a Scottish tour by Mrs C. T. Studd in March 1918. Meetings took place in Edinburgh, Dundee and Aberdeen. Herself a powerful preacher, Priscilla Studd had large audiences: 1,000 at Charlotte Chapel, 500 at Tynecastle

Parish Church. DP's best was 600 at Queen's Cross UF Church, Aberdeen. He was most pleased by his evening meeting at Gallowgate UF Church, Aberdeen:

> I found an expectant and warm hearted company of about 40. There was a real atmosphere – charged with spiritual power and I spoke on the HAM, our work, with much freedom and power. There was a splendid response – many enrolling in the Crusade and purchasing magazines. The missionary of this church – Mr Allison – is a very saintly man and withal every inch a man. I was much cheered – this being the warmest and most congenial gathering I have enjoyed in the Granite City.

Being Scottish Organiser and Deputation Secretary for the Heart of Africa Mission, even in wartime conditions, gave DP a hearing far beyond what he would have had as a young itinerant evangelist. He concluded 1917 with the reflection:

> The close of a memorable year – a year brimful of glorious and boundless possibilities – a year in which I can gratefully and adoringly record the wonderful grace and unmistakable leading of God.

Reading DP's diaries during this period, it takes an effort to remember that during 1917 and 1918 the outcome of the First World War was still undecided; that the trenches still devoured the armies, and that revolution blazed in Russia.

D. P. Thomson recorded in *Personal Encounters* that he 'parted from the Heart of Africa Mission', 'under circumstances which compelled me to challenge some of its basic concepts and methods of working.' This breach occurred at the annual Convention of 1918, less than a year after he had begun his association with the HAM. The first fortnight in May saw a sequence of Annual Meetings held by the interlocking societies associated with the 'holiness' movement. DP had travelled to London by train; his accommodation was arranged by the Mission. First came the Annual Meeting of the Pentecostal League. Next came the HAM Annual Meeting, at which DP was part of the platform party and opened the proceedings with prayer. During the course of that day DP featured twice on the programme and thereafter he had a fairly full programme of engagements in the London area, speaking for HAM in Leytonstone, Willesden and Surbiton and leading the local weekly prayer meeting at Ashley Gardens. He saw a lot of Miss Blakeman, his original sponsor, and it appears they confided mutual problems:

> Thursday, 9th May [1918] . . . I returned to 17 Highland Road [*the HAM headquarters and Mrs Studd's home*] in the evening and had a long conversation

> with Miss Blakeman. We are agreed that things are in a bad way with HAM – that probably we shall protest against (1) Bitterness (2) Uncharitableness (3) Bombast (4) Advertising (5) Not telling candidates (6) and deceiving the public, and that we shall resign.

The contrast between this diary entry and those recording his fairly successful and certainly enthusiastic speaking engagements to promote the Mission is quite stark – and nowhere did DP elaborate on this list of criticisms. He appears to have retained confidence in the evangelistic vision of the Mission, while becoming disenchanted with its leadership and organisation.

D. P. Thomson now began a short series of personal calls on leaders of the Mission, seeking to win further support for his point of view. The Annual Meeting of the JEB followed on Tuesday 14th May, and later the HAM Executive Committee met:

> I made for the Wesleyan Central Halls, Westminster, where the HAM Executive Committee was sitting. I was admitted as they finishing tea, and wasn't long in observing that the general attitude towards me was hostile rather than sympathetic. One by one I read out my points, and volleys of talk including some hard and unpleasant things followed each. At last Mr Barclay clinched the matter by avowing that the committee were there solely to back up Mr Studd in everything he did and not to criticise him. That settled it, although they concluded by shewing a distinctly more sympathetic spirit and by refusing to accept my resignation; I felt I must go. I was asked to reconsider the matter and they promised to call another meeting of all the Executive. Afterwards, I had dinner with Miss Blakeman at Victoria and from her I learnt what had transpired at the meeting before I was brought in. It appears she had raised most of my points, which had been indignantly repudiated by the Committee. We agreed that the only course open was for both of us to resign.

As DP noted, the key to this was the inability of the London Committee to criticise C. T. Studd himself. Until his death in 1931 Studd remained in Africa, necessarily separated from his wife, himself still in overall command of a Mission that was – in Africa – steadily growing larger and yet also increasingly controversial back in Britain. It was to be C. T. Studd's successor, Norman Grubb, who was to bring HAM's successor, the World Evangelisation Crusade [WEC] out of the disaster that had almost overcome it by the time of Studd's death. The 'manner of working' from which DP had come to dissent was certainly the effects of the one-man-rule of C. T. Studd who, while harshly disciplining himself, also demanded from others obedience to his understanding of the directions of the Holy

Spirit, interpreted argument as disloyalty and met what he perceived as opposition with fluent hostility. DP's reference to 'advertising' may have referred to difficulties in working out the principle, certainly a 'basic concept' of HAM (and still of WEC), passed down from Hudson Taylor, of not appealing for funds but relying on God's Spirit to lead people to offer support as and when it was needed. 'Deceiving the public' may have referred to the fact that, though part of the 'holiness' movement, while in Africa Studd neither enforced teetotalism in his stations nor took any firm line on the baptism of the Holy Spirit. Some new missionaries had hence, on arrival, been profoundly shocked and may also have felt deceived.

On return to Scotland in May 1918 DP faithfully fulfilled his booked engagements on behalf of HAM, his last being on Sunday 26 May:

> At 6.30pm I conducted the service and preached at Westbourne Church, Glasgow to some 120 people. I was 'in a tremble' – unusual for me, nowadays, this being, from a carnal viewpoint, the most important church I have yet preached in. However He who never fails stood by me, and I spoke the word with boldness (The Change that Christ is Making - Isaiah 9,2) There were tears in some eyes, and most gave rapt attention to the message . . . the great day may show some fruit of this my last HAM service.

The next day brought a letter from Priscilla Studd: 'Monday, 27th May A letter from Mrs Studd this morning, – cold and formal – chilling in the extreme,' and the next week a final letter of severance came:

> Monday, 3rd June [1918] Morning post brought me a letter from Rev. G. A. Barclay SCF, Chairman of the HAM Executive, it accused me of all manner of shortcomings over the regrettable business of my leaving and I was especially wounded by one passage: 'No possible good to the Mission could have come out of your action, it is quite clear. What was your motive? I am reluctant to believe that you sought to air your own opinions at the expense of the Mission, and the Kingdom of God. Permit me to add that if you had approached us in a humble spirit (you were the youngest person present at the Committee) instead of in a menacing, aggressive and dictatorial manner, you might have helped us considerably. Instead of which you have sown discord and strife amongst us.' If this be true – woe is me – I have disgraced my Lord and Master. All day this letter has darkened my horizon.

Perhaps it is possible to read in this letter an admission that the Mission did in fact require to be 'helped'. Accounts of the disputes within HAM during the 1920s, however, suggest that no-one, not even Priscilla and certainly no committee, could ever restrain C. T. Studd or persuade him to moderate his views.

This was not D. P. Thomson's final meeting with the network of English evangelical leaders associated with the Heart of Africa Mission. In August 1918 he attended another JEB Convention at Swanwick. His diary makes interesting reading:

> Thursday, 15th August [1918] We have had very solemn and impressive meetings and I have been more or less under conviction all week. Rev. Barclay F. Buxton, Rev. J. M. Pollock, Rev. Herbert Wood, Mrs Reader Harris, Mrs Rue etc have been God's messengers to us. I have been so happy and feasting so much all day long that I have scarce put pen to paper all week . . . In conversation with Pastor J. D. Drysdale (of Emmanuel Church, Birkenhead) Pastor Geo. Hart (of the Bethel, Paisley) Rev. D. P. Robinson (of the Africa Inland Mission) Pastor Owen (of the Baptist Church) and others I have criticised both addresses and speakers freely – and said several unkind things about Holiness people. Several of the brethren have dealt faithfully with me and have sought to show me from the Scriptures the possibility and the necessity of Entire Sanctification. I have been unable to see it, and by no means at ease, as I do know these brethren have got a secret (of joy and happiness) that I fain would make mine. This afternoon Pastor Smith (of Bethesda Mission, Huddersfield) and Rev. Herbert Wood and I went to Ripley on business and for lunch and again I indulged in criticism. This evening at the Convention Mtg, God spoke directly to me thro Mr Wood and the Book. I almost wished the ground to open at my feet that I might hide myself and immediately the meeting was over I rushed to my room and flung myself on my bed more deeply convicted, I think, than I have ever been in my life. I dared not seek sleep until I had had the matter out. I told the Lord I was ready to be dealt with, and that I was quite willing to be dealt with alone by Him if He wished, although I would rather that He sent Pastor Drysdale to deal with me. I waited His answer and it came in the shape of a knock at the door. I knew that it was dear brother Drysdale, and in he came. He had gone upstairs but the Lord had bidden him come down to see me. He put his arms round my neck and we had a sweet and precious time together. Altho the load was partially lifted, I did not yet have peace, but after a short session of prayer, I lay down to sleep.

Criticism of the leaders of the 'Entire Sanctification' or 'Holiness' movement was understandable. DP had heard 'hard and unpleasant words' during his break with HAM, and we should not underestimate the sense of hurt he may have felt. For his part he had done as faithful a job as he could to represent the Mission, and his criticisms had stemmed from genuine youthful idealism – as well, no doubt, as from youthful arrogance. Christian leaders he had admired since his teenage years had overridden him, and it seems that he fell into the same temptations that he had accused others of: '(1) Bitterness (2) Uncharitableness (3) Bombast.' An emotional crisis of repentance resulted, an event sufficiently significant to appear also in Drysdale's own autobiography.[4] DP as a young man was impressionable and could be roused by a variety of triggers. That night-time crisis was but the first of three he experienced at Swanwick.

The JEB Convention sought to inspire young men to offer themselves for missionary service under the inspiration and leading of the Holy Spirit, and this was embodied in a formal ceremony at the end of the Friday Missionary Meeting:

> Friday, 16th August [1918] Today was the Missionary Meeting ... It was a very hallowed season and at the close the thank-offering was received. A table was spread at the front, below the platform and row by row we went forward to present our gifts. Those who the Lord had called to the foreign field and those who were willing to go, whenever and wherever He called, stepped quietly over to the right hand corner and there, in reserved seats, knelt in the silence before the Lord. I was trembling with apprehension lest I should have to be the first to cross over, but glory to God, Lieut. Donnithorne led the way and close behind I followed. It was a very solemn and searching and impressive time. Over and over again the audience kept singing 'When I survey' while the young people were coming forward. In all 40 laid themselves on the altar and over £300 was put on the table.

This act of public commitment to Christian service by DP was an emotional response within a liturgical context and it also flowed from his long history of interest in mission, now enhanced by a new ability in evangelistic speaking for Christ. 'When I survey the wondrous Cross', Isaac Watt's hymn, appealed for the sacrifice of 'all the vain things that charm me most', characterised Christ's death on the Cross as 'Love so amazing, so divine' that 'demands my soul, my life, my all' and thus closely linked core evangelical doctrine with the plea to go 'whenever and wherever He called'. Missions in the tradition of Hudson Taylor indeed looked for sacrifice, faith and holiness. There is no reason to doubt DP's sincerity: having surrendered his HAM appointment, he was looking for God's leading for his life. Thoughts of overseas service had surfaced again at the end of the May 1918, just as he received his 'chilling' letter from Mrs Studd:

> Monday, 27th May [1918] A letter from Mrs Studd this morning ... Went in the evening to the Christian Institute to hear Rev. Howard Moull of Toronto lecture on work in the Far West of Canada – most interesting – almost thrilling – whole communities who have never seen a parson or

> had a service for 30 years. Areas where 90% of the population return themselves as of 'no religion.' I felt the old impulse to go out on an evangelistic mission to these parts – to tour the missions and churches at home first for funds – to seek a 'Paul' to accompany me, and on my return to tour the assemblies again giving an account of the work done. Who knows?

His breach with the HAM had not killed DP's interest in mission, nor much repressed his romantic, impulsive nature.

Finally the JEB Convention was an occasion when D. P. Thomson received a special blessing from the Holy Spirit. The teaching associated with the 'holiness' network, described as 'the possibility and the necessity of Entire Sanctification,' did not claim that Christians could be freed entirely from all desire to sin. What it did, however, claim was that a heart fully surrendered to the Holy Spirit could successfully combat all temptation. The movement sharply separated being saved from being sanctified, and linked the latter with a further act of surrender and a blessing or filling by God's Spirit. This was the doctrine that DP had previously questioned: and, indeed, it is one that conservative Christians in the Calvinist tradition still criticise for too strongly dividing justification from sanctification, for insisting on a two-stage model for the Christian life. Such teaching had been associated with the JEB for a decade.[5] At the 1918 Convention the scene was set for a further public act of confession and surrender.

> Saturday, 17th August [1918] This forenoon there were special meetings for Ladies and for Men. The ladies meeting was on the subject of Rescue work in Japan and the men's on revival. After a very interesting address by Pastor Geo. Hart (of the Partick Bethel) and another brief message by Mr Drysdale, we had a time of heart searching before God. The leaders felt led to invite those who, at all costs, would seek the blessing of the Baptism of the Holy Ghost to quietly stand and one after another stood and, briefly, poured out their hearts to God in confession. It was a very hallowed hour and one pregnant with immense possibilities for the Kingdom of God. The first to rise was Brigadier General [Charles] de Winton C.M.G., who confessed that his past Christian life had been 3rd rate, 4th rate, and asked God's grace and strength to claim the blessing. Vice Admiral Currie was the 2nd to rise, and I was constrained to burst the shackles of unbelief and rise to claim the promised blessing, and in token of entire surrender. I had somewhat reluctantly to leave before the meeting finished, as I had arranged to take darling Mother and little Kathleen Lees into Nottingham in the afternoon. Walking into Ripley to catch the car, the words of a dear brother, I forget who, flashed across

> my mind: 'You must get rid of inbred sin before you can enter the Saviour's presence. If death can remove sin, then death is a mightier power and a better friend than the Lord Jesus Christ.' I saw quite clearly that death could certainly not remove sin and that there remained but 2 alternatives. Either I interposed an intermediate state for purification, between death and the glory, or I must admit the possibility, and hence the necessity, of being wholly cleansed here and now. I saw it in a flash and there and then I said: 'Lord, I will. Make me clean.' Shortly there came to my mind a sweet peace, and on the top of the car on the way to Nottingham I received an outpouring of the Holy Spirit. I was filled with joy, and felt like shouting Hallelujah and hugging everybody when I arrived at Nottingham. I was so overjoyed and so full that I could hardly wait to get back to Swanwick for the testimony meeting, so eager was I tell out to others what great things the Lord had done for me.

In passing, the position of those attending this Convention may be noted: a Brigadier General and a Vice Admiral, no less, stood to confess and to seek the blessing of the Spirit, and ex-Lieut. Thomson then followed.

DP returned to Scotland keen to deploy some of the Swanwick methodology and to share his experiences. On Thursday 29 August, at a midweek meeting at the James Street Hall, Dunfermline, he invited all seeking the blessing of the Holy Spirit to come forward and handed out copies of Mr Buxton's *Baptism of the Holy Ghost.* The same sermon was repeated at the evening service at Wallneuk UF Church, Paisley, the next Sunday, and he spoke on his impressions of the Convention at its midweek prayer meeting.

Towards the Recognised Ministry

D. P. Thomson's active connections with the 'holiness' strand of evangelicalism continued for some time. He attended a Missionary and Holiness Conference at the Pentecostal Church of the Nazarene, Parkhead, Glasgow and was invited to undertake work with the Pentecostal Church in Paisley. He spoke at Faith Mission Conventions in Dundee and Dunfermline, and also spoke on the Second Coming of Christ at the James Street Hall in January 1919. He attended the Annual Faith Mission Convention at Bangor, Northern Ireland, in 1919, issuing the key invitation to spiritual surrender. One young evangelical wrote around this time to compliment him as 'the hottest bit of stuff I've had the pleasure of running up against for some considerable time'. Nevertheless events were now drawing him in the direction of the United Free Church, the denomination of his family. While working for the HAM, DP had begun his courses of study: with the Bible Training Institute of Glasgow, and a Christian Workers' Course with the UF Church's School of Study and Training, also based in Glasgow. D. M. McIntyre, Principal of the BTI and an active United Free Church minister, was an irenic conservative and – important to DP's spiritual development – neither a dispensational pre-millennialist nor a doctrinal rigorist, being content to leave ultimate theological questions unanswered and refusing to condense his understanding of the Cross to a single theological concept.[6] On Sunday 24 February, 1918, DP noted that he had heard 'Rev. D. M. McIntyre preach a thoughtful and suggestive sermon on the Second Coming in Finnieston UF.' Within the secure fellowship of an evangelical – and Scottish – Bible College, DP was learning a less narrow approach to Christian doctrine. Such theological development no doubt facilitated his acceptance of (and by) the UF Church, a broader-based denomination than the Brethren and Mission Hall congregations of his early ministry.

In the aftermath of his breach from the HAM, DP accepted first one and then another offer of employment as a locum with UF congregations in the Glasgow area. Such employment was required by a student with few other sources of income: together with his studies at the UF College, it also served to bring him into regular fellowship within the UF denomination. Between June and September 1918, DP was locum at Wallneuk UF Church, Paisley, while its minister undertook wartime Huts and Canteens work for the Forces chaplaincy. The invitation came because of a recommendation from someone who had heard his preaching: he had no other qualification. And it was offered at just the right time, within days of DP's return to Scotland from the HAM Annual Meeting. Although he was to look back warmly on his time at Wallneuk, initially the experience was somewhat humbling:

> Sunday, 2nd June [1918] And what shall I wrote of this day, looked forward to for so long, prayed for by so many? Shall I run thro' the facts baldly first. Rose late, washed, dressed, prayed very briefly, breakfasted, then off to Church. A good attendance – 300 or more, probably more. My prayers seemed stilted, my children's address was too long. I forgot to intimate the collection and in my sermon, forgot many important points and said a great deal in a way I hadn't meant to say it. To crown all I finished at 12.40 and got gentle hints about length – the collection – the ridiculousness, the impossibility of a Wednesday prayer meeting in summer . . . only 70 at the evening service. God help me, but it was a stunning

> blow. My sermon seemed hopelessly insipid – lacking fibre and fire: my pen refuses to record more.

All trainee worship-leaders who have, to the ire of local office-bearers, forgotten the collection, may take heart from this record! For someone engaged for a mere four months, DP tackled his ministry at Wallneuk aggressively. He did in fact run – contrary to those nay-sayers who thought it impossible during the summer – a midweek prayer meeting, and he 'threw the meeting open to others', allowing extempore prayer, which the congregation's minister had never done. On Thursday 1 August he recorded:

> Thursday, 1st August [1918] Mr W. M. Southwell, Session Clerk of Wallneuk, came to see me. We had a very straight talk – I trust it may not be without effect.

Even if DP's idealistic assurance that he knew what pattern of meetings was needed while he was locum was not conveyed in the 'menacing, aggressive and dictatorial manner' perceived by the HAM Executive, there was clearly something of the young officer about his approach. But, despite the dreadful start and possibly shaky relations with the long-term office-bearers, he found fulfilment especially in the midweek fellowship and in the personal work associated with a young communicants' class, where he saw a number of conversions. Looking back from the safety of 1951, DP wrote:

> I went to Wallneuk and for four months, at the age of 22, and with no thought then of entering the ministry, I had full charge of a congregation of some 700 members. It was one of the things that could only have happened in wartime. But it was that four months' experience which ultimately sent me into the ministry.

Paisley: Wallneuk gave DP for the first time practical experience in regular preaching and in the combination of preaching, teaching, pastoral work and congregational leadership particularly associated with the full-time ministry. He began to sense God's call with new definition.

Next came an assistantship at the Wynd UF Church, Glasgow, during the autumn of 1918, and another at Renwick UF Church, Glasgow, from January to September 1919. The first was undertaken with guidance from one of the United Free Church's venerable evangelical ministers; the second was a congregation described as:[7] 'a busy hive of Christian effort . . . It is a strong centre of the Christian Endeavour movement, its Bible Classes and Sunday Schools are large and prosperous and splendidly staffed, and much aggressive evangelistic work is carried on.' Meanwhile he also continued his courses of study and his December examination results were encouraging:

> Tuesday, 17th December [1918] We have had an exam from Rev. D. M. McIntyre at the BTI this morning and one from Prof. Clow at the School for Christian Studies this evening. We also got out the results of Rev. J. A. Hunter's exam (O.T. Intro). I was first with 84% – two others very near with 79% each (Bowers and Blackwood). Mr Hunter strongly advised me to enter the Hall. He said he thought I was wasting my chance. I am seriously considering whether I look to take this step when the way opens up – my objection has always been the Higher Critical Teaching.

Under post-war regulations access to university courses was eased, to offer a path that many ex-service men were considering. Perhaps DP was also encouraged by the examples of his sister, Christine, and his younger brother, Robert, both of whom were by now university students. Christine graduated M.B., Ch.B. (with Distinction) at St Andrews University in July 1921 and she received an M.D. in June 1925 for a thesis entitled 'Notes on the Pathology of Foetal Maceration'.[8] DP's younger cousin, Gladys Burnet (with whom he 'spooned' around this time in the woods beside her father's manse) was now also a medical student. To enter the ministry, DP would need first to obtain entry to a university arts course and then successfully to graduate. He would then have to satisfy the Church's requirements at a UF Divinity Hall – a long overall programme, during which he would have to finance himself. The way did open up. Success in his evening classes brought access to Glasgow University, the degree of M.A. in 1922 and thence entry to the UF Divinity College in Glasgow. He moved from Renwick UF to Glasgow Central UF as assistant in the autumn of 1919, remained there as locum through 1920 and continued to secure congenial if essential employment throughout his training.

The availability of these successive posts and a multitude of *ad hoc* pulpit supply requests, with the very real fellowship within the UF fold that they brought, together with the sense of fulfilment, together with the advice of his friends, together with an inward sense of God's leading, culminated to persuade DP that his calling was to be an ordained minister. This was no light decision. DP's Diary for 1918 was appropriately marked up in capitals with the end of what he called his third, and the beginning of his fourth, year of public ministry:

> Wednesday, 31st July [1918] The closing day of the third year of my ministry in the Gospel. It has been my privilege to proclaim the unsearchable riches of Christ on 172 occasions during the past year – in

> fact during the past 9 months I have spoken for my Lord on 160 occasions. Today I have studied on 'The Lord's Return'. Thursday, 1st August [1918] 4TH YEAR OF MY PUBLIC MINISTRY

This 'public ministry', albeit in no recognised denomination, had been and was very real to him. He felt called by God to it, and believed that God had blessed his preaching and evangelism. Many (most? all?) of the missionaries and evangelists he had admired since his youth – Livingstone, Finney, Moody, Hudson Taylor, both C. T. and Mrs Priscilla Studd – had not been ordained: the Gospel Hall tradition often looked askance at gowned and degreed ministers. His own father had an occasional preaching ministry though not ordained to the ministry of word and sacrament. Now DP was being asked to submit to the discipline of a national church, with its presbyteries and national committees, with its church law and church procedures – and with its breadth of theology, largely based on the higher critical method of assessing the various books of the Bible in terms of their historical context or literary form. Nevertheless the decision pressed itself upon him:

> Sunday, 16th March [1919] . . . Today I felt definitely led to contemplate entering the recognised ministry – my friends have been urging me to this for a long time.

One of DP's professors had a large part in claiming him for the ordained ministry of the United Free Church of Scotland. On holiday in Arran during the summer of 1919, DP – having then begun his theological evening classes – was asked without much warning to stand in to preach in a country church. The sermon he picked, 'Christ's Conditions of Discipleship', owed much to Prof. W. M. Clow, Professor of Christian Ethics at the UF College, whose preaching had impressed him back in 1914. As it happened Prof. Clow was also on holiday in Arran and in the very same congregation that Sunday to hear his own sermon re-preached to him! An invitation to lunch and friendship followed. Later, in 1924, when DP and a friend were running the small publishing company of Thomson & Cowan, he produced a volume entitled *United Free Church Sermons* and one of W. M. Clow's sermons, 'Missing the Highest', was among those selected. The preaching and example of such leading UF evangelical churchmen certainly played its part in persuading DP to enter the ministry and, in the case of Clow, he acknowledged the debt in *Personal Encounters*: 'It was largely owing to his wise advice that I went on, first to take a full theological course, then to get the pastoral experience which an actual charge alone could afford.' This two-stage process urged by Prof. Clow turned D. P. Thomson also into a churchman when he might well have continued an un-ordained vocation among the evangelical missionary societies, and he remained grateful.

In the years after 1917 DP was thus faced with the choice he described in *The Road to Dunfermline*: 'I had to choose whether my life's work was to be with the County Christian Unions and the Mission Halls, or in the wider stream of the Church's life. When the time came I had no difficulty in making my decision.' As DP put in it 1951:

> It meant . . . the realisation of the weakness as well as the strength of the mission hall as an institution. It has been, like every similar centre, the gateway of heaven to many, a training ground for Christian workers, a centre of happy fellowship, a place at which men have learned the secret of prayer and have found the hidden treasures of corporate Bible Study. But, as W. M. Clow was to teach me in later days at Trinity College, there is no continuity in the mission hall, there is no real conservation of gift and of experience; there is an over emphasis on certain aspects of truth to the exclusion of others equally vital; and there is a want of that salutary discipline which comes in the ordered life and stated form of a church whose background is at least nation-wide, and within whose fellowship are to be found other schools of thought and forms of worship than those we designate evangelical.

I suggest, in fact, that DP took longer over this decision and found it harder to take than he admitted in retrospect. He had to learn the hard way, while in conflict with the personalities of HAM, the truth behind this realisation of the 'weakness as well as the strength' of independent evangelical institutions. The 'ordered and stated form of a church' had checks and balances designed to allow participation in the process of determining the will of God. As well as experiencing a pull toward the United Free Church, DP had also experienced a push away from the associations of his early ministry. Yet his decision for the UF Church took time. He retained close friends in other denominations, so that at the end of 1920, he recorded 'The feeling grows stronger upon me that I am shortly to be called to a Congregational Church and that it will open a new epoch in my life.' In these early years after the War he was exploring his vocation.

There were other, personal, decisions that at this time troubled DP, always an emotional, romantic man:[9]

> <u>Wednesday, 1st January [1918]</u> . . . This has been an eventful day for I fell in love with Mr H's daughter, J., who attracted me strongly the first time I met her but who took my heart by storm today.

Saturday, 4th January [1918] I spent as much of the forenoon and afternoon as possible in J's company, having fallen a willing victim to her charms . . . I have reason to think that J. cares for me a little – perhaps I am mistaken but so I fancy.

Friday, 17th April [1918] Among the guests who arrived were the Ls – Ena, G and M. With Ena especially I had very close fellowship. We walked to and from town very often together – she is a delightful girl of about 24, out and out for the Lord, practical, thoughtful and talented.

Wednesday, 7th May [1918] At Bangor I saw less of J. than I had expected and Ena's coming on the scene altered the aspect of things for a little. For a day or two after coming here I was in a strait betwixt two – or thought I was; last night I decided that I was not and had not been in love with Ena; whereas I was most decidedly in love with J. Ena is older, further on the spiritual life and better fitted in every way to be a help to me, but . . .

Tuesday, 15th May [1918] Travelled to Edinburgh again and spent an hour at . . . J. struck me as somewhat colder and I was unable to make any advances, despite the fact that we were alone together for quite a time.

Thursday, 11th September [1919] Here I record the fact that I find myself in love with Ena – Ena whom I met at Bangor and with whom I have corresponded since. I don't know exactly how or where it happened but my liking for her conceived at our first meeting has steadily grown and ripened into something more. A letter received from her last Monday gives me distinct reason to hope that she likes me and will yet be led to love if the Lord will. I won't set down my feelings here – it would take too long and be by no means easy.

2nd January [1920] – Met Ena at 8.15. She desired to visit my digs. I had not contemplated this and found my landlady unprepared and greatly taken aback. We did not just have the happiest of evenings – I was too nervous and oppressed by thoughts that I must break off our intimacy for Ena's sake; my future hopes being so uncertain.

DP was still a young man: a young man from a loving home and a close family, and subject to all the hormonal and social pressures common to those of his age. His decision to start on the long path towards a degree and some form of ministry impacted on both girls with whom he might have had a deepening relationship. There could be no hope of his yet being able to commit himself to family responsibilities of his own as a married man: 'my future hopes being so uncertain'. Still, he continued to fret over his lack of relationship with Ena: 'Tonight I was very hungry for Ena and found myself painting pictures and dreaming dreams of the future.' All this time he was living in lodgings and, as he remembered in *Personal Encounters*:

> This was not home; there were no children; there was no family table or fireside; and for all these things, I confess, I pined.

There were other pressures, too, pulling in different ways.

> Sunday, 24th July [1921] . . . I am struck by the number of people who agree that it might be the best thing for me to return to business after finishing my College course and do evangelistic work at my leisure.

If, looking forward, there was the thought of marriage and future family prospects, there were also his ongoing responsibilities from the past as the oldest surviving son of James and Helena Thomson. The postwar years were not easy for the family at Hyndford Terrace. Mrs Thomson faced major surgery in 1921, and took time to recover. Though inheriting something of his own father's status in Dundee, James Thomson had made his way as the sole practitioner of a solicitor's practice and faced a financial crisis after the War. By 1921 DP's 60-year old father was almost bankrupt. One solution would have been for his eldest surviving son to have abandoned or curtailed his studies, gone into business, begun to earn and support his parents:

> Wednesday, 10th August [1921] . . . All evening we discussed business. I found this very black – Father owes £570 against which he has only an unsaleable Roperie bond – Aunt Lizzie refuses help and has written very bitter and unkind letters . . . ordering Christine to dismiss the maids and upbraiding Robert for not being at work. They have decided to leave Hyndford at the end of the month and are doing all they can to get it sold. The maids are getting notice, part of the furniture is to be stored and the rest to be sold, Father and Mother are to take turns in the country within convenient distance of Dundee, Christine goes into residence at the Infirmary and Robert hopes to get a job in London. If the house is not sold by the end of the month it is to be left empty. We agreed to ask £1,550, but to let it go at £1,200 or £1,050 if need be. It is bonded up to £800 and the residue will go towards the bank overdraft. We sat late discussing plans – it will mean a big upheaval for Mother.

Besides, quite apart from this family crisis, business remained attractive to DP: he believed (almost certainly wrongly!) he had an aptitude for it. To assist with the costs of his student days he attempted to make money by trading. A schoolboy enterprise in buying and selling postage stamps was briefly revived in 1919-1920; rather more useful, perhaps even hopeful, was the attempt in 1921 to go into reselling second hand theological books.

DP reckoned he could store 800 books in his lodgings; he looked to buy up ministers' libraries and resell at the BTI and university. In September 1921 the family emergency was postponed by the sale of 1 Hyndford Terrace for what was then the huge sum of £1,100 and by Robert securing a post at St Andrews University that would also enable him successfully to complete a Ph.D. The crisis was to return in 1922, though it should also be said that James Thomson completed his legal career still practising as a solicitor and notary public, and as Clerk to the Justices of the Peace for Forfarshire.[10]

The immediate past also retained its attractions. In August 1921 a letter arrived asking DP when he would be free to undertake an evangelistic tour of a remote area of New Zealand as his ministry in Salonica was remembered by some of the evangelicals within the Anzac forces. There must, too, have continued to be tensions between his ties to the UF Church and those to his Gospel Hall friends, some of whom considered the UF ministry as a whole to be spiritually dead. Was he really on the right track? As well as his regular preaching, DP now developed an evangelistic missionary-based lantern lecture, 'The Challenge of a World's Need', and he reappeared on platforms for missionary meetings with Mrs Priscilla Studd, with whom he was again on calling terms. Service overseas remained his dream, but a dream he was aware that was challenged by reality. There was the continuing issue of his health. The pressure of campaigns could reawaken his heart condition:

> Saturday, 8th April [1921] . . . After a hunt around I got Dr F. W. Martin at his house at 1.30 and he examined my heart. The verdict was what I had feared namely that my heart is much dilated again and from about 10% I am back to at least 30% – Martin says 3 weeks on my back would put it right but he wouldn't prescribe it under the circumstances. He advised me not to consider the foreign field but thought I could go out at home. This was rather a setback to me and gave me much food for reflection.

Medical advice continued to block thoughts of missionary work – and possibly of marriage as well. There was also the question as to whether he was really the colonial missionary 'type' compared, for example, to 'Ralph Connor', an alias for Rev. Dr. Charles W. Gordon, a best-selling author and a leading Canadian presbyterian minister, who had served in the North Western Territories:

> Friday, 15th July [1921] . . . In the mirror that Ralph Connor held up before me I see how woefully and pitifully inadequate my equipment is for the Master's service – a pleasing personality, a gift of

> conversation, an emotional nature, a genius for organisation, and the power to preach compellingly and persuasively – against these, and I have exaggerated them – must be set the fact that physically I am far from robust, I excel at no manly games, I can neither ride, cycle, swim nor skate, I can neither sing nor play, I have none of the arts wherewith to claim men and none of those manly gifts which win respect – nor am I even handy or adaptable. What a useless lot of lumber – can it be that my work lies at home where my equipment does count for something, or is it possible for me to develop the things that are lacking and yet make the world my parish? The answer is with Him and time will tell . . .

John Wesley's 'the world as my parish' was D. P. Thomson's longest held ambition, and he believed in the positive value, under God, of having high ambitions.

Three main streams of Christian experience helped to shape D. P. Thomson during the first stage of his vocation. There was the stream associated with the JEB, the HAM and the broader Keswick holiness theology of a mainly English evangelicalism that linked in Scotland with the Faith Mission and the Gospel Hall culture. He also came better to appreciate the evangelistic commitment and other strengths of the United Free Church in which he had been brought up, albeit not exclusively. Underlying both these streams was the lasting Atlantic-wide legacy of the evangelist D. L. Moody. These streams could flow in different directions and, while we now know the outcome, we need too to appreciate the choices and pressures DP faced during these years. The HAM we have met; Moody we will look at again. The ethos of the United Free Church now needs further examination.

The United Free Church amalgamated with the established Scottish church in 1929. Its character and its contribution to the united Kirk have, regrettably, been overshadowed by the continuance of the name of 'The Church of Scotland' as that of both the pre-union Established Church and that of the new, potentially different, denomination created by the Union. Evangelism was widely practised in the UF Church: it was during a campaign in their McCheyne Memorial Church that, aged, 11, DP responded to the appeal of the evangelist. Such weeks or special addresses were a regular part of congregational life. The interest of such good numbers of UF congregations in, for example, the tiny Heart of Africa Mission went hand-in-glove with evangelisation at home. Moreover evangelism was officially encouraged by central structures of the UF

Church. Reports of campaigns and analysis of strategy filled pages of the annual volumes of *Reports* to the United Free General Assembly in the 1920s with an ethos that was lost after 1929. In 1922 D. P. Thomson was elected the representative of the Glasgow Divinity Hall to his denomination's Central Campaigns Committee: he was then appointed to its Executive, the body responsible to the General Assembly for planning centrally-backed campaigns. In the later 1920s numerous UF presbyteries supported 'Active Evangelism', following a model promoted by their General Assembly's Home Mission and Church Extension Committee. The recommended methodology included co-operation with other churches; securing the support of the host congregation through preparation in advance via study circles and prayer groups; house-to-house visitation; open-air occasions and sectional meetings 'for women only, for men only, for adolescents, or for any classes in the Community'. The whole was to be undertaken only after a survey of the area had been undertaken, so that 'the changed habits and social circumstances of the people' might be born in mind. 'The utmost flexibility in the method of Evangelism is now called for.'[11] Of particular interest, in the light of future discussions, was the UF insistence that renewal of the church came through engagement in evangelism and was not a prerequisite.[12] This insight would be rediscovered by the Scottish churches after the Second World War.

The evangelistic ethos of the UF Church was, for a time, part of its legacy to the united Kirk: a legacy the more significant because it was an ethos that was less in evidence in the pre-union Established Church of Scotland. As the 'Auld Kirk' mainly understood it, people came to Christ, not through campaigns but within the ordinary ordinances of Sunday worship, Sunday School and Bible Class, through baptism and membership classes. Missions were not for the population as a whole but for those abroad; or, through the limited non-parochial institutions of the Home Mission and Highlands & Islands Committees, for those in need or on the margins of society. Even in the UF Church there could be a sense that a respectable urban congregation ought not to be addressed in a personally challenging evangelistic mode, as DP was once told:

> Tuesday, 17th May [1921] . . . I heard from Mr Herringshaw at teatime of a St James man who had been giving vent to his feelings in a butcher's shop and asking what right I had to preach such sermons in St James! I ought to be either in a Mission Hall or in Central Africa!

Evangelist at Kilmarnock: Glencairn

During the winter of 1920-21 D. P. Thomson found that he could not ignore his intuition that evangelism was to be his calling. His congregational experience had thrilled him as young men and women had committed themselves to Christ while he led communicants' classes (at Wallneuk UF), or Bible Classes (Renwick UF and Glasgow: Central UF) or the Boys' Class at Central. In addition while at Glasgow: Central he had acted as chaplain to the Quarriers City Orphan Home. Though he could still lapse into somewhat juvenile behaviour:

> 20th July [1920] I played a very coarse game [*of football*] and laid out quite a number of the boys – overdid it and had pangs of remorse.

. . . he was also developing broader sympathies of mind, both socially:

> Friday, 28th May [1920] Coming home I was greatly moved about Central Europe and feel lately about giving up my pleasures and plans for the summer and stumping the country in a passionate endeavour to bring home to the nation the awful distress and our tremendous responsibility. I pray that I may be led aright. Golf seems tawdry besides this.

. . . and theologically:

> 1st January 1921 I chatted with Mr Sloan [*Walter B. Sloan, Keswick Convention Secretary*] who was deeply interested in all I had to say about student life and its attitude to dogmatism and Biblical interpretation – I was delighted with the breadth and charity of his views.

Now aged 24, DP was questioning the dogmatism of his youth and, taking a less rigid view of Biblical interpretation, he was pleased to find that the Keswick Convention Secretary could empathise with him.

DP was also more self-aware and self-critical than he had been as a younger man – more able to understand and to channel his surges of enthusiasm: 'Why do I want to shine as an impressive preacher and not merely to glorify God as an earthen vessel used by sovereign grace?' he asked himself. 'Troubled with self admiration, vanity and desire for honour,' he prayed 'Oh to be wholly His and all self to be gone!' DP did in fact help to raise funds for the post-war, post-revolutionary crisis in Europe. He also postponed a possible evangelistic tour in the United States, recognising the fantasy in the concept while he had serious work in hand with Orphan Home boys. Neither his American nor his World Tour plan ever did prove possible. Out of this period of reflection came a conviction that he must really *engage* with evangelism, and evangelism particularly among young men and women:

> 2nd February [1921] . . .Last night in prayer I seemed to get my marching orders – to go out into evangelism as an evangelist to young men and women – continuing with College meanwhile and taking missions as the Lord shall lead. Everything – experience, preparation, blessing, seems to have been leading to this for some time.

So DP contacted a number of friends – Horace Govan of Ardrossan, Robert Steel of Dunfermline, Rev. W. A. Thomson of Dalmellington and Rev. Geo. Steele Jeffrey of Kilmarnock – to share with them what he was thinking and to ask if they knew of any opportunities. Three offers came back, from Kilmarnock, Ardrossan and Saltcoats, all of which he accepted:

> Wednesday, 16th February [1921] Last night I received a letter which may mark an epoch in my life . . . I heard from Mr Jeffrey – his own church had experienced a gracious revival under Wm. Thomson in November when 300 decided and it was hardly the time for another mission, but his friend Rev. John Hunter of Glencairn Church had been wanting all winter just such a mission as I proposed.

The United Free Church of Kilmarnock: Glencairn was therefore to be the first to invite D. P. Thomson, as its guest evangelist, to lead a full week's special mission campaign.

Deciding to set several weeks at a time aside to be the leader of a series of evangelistic campaigns was no light matter. Besides the spiritual responsibility there were other matters to consider. DP's invalidity pension from the Army was being reviewed, so perhaps the responsible course would be to be content with taking further assistantships, which could offer a regular income that ad hoc special missions certainly would not? The 1920s saw massive unemployment in Scotland, financial and economic crisis: DP would have known of the occasion in 1919 when the UK government deployed troops and tanks in the streets of Glasgow to repress socialist radicals. And what about finding time for his courses of study – and what, too, about any possible future with Ena?

> Kilmacolm might call me for 3 to 4 months with hospitality, £33 per Sunday, probably a presentation at the end, plenty of time for study and no work through the week. I thought of what that would mean in the way of quiet preparation for the future, of influence in a wealthy church, and of saving for Ena – I faced it all and felt that if the way opened, the more uncertain and exacting field of evangelism was the one the Lord would have me enter.

Hudson Taylor's sacrificial modelling of living by faith; the example of the Inland South America Missionary Union and that, even, of C. T. Studd, had not been lost on D. P. Thomson. In a not very dramatic and yet ultimately critical way, this was when DP fulfilled his earlier commitment to his Master to go 'whenever and wherever He called'. It was, however, typical of him that he *also* undertook a locumship at Kilmacolm: St James during 1921. When this finished, he continued to preach and run young people's activities on a regular basis at Kilmacolm: St Columba's. These engagements brought contacts with some of Glasgow's wealthy evangelical businessmen, especially with Joseph Maclay, 2nd Baron Maclay, for whose advice (and occasional donations towards campaigning projects) Thomson became a fairly regular visitor at Duchal House.

The Glencairn Church mission (19 - 28 March 1921) was explicitly directed towards young people, of whom there were a good number connected to the congregation: 80 in the Bible Class, over 40 in a Christian Endeavour Group. The aim of the week was thus to convert young people who no doubt had been baptised as infants and were well integrated into the organisations of the congregation. They still needed to make their own decisions to commit to Christ. The mission consisted of 12 meetings spanning eight days and DP's diary narrative of the week was a full one. He was concerned to record the occasion and the topic on which he spoke, not always with a text annexed. Comments were added on how he felt while speaking: variants on the old themes of liberty, power and impression. These addresses did not follow any preset theme. Indeed he settled on his title for each evening earlier that day after thought and prayer, and according to what he believed was the Spirit's prompting. His sermon on one occasion at least was written on the train and in the vestry immediately beforehand. DP was a 'just-in-time' composer of sermons. In practice he selected different Biblical exemplars for the need to decide, though towards the end two addresses focused on issues of living the Christian life. The invitation to receive the Holy Spirit's blessing was issued after the official end of the week, showing a continuing distinction and practical separation between salvation and sanctification.

Choreography included features of evangelism familiar since the days of Moody and Sankey. There was an enquiry room, to which those under 'impression' or 'convicted' were invited to come; alternatively, there was the 'after-meeting', for the same purpose but with a speaker further urging decision. Singing and prayer added to an emotional atmosphere that fostered a sense of crisis, of urgency. Before the mission DP questioned aspects of this methodology with his friend and BTI fellow-student Frank Millard. The then normal method of appealing for decision was publicly to ask the newly convicted or converted to stand – and *to keep on asking* until someone did stand. At Kilmarnock, in fact, DP did not use such blatant manipulation. He simply intimated that those who wished might stay behind and thus allowed the majority of the congregation their opportunity to leave. Still, the event was understood as a struggle, as a battle to break the grip of the Devil (mentioned twice in DP's narrative of events at Kilmarnock), and the evangelist's task was to win victory by all means at his disposal: his faithful use of Scripture, he (and others) bathing the event in prayer; the impact of his personality; the methodology of the meeting. It was the Glencairn minister, DP's host John Hunter, who at the beginning of this week recommended that an evangelistic address should be four-fifths appeal and one fifth Biblical exposition – a recommendation DP took to heart thereafter.

Theology, too, played its part. Friends of DP's, students at the BTI, believed that no-one could be truly converted without understanding that Christ died on the Cross to pay the penalty for his or her sin. If this doctrine of penal substitution, alone, could explain and enable atonement, it would then follow that every evangelistic address must focus on the Crucifixion. DP did not wholly agree, not because he did not accept that particular explanation of the atonement, but because he was prepared to distinguish what was understood at any one time by a human mind from what God was achieving for eternity in the soul. John Hunter, however, also took a firm view of the essential place of the Cross in evangelism, and DP was at least to some extent persuaded, in part also because of his preparatory reading in James Denney's *Studies in Theology*. On Friday 25 March 1921, DP therefore preached on 'The Message of Calvary' and there were four enquirers. The Cross was, however, only one of the notes he struck that week: others were God's final judgment, the fulfilment to be found in Christ, and Christ's call to service. Behind all the apparatus of evangelism DP looked to find the Spirit of God working in answer to the faith and prayer of Christian people.

By the end of the week what had happened? DP summarised the 'fruits', as he understood them:

> Thus ended my 1st Campaign. What are the fruits, so far we know them? 1st A deeper sense of my own utter inability to win men and women for Jesus. 2nd A realisation of His wondrous goodness and power in answer to simple trust and believing prayer. 3rd Real blessing among the Christians of Glencairn – a number begun to testify for the first time; and one at least begun to lead others to Christ, one volunteered for the foreign field

> and several delivered from the burden of sin and evil habits; backsliders restored and about 20 in the Saviour's fold for the first time. How good God is. Mr H and I rejoiced quietly together.

He had found it hard. On the Monday, he had almost despaired of being ready in time:

> Monday, 21st March [1921] All day I was in a maze as to what I should speak on at night – I could get nothing done and no light. Oh how I longed to get out of a meeting for which I felt so unready!

On the Tuesday evening he had been entirely out of his depth dealing with girls in floods of tears:

> I felt hopelessly at sea in dealing with the anxious souls and feel that I bungled it badly. Oh for a 'clinique' where individual dealing is taught . . . Kilmarnock will be a great test as well as a great field.

Through it all ran his consciousness of the support of the congregation's more experienced minister and of his need to learn from him: 'It is good to have such a man by me to guide me,' he wrote on the Monday night. From all of this came the deeper realisation that he could not by himself 'win men and women for Jesus' – he had continually to look to God, to 'His wondrous goodness and power in answer to simple trust and believing prayer'.

This week of special mission had built on the normal life of the congregation of Kilmarnock: Glencairn, just as similar weeks slotted into congregational life across the country. The pattern of a week of meetings with a guest preacher was a familiar one: the young people of the congregation were invited, and so they came. What it meant to be converted was also understood: meetings could be advertised for 'young converts' with some confidence that they would be attended. Emotional distress and its resolution through counselling was an accepted part of religious behaviour. For some, the mission was about internalising and personally acknowledging the faith in which they had been brought up, about learning to speak in public about their faith. DP wrote of one boy,

> J, who came through to victory on Friday night, came to volunteer for the foreign field. His father, who is Sunday School Superintendent and President of the Boys' Brigade, came in later to see me. He himself had great blessing during the mission and is quite willing that his son should go – the way may open up for his entering the BTI in September.

This mission was directed at older teenagers of the sort of age that DP was when he first starting writing the Diary of My Life. The minority were still at school, most were probably in (or looking for) work. These were young men and women on the brink of adulthood, facing decisions about their future in the highly unsettled post-war world of the early 1920s. To choose to offer for foreign mission was, for the sincere, to follow a well-beaten Scottish path. Nevertheless it is interesting that it was the girls that appear to have been most affected by the mission: belonging to the Church was still part of what it meant to be an adult for many British women until, perhaps, the 1960s.[13] DP's first campaign was conducted according to the established patterns of his day, with a vocabulary he shared with his audience and their parents, part of a spectrum of behaviour and belief that linked the presbyterian UF Church with the Brethren and the Gospel Halls. In time, this pattern would come to be described as 'the old evangelism', and its effectiveness would be considered to be at an end.

Meanwhile DP moved from the Glencairn mission to the Ardrossan mission, which included factory gate meetings and was directed more at adults and especially men. Then came Saltcoats and then in the autumn a second series of missions: at Alloa, at Dalry in Ayrshire, and at Govan. Results were mixed. He returned to Saltcoats in early 1922 to speak to the Christian Endeavour group and was delighted. At Alloa, however, apparently few decisions were made. All this time he was finishing his Arts course to graduate M.A. in 1922 and also preaching regularly in Glasgow and Kilmacolm. From Sunday appointments, too, decisions flowed. By the end of 1921, DP had confirmed in his own mind his calling to be an evangelist:

> Sunday, 13th November [1921] There are many fields tempting me sorely just now – social purity, missionary pleading and organisation, the cleansing of public life, the proclamation of an ethical gospel etc, but more and more do I come to feel that this is essentially the age of the specialist and if I am to do my real work in the world – having only one short life to live – I must specialise in evangelism. It is at once the easiest and hardest of fields and it is certainly the greatest – it is easy to score a cheap and showy success, definitely hard to succeed in a way that will endure but with Him all things are possible.

Despite the various crises that had come his way since Salonica, DP was able to look back over these four years with gratitude to God:

> Sunday, 27th November [1921] Here I am at Kilmacolm again, another year having nearly run its course. Looking back I praise God for his goodness in the 4 years that have elapsed since I got my discharge from the Army. Told then that I would be a semi-invalid all my days, I can look back on 4 years during which I have not had 3 days in bed at any time and

> not 10 altogether. I have preached some 650 times, have travelled up and down the country as a Deputation Secretary, been Locum in 3 churches and Assistant in 3 others, have launched into evangelism and engaged in 6 campaigns and all the time studied to good effect, taking a high place at the BTI, passing with distinction in 7 subjects at the Christian Worker School, and getting through 5 subjects for my M.A. How very good God has been.

Events and people had and could upset him: but his freedom from any enduring bitterness, his forswearing of personal animosity, remained one of his attractive traits.

EVANGELIST IN TRAINING:
III - With the Students, 1922-1928

> We must go to the people – our cushioned seats and comfortable pews have seen more of us than have the multitudes that flow past our church doors like sheep without a shepherd. If the men of the 1921 Revival can draw crowds in the open air in the cold of a northern winter night, the mighty potential army of Christ in our town and city congregations can arrest and win the indifferent masses by a combined and whole-hearted effort to reach men in the streets and lanes of the city.
>
> D. P. Thomson, 'A Student's Impressions' in *The Record*, February 1922.

> Friday, 5th October [1923] Only last night I became acutely conscious of lost spiritual power – John and Joe both feel that my message lacks the old bite and Joe puts it down to the thorough change in my intellectual outlook – I don't. I regard the trouble as spiritual and I am out to put it right in the only possible way – by getting right with God.
>
> D. P. Thomson, The Diary of My Life part 8.

In 1922 D. P. Thomson entered the Glasgow Divinity Hall of the United Free Church. Like many others at that time, after the close of the war, at 26 he was older than subsequent year-groups of divinity students would be. DP's generation had already lived through the heart-breaking experience of disastrous (if victorious) world war, and the equally heart-breaking disillusionment of the peace; through the collapse of empires and the birth of Bolshevik revolution. The war and its aftermath posed immense questions to the Christian churches of Europe. The world and theology appeared to enter a new age. Many were determined that steps must be taken to ensure that such a blood-bath could never recur. Some concluded that the hour for Christian unity had struck; others, that effective evangelism was the pressing need. Faced with ruin and revolution in eastern Europe, Karl Barth's theology of crisis turned its back on the optimism of liberalism. The Church of Scotland and the United Free Church now stepped up negotiations towards their union. DP became a candidate for the ministry of the United Free Church with some reputation as an itinerant evangelist: by 1930 he was a parish minister of the Church of Scotland. Besides his theological studies, he continued regular preaching. Besides his preaching, he also created the Glasgow Students Evangelistic Union and ran campaigns across Scotland. Besides these campaigns, he also stepped up his business enterprises to assist with his continuing family financial problems, masterminding the publication of a series of evangelistic handbooks. At times the pressure of all this became too much and he endured a difficult period of vocational and spiritual crisis while his approach to theology continued to diverge away from dogmatic fundamentalism. To meet the need of the 'new era' DP embraced the call for a 'New Evangelism'.

The Glasgow Students Evangelistic Union

D. P. Thomson was a life-long evangelical, if that word describes a broad segment within the British churches that emphasised conversion and a life given in active service to Christ, accepting the authority of the Bible and relying on Christ's death on the Cross.[1] Thinking of himself as an evangelist, able to speak for Christ in the formal and informal, the planned and the unexpected, and looking for God's Spirit to lead hearers through the experience of conversion, DP also thought of himself as an evangelical. The strand of the life of the church underlying the whole period of his ministerial formation was the legacy of the American evangelist, D. L. Moody. 'Moody is the man from whom I have learned most,' DP chose, with the benefit of hindsight, to acknowledge in *The Road to Dunfermline*. While in Dundee as a young man his reading and sermon-tasting had been much influenced by Moody's associates. He admired Moody's career as an evangelist: 'Today I have a shelf of books dealing with his work'; he admired Moody's principles: 'Moody took long views . . . he brought local ministers right into the centre of the picture . . . above all Moody remained a learner until the end': and he admired Moody's legacy in Scotland – the human legacy of those converted during the missions of 1873, 1881-2 and 1891-2. 'Sound in strategy', 'thorough in organisation' (as DP put it), and supported by his musician colleague and soloist, Ira Sankey, Moody's success had confirmed a pattern for evangelism – the publicity, the mass meeting, the singing, preaching for decision, personal counselling – that was to endure and deeply influenced DP's own early practice. Moody's, and DP's, purpose was the conversion of the individual.[2] DP was not alone in recognising Moody's work in Scotland:

the centenary of Moody's birth was widely celebrated across the Kirk in 1937.

In looking to Moody as his model, 'a simple, direct, forthright preacher, with a marvellous gift of experiential illustration', DP was looking to a self-taught man without formal theological education, who steered clear of the doctrinal controversies that as the 20th century progressed tended to divide evangelicals. Moody avoided identification with the extremes of the holiness movement, just as he avoided the extremes of pre-millennialism. As DP later said in a BBC interview and printed in *Why I Believe*: 'If you were actively engaged as I was in work all the time, and if you were seeing the Spirit of God working in the lives of men, you had this to set over against any theories that might be in danger of gripping your mind temporarily.' The reality of spiritual life and new birth meant far more to him than debating doctrinal divisions. Thus when in 1922 the Student Christian Movement [SCM] in Glasgow University split on the creation of the Christian Students Fellowship [later the Christian Union or CU], 'a group of those who were prepared to confess to an allegiance, to subscribe to a creedal basis, and to adhere to a formulated policy' as part of the then developing Inter-Varsity Fellowship [IVF], DP recorded that 'There was a large exodus of evangelicals from the SCM, and I found myself one of a very small minority [*ie of evangelicals*] remaining within that fellowship.'[3] In its origins and into the 1920s the SCM organised student evangelistic campaigns: it had been a sponsor of the 1910 Edinburgh missionary conference. For years DP subscribed to the SCM Press book club. Nevertheless he had been voted off its newly-formed Glasgow committee in 1920 after only one year: perhaps he was too abrasive or too conservative? Who now knows! This rejection meant that it was not to be to the SCM that DP was to give his energy as a theological student, but rather to his own independent creation, the Glasgow Students Evangelistic Union [GSEU].

DP's first series of missions, in the spring and autumn of 1921, beginning with Kilmarnock: Glencairn, had been conducted by himself, or by himself and Frank Millard, in association with the local minister or ministers. Then came the Fraserburgh Revival over the winter of 1921-22, associated with the independent evangelist Jock Troup. DP and a fellow student, Alec Smart, went north to the fishing town to see what was happening, encouraged the local presbyterian congregations to become involved and (very briefly and somewhat nominally) led the movement after Troup had departed. Thereafter DP addressed a large number of meetings in southern Scotland on the subject of 'The Revival', substantially boosting his connections and reputation. The UF Church's monthly magazine, *The Record*, published an article he wrote on lessons to be learned from the Revival:[4]

> We must rid our minds for ever of the idea that that dignified dullness which passes for Christianity – the stilted respectability that claims lineage with Pentecost – has any real relation to the vital and living religion of the New Testament. We must find a spiritual home for the red-hot enthusiast and a place for 'Hallelujahs' and 'Amens,' . . . we must shed some of our ecclesiastical vestments and scrap some of our machinery if need be – above all, we must get to our knees and we must go the people . . . We must go to the people – our cushioned seats and comfortable pews have seen more of us than have the multitudes that flow past our church doors like sheep without a shepherd. If the men of the 1921 Revival can draw crowds in the open air in the cold of a northern winter night, the mighty potential army of Christ in our town and city congregations can arrest and win the indifferent masses by a combined and whole-hearted effort to reach men in the streets and lanes of the city. Wesley and Whitefield roused the England of their day and shook it from end to end because they went to the people – went to them whenever and wherever they could be found . . .

A live, practical faith; an out of doors faith; an outgoing church; a church not just of the ministry but of the whole body of Christ: these were lessons that were to remain with D. P. Thomson. John Wesley was to remain one of his Christian heroes and exemplars, from whom DP learnt 'We must go to the people'. His article also contained a summary of the gospel preached at Fraserburgh, a useful account of DP's own core message at this time:

> The message of the revival has been the message of every great spiritual awakening – a tender, pleading, passionate appeal to commit the heart and life to Christ in one definite act of surrender and faith – an appeal based on personal experience, on the deep need of the human heart and the wonderful efficacy of the atoning work of Christ. Man in his sin and need, God in his righteousness and love, Christ in his substitutionary work and soul-satisfying power – these have been the notes of the Evangel struck by the speakers in this Revival. Hell has been preached but not unduly stressed; the terrors of judgment may have formed a dark background to the appeal of the preacher, but it was a background which only served to set forth more clearly and winsomely the offer of salvation – the revelation of a heart of love that found expression on a Roman cross.

The formation of the GSEU was intended to offer some structure, and to recruit some helpers, for what had begun in 1921. Now in early 1922 DP and four others founded the GSEU to be a disciplined fellowship of students to conduct evangelistic campaigns at the request of local churches. Its basis of membership was not any doctrinal statement but the preparedness to take part in campaigns to proclaim Christ: it thus accepted participants from both the SCM and the IVF.[5] From the start it was ambitious, even visionary, as DP admitted in 1951:

> No movement of the kind began its work with so small a group of men and so ambitious a set-up. We started with five members, four of whom were office-bearers, and we began with an Hon. President and seven Hon. Vice-Presidents, to say nothing of a library, a headquarters, and a financial appeal aimed at bringing in not less than £200. But our optimism was justified, and within a few weeks we had established ourselves as a force to be reckoned with in the life of both Church and College . . . 'The primary aim and purpose of the Union,' I read [*from a report issued in June 1922*], 'is to equip and qualify its members by a wide and varied practical training for an aggressive evangelistic ministry at home and abroad. With this end in view the GSEU undertakes the supply of pulpits, the temporary oversight of church and mission districts, and (more especially) the conduct of evangelistic campaigns.'

At the meeting of the Executive of the GSEU on 16 March 1922, D. P. Thomson was appointed President, with Alec Smart as Secretary and David Cowan, Treasurer. In time all three would enter the ministry, first of the United Free Church and then of the Church of Scotland.

GSEU campaigns revolved round meetings: following a Saturday welcome meeting, the students would preach at their hosts' Sunday services, hold afternoon and evening rallies, run a series of week-day evening meetings, and conclude with a final 'mass' meeting. Daytime visits to speak at schools and factories were sought. 'After meetings' were offered as opportunities for individuals to be counselled about the meaning of commitment. Personal interviews with the evangelists were encouraged. Publicity, to bring in the people, 'to stimulate curiosity and to set folk talking' was essential. Stunts might be employed to attract attention – parading with sandwich-boards, the use of bands, setting up soap-boxes at street corners were all popular. While on campaign the team often lived together in a church hall, beginning and ending crowded days in corporate prayer. Spawning sister-unions at Aberdeen and Edinburgh, the GSEU later was part of the Scottish Student Campaign Movement which DP served as Chairman in the 1930s, twice leading campaigns during his ministry at Dunfermline: Gillespie Memorial.

#7: CAMPAIGN TEAM, GALASHIELS 1928: DP 2ND FROM LEFT

Alloa, Armadale and Broxburn, Ardrossan, Kilmarnock, Airdrie, Wishaw, Galashiels, Selkirk, Falkirk and Dumbarton, besides Edinburgh itself, were soon to hear the students' proclamation of Christ. The success of the GSEU was such that by July 1923 D. P. Thomson knew the burden and satisfaction of being 'an Evangelical leader – a preacher – a man in the public eye'. By August that year he had been involved with 21 Campaigns and had yet to be licensed as a preacher by the UF Church, never mind finally ordained. The sense of fulfilment that DP experienced 'With the Students on Campaign' never left him; these years confirmed all that he perceived of his vocation, to specialise in evangelistic work, and he devoted a good proportion of *The Road to Dunfermline* to this period.

The first Union campaign was an inter-denominational effort in Greenock, attempted when the movement was barely weeks old. On reading DP's diary's account, what stands out is his shift of focus since his own first campaign. During Kilmarnock: Glencairn, he wrote about the actual meetings of the campaign; during the Greenock Campaign, his underlying concern was the development of the GSEU. Because there were others involved, he did not require to be in Greenock all the time and nor was he. He had several other preaching engagements; he was getting on with his studies; he was making arrangements for future campaigns. He and Alec Smart, with whom he shared rooms, were changing their digs, and premises had also been acquired as a store and meeting room for the Union. With all this going on besides the campaign, DP's accounts of the individual mission services at Greenock were less detailed, though his interest in counting decisions was undiminished.

Even while the Greenock Campaign was in process, DP was also negotiating about further missions at Saltcoats and Auchinleck, and discovering that a project for the GSEU to run its own evangelistic Tent in Ayrshire during the summer had been pre-empted by the Ayrshire Evangelical Union. An elaborate plan to evangelise the area around the UF Church of Glasgow: Young Street was drawn up, to add to an existing commitment of the Union to offer regular pulpit supply at Glasgow: Albert Street. He himself still maintained links with the City Orphan Home and the Kilmacolm: St Columba's and Glasgow: Renwick UF congregations; and he preached midweek on 26 April at Newlands UF Church. On Sunday 23 April he took some part in five services or meetings, none in Greenock but including one in the open air and a Revival Demonstration, planned to oppose the communist and radical-socialist sentiment then current around the Clyde. Meanwhile he spoke 12 times during the two week campaign at Greenock, tackling the first week himself and leaving the second week largely to his colleagues. No doubt the fact that he was recycling stump sermons assisted DP to manage such a schedule. His unease with his performance may also have stemmed from over-busyness and over-familiarity, from the difficulty of remaining fresh with pre-used material. From his own record, it appears that the bulk of the 60 or so recorded decisions took place during the second week, as a response to the ministry of his colleagues.

One or two of the incidents of the Greenock mission are worth further consideration. On occasion DP foreswore the practice of 'button-holing', the active encouragement of individuals into the enquiry room; but at Greenock the persuasion appears to have been somewhat heavy. Although he preferred to use an enquiry room rather than asking those making a decision to stand there and then, he did use the final meeting to ask for a public declaration of a recent conversion, perhaps drawing on his own JEB experience at Swanwick. As at Glencairn, this mission was again successful with the younger men and women, perhaps because of the deliberate targeting of meetings on this group; perhaps because the evangelists were younger people themselves. The conversion of the daughters of the minister whose church hosted the main campaign meetings and the conversion of a Sunday School Superintendent again emphasise that, despite the picketing of football crowds and the holding of open air meetings, the converted appear to have been largely those already within the organisations of the congregations concerned. 'Into the great community lying outside the scope of the Church's work they [*the campaigns*] only just penetrated,' he was to write in 1951. Nevertheless at the end of their time at Greenock, the members and friends of the GSEU had been encouraged. So, too, was the minister of Crawfordsburn Church, in which the main meetings had been held:

> Thursday, 27th April [1922] . . . We travelled down to Greenock on the 3.10. Alec and I were met by Mr Cameron with whom we talked and tead. He is overjoyed at the Campaign which has far exceeded his expectations. He told me that it had been the greatest thrill of his ministry.

What brought young Scots to decide for Christ? Clearly no sweeping answers can be gleaned from DP's diaries: he had his own particular views and experience, and he seldom recorded individual cases. There was a social or communal element to evangelical practice. Young men and women came in larger groups to meetings; they often stayed behind to after-meetings in twos or threes; they often decided when collectively counselled. When asked publicly to stand to testify to their new faith or to attend Young Converts meetings, again this was done together, in company. DP sometimes had qualms about the spiritual reality of such proceedings. On 9 October 1921 he wrote: 'I feel that the after meeting work has not been systematic enough – nightly I have dealt with the young people in a group, whereas individual dealing is really the only satisfactory way;' and after a meeting he attended in November 1921:

> On Monday night I came down to Mr Stewart's meeting and again on Friday. [*Stewart was conducting a week of lantern services in the Kidston Halls for children*]. On Friday over 80 waited to the afternoon meeting, I dealt with 8 boys of over 14, three of whom decided, two being the Paterson boys. After 25 minutes talk I got them all to their knees but none decided – it was only after the others had gone that I got these three to the place of decision. Mr Hope Robertson got 14 names of boys between 12 and 14 who professed – I have grave doubts about these wholesale conversions.

Younger teenage boys might well be expected to be sensitive to the group dynamics of whether to wait for an after-meeting; of whether or not to signify decision. DP's 'grave doubts about these wholesale conversions' are very understandable. The practical ratios of evangelists to enquirers meant that enquiries and decisions were often not handled on a one-to-one basis. It is easy, however, to see how such a shared dedication to Christ could leave a congregation stronger and more determined in its life and witness. Rev. T. Ralph Morton, no enthusiast for the older evangelism, later acknowledged that such campaigns could be helpful in bringing to decisive, active Christian service young people brought up in an emotionally drier, primarily doctrinal Calvinism.[6]

There were of course conversations and encounters with individuals that made a deep impression on D. P. Thomson:

> Sunday, 16th October [1921] The fellow I got – a fine young chap of 19 – seemed in deadly earnest. While unable to remember his exact words, I recall them as something like this. 'I am right up against it tonight – I have never been up against it like this before. I will be 20 tomorrow and I've got to make up my mind what I'm going to do. I have to decide for life tonight!' He seemed to be quite clear, had counted the cost of open confession and coming right out, wanted to make sure that it worked, and to know why some who had made profession showed no difference in their lives. He gave his heart to Christ and then I learnt that Parker was dealing with his greatest friend. He was obviously deeply moved and gripped my hand like a vice, saying 'I have given my heart to God tonight'. How we praised the Lord together. I don't know when I have seen young fellows of that class and age so deeply moved as to the necessity for and meaning of decision, or so desirous to press right through.

Conversion for DP was a two-way transaction between Christ and the individual. Even if he wasn't as certain as some of his fellow-students at the BTI had been that an understanding of the doctrine of penal substitution was essential, yet his understanding of the conflict in the human heart between sin and the gospel led him to accept, in adults, evidence of spiritual and emotional crisis:[7] 'Salvation must be a crisis and there must be definite and personal acceptance of the Saviour and His atoning work.'

D. P. Thomson reflected on these issues publicly in his chapter 'The Conduct of Children's Meetings' in *Winning the Children for Christ.* Much in this chapter appears to reflect DP's own personal upbringing and entry into Christian service. He, personally, had not begun his Christian walk with a crisis of guilt and repentance: such a 'catastrophic' experience was not for children, he wrote, to be taken as normative:

> But at all costs care must be taken to avoid creating the impression that life is generated and cradled in sin and shadowed by guilt and condemnation from its very entrance into the world, and that only by the

> way of repentance and cleansing – by heartfelt conviction and catastrophic conversion – can young or old come into the Kingdom. Such teaching is altogether alien to the spirit of the New Testament and does violence not only to the character of our Lord, but to the sensitive mind of the child.

In his own teenage years he had heard his Master's challenge to a life of Christian service; and in 1924 he wrote of the positive invitation, welcome and summons of Jesus, of both 'the inalienable right of every child to a place in the Kingdom of God, to his share of the Heavenly Father's love and care' and 'the sense of something big enough to demand all they are and have, and the knowledge of One Who is worthy of all their devotion and service'. Again, the detail of doctrine is in the background, the engine unseen under the bonnet of the car, 'however necessary such creedal statement may be for the fully developed intelligence'. This line of argument was that of Newton H. Marshall, *Conversion or the New Birth* republished by Thomson & Cowan in 1924. In 'The Conduct of Children's Meetings' DP wrote that Jesus' 'two-fold nature', 'the God of the catechism' and 'the substitutionary theories of the theologian' were alike unsuitable for children. So, too, was the prewar optimism that reduced Jesus merely to a model to be emulated:

> In presenting the Christ of history and of experience to the child-mind he must beware of leaving the impression that Jesus is little more than a Hero to be admired, or a great Teacher and Wonder Worker. He must set forth Christ as both Saviour and Lord – as Master and Friend.

That Christ is the Saviour from sin and death, who offers forgiveness, was undoubtedly one of the fundamental truths dear to D. P. Thomson in 1924, yet in his own early diaries DP's favourite term for God was not 'My Saviour' but 'My Master.' From the 1920s he insisted on a holistic view of Jesus, understood from both sides of the Cross: 'Christ as both Saviour and Lord – as Master and Friend.' This, he believed, was 'the interpretation that appeals to the boy or girl entering on the adolescent stage.' In consequence DP was content when young people 'decided brightly', as he had, to surrender their lives to Jesus and to follow Him.

The GSEU's early months held D. P. Thomson's massive enthusiasm. He admitted in *The Road to Dunfermline,* however, that initially they had bitten off far more than they could chew.

> The organisation of pulpit supply proved rather a controversial matter, and although carried on for some years, with a Pulpit Supply Secretary as one of the regular office-bearers, it was ultimately dropped . . . The oversight of vacant congregations and mission districts for months at a

> time proved too heavy a strain for all but the first group of members, and that part of the work disappeared even more rapidly. What remained as the permanent sphere of this new student body was the organisation and carrying through of United Evangelistic Campaigns.

During the activities of his student years, D. P. Thomson had to face opposition to the GSEU from within the UF Divinity Hall as well as personality clashes and upsets within its own membership. He was tempted to think that trying to work with a team was a mistake. Within months the original office-bearers had found the strain too much:

> Saturday, 6th May [1922] Cowan is resigning as Treasurer and Alec wants to be relieved of the Secretaryship.

DP now resigned as President in order to become Organising Secretary, causing a further crisis, resolved by a face-to-face meeting during a boat trip:

> Thursday, 13th July [1922] A letter from David Cowan threatening to resign because not consulted about the change of President took me to Craigendoran and thence on his boat to Rothesay. He was very nice.

Joe Haldane succeeded DP as President and proved a good leader. A party from the GSEU travelled together to the Keswick Convention of 1922, and thereafter the teething troubles within the Union appear to have been resolved. More serious was the problem that erupted in January 1923:

> Saturday, 20th January [1923] What a week has gone by – it has changed everything and I feel it has aged me a little. I have been sobered by its events . . . Tuesday saw the first bombshell of the week launched – a spirited attack on the Union at the College dinner table on the grounds of usurping supply functions – it looked as though we would have difficulty in weathering the storm.

It seems that other ministry candidates resented the Union's organisation of pulpit supply, which was valuable to them all for both experience and income. Perhaps some thought that the GSEU was attempting to monopolise available opportunities.

All these storms were weathered, however. DP had a pushy leadership style that could cause problems. He wanted to organise everyone around his vision; he had little time for teams he did not lead. Yet DP also had a vision for reconciliation, and an ability to communicate his enthusiasm for his Master's work as he saw it, that held the GSEU together and made it an effective evangelistic agency. He retained into later life the friendship of many with whom he campaigned in these years. GSEU had not been

#8: POSTER, STUDENTS' CAMPAIGN 1925

narrowly conceived and its breadth of approach remained important. Speakers at its fellowship meetings, 1926-27, included Rev. Principal W. M. Clow on the history of evangelistic method (17 Nov. 1926); Rev. R. C. Mackie on the message of the SCM (24 Nov. 1926) and Rev. James Barr B.D. MP on socialist teaching in the Christian Church. During a 1927 lantern-lecture review of their first five years, DP highlighted 'The Catholicity of the Union', with seven countries represented in its membership (Scotland and England being two), nine denominations and seven faculties. Their refusal to sell a line other than the heart of the Gospel was one reason why the students appear to have been well received in the towns in which they campaigned.

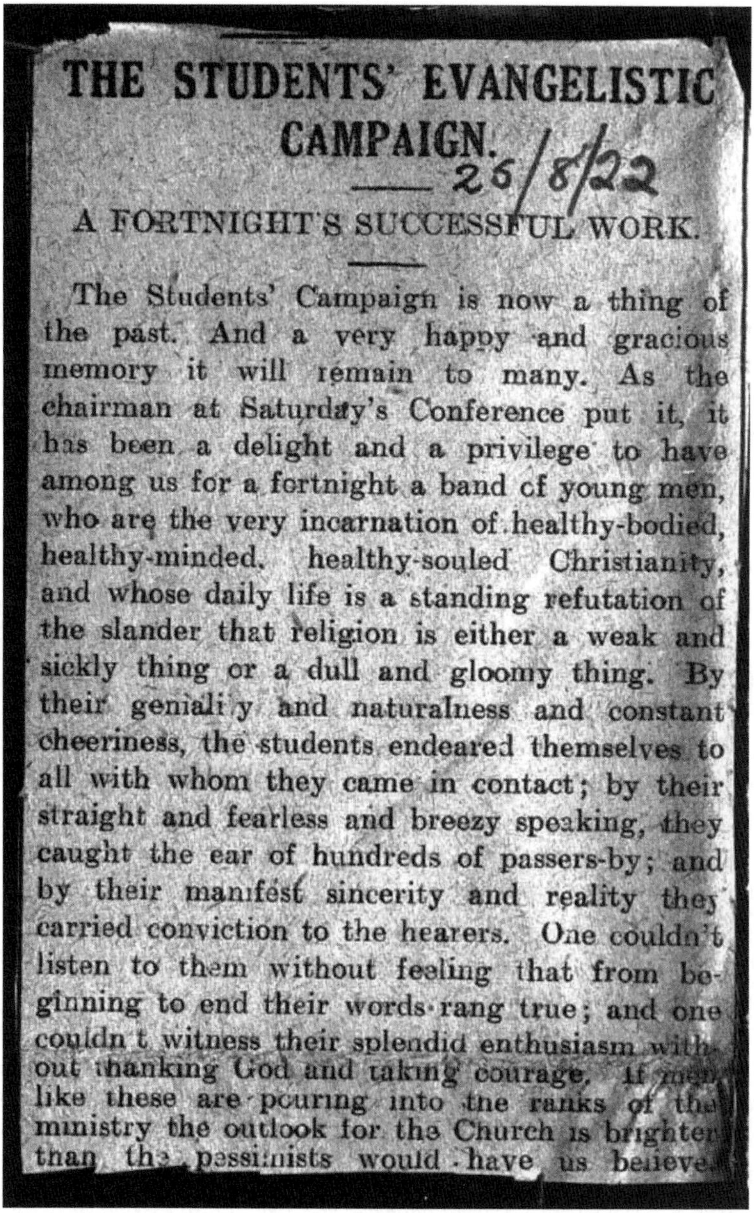

THE STUDENTS' EVANGELISTIC CAMPAIGN.

25/8/22

A FORTNIGHT'S SUCCESSFUL WORK.

The Students' Campaign is now a thing of the past. And a very happy and gracious memory it will remain to many. As the chairman at Saturday's Conference put it, it has been a delight and a privilege to have among us for a fortnight a band of young men, who are the very incarnation of healthy-bodied, healthy-minded, healthy-souled Christianity, and whose daily life is a standing refutation of the slander that religion is either a weak and sickly thing or a dull and gloomy thing. By their geniality and naturalness and constant cheeriness, the students endeared themselves to all with whom they came in contact; by their straight and fearless and breezy speaking, they caught the ear of hundreds of passers-by; and by their manifest sincerity and reality they carried conviction to the hearers. One couldn't listen to them without feeling that from beginning to end their words rang true; and one couldn't witness their splendid enthusiasm without thanking God and taking courage. If men like these are pouring into the ranks of the ministry the outlook for the Church is brighter than the pessimists would have us believe.

9: THE SALTCOATS STUDENTS' EVANGELISTIC CAMPAIGN PRESS-CUTTING, 1922. ONE OF DP'S LANTERN-SLIDES, SOURCE NOT ATTRIBUTED

Handbooks of Modern Evangelism

It takes some effort to recall that DP entered his preaching career on no better basis than a church upbringing little different in quality from that of countless other young Scots of his age. Fortunately DP left sufficient record of his Divinity College years to venture some comments on their impact on his theological formation. Some 40 years later he was interviewed about his faith for BBC Scottish television and his questioner asked whether his academic course had shaken his faith? DP was then willing to admit, and to publish in *Why I Believe*, that he had moved away from 'a more rigidly fundamentalist' view of Biblical inspiration, held in his pre-war youth and the early years of his ministry, to 'a richer understanding of the meaning of the word Revelation, of inspiration, and a new understanding I think particularly of the relationship of the Old Testament to the New'. He also denied, however, that his theology had become 'liberal'. Bishop of Woolwich J. A. T. Robinson's *Honest to God*, the classic book popularising the liberalism of his day, was published in 1963, the same year as the interview. With Robinson's rejection of the age-long view that God was made flesh in Jesus, and with his attempt to find a basis for speaking about 'God' not as any beyond-the-universe reality but instead in human consciousness, he brought to public notice conclusions to which academic theology had been moving for some decades. It was not surprising that in his 1963 BBC dialogue DP sought to distance himself from the suggestion that his theology had been 'liberal' for more than perhaps a few months. His essential beliefs were far more traditional than those of Robinson. D. P. Thomson's God was truly supernatural, both in his transcendence and in his Spirit's immanence.

Involvement with books – buying, reading, writing, publishing – was to be DP's default activity, lacking a current campaign, all his working life. In his college days he started a small business with William Cowan, his friend David's brother, under the imprint Thomson & Cowan, 8 Blythswood Square, Glasgow. 1923 and 1924 saw the publication of four books 'designed to discuss present day needs and problems in the light of the most competent scholarship and the widest practical experience'. These were marketed as a series of *Handbooks of Modern Evangelism*, of which the first was *Evangelism in the Modern World*. Very quickly after this followed *The Modern Evangelistic Address, Modern Evangelistic Movements* and *Winning the Children for Christ*. All four volumes were at first attributed to the editing of 'Two University Men', later revealed to be DP himself and his younger brother and closest friend, Robert. DP described Robert, by 1924 a lecturer in Physical Chemistry, as:

> . . . a teacher and thinker at once intellectually more stimulating and aesthetically more satisfying than almost any I have sat under. In theology, in psychology, and in philosophy, he could take me out of my depth with ease . . . In adult life he was my mentor, my guide, my adviser, and my unfailing council of reference.

We cannot, of course, know whether there were aspects to these publications, not now easy to identify, where Robert's influence predominated. His advanced university education in the physical sciences was far removed from DP's more amateur historical and ecclesiastical interests. Other projected volumes – *Present Day Methods in Evangelism*, *The Psychology of Evangelism* and *The Ministry of Personal Dealing* – failed to appear; and this failure related to Robert's tragically early death in November 1924, aged 25. Yet DP's diaries suggest that not his brother but he himself was the main executive of this publishing enterprise, writing the introductions, soliciting articles from contributors, editing submissions and checking the proofs.

'The Editors' collected specially commissioned chapters from men they considered to be British experts. No explicit party-line was followed: indeed, the preface to *The Modern Evangelistic Address* made it clear that the principle used was the 'utmost catholicity', so that each book might contain 'widely different schools of thought'. Catholicity is of course itself a criterion and not one that all choose to follow. The repetition of the word *Modern* for the series and in the individual titles was clearly intended as a keynote, yet 'Modernism' between the wars had a range of meanings as a descriptive shorthand. It could stand for one side in a fiercely-contested theological controversy between fundamentalist and modernist presbyterians in the USA.[8] Scottish presbyterian opinion was less polarised than that across the Atlantic, however, in part because the 'modern' movement was far more dominant.[9] Undoubtedly aware of the polemical sense of the word, the Thomsons defended their use of 'Modern' as a generic commendation of contemporary practice rather than as denoting allegiance to a school of thought, as least when using it to describe organisations to whom the attribution of modernistic theology could have been offensive.

While the editors affirmed that they 'could not accept responsibility for individual views expressed' in *Evangelism in the Modern World*, nevertheless they did chose to publish without any counterbalance the chapter on 'Evangelism and the Higher Criticism', a chapter fiercely critical of fundamentalism, by contrast calling for the Gospel to be restated in modern terms. The author, Prof. George Jackson, had had painful personal experience of fundamentalism: an attempt had been made in 1913 to reverse his appointment to the chair at the Didsbury Methodist College on the grounds that his acceptance of the principles of higher criticism disqualified him. The case had attracted attention across Britain. A man respected in Scotland for his creation of the Methodist Central Mission in Edinburgh, Jackson's devout *and* modernising stance, and the controversy it had evoked, cannot have been unknown to the Thomson brothers.[10] DP had called personally on Jackson during a visit to England to arrange articles for the *Handbook*. This choice of contributor to *Evangelism in the Modern World* associated the 'Two University Men' with the modernising majority of British ecclesiastical opinion.

The sentiments expressed in Prof. Jackson's chapter on the Higher Criticism were, indeed, very largely those of the Editors of *Evangelism in the Modern World*, as their own introductory chapter revealed. This 'Introduction', written in 1923, was to a considerable extent recycled and expanded by DP when, in 1968, he offered the fruits of 53 years' experience in *Aspects of Evangelism*. The rejection in 1923 of 'a blind literalism and an obstinate obscurantism which have repelled enlightened minds in every communion . . . an unlovable dogmatism altogether alien to the spirit and teaching of Jesus Christ' was to be repeated by DP word for word in 1968 and hence it can be taken truly to express his considered and enduring opinion. With only a very few changes, one entire passage was reprinted:

> Evangelistic preaching is at once direct and personal, urgent and compelling, simple and clear, calculated to enlist reason on its side, and at the same time awaken a responsive chord in the heart. Such preaching constitutes the legitimate demand of every age and forms the adequate response to the need of every individual.
>
> The Church of today is met by a demand not merely for Evangelism, but for a *New Evangelism* that will do justice to the needs and problems of the present hour. The inherent justice of such a demand must be immediately conceded. The evangelist can speak with authority and power only when he uses the language of his day, bases his message on current conceptions, and appeals to the dominant aspirations of his time. The great evangelists of every age have dealt with Christian truth in such a way as to make God intensely real to the men and women of their own generation; and the timeliness of their appeal is no less striking than the genuineness of the experience that gave it birth. The Evangelism of today will fail in its purpose unless it comes to men with a message at

> once fresh and compelling – a message instinct with spiritual power and beauty, embracing the eternal truths of Christianity, and applying them with spiritual insight to the problems of the hour. What we need today – and need supremely – is a daring application of the mind and teaching of Christ to the whole field of contemporary life.

The logic behind the entire *Modern Evangelism* project was very simple: that the changed world of the post-1918 era needed fresh language and a *modern* approach – a 'New Evangelism.' In a 1923 passage DP did not reprint in 1968 the Thomsons spelt out what they saw as the implications of this demand:

> In the light of modern scientific thought and psychological research the evangelist is called on to rethink his message, to revise his methods, to restate his Gospel, and to relate his appeal to contemporary needs and modes of thought. With the richer background Biblical Criticism has given him, and the fuller content the social consciousness has discovered in his Gospel, he can face this task with every confidence and still look forward to presenting Christ as the Lord of life, who alone can fulfil its hopes and complete its ideals. He can base his appeal on that singularly lucid and convincing exposition of the message of Jesus Christ which is the fruit of modern scholarship, and look forward to recruiting for the Master's Kingdom multitudes whom the older Evangelism left untouched, and who remained unmoved by its appeals.

The chapters commissioned for *Evangelism in the Modern World* thus covered, besides what might have been accepted as mainstream subjects – sin, the Cross, The Kingdom of God – also 'Evangelism and the Higher Criticism', 'Evangelism and the New Psychology', 'Evangelism and the Materialist Spirit of the Age' and 'The Approach to the Modern Mind'. The underlying logic of the volume was that Christ speaks to people as they are: and, hence, anything that helps the evangelist to understand people as they are may help to win entry for the Word of God. Rev. A. Herbert Gray D.D. of the Student Christian Movement thus insisted in his chapter on the Kingdom of God that the 'old evangelism' had been too individualistic, too inward looking, and that only an evangelism that also contained a call to service, to the expression of love and to concern for the needs of world, would touch the hearts of those younger generations looking for 'a Leader who means to rebuild the world'. The emphasis of liberal-evangelism on human experience rather than on historic doctrinal statements recognised that, in the past, evangelism had often been reduced to obtaining a mere assent of the mind.

D. P. Thomson had travelled some theological distance since his Salonica and Heart of Africa Mission days. As a theology student he was part of the liberal-evangelical world.[11] Indeed, DP acknowledged a debt to the President of New York's Union Theological Seminary, Prof. Henry Sloane Coffin, whose Warrack Lectures on *What to Preach* he read and admired in 1926. In 1950 DP wrote 'How great a debt I owe to Coffin for the content and form of my message. It would seem to me now, looking back, that he confirmed and intensified and greatly developed my approach along the lines it had already begun to take.' Coffin was no literalist, preferring to think of the different Biblical authors and early Church communities as crafting their own 'portraits' of Jesus very much as artists might, some more photographically, some more impressionistically, reflecting their own spiritual circumstances and history.[12] Believing that each generation had to make its own response of faith in terms of its own age, Coffin led opposition to attempts within the Presbyterian Church (USA) to bind the Church to particular doctrinal formulations.[13] Prepared to acknowledge a debt to a progressive such as Coffin, D. P. Thomson was no longer a fundamentalist and this change in outlook can be dated at the latest to October 1923: 'John and Joe both feel that my message lacks the old bite and Joe puts it down to the thorough change in my intellectual outlook – I don't.' Neither, however, was DP a theological liberal in the 1960s sense of the word. From all that we know of him, at the heart of DP's own faith was a living experience of fellowship with the supernatural, living God whose providence ruled a created cosmos. We may associate DP with Graham Scroggie, the pastor of Charlotte Chapel in Edinburgh, with F. B. Meyer and with others who around 1923, distinguishing themselves from aspects of American Fundamentalism, were not prepared to reject new methods of Biblical analysis out of hand.[14] Scroggie and Meyer were both main speakers at the Keswick Convention of 1922 that DP and fellow GSEU members attended with appreciation. Scroggie offered to use his American connections to obtain pulpits for DP for his contemplated USA tour.

In his preaching DP sought to challenge young men and women to accept the call of Christ to a life of 'dedication to a great and worthy cause . . . adventure, with the element of real hazard in it' in a world where 'the vested interests of evil seem so securely lodged, and the forces of a narrow nationalism and a gross materialism look so strong'; where the nations 'are all busy feverishly arming at colossal cost for a war that will shatter the world' – the quotations come from his *When Christ Calls*. Because he held such a high view of the Christian calling, he sought true conversions, full surrender to Christ and an entry into life with his Spirit. His 'new evangelism' was an evangelism not solely individualistic but incorporating a belief in the fellowship of the Church and of the Church's calling to pursue peace and justice in the world: an evangelism not just based on intellectual assent to doctrine but on acceptance of the living Christ. Such a content, of course, did not by itself undercut the methods that Moody had employed – the preaching, the call for decision, the counselling, the open profession of faith – or the older reliance on the specialist with the preaching gifts and the practical understanding to assist the convicted to surrender to Christ.

The man responsible for reshaping DP's attitude to theology was Rev. Dr W. M. Clow, professor and in time Principal of the United Free Divinity College at Glasgow, his Professor of Christian Ethics and of Practical Training for the Ministry, of whom he was to write [in *David Inglis Cowan*] that he was: 'one to whom men learned to look back with a growing sense of indebtedness the longer they were in the ministry'. In 1908 Clow had published, as a collection of his sermons, *The Cross in Christian Experience.*[15] He sought to teach the primacy of the doctrine of atonement through Christ's sacrifice on the Cross as the organising centre of all Christian thought, but not by expounding passages of Scripture. Rather, Clow argued from his 'study of Christian consciousness', by calling on 'my fellow-believers experience and my own', and that of Jesus himself. He recommended the truth of doctrine by illustrating its power in the heart and soul. Indeed he could write: 'The Bible is not the supreme revelation of God. That is to be found in the human heart.' Unlike those of his day and later who founded their theology on the principle of God's full revelation of his truth in a Bible factually inerrant, Clow was prepared to accept that even the New Testament books might be 'only large and loose reports', provided that the truth of the death of Christ for our sins was proclaimed. 'As for me, the Scriptures are the sure and reliable Word of God,' he accepted; and this confidence came from the fact that the Bible found its coherence in the Cross, whose truth he acknowledged in his mind, and found in his own heart and in human experience. He sought, therefore, to show the experiential truth of traditional doctrine; to show, for example, that the guilty conscience is purged by the sacrifice of Christ on the Cross; that 'the Cross takes the sting out of the memory of sin' and makes it a means of grace and a spur to service.

W. M. Clow's theology of the Cross was one that recognised the inherent sinfulness of the human heart and of human experience. 'History is . . . the revelation of human greed and pride and prejudice and passion. It is the story of how men have striven to thwart the will of God.' Clow saw the grief and pain and separation from God that men and women experienced. Rejecting the optimism of some of his contemporaries, he believed that it did not lie in humanity to rise above this fallenness, but rather that it took an act of God, in grace and mercy. Clow argued, both from Scripture and from human experience, that the Cross of Christ had to be understood as the vicarious suffering of the incarnate Son of God for the sin of humanity, a willing sacrifice in the midst of history. He distinguished himself from more progressive theologians, presenting his congregations with Jesus Christ, not just as 'the captain of a host' but also as the unique Mediator, in whom alone was redemption. W. M. Clow, then, was one example of what we now know as a Scottish liberal-evangelical: liberal, because he accepted some at least of the conclusions of contemporary literary and historical study of the Bible; evangelical, because he avowed that, to be saved, men and women had to accept the evangel's call to submission to God, to a repentance that sought reconciliation with God only through Christ's death on the Cross. In his sermons, he called for personal repentance and faith in Jesus Christ:

> But let me press upon you the natural question of our text. Are you justified by faith, and have you peace with God through our Lord Jesus Christ?

The chapter 'The Preaching of the Cross' in *Evangelism in the Modern World* was by Principal W. M. Clow D.D.

When DP published *United Free Church Sermons*, a volume of sermons representative of United Free Church practice, he did not choose one that unpacked the doctrine of the Atonement. His magpie, big-picture mind, saw the work of Christ as a whole and refused to focus theology round the single concept of sacrifice. Thomson & Cowan did, however, publish in 1924 *The Significance of the Cross: a New Testament Study*, the outlines of three sermons by George H. Morrison, minister of Wellington UF Church, Glasgow, and heralded it in their publicity as:

> . . . the central theme of the Christian Faith reverently and courageously handled by one of the foremost preachers of the day. Nothing is more needed at the moment than just such an interpretation of the Cross as Dr Morrison offers us here – an interpretation that does justice to the whole range of New Testament thought, and that brings home its great dynamic inspiration to the men and women of our own day.

Morrison himself acknowledged his debt especially to James Denney and defended the view that the sacrifice of Christ on the Cross must be thought of as the pivot of history, at once the supreme testimony to the love of God and an event necessary to uphold the justice of God. And in his turn, when help and guidance was needed, D. P. Thomson looked, among all the ministers he knew, to George Morrison, the honorary President of the GSEU.

There were, of course, those who rejected Biblical criticism as a discipline and repudiated its findings. Those Methodists who sought to condemn George Jackson did so because they believed that his methodology attacked the authority of the Bible, subverting orthodox Christian doctrine, and especially teaching about Jesus Christ himself and any understanding of his death on the cross in terms of sacrifice. The Cambridge Inter-Collegiate Christian Union [CICCU] had disaffiliated from the SCM as early as 1909-1910 in order to maintain their view of the infallibility of Scripture, the sacrificial nature of the Cross and their expectation of Christ's return.[16] Student groups of the same mind as CICCU met in an annual conference, the Inter-Varsity Conference of Evangelical Unions, [*later the Inter-Varsity Fellowship or IVF and then the UCCF*] and in the 1924 Conference approved a new constitution that laid down a theological test for membership: 'That the object of the Conference shall be to stimulate personal faith, and to further evangelistic work among students by upholding fundamental truths.' The first of these eight truths was intended to turn back the tide of Biblical criticism: 'The divine inspiration and infallibility of Holy Scripture, as originally given, and its supreme authority in all matters of faith and doctrine.'[17] As time progressed, this conservative evangelical movement was to grow in strength and to move from its English and Welsh heartlands into Scotland, where the Free Church and Free Presbyterian Church already stood for the doctrinal formulations of the 17th century Westminster Confession of Faith without modification. In 1910 the Established Church of Scotland had altered the promise required of those it ordained, limiting adherence to the Westminster Confession as commitment to believe in 'the fundamental doctrines of the faith contained therein'– but without any guidance as to what these doctrines might be.[18] As the 20th century progressed, what marked out conservatives in both the USA and in the UK was their determination to define clearly just what were the 'fundamental doctrines' of the Christian Faith. As a student and ministry candidate D. P. Thomson sought to remain on good terms with the members of the Christian Union in Glasgow, but their focus was not his focus. Like the CU he sought to 'further evangelistic work among students', not however by 'upholding fundamental truths' but rather by engaging in the field, by doing evangelistic work.

There were those at the United Free Church College in the early 1920s who took an entirely different approach from either the GSEU or the CU. Scotland being the small country that it was and is, the men DP met when they were student ministers together would be men he would meet again. In *The Road to Dunfermline* he claimed that his generation 'was one of the most brilliant groups any Theological College in Scotland had seen for many years', and he cited the senior positions later held by many of these men. Two of those he listed in 1951 may be introduced: T. Ralph Morton, who was later to be Deputy Leader of the Iona Community; and R. C. Mackie, who served on the staff of the British SCM, the World Student Christian Federation and the World Council of Churches.[19] Both ministers would be involved with the formation of policy on evangelism in Scotland in the later 1950s. Both were close friends while at Divinity Hall and afterwards, and some of Morton's letters to Mackie have survived.[20] His views were in many ways diametrically opposite to those of D. P. Thomson. DP had from his youth been in contact with the holiness movement symbolised by the Keswick Convention. Morton's views on Keswick, however, were trenchant: 'It's terrible when a place gets such a bad name that only those who cannot be accused of having any interest in religion can go there without danger to their reputations.'

Similarly whereas DP greatly admired Rev. Prof. W. Clow, Morton challenged what Clow stood for. 'Fanatic', it seems, was the worst description available in Morton's vocabulary, and to him Clow, who supported traditional evangelical campaigns, was the worst of the worst. If DP simplified theology down to a decision for Christ, Morton could not believe that truth was simple. He recognised that he spoke a different language from fellow-Scots who were evangelicals: 'Their manner of thinking riles me and mine mystifies them.' While DP (together with many in the UF Church) campaigned in 1924 for the 'No Licence' plebiscites on local prohibition, to block all selling of alcohol, Morton saw temperance as an issue for fanatics, that by its dominance in the minds of the Scottish churches prevented them from addressing deeper societal issues. In 1924 he attended COPEC, a major ecumenical Conference on Politics, Economics and Citizenship, held in Birmingham, and came back convinced about the importance of faith impacting on all these areas of life. Though D. P. Thomson also preached on 'COPEC - Its Meaning And Its Message' in April 1924, his long-standing approach was that of the separation of faith from party politics. In 1913 he recorded (after hearing a Presbyterian from Northern Ireland preach): 'The resolution I hereby make is that 'God helping me and the Holy Ghost sustaining me with His grace, I will never again take any side in party politics but will truly follow the Spirit'. Finally if DP's ambition as a preacher was for individual conversions, Morton's was more socially oriented, about relationships. Through the SCM, in 1924 T. Ralph Morton was invited to China to work with the YMCA. Later Morton would be a district missionary in China until his return to Scotland in 1937. Neither Morton nor Mackie were close associates of D. P. Thomson while they were all at the Glasgow Divinity Hall, though on occasion their paths crossed on the golf course. When he was the ministry students' 'Moral Censor', R. C. Mackie's public reception of *Evangelism in the Modern World*, as recorded by DP in *David Inglis Cowan*, was one of humorous condescension.

Crisis, Recovery and Eric Liddell

While D. P. Thomson's evolving patterns of thought did not involve (in his own eyes) the theological crisis that sometimes befalls candidates for the ministry, he nevertheless went through a complex spiritual and vocational predicament in these years. DP's diaries record this story, endured in the midst of a theology course – in the midst of GSEU campaigning – in the midst of preparing the *Handbooks of Modern Evangelism* – a crisis which lasted from December 1922 to June 1924, to and beyond the end of the Eighth Diary. He went through a very dark time indeed – but one from which he sought to learn.

This was a period when DP was under very considerable pressure. He, very much a family man at heart, was lonely. We have seen his dismay and frustration at his own inability, 'my future hopes being so uncertain' to develop his relationship with Ena. During 1923 he had another intense but short friendship with an Ardrossan girl 'without staining our honour'. He continued to suffer from problems of the heart in the physical, bodily sense, as well as from other ailments. And beyond the purely personal, as 1923 began his family's financial emergency had erupted again in January:

> Saturday, 20th January [1923] . . . Father wrote to say that the Bank was foreclosing – and that he hadn't a penny left. I was stunned – had known things were precarious but was hardly prepared for the blow falling so suddenly. I consulted John S. Paterson and Lord Maclay, who agreed that I should continue at College, devoting all the time I could to remunerative spare time work.

This was part of the context behind DP's determination to earn his way by running his own profitable business: 'remunerative spare time work' seemed essential. By the end of June he had created the Thomson & Cowan partnership, not simply as Christian publishers but also as Merchants and Commission Agents, securing a bookselling agency from Pickering & Inglis and an insurance agency from the Alliance Assurance Company. New and second-hand books, and golf clubs, were their stock in trade. Evangelical 'Blythswood posters' were also published. They opened new premises with a Sale in March 1923. Given his father's near-bankrupt state, in retrospect it looks rash for Thomson & Cowan to have funded their business on the basis of at least one £100 loan, but DP's father and uncles ran their affairs on the leverage of debt. The dictum 'Never a borrower nor a lender be' was missing from DP's inherited ethical code. His father's problems dragged on. It took until February for the bank to come to terms, and DP – already unable to think of marriage or any family life of his own – now agreed with his brother Robert and sister Christine to guarantee part of his father's debt: 'Father has got a settlement with the bank – we children are to stand security for £700.' When DP wrote in May 1923, 'I have been an arrant hypocrite and a rank outsider. My life has been a living lie these many months,' among other matters he may have sensed the tensions inherent in needing to secure income from speaking engagements, of welcoming invitations from congregations as opportunities to sell books rather than to win souls. Of course, his life's ambition had once been to succeed in the world of business: he was susceptible to this temptation to alter his life's course. Some of his friends still urged this path on him instead of full-time Christian ministry. Perhaps the two could be run together?

> Sunday, 1st April [1923] . . . I am busy planning for the future of our business – have decided to devote myself to Evangelism in business as well as in service – we will endeavour to have the best stocked evangelistic bookroom in the country.

Such conflicts of interest did not go unnoticed:

> Friday, 18th January [1924] Wednesday saw a regular blaze up on my part at the Executive Mtg – against charges of using the Union [GSEU] name for private and business purposes. It was far from pleasant and a very humiliating experience.

Soon after, DP was ruefully noting that he was 'misunderstood and misinterpreted on every hand'.

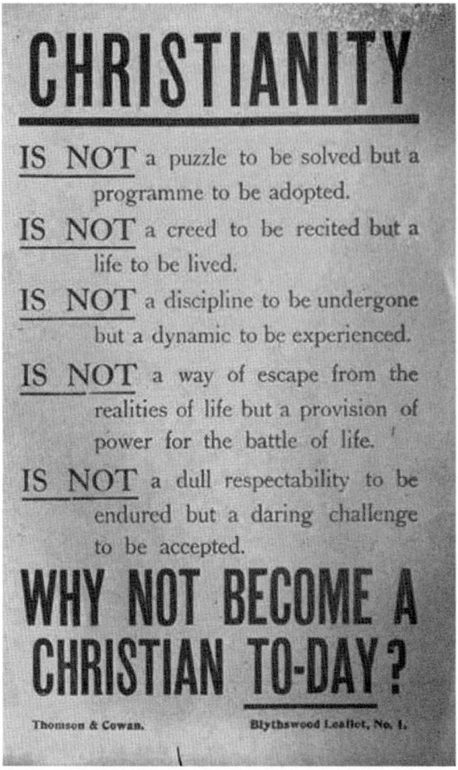

#10: THOMSON & COWAN, BLYTHSWOOD LEAFLET NO. 1: CHRISTIANITY

The source of support and encouragement that DP received during his crisis was of considerable importance to his later practice as an evangelist:

> Friday, 4th May [1923] Perhaps the great red letter day of my life. I have been an arrant hypocrite and a rank outsider. My life has been a living lie these many months. Prayer has died down in my heart. Bible Reading has to all practical purposes ceased – the passion for souls has been a fleeting flame – the cankerworm has been eating at my heart – pride has been full blooded and full-blown . . . And now – . . . I have risen from my knees in the power of a new life and quiet determination. What has been the instrument in God's hands of bringing about this wonderful change? A book of Harold Begbie's called *Life Changers* – the story of Frank Buchman's work in Colleges and Universities – of how he used the knife and extorted confessions from the most unlikely men. Buchman insists on confession – confession to men as well as to God. It is a hard road that I must travel but travel it I will, – Joe and Bob Dobbie must come first. Tomorrow I will see them – the one will be horrified, the other, I think, will be helped.

> Saturday, 5th May [1923] Oh how happy I am. I have never known life quite like this. All – all – is different now. I confessed to Joe – it hurt. I saw tears in his eyes – but what a handshake he gave me!

By May 1923 DP had been struggling spiritually for some time and his existing methods of spiritual discipline had brought no success. Now he read of a man – an anonymous 'manly' sportsmen and an elite Oxford undergraduate – who had found victory thanks to counselling with Frank Buchman:[21] 'I told him the whole trouble, everything.' So DP put this new method into effect and confessed his failings to Joe Haldane, GSEU President and by now also a fellow UF ministry student.

Frank Buchman, whose teaching on the need for man to man confession DP now found so liberating, he had encountered at a reception at Keswick in 1922. DP had thus met Buchman very close to the beginning of the latter's long international career. A minister of the Lutheran Church of the United States but converted to evangelical Christianity at the Keswick Convention of 1908, by 1923 Buchman held the, perhaps somewhat nominal, position of Second Vice-President of the International Union Mission, based in New York. Essentially, he was propagating his personal society, 'A First-Century Christian Fellowship'. He centred his teaching around the need for, and the power of, personal experience of Christ. Begbie's 1923 book, *Life Changers,* was based on accounts of personal transformations resulting from Buchman's 1921 visit to Cambridge during which a man of Scots descent who was to become one of his closest associate, A. S. Loudon Hamilton, was converted.

At much the same time as DP was confessing to Joe Haldane, Hamilton explained the purposes of 'The First Century Christian Fellowship':[22] teaching that had much in common with DP's own practice – charismatic, practical, concerned with conversion and rather less with the details of doctrine, recognising the importance of personality. Connections can be made with W. M. Clow's hermeneutic of experience and with the JEB Holiness Convention's demand that those seeking to confess failure stand publicly to seek a filling by the Holy Spirit. Buchman's particular slant on this was to bypass the public meeting, emphasising rather the importance of fellowship, man to man and woman to woman, so that the Christian life and faith might spread from person to person. Open, one to one confession thus had for Buchman and Hamilton a double significance. On the one hand, it testified to the Spirit's cleansing power and reality; on the other, it removed the barriers of formality which kept faith under lock and key. Around 1930 the 'First Century Christian Fellowship' became known as the Oxford Group Movement and its opponents would argue that 'Buchmanism' placed more trust in its methods than in Christ, that constant confession could dull the sense of shame, and that their emphasis on personal guidance rendered Scripture redundant.[23]

For the moment, however, D. P. Thomson welcomed what he had gained from reading *Life Changers*, and – while he had no personal connections with Frank Buchman, or until 1930 with Loudon Hamilton – their reported methods began to influence his own practice of counselling. One of the accusations later brought against Buchmanism was that it concentrated on sexual matters to the exclusion of perhaps more weighty sin – that, somehow, public confessions rarely if ever involved owning to crimes that might involve prosecution. This, if true, may rather reflect Buchman's social acceptance among upper class England, where crime was (perhaps?) less usual than sexual temptation. DP's diaries do suggest that, in the climate of the period, his own sense of crisis was commonly shared and that a measure of openness brought release: 'nothing vital could be done until we got the trouble out into the open.'

DP's complex spiritual, financial and vocational predicament was not easily resolved. It was not resolved when his Eighth Diary concluded in June 1924. He was, in fact, still in debt by 1931. Working on his accounts was, life-long, invariably at the very end of DP's list of priorities. He was too susceptible to new enthusiasms, which he sometimes understood as the Spirit's guidance. To his already over-busy life he had added a further complication, an enthusiasm for psychology:

> Saturday, 20th October [1923] . . . This has been a formative week – altho' there may be little to show in the way of active work . . . I have planned three books on which I will be working all winter:
>
> The Psychology of Evangelism
> The Fact and Features of Conversion
> and The Ministry of Personal Dealing
>
> This week I have received a call to what may be my lifework – Evangelistic Psychology. I have begun to amass a copious library on the subject and look forward to publishing the results of my research not only in books but in magazines.
>
> Saturday, 27th October [1923] My psychological studies are proving extraordinarily fascinating . . . Last night I was at Duncan Heriot's where he, John Kent, Joe and I got down very deep to the big things of life. We discussed the New Psychology, the difficulties of personal dealing . . . It was a most vital discussion. I am making application to the Senatus for enrolment as a Research Student in Psychology at the University – with a view to a thesis on 'The Psychology of Conversion' for the Ph.D. degree.

Robert Thomson by now had his Ph.D.; Christine Thomson was to qualify as a doctor with both an M.D. and a Ph.D., so did David Patrick Thomson wish to compete? Whatever the reason, 'psychology research' was added to the all too long list of things to be done that autumn – a paper was promised, written and read to the College's Theological Society – and the result was a vocational crisis. DP had far too many pots on the boil; he was conscious that he was letting many people down, and that his increasing debt threatened financial disaster. The question was, what was to be abandoned? The question also was actually: 'What may be my lifework?' Was DP really called to the ordained regular ministry of the United Free Church? He no longer wholly believed he was:

> Thursday, 13th December [1923] . . . I have come to a momentous decision tonight – to give up College. This is the situation:
>
> 1) Nothing is being done well just now – College work is a farce. I am making nothing of it and creating endless misunderstandings. North Woodside is suffering. Business is getting more and more into the mire – GSEU work is suffering too – these things create a profound sense of dissatisfaction.
>
> 2) I have lost all real interest in Theology – Psychology claims me more and more. I am clear now that I have no bent or calling for the regular ministry.
>
> 3) My personal financial position is precarious – I can't live within my income – my salaries together only come to £120 – I am likely to lose some of that – and am not earning it just now. My pension I am likely to lose in April.
>
> 4) I have lost £100 in the business and will lose another £100 in the next 6 months unless I give myself to it with all my strength.
>
> This is the crossing of the Rubicon – the parting of the ways!

Two days later his mind was marginally changed during a family meeting: he would, perhaps, not totally abandon his course but reduce his classes to one only. The turn of the New Year found him depressed . . .

> Sunday, 30th December [1923] I woke this morning with a crushed and hopeless feeling when I looked back on the past year with all its failure and misunderstandings and forward to the coming year with all its gloom and uncertainty. Can my back weather the storm?

. . . and in February 1924 DP did drop out of his ministry course: 'I have taken the long premeditated plunge and left College, for the time being at least!'

D. P. Thomson was neither such a saintly figure that he lived untroubled by the conflicts that afflict others; nor – like D. L. Moody – was he the most profound of theologians. Yet his academic ability should not be underestimated. Despite all the pressures on him he did well in his university examinations; his classical prose stands rereading. The *Handbooks of Modern Evangelism* offered a thoughtful, coherent and passionate approach to their topic even if they owed much both to DP's teachers at the UF Divinity Hall and also to those to whom he looked for inspiration. During an English tour of 1923 he rejoiced to meet – besides Rev. J. Stuart Holden and others – another 'prophet of the New Evangelism', Thomas Toplady:

> Sunday, 20th May [1923] . . . Then I came to the last most fruitful interview of all. Rob and I travelled down to Lambeth Central Hall and had a most illuminating and stimulating half hour with Thomas Toplady, Supt. of the South West London Mission. Toplady is a genius – a prophet of the New Evangelism, we found him in a study littered with books and papers – and littered in one little bit with cigarette ends – a weird miscellany – a most striking man – young and dark and gaunt – army chaplain, an uncompromising realist, a burning social reformer – a whole hearted evangelist – he has written books and booklets that could have made other men famous. His witness flows with passion and bites home in tense, gripping sentences. I left London feeling that I had made a real discovery . . .

It must not be thought that because D. P. Thomson was primarily concerned with evangelism that he was uninterested in the social conditions of his time. What attracted him to Toplady was the combination of concerns: 'uncompromising realist, a burning social reformer – a whole hearted evangelist'.

It was because DP *was* burdened for the conditions he described in *Evangelism in the Modern World*:

> the hideous welter of after-war conditions, the pathetic helplessness of rulers and people alike in face of the pressing problems of the hour, the sin and self-seeking that flaunt themselves openly and unashamedly in our midst, and the intense hunger for spiritual satisfaction manifesting itself on every hand . . .

that he believed 'Never was Evangelism more urgently needed than today'. He did not discount the other ministries of the Church and of the para-church: in *Modern Evangelistic Movements* he celebrated such diverse organisations as the Salvation Army and the Church Army, the YMCA and YWCA, and the Industrial Christian Fellowship. He was also sure, however, that outreach which called men and women to true, dedicated,

#11: Lantern lecture slide: My year with Eric Liddell

Edinburgh Evangelistic Union
SPECIAL SERVICES
FOR YOUNG MEN AND WOMEN
(5th to 17th May)
Sundays USHER HALL . . at 8.0
Week-days St. George's U.F. Church at 7.30
Convener
Mr. ERIC H. LIDDELL, B.Sc.
Leader
Mr. D. P. THOMSON, M.A.
Note.—The Sunday Night Meetings in Usher Hall at 8 o'clock are open to everybody—old and young.
B. S. O.
P.T.O.

#12: Invitation card, EEU campaign headed by Eric Liddell, 1925

sacrificial service to Christ was essential to underpin all the moral and social work of the churches; and he believed that his Master had called him to specialise in evangelism. Through the GSEU he set out his stall as an evangelist and a leader of campaigns. Through the *Handbooks,* together with Marshall's *Conversion or the New Birth* and Morrison's *The Significance of the Cross*, he put his manifesto before the church, a manifesto to which he sought to dedicate his life:[24]

> Evangelism is at once the primary work of the Church and the most urgent need of the hour. It is hardly possible to exaggerate its urgency or to overestimate its importance. The Church of Jesus Christ may cultivate a reverent and brilliant scholarship, maintain an inspiring and progressive ministry of teaching, and achieve a dignity and beauty of worship appealing to the most aesthetic sense. She may acquire a social conscience keenly sensitive to the needs and problems of the hour, an outlook at once broadly catholic and deeply sympathetic, and a charity sufficient to excite the admiration of the most fastidious. But if she fails to display a living and vigorous evangelism, she has failed in her essential and ultimate mission, and the days of her influence are numbered.

If 1923-24 was the nadir of D. P. Thomson's student years, the high point was 1924-1925 when he collaborated with the Olympic gold-medalist Eric Liddell, celebrated in the 1981 film *Chariots of Fire.* Indeed it may not be too much to say that, while DP introduced Liddell to Christian mission, Liddell saved Thomson for the Church's ordained ministry. Eric's brother Bob had been an early member of the GSEU. Eric himself was recruited by DP to support the Armadale Campaign on 5 April 1923, by which point he had already gained fame as a Scottish rugby internationalist and a British athlete:

> I saw Bob Liddell and Eric Liddell and arranged for both to come here tonight to address a special mass meeting for men – this may mean a great deal for the future of the Kingdom of God in Scotland – Eric is the champion sprinter, famous rugby internationalist and most outstanding athlete in Scotland. He is a modest, unassuming and very popular man.

DP and Eric Liddell became friends and Eric helped to form an Edinburgh branch of the GSEU later, while he was studying in preparation to go to China as a missionary. When DP dropped out of College early in 1924, his intention appears to have been to resolve his financial difficulties by the publication of the *Handbooks*, to give due attention to his Assistantship at Glasgow: North Woodside and, as Organising Secretary of the GSEU, to manage its campaigns. Summer 1924, however, was when Eric Liddell famously won the Olympic gold medal in the 440 yards sprint, having refused to run in his main event because it was scheduled for a Sunday. Independently of the GSEU, DP now managed a British evangelistic tour with Eric Liddell, the 'Manhood Campaigns', during which they both spoke for Christ in London, Manchester and several other English centres and schools besides the Scottish cities. Thomson was deeply impressed by Liddell:

> Eric has made great strides as a chairman, a leader, and a speaker. You would hardly know he was the same man as six months ago. We are getting on very, very happily together. I have never known a finer character in all my varied experience . . . There has never been a hitch or a shadow in our friendship, and it is due to him almost entirely. He is pure gold through and through.

A call to commitment to Christ: and, beyond commitment, a call to whole-hearted service was central to Liddell's appeal. Successful management of their joint Campaigns, with the Valedictory Meetings for Eric Liddell in Glasgow and Edinburgh before he left for China, appears to have provided the renewed confidence that Thomson needed to restart his ministerial training later in 1925 and, finally, to bring his studies to a successful conclusion. Eric Liddell died in a Japanese interment camp during the Second World War and DP initiated the efforts to honour his memory. The Eric Liddell Memorial Committee and a series of biographical pamphlets and books were in a sense the repayment of a profound debt.

PARISH MINISTER AND EVANGELIST:

I - Gillespie Memorial Church, Dunfermline, 1928-1934

Wednesday 5th August [1953] . . . Gillespie today, dear Gillespie of such happy memories. Was there ever just such a Church or just such a ministry! I am looking forward greatly to the evening I hope to spend there!

D. P. Thomson,
The Diary of My Life part 21.

Having finally completed his theological training, the Rev. D. P. Thomson was inducted as minister of Dunfermline: Gillespie United Free Church in February 1928 and remained there until November 1934, by which time the congregation had participated in the 1929 Union of the United Free Church with the Church of Scotland and hence become a Parish Church. Even

#13: THE GILLESPIE MEMORIAL CHURCH, DUNFERMLINE, C.1930

though 'it was with the evangelistic opportunities of the regular ministry I had to concern myself while in Dunfermline', as he claimed in 1951, DP's conception of these 'opportunities' was certainly broader than simply his responsibilities to his congregation. Just as his day job as an ASC lieutenant had offered opportunities for preaching at Le Havre and Salonica – just as his status as a student had offered a base for building the GSEU – now DP was to use his position as a parish minister to initiate 'experiments', a series of new ventures: a Presbytery travelling bookstall; a Social Club for Lodging House residents; a new Council of Churches for Dunfermline; involvement with the Oxford Group movement; a regional Retreat Centre; a Missionary Training College. These, if they did not prove as significant to the Scottish church as a whole as his ambition had hoped, nevertheless did help to shape his own experience and future ministry. Nor did DP's involvement with evangelistic campaigns altogether end during this period. It must also be said that when he left the congregation after six and half years, it was after a mutually fulfilling ministry and he looked forward to occasions when, as in 1953, he received an invitation to return.

Minister at Dunfermline

What were DP's aspirations as he moved to Dunfermline? In *Personal Encounters* he suggested that Prof. W. M. Clow and, presumably, others had persuaded him that, even if evangelism was his goal, he ought to serve first in a parish:

> . . . if an evangelist is to have any real standing with his fellow ministers, he must be not only a man as fully trained and equipped as they are; he must also know their problems at first hand by having shared the drudgery and discipline, as well as the rich opportunity and privilege, of regular congregational work in at least one charge.

During 1930 and 1931, however, he believed that his calling was to exercise an evangelical ministry in West Fife, building on his call to Dunfermline's Gillespie congregation.

> <u>Sunday, 17th August [1930]</u> . . . I began to feel that personal influence quietly and steadily exercised rather than an official position, and presbyterial activities rather than denominational may be my sphere.
>
> <u>Monday, 15th September [1930]</u> . . . I came here on Saturday feeling – as I had done for days – that I might very well remain here for good – it suited me so well, offered such growing scope: I was digging my roots steadily so much deeper in West Fife as well as in Gillespie.

Sunday, 16th November [1930] . . . I am growing attracted to a one ministry career – growing in insight, influence and power. And yet I cannot hardly deny myself to the city if it call, and offer what is right!

For much of his first period of parish ministry, the issue was not whether Thomson should resume the calling of evangelist but whether he should leave the Gillespie Memorial for a more prestigious city parish. By the end of 1930, not two full years since his induction, DP had received approaches from vacant parishes and even explicit offers from within the Presbytery of Glasgow to preach as sole nominee – offers that all but guaranteed election by the congregation. Some he turned down. Some never developed beyond informal soundings or rumour. Had matters turned out otherwise, had the vacancy committees of Renfield Street or St Mark's-Lancefield or Aberdeen: North made him acceptable overtures, D. P. Thomson might well have sought 'insight, influence and power' as a prominent city-parish minister.

What did DP experience of what he described in *Personal Encounters* as 'the drudgery and discipline . . . the rich opportunity and privilege, of regular congregational work'? Sundays were of course busy: Gillespie offered regular morning and evening worship, though not the afternoon session that some city congregations also maintained at that time. As well as these two sermons and an additional forenoon children's address, DP's Sunday duties also included his Bible Class and, seasonally, a Communicants' Class for potential new members. Both these classes were given an address, and discussion was not encouraged. At North Woodside, for example, he had offered their Bible Class a series of addresses on 'The Life of Christ'. Those intending to join the church received a course on the essentials of faith. He also on occasion visited the afternoon Sunday School classes to keep in touch with children and teachers, and sometimes to take part. Sundays were thus often crowded – but their duties did not necessarily impact much on the rest of the week. DP's sermon preparation was still of the 'just-in-time' variety: 'Saturday, 4th October [1930] . . . I am terribly behind – not a sermon or address written and 'on' four times tomorrow!' DP's not especially systematic preaching was, on the whole, designed to teach and inspire his congregation, rather than to convert them. Short series of evangelistic, campaign-style, sermons were, certainly, given once or twice each year. Preaching was important to him – he was delighted both by good attendance and by positive feedback . . .

Saturday, 11th October [1930] I am mightily encouraged by the knowledge that my 'Human Drama of the Bible' sermon of a fortnight ago, largely

> extemporised from a few notes hurriedly made at Perth, seems to be regarded as the best I have preached since coming here. It is a strange world!

. . . but what he especially valued about his position at Gillespie were the twin opportunities for evangelical counselling and evangelical experiment.

Given that his ministerial vocation originated in evangelism, it is hardly surprising that D. P. Thomson looked for conversions as fruit from his ministry in Dunfermline. That these came slowly, he found both depressing and personally challenging – especially when neighbours appeared to be outperforming him. Conversions came by two main routes. On the one hand, there was the normal working of congregation life. Graduates of the Sunday School and Bible Class, young people already part of the life of the Gillespie Memorial, might in due course be expected to seek to become full, communicant members of the kirk, entitled to vote for a new minister and to take an adult part in congregational affairs. By November 1930 the horizon was brighter on this score . . .

> Sunday, 16th November [1930] . . . a visit from Willie G. to ask if he was old enough to join the Church. Somehow I feel I am going to have a record Catechumen's class this quarter. It ought to be! Hitherto the ingathering has been very gradual.

. . . and this impression was confirmed when DP came to interview personally the members of the class:

> Thursday, 11th December [1930] . . . Interviewed 5 Catechumens – all very emphatic about how clear I had made it. Willie G., as I expected, begotten under my ministry . . . all seem to be getting something vital under my ministry.

By Monday 15 June 1931, DP was able to record: 'Yesterday I baptised 3 adults at 10.30 and admitted 22 catechumens at the Forenoon Service – by far my biggest number so far.' Over D. P. Thomson's time at Gillespie, adult church membership showed a net increase from 656 in 1928 to over 750 in April 1934, a total he claimed to be the largest in its 182-year history.

The unplanned processes of personal contact and of individual need could also bring a minister opportunities to introduce people to Christ. One man simply walked in off the street:

> Monday, 9th March [1931] . . . Tonight I had an immensely cheering call – a man who came last week in real desperation – an entire stranger who had seen 'Manse' on the gate – had to get someone to pray for and with him – wife at death's door – had been giving way to drink – sorely

> convicted – came through! Back tonight to say 'a new man.' Previously had said prayers – now really praising – Old desires gone – had had a real moral clear-out! A fine case.

For such pastoral work DP used the methods he had learned on campaign, in the after-meetings and counselling sessions that followed evangelical addresses. Repentance had long been important in Christian doctrine. Since his reading of Harold Begbie's *Life Changers* and his exposure to Frank Buchman's emphasis on personal acknowledgement of sin, seeking confession had become a regular part of DP's practice.

> Friday, 19th September [1930] . . . A trying couple of visits to mothers involved in forced marriages – one only properly repentant.

Yet D. P. Thomson was not an excessively judgmental pastor. On one occasion he hosted a friend home from India, enjoying a full day's golf at Aberdour in his company:

> We farewelled a Scotsman from Chittagong at 9am this morning. We open our doors to a Cornishman from Edinburgh at 10.30. We heard the Scotsman describe with gusto his whisky and sodas: the Cornishman is the General Secretary of the Scottish Temperance Alliance! They will both sleep in the same bed . . . [*The man from India*] is a good mixture — Sunday School Superintendent & Literary Society Leader at the famous Wellesley Square Church, Calcutta — drinks, swears, gambles etc! But all within strict limits and with a business code of honour and a private code of morals that would give points to many distinctively 'Christian' workers at home.

Between rounds and over lunch, B. had a beer, a Bass; DP (always teetotal) enjoyed a dry ginger ale. While disciplining himself, he was able (within the limits of his time) to accept that different people might follow different paths.

Ministers, of course, were not expected simply to wait for people to come to them. Visiting was part of DP's pattern of work:

> Tuesday, 21st April [1931] . . . Yesterday afternoon and evening I was out visiting – in the new parochial area where I met with a surprisingly cordial response. I think some 20 new members will come out of that . . .
>
> Wednesday, 22nd April [1931] . . . In the afternoon and evening I visited in the district, again with real encouragement.

Then there were visits to be paid to the sick and dying, visits to the hospital, visits to the new Hostel for Dunfermline's College of Hygiene and Physical Education, visits to the most recent 'Gillespie' baby to arrange for baptism. Sometimes it all became too much:

Tuesday, 16th June [1931] Tonight I touched 'rock bottom' . . . How shockingly I have neglected Gillespie – and failed the Parish.

Mention of 'The Parish' should not be taken for granted. Before 1929 congregations like the Gillespie United Free Church had not thought of having 'parishes' of their own – designated streets within which to exercise Christian ministry. Rather, their ministry had been to those who choose to attend, to whose who (from where-ever) connected themselves to particular ministers. After the Union, however, all congregations of both the former Established and the former United Free denominations were allocated 'new parochial areas', 'delimited' or demarcated areas where, within the discipline of the united Church of Scotland, they would have exclusive pastoral and evangelistic responsibility. The Gillespie Memorial thus acquired a Parish with the Union, and DP adjusted the mechanisms of the congregation accordingly:

Monday, 24th November [1930] . . . Kirk Session met afterwards and agreed to carry through the district visitation.

#14: GILLESPIE'S KIRK SESSION AND THEIR MINISTER, 1929

> Tuesday, 20th January [1931] Just in from our 3rd Congregational District Social – a most enjoyable affair.

He personally undertook some door to door visiting; he organised the Parish into smaller districts, arranged for the elders of his Kirk Session to visit these districts, and held inaugural District Socials by way of welcome and fellowship. His speed of work could pose problems – one senior elder complained in September 1930 that 'the Session was being driven not led', threatening to resign. DP was much later to recollect three such independent personalities on the Session, including one who moved a vote of censure against him, but on the whole the Gillespie Memorial Church under DP's leadership successfully tackled the challenges of the Union.

Much has been written about the Union. Here it needs to be emphasised that, while the doctrinal and legal experts of the two denominations concentrated on such matters as the relationship of the newly united church with the state, and on the church's ability to maintain or redefine Christian doctrine while remaining true to its constitution, for many the key issue was how best to evangelise Scotland. Union was seen as a route to an effective and efficient structure to enable the existing resources of the two churches to meet new challenges.[1] 'It is said that we have entered on a new age,' wrote the Very Rev. John White, leading spokesman for union from the side of the Established Church.[2] Arising from the First World War was a new concept of the world as one community, embodied by the League of Nations. There was a 'growing sense of the unity of mankind', he affirmed: hence it was also necessary for Christendom to be reunited, so that the Church might speak with an authoritative voice. Within Scotland, White argued that the motive impelling the union of the two largest presbyterian churches was the moral, social and religious wellbeing of the people of Scotland. Following the War: 'Great and increasing as had been the work of the Churches, the successful evangelism of our nation had not been accomplished.'

A minister ordained in the United Free Church, DP had chosen with the vast majority of his colleagues to enter the 1929 Union with the Church of Scotland, seeing its missionary potential. A minority dissented, constituting the United Free Church (Continuing). 'I was from the start a Unionist (but not in politics!)' he asserted in *The Road to Dunfermline.* He did not easily categorise or exclude when it came to fellow-Christians. Rather, he sought to include: 'That union is strength, we proved again and again.' Catholicity had been the guiding principle of the *Handbooks of Modern Evangelism.* The GSEU's teams were theologically diverse: 'from an avowed modernism to a fairly rigid fundamentalism. That catholicity was at once our strength and our weakness.' As minister in Dunfermline, DP encouraged connections and joint services between his former United Free congregation and that of its former Established Church neighbour:

> Monday, 3rd November [1930] This has been a gruelling weekend . . . At 2pm we had our historic United Communion Service with St Andrews Parish. The attendance crowded the floor of the Church. Hutchison conducted the first part of the service and I administered the Sacrament. Very impressive. We came down the aisles in procession, elders turn and turn about . . . In the evening we had a joint Thanksgiving Service. I presided and Hutchison preached, about 500 there.

During 1930-31, D. P. Thomson's vision helped to create the Dunfermline United Christian Council and he later rejoiced that it was both the largest of its kind and 'so far as I know, the most broadly based' in Scotland, with representation from such bodies as the YMCA and the YWCA besides the denominations. Even earlier in his ministry at Gillespie, on 20 June 1929, he had taken part in a Service of Commemoration for the completion of repairs to the Abbey on Inchcolm Island, in the Firth of Forth: a service at which leaders from both the Presbyterian and Episcopalian traditions participated, a collaboration exceptional for its time. The press noted DP as the 'reverend young brother' whose 'thunderous voice', alone of the clergy present, managed to reach the congregation above the noise of aircraft circling overhead.[3]

#15: ECUMENICAL CELEBRATION AT INCHCOLM ABBEY, 1929: DP IS AT THE CENTRE OF THE OFFICIATING GROUP BEFORE THE WALL.

While at Gillespie D. P. Thomson also served on national committees of the Church. One was the Executive of the Forward Movement of the Church of Scotland (1931-1933), to which we shall return. Another was the Foreign Mission department's sub-committee on Lantern Lectures, which was impressed by the materials he had developed since his days promoting the Heart of Africa Mission. As the 1920s had progressed DP had promoted himself as a popular lecturer on a variety of topics, particularly through the medium of lantern slides. By 1922 he had had six

#16 & 17: LANTERN LECTURE SLIDES: HERALDS OF THE DAWN & WOMEN OF THE SCOTTISH CHURCH

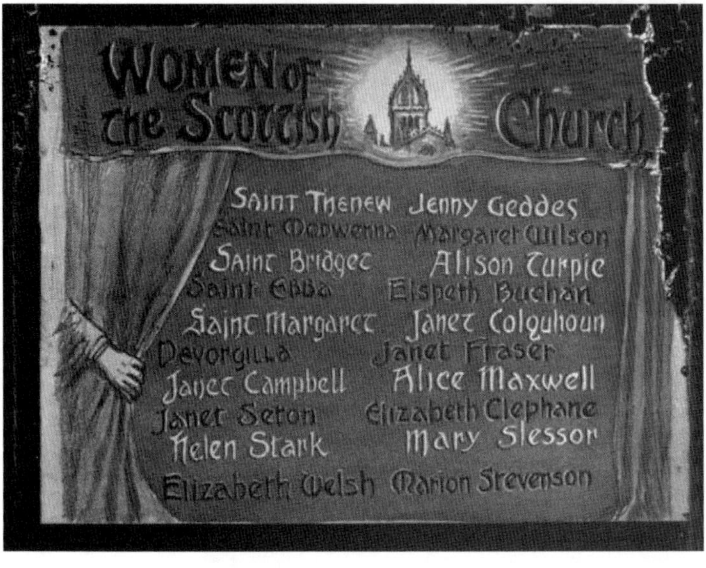

Aggrey's Favourite Illustration.
Harmony — Cooperation
Embodied in the Shield of the Prince of Wales College, Achimota Gold Coast
The foundations of whose success he laid.
"You can play some sort of a tune on the white keys of a piano: You can play some sort of a tune on the black keys: but to produce real harmony you must play both the black and the white keys" — J E Kwegyir Aggrey

#18: Lantern lecture slide: Aggrey's Favourite Illustration, from the set 'Sons of Africa'

sets in hand: two missionary, 'The Challenge of a World's Need' and 'Scotland's Part in the Great Campaign'; and four lighter, popular shows based on his holiday tours: 'Wandering in the Western Isles', 'From Peebles to the English Lakes', 'Wandering in the Highlands' and 'From Chester to the Wilds of Wales'. During his time at Gillespie he added to these 'The Romance of the Scottish Kirk', 'Summer Days in the Emerald Isle', 'The Romance of Natural Science' and 'Sons of Africa'. Later, during the 1940s 'Pilgrim's Diary on the English Road', a set on Jamaica, 'Historic Scottish Communions', 'Communion Hymns: Their Stories', and 'Women of the Scottish Church' would be created. It was, of course, 'Sons of Africa' that especially interested the Foreign Mission Committee in 1930. This was a set that lauded the Christian witness, not of European missionaries, but of such Africans as Prophet Harris, the 'apostle of Ivory Coast' [c1860 - 1929]; James E. Kwegyir Aggrey [1875 - 1927] of the Gold Coast; and Khama Boikano, the paramount chief of the Bamangwato who was baptised in 1858. DP had his own vision for Africa which he set forth in two challenges: 'Africa tomorrow: cooperation or conflict' and 'To build a new Africa together' asked for racial respect; and 'The future of Africa: Crescent or Cross' sought to challenge growing Islamic influence.[4]

DP was an inveterate publicist: writing came easily to him and, besides, could be profitable. 'I have accordingly conceived the bright idea of paying off my debts by the steady five article a week service of my pen! Might be done!' he wrote in 1930, and: 'An article a day keeps the [pawn] broker away.' 'From a Study Window' was the title of an occasional column that he wrote for the local paper, the *Dunfermline Press*, while minister at Gillespie Memorial.[5] For the edition published 2 December 1933, he wrote an article on 'The breakdown of the parochial system' that showed a continued interest in the renewal of church structures in the interests of missionary efficiency:

> An instance of the drift away of churchgoers from the district in which their particular house is situated, and of the almost total want of personal relationship in which a parish church may stand today in the area it is supposed to serve, was given at the recent Commission of Assembly when it was mentioned that in the case of one Glasgow Church of 850 members, only six families represented on the communion roll resided within the parochial area. This, of course, means that, while the minister's energies are dissipated in journeying here and there over the city to visit his scattered flock, the needy population within the area is left practically shepherdless . . . A review of the whole parochial system is urgently called for.

DP went on to commend, in the light of this breakdown, what he described as 'the bold experiment' of the new parish minister of Govan, George F. MacLeod, presently to found the Iona Community, who had declared he would only visit within his parish bounds. MacLeod was to publish, three years later, his *Are Not the Churchless Million Partly the Church's Fault?* that also protested against the failures of the parish system. MacLeod and Thomson were men of very much the same age (MacLeod was born 17 June 1895: Thomson, 17 May 1896) and they shared much the same missionary zeal and energy. Both were noted preachers. Whereas DP had left school for work, however, MacLeod, the son of a baronet, had gone to Oxford University before the First War. After his distinguished military service and theological courses at New College, Edinburgh, and Union Theological Seminary, New York, and an appointment with Toc H, he was appointed assistant at St Giles' Cathedral, Edinburgh in 1922 and thus had several years' seniority over DP as well as a vastly prestigious debut in the Kirk.[6] DP certainly respected George and welcomed his induction at Govan. In later years, however, MacLeod could be viewed as DP's more successful rival for influence within the church, and their paths diverged.

DP's 'From a Study Window' articles also show that during his ministry in Dunfermline his theological approach continued to be liberal-evangelical.

In his 'Window' for 4 November 1933, DP sought to defend his friend Rev. Hamish Mackenzie, whose recent address to the Glasgow Provincial Sunday School Union had 'brought a flutter in the dove-cotes and a hornets' nest around his ears'. Mackenzie, the *Scotsman* had reported, had said that parts of the Old Testament were incomprehensible and that parts could pose moral dangers to the young.[7] The Scottish press printed the Scottish Sunday School Union's leadership's dissociation from these remarks[8] and also a series of irate letters defending the Old Testament on the basis of the unity and inspiration of the Bible, and of the credence Jesus himself gave to it.[9] DP wrote in support of Mackenzie:

> Correspondents in the *Glasgow Herald* and the *Scotsman* and the other papers have overlooked the main points of his address: first, that the Old Testament could in no sense be equated with the New as a manual of instruction in Christian principles, as it too often seemed to be; and second, that by its very nature, it was much more suited to advanced study than to use in the Junior department in the Sunday School, from which it ought be kept until the essentials of the Christian faith had been mastered and a distinctively Christian point of view attained. Mr Mackenzie would be the last to deprecate the value of the Old Testament for an understanding of the preparation of the world for Christ, and of the progressive self-revelation of God to men in the ages before He came. As a matter of fact he spoke with a sincere appreciation and understanding of what might be accomplished in this respect.

This defence of a methodology deduced from the conclusions of Biblical Criticism suggests that DP's own position on this issue had changed little over the decade since in 1924. In 'From a Study Window' for 7 October 1933, however, a short paragraph had discussed the results of archaeological excavations in Iraq and ventured that they supported the historicity of the Old Testament, 'leading to conclusions the very reverse of those which were reached by German critics of a generation or two ago'. Such an appeal to what were thought to be archaeological facts was a common liberal-evangelical reconciliation of Scripture with Biblical Criticism.

Some of DP's columns in the *Dunfermline Press* expressed views radical for their day. Relations between protestants and Roman Catholics in Scotland were fraught and sometimes violent. The 1920s and 1930s saw what one historian has called 'a frenzy of anti-Catholicism' as Church of Scotland leaders like John White persuaded the 1923 General Assembly to resist Irish immigration as a threat to the protestant character of the Scottish nation.[10] The Church of Scotland in 1921 had reaffirmed in its

'Articles Declaratory' its adherence to the *Westminster Confession of Faith* [1646 AD], which held that the Pope was Anti-Christ. Moreover the issue was a live one for Dunfermline's presbyterian ministers, as the development of the Fife coalfield had brought a substantial Roman Catholic population into Fife. D. P. Thomson, in fact, played a leading part in local protests against a Roman Catholic pilgrimage to the historic Dunfermline Abbey (foundation 1072 AD), the home of the town's leading Church of Scotland congregation. His 7 October 1933 'Window', however, included the following:

> The whole question of possible cooperation between Catholic and Protestant is one that many communities have not yet brought themselves to face, and strained relations not infrequently exist where a happier spirit might well prevail. In the Yorkshire town of Stocksbridge there is held annually what must be a somewhat unique festival. At the time of the yearly Sunday School celebrations Roman Catholic, Episcopalians, Methodists, Congregationalists and Salvationists march in the one procession, bearing striking tribute to the underlying unity of their aim and faith.

Such a general acceptance that Roman Catholics and protestants shared an 'underlying unity' of 'aim and faith' may, for that period, properly be described as radical.

DP's attitude to women remained confused: 'Wednesday, 4th March [1931] . . . My attitude to the other sex requires a terrible lot of adjustment yet.' He could enjoy himself in a traditional social setting like a small wedding reception . . .

> Saturday, 4th April [1931] . . . just 15 or so friends in Andrew Thomson's house. We cracked, listened to the gramophone, danced and made merry. I was inveigled into the Grand Old Duke of York and found myself compelled to bestow 4 separate kisses on the bride! I left at 11 after proposing the toasts.

. . . but new styles of dancing disturbed him:

> Wednesday, 4th March [1931] I am just in from the Choir Dance. Difficult to know what to do about these things. Perhaps I tend to take the line of least resistance. I confess I don't at all like it! The more I see of these modern dances with the close embrace the less I care for them and the more I doubt their wholesomeness. Personally I couldn't stand it for 60 secs. and I am not alone! A few hours of that in the heated atmosphere of a ballroom cannot be good for young folks of either sex.

He could be disturbed by any emotional intimacy that might develop, whether with a visiting acquaintance or with his personal secretary. D. P. Thomson, even before thinking of entering into a closer relationship, had in mind that 'A Minister Needs a Wife', to use the title he gave to a chapter in his biography of his fellow-student David Cowan. In this area of life, as with his theology, DP learnt from Prof. W. M. Clow:

> It may have been that David Cowan's mind harked back during these days – as my own often did – to the lecture on 'The Minister's Wife' – given by Principal Clow each year in his class of Practical Training. There were men who smiled – and others who poured the vials of their scorn on that particular utterance, as they did on so much else that Clow said. There were others, however, who realised increasingly, as they went about the country, the debt they owed to a man who had the courage to speak his mind, and so to draw on the width and depth of his own experience of the ministry, not only in light but in shadow. Cowan, I think, was one; his biographer was certainly another.

For one with the vocation of an ordained minister it was not sufficient to be in love: the prospective wife also needed to have the qualities of a minister's wife, 'fitted in every way to be a help to me' as DP had thought Ena in 1918. For decades to come the assumption of most congregations was that the minister's wife would be a subordinate full-time church worker: President of the Women's Guild, visiting homes on her own account and with her husband, setting a tone and a standard – and bringing up a family, keeping a hospitable manse and occupying the manse pew twice on every Sunday. Even in the 1930s this was not a calling for every educated Christian girl. On the other hand DP was also a romantic – he could not make himself love a girl simply because she might be a perfect lady of the manse:

> Monday, 18th February [1923] . . . I like [A.B.] immensely – it is one of my regrets that I haven't fallen in love with her – she would make such a fine wife.

D. P. Thomson's debts, too, argued against his opportunities for marriage: by January 1931, he still had a capital debt of £300 (at least a year's stipend) to repay from the business ventures of his student days.

DP nevertheless appreciated the independent spiritual gifts and ministry of women.[11] DP had, after all, worked closely with Mrs C. T. Studd, admiring Priscilla's personality and preaching gifts. Two of the girls with whom he had fancied himself in love as a young man had been active in the Faith Mission; Ena had left Scotland as a missionary to Japan in 1922. In the summer of 1931 he led a 'new evangelism' tour of young Scots ministers, divinity and medical students to London. Besides visits to the Clubland Church, the Church Army, Toc H and Regnal House, they made a point of visiting, for tea on the terrace, the noted female preacher and social reformer Maude Royden D.D. at the Eclectics Guildhouse.[12] With his 'Window' for 2 December 1933 DP revealed his disappointment that opinion was growing against the admission to women to the eldership of the Church of Scotland:

> It looks as though the ladies would require to wait for some years yet before this important step is taken. There are, it should be noted, women elders in the English Presbyterian Church even in such an exclusive congregation as that at Oxford, and in the United Free Church [*ie Continuing*] women ministers as well as elders. In the Church of Scotland, however, it looks as if the diaconate would be as much as the women can hope for at the next Assembly.

D. P. Thomson's preparedness in the mid-1930s to accept women as elders shows that on this issue, as on others, there was a modernist element to his mind, so that debate was not necessarily settled by a strict, literal reading of key Biblical texts. The Church of Scotland would not accept the ordination of women on the same terms as men until 1966 for the eldership and 1968 for the ministry of word and sacrament.

#19: THE 'NEW EVANGELISM' SCOTTISH TOUR VISITING THE CHURCH ARMY HEADQUARTERS, LONDON, 1931: DP 4TH FROM RIGHT

A bachelor parish minister, DP had a large number of contacts and a small number of close friends, mainly from his Glasgow days and from the GSEU. Reluctant to let go a period of life he had found exhilarating, he had widened the original GSEU concept over time and in two directions. Further Evangelistic Unions had developed at Edinburgh and Aberdeen: these then became the basis of the Scottish Students Campaign Movement [SSCM], which had a Council on which of course DP served for some time as President. If the SSCM offered breadth and a way for graduated, ordained and senior members to offer leadership to a student movement, the Former Members Fellowship [FMF] of the GSEU offered depth. Of all ministers outside Dunfermline, D. P. Thomson most valued the opinions of the Rev. John Kent, though he much regretted being unable to attend his induction to Glasgow: Cathcart South in September 1930. Kent was the first FMF President, and when in Glasgow DP frequently met him for a coffee at 'Miss Cranston's Tearoom' and they spoke often on the phone. It was John that DP chose to phone soon after midnight on New Year's Day, 1931, and, indeed, on at least one other occasion. DP could be demanding of his friends, valuing trusted faces around him in fellowship. Hamish ['Ham'] C. Mackenzie, minister of Bridge of Allan: Chalmers, whose views on the Old Testament DP had defended, was another former campaigner, now serving in a parish, with whom DP frequently had a 'crack' on the phone very late at night.

The future of the student campaigning movement still meant a great deal to DP. He was unable to attend the induction of another close friend, Rev. Jim Munn, because he was supporting a campaign in Perth at the time. As 1931 began he was concerned that the annual GSEU Retreat had had to be cancelled. Once again personality (or perhaps theological) difficulties were part of the problem, and DP tried to mediate. During February and March 1931 he led the Stirling Churches Campaign – John Kent was one of 15 ministers involved,[13] evangelists brought together under the auspices of the SSCM.[14] In March, he called in on the Glasgow: Bridgeton Churches campaign, called – provocatively, at a time of massive unemployment and economic depression – 'The Bridgeton Prosperity Fortnight':

> Friday, 20th March [1931] . . . foregathered with John Kent at Cranstons, discussing Stirling, Oxford Group, FMF and GSEU . . . with him to Bridgeton to see something of the Campaign in progress there, Jim Munn arriving a few minutes after I had gone! Jock [*Stewart*] and I were roped in at the Bridgeton Prosperity Fortnight's Open Airs – I spoke at Tullis' Leather Works, then had to leave for town. Jock stayed on to speak at a women's works gate and to lunch with the campaign party and attend their Committee Meeting.

In April 1931 DP visited the Aberdeen Student Campaign in Fraserburgh, following rumours of new and perhaps unsound methods being used by the new generation. The next month saw a FMF Reunion held at DP's new Retreat Centre, to which the leaders of the Glasgow, Edinburgh and Aberdeen Unions were also invited, along with John Kent:

> Saturday, 22nd May [1931] 11.40pm . . . We had a great time at Glassiebarns – a memorable conference – Johnny Graham chairing and I acting as scribe – Jock Stewart, Harry Thornton, Ian Cameron, Charlie Duthie also for the whole time, and John Kent for one session. We reviewed the whole 9½ yrs of the Union's history, examined its relation to other movements, estimating its present personnel and capacity, and arrived at far-reaching conclusions affecting its future. Altogether a memorable and creative experience – drew us very much more closely together. Much will come out of it in every way – it may be the first of many such gatherings.

Between 1928 and 1934 D. P. Thomson was a parish minister; yes, but he also retained his older ambitions to be involved with evangelism on a national scale, and the SSCM and the FMF were vehicles by which this ambition was promoted.

The Oxford Group

By 1933 DP had learnt to value the evangelical power of ordinary Christians, enabled as congregational groups or teams comprising both women and men. In his student-days DP had appreciated Buchman's emphasis on personal confession as a route through spiritual struggle. While at Gillespie DP was directly involved with Frank Buchman's Oxford Group Movement, as the 'First-Century Christian Fellowship' was called by 1930. Though the Oxford Group Movement changed over the years, being in time reconstituted as Moral Rearmament or MRA, DP was still prepared in *Personal Encounters* to acknowledge that he had learnt valuable lessons from it:

> My debt to the Group I am more than happy to acknowledge. Never since these days have I been tempted to undervalue the self-examination, the 'sharing in depth', the daily seeking for divine guidance, and the vital fellowship of a mixed team, both as a means of grace and as instrument for service, which its leaders then so rightly stressed.

Frank Buchman's movement had moved into a new phase of its life in 1928 as he, his close associates and volunteers began an ambitious global outreach programme with the innovation of travelling teams that began in South Africa and by 1932 had reached Holland, Germany, Geneva, Egypt and Scotland.[15] Large public meetings were held, using the conventional style of an evangelical campaign except that stress was laid on the team: several individuals would offer testimony. Buchman personally brought a team of 60 to Edinburgh in April 1930.[16] His Scottish-connected senior associate, A. S. Loudon Hamilton, now moved to Edinburgh to lead developments. From the first there was questioning and outright opposition. Was there sufficient understanding of the Cross and of atonement in Christ? Was the emphasis on daily guidance either fanatical or petty – or both? Was group confession 'morbidly unhealthy', concentrating on sex? Yet many also believed that the revival apparently due to the movement was an answer to prayer.

The Oxford Group's impact in Scotland and in the Church of Scotland was well known to D. P. Thomson, as attuned to publicity and church news as he was. By November 1930 the Group was operating in Ceres, Fife. Loudon Hamilton followed up the Ceres campaign with an appointment at the Dunfermline ministers fraternal – and DP stole the show by recycling criticisms, a lack of courtesy of which he quickly repented. His closest ministerial colleague in Dunfermline, however, Rev. George Dryburgh of Dunfermline: St Columba's, favoured exploring further the potential of 'The Group':

> Tuesday, 11th November [1930] . . . Dryburgh came last night and stayed till after 12. He feels that I put my foot in it badly at the Fraternal over the Oxford Group with my criticisms and that big things might have happened had I refrained. I am meditating a letter of explanation and apology.

DP now accepted an offer by Group member and Scottish rugby internationalist Harry Polson to address Men's and joint Bible Class meetings on 23 November and at least one of DP's acquaintances became a 'Buchmanite' around this time: Jim Watt, a former Communist organiser in Fife, now converted to Christ. Next, DP ran up against young people he believed to have been positively influenced by the Group when he led the United Churches Campaign in Stirling in February/ March 1931. He wrote to *The Stirling Observer* that the local Group had, in fact, supplied the campaign with its best volunteers.[17] It was a strong, public commendation, written to supplement an earlier and fuller campaign report in the same weekly, and penned immediately after a visit he paid to a meeting of the parent Edinburgh Group. Any possible contribution to effective evangelism went to the heart of DP's concerns. Was the SSCM going to embrace or reject this new movement for young people? His instincts were always for unity, for co-operation:

> Thursday, 9th April [1931] . . . I do pray that I may be used to build a bridge between the movements – Forward, Oxford Group, Student Campaign. More and more does the Ministry of Reconciliation come to mean to me.

While aware that several of his friends still disapproved of the Group – Hamish Mackenzie threw in the fire a notice of Hamilton's proposed visit to Stirling – DP now took what he realised might be the turning point of his ministry: he invited the Oxford Group Movement to send a Team to the Gillespie Memorial.

During March, April and May of 1931, D. P. Thomson's congregational ministry largely revolved around a series of involvements with the Oxford Group; by June his enthusiasm was waning and his energy was directed elsewhere. During those months, however, the engagement was intense and it left a lasting impression. A visiting team came to Gillespie, giving testimonies at a Sunday evening service. An after-meeting followed. The pattern was repeated the next week, and by that stage conversions were being reported among Gillespie's young people. What really hit DP, however, was a late-evening meeting, after the second Group weekend, with one of his congregation, a young man from Switzerland, then working in Scotland:

> Tuesday, 31st March [1931] . . . I hurried home just after 10pm . . . Hans B. was waiting for me. He stayed till 12.15. These 2 hours can never be adequately described. He told me his story – I was just nowhere – nowhere. All these years I had thought him a nominal and mildly interested churchman – and he had been cherishing, and preparing for, a life purpose of magnificent idealism and sacrifice – the hour had come when he stood at the crossroads and he had come to me for counsel and help – a Swiss run blind asylum in Syria wanted a teacher of weaving. He told me much more – 7 years of hunger for fellowship in the deeper things never satisfied. No-one can meet him on that level – Gillespie hadn't. I hadn't. He had been fighting loneliness and temptation in his digs, a stranger among strangers. These last 2 Sunday nights had been the coming of springtime, the first taste for 7 years of a fellowship he had known across the seas. Little wonder if I sat long or late after he left – we sat in silence by the study fire after he had told me all . . . 'Pray for me' and I did. And then he prayed – and broke down – and haltingly carried on – and we rose to a new day. Yes, the church has failed – there are 1st century elements wanting. Of that I can have no possible doubt now. I am going to form a young fellows' group immediately. Thursday night.

And indeed DP did now begin a congregational weekly Group meeting; a Ministers' Group also began for prayer and Bible study at 8am on Saturday mornings. Group testimony services were also held in Dunfermline: North, Dunfermline: St Columba's and Dunfermline: St Margaret's. The Gillespie Group received visits from the Groups of Edinburgh and of Stirling; and it sent teams to offer testimonies at Stirling, Edinburgh and the parish church at Mossgreen, Fife. DP was, frankly, thrilled:

> Sunday, 3rd May [1931] A memorable day and I am all keyed. Today, after 3 years and 3 months ministry I am to lead the hosts of Gillespie over the top! This afternoon I go to Stirling with a band of my young folks to witness, in the South Church. I have led student teams and ministerial teams – but a team from one's own flock! I am thrilling at the prospect.

Involvement with Oxford Group methods and people opened windows in DP's mind – he was always a man of enthusiasms.

What Hans B. had brought DP to realise was the poverty of fellowship offered by the model of congregational life then followed in the newly united Church of Scotland. Ministers preached to congregations and lectured to meetings and classes. Following their own academic education, they taught as Scots school-teachers and university lecturers then did, preferably without interruption and offering limited or no opportunity for discussion. People talked about and discussed their faith, if at all, personally with the minister, or perhaps with an elder, but not in groups; not with fellow-members of the congregation. When Loudon Hamilton wrote of the importance of team-work and of removing all barriers to mutual understanding; of the 'need to recapture the genius of fellowship'; when he asserted 'We suffer mostly from an over-emphasis on the intellectual', he was addressing a real need in Scottish church life.[18] Hamilton, who had fought in the First War and then gone to Oxford University, had an appeal beyond students. At a meeting of the Stirling and District Church of Scotland Office-Bearers' Union in March 1931, he was accompanied by Sheriff J. Gordon Jamieson K.C., who spoke of the joy he had found in Group membership and had failed to find in what fellowship was offered by congregational life.[19] No doubt the Sheriff brought a similar message on 'the lack of an essential something in the average Christian's life' to the elders of Gillespie Memorial when he met them after an evening service in May 1931:

> Sunday, 31st May [1931] . . . In the afternoon went to Inverkeithing to meet Sheriff Jamieson, off the Edinburgh train . . . At 6.30 I accompanied the Sheriff to the pulpit – he gave a very fine address on 'The Cross' – finely thought out and expressed both. A capital attendance for so wild and wet a night. He spoke well to the elders in the Vestry afterwards.

Students, sheriffs, former communist organisers, sportsmen: the Group Movement in Scotland had a fairly broad appeal. Its 'witness and challenge', DP wrote in his 'Preface' to *Eric H. Liddell: Athlete and Missionary*, played a significant part in Eric Liddell's Christian development. Though the Oxford Groups often attracted (and targeted) people of wealth, those who joined the Gillespie Group were the ordinary young people of the congregation, who would have attended a Young Converts meeting in the 1920s. One attraction may have been the essentially egalitarian nature of Buchmanite methodology. Everyone had a say, and the contributions of both young women and young men were equally valued, though they sometimes met separately for intimate discussion. Both women and men were chosen to participate in the visiting teams and to give their testimonies: when the Gillespie group visited Stirling, DP took along '14 in all, 11 men and 3 ladies'. 'The vital fellowship of a *mixed* team, both as a means of grace and as instrument for service' was one of the enduring lessons DP reported in *Personal Encounters* from his flirtation with Buchmanism. Moreover DP also discovered that young people could lead others to Christ: 'Too long I had thought of myself as the expert – the clinician.' This, too, would be an enduring discovery from his experience and experiment with the Oxford Groups.

Some historians of Buchmanism comment on the excesses of 'groupism',[20] the increasingly obvious nature of Buchman's own assertive leadership, his pre-1939 flirtation with Hitler and the Nazi Party, and the movement's drift away from evangelical Christianity after 1938. What struck DP in 1931, as he saw the witness of young people winning others for Christ, was rather the movement's potential to bring something of the dynamic of the mission team, or perhaps of the holiness convention, into ordinary congregational life. Moreover the Group in its origins clearly sprang from the liberal-evangelical wing of the Church and it engaged with psychology, another of his former enthusiasms; it sought to be up-to-date, modern. All of this must have attracted him. Besides being a man of enthusiasms, he was something of a magpie, collecting ideas for their practicality and for his purposes. Still, he was aware of the potential dangers of the Oxford Group Movement, *hearing* and, even in the spring of 1931, *voicing* warnings as well as appreciation. By the early summer a certain disillusionment had set in. Reports of mental disturbance associated with Group activities circulated. George Dryburgh, who had at first encouraged and then shared in DP's sponsorship of the movement, began to have second thoughts. Some of their initial recruits were showing signs of relapse: DP was distressed by the lack of discipline shown by some members of both his own and of the Stirling Group he had persuaded to come to help with Gillespie's annual Boys' Brigade Camp. Then in August 1931 Hans B's employers moved him to Edinburgh: 'One of the lights gone out of my life here,' DP wrote.

Key SSCM leaders continued to hold reservations about the Oxford Group as a whole, even if they could share in joint events that DP arranged. May 1931 was the last time DP appeared on a platform to support the Oxford Group Movement at any major public meeting, though after the Second War he continued to appreciate aspects of the work of MRA. It is certainly true that during the first six months of 1931, and like a good number of Church of Scotland ministers who then believed that the movement was essentially about personal evangelism,[21] he could be described as an adherent or supporter of the Group. Its influence, however, served to highlight for him truths he had already perceived from within his evangelical tradition without diminishing what was ultimately his Christ-centred vision. He was never Buchman's man, but rather remained his own, and God's.

Residential Fellowship and other Experiments

One theme that now was consistent through DP's career was the Oxford Group insight into the importance of Christian fellowship in generating spiritual growth. Yet this was not really new to him. The work of the GSEU had been double-focussed: the campaigns themselves clearly sought to win people for Christ, *and* they also offered training to the young men of the teams. Membership was offered to those who sought 'training for an aggressive evangelistic ministry'. DP placed emphasis on the communal fellowship of the short-term, residential team during student campaigns. The pre-mission and New Year retreats of GSEU had been significant for him and now the united Kirk's Forward Movement acknowledged the Oxford Group emphasis on fellowship.[22] Since August 1930 he had had the 'Big Idea' of the creation of a residential camp or centre to cater especially for retreats for congregational and student Christian organisations, offering (as he wrote in *The Road to Dunfermline*) . . .

> . . . a small, secluded centre to which groups might go, who wished to be right away by themselves, undisturbed, for a short time of really intimate fellowship. There in the quiet, together, with the beauty of nature about them, they might come closer to one another, and be able to travel further in their thinking and their planning, in a very short space of time.

This was the concept of gathering a group apart to share fellowship for its own sake, without the demands of an actual campaign. Maybe a reflection of DP's experiences at Swanwick and Keswick can also be seen in his promotion of residential centres in the service of the Scottish churches.

DP's adventures in Christian camps and centres restarted with a January 1931 retreat organised for the Edinburgh Colleges Evangelical Union [ECEU] at Deepsykehead, West Lothian. The students bedded down in a borrowed bothy, 'It's a wonder any of us survived' one wrote,[23] while their older leader slept in a hotel, five miles away! Next came a formally organised centre within reach of Dunfermline at Glassiebarns, where a 'but-and-ben' supported by bell tents was advertised as 'A Retreat and Conference Centre for Experiments in Group Fellowship':[24]

> Glassiebarns provides sleeping facilities for twelve indoors, and for as many more in the garden as bell-tents may be available to house. (At present there is only one, which means perhaps another eight people!) Parties using this Centre for Quiet Days, Retreats, or Conferences – and it is designed for all three – are required to make their own cooking and catering arrangements, but find on arrival that crockery, cutlery, and cooking utensils have all been provided for them, that there is an excellent kitchen range, and a paraffin stove in addition, and that if the weather is fine, meals can be enjoyed in the garden, amid scenery at once delightful and full of historic interest. It is one of the beauties of Glassiebarns, and one of the essential features of this experiment, that there is no caretaker and no staff, and that groups, who go there for a period of retirement and fellowship, have the place entirely to themselves, and can make their own arrangements as to places and hours for meals, and as to time and mode of retiral. One or two stipulations the Board of Management does make. One is . . . that every party must have a definite programme of which the Board approves, and must make a full entry in the 'Log', of who they are, and why they came, and what they did during their stay, as well as subscribing their names in the visitors' book.

It was DP's way to embody such enterprises in ambitious constitutions, so the West Fife Retreat and Conference Centres movement had a Board of Management (DP was Chairman) originally consisting of Jock Stewart from GSEU and Harry Thornton from ECEU, with Hans B. and Eliza Hutton from the Service and Social [Young People's] Guild at Gillespie (and also from the congregational Group) and the minister of Crossgates Parish Church. The Presbyterial Girls' Association was also represented. Glassiebarns was 'set apart' at a service led by the Moderator of the local Presbytery on 15 May 1931. To Glassiebarns came groups from the universities of St Andrews and Edinburgh; from the Scottish Student Campaign Movement and from Gillespie Memorial Church itself, particularly for a series of Missionary Days, shared with staff home from overseas. DP chose to end *The Road to Dunfermline* on a high note, as the demand for the experience Glassiebarns offered outstripped its accommodation:

> By 1933 Glassiebarns had become too small, and another, and bigger, centre had become an urgent need. It was at St Ninian's, Lassodie, that still more far-reaching experiments were to be made, and it was there, at a conference of the students of the Divinity Halls of the four Scottish Universities, that George MacLeod first adumbrated his proposals for what later became the Iona Community.

Glassiebarns was one of DP's 'far-reaching experiments', the initiation of which were a mark of his Dunfermline ministry. Indeed, it was experiment number two:

> Monday, 15th June [1931] . . . Thereafter I met the workers who have volunteered to help at the Chapel St. Social Club and explained the scheme to them. That is experiment no. 3 – 1 was the Bookstall, and 2 Glassiebarns – 4 the Churches Council. And so we go!

All these four projects reached beyond DP's own parish and congregation. Their tracks of development interweave through his Ninth Diary, evidence of his ambition to make a mark in West Fife. 'The Bookstall' was a travelling bookstall sponsored by the Literature Committee of the Presbytery of Dunfermline & Kinross, staffed by volunteers from local youth groups and thus combining opportunities for outreach, fellowship and service. The 'Social Club' offered a base, a lounge and a place of fellowship for the near-destitute residents in Dunfermline's Model Lodging Houses. Again staffed by volunteers from the churches, its inspiration may have been the larger and longer-established Glasgow Lodging House Mission. Glassiebarns and the Dunfermline United Christian Council we have already met, if briefly: the latter brought together 11 denominations and '34 separate units', and ran standing committees for evangelism, social problems (including housing conditions) and the promotion of overseas mission. DP could work very fruitfully with others. These experiments required other ministers and church leaders to be persuaded, funds raised, committees formed, publicity arranged, articles written for *Life & Work*. Motions had to be made and votes had to be won in Presbytery.

There was also a fifth experiment: a private Missionary Training College:

> Friday, 10th July [1931] . . . the Dunfermline and West Fife Missionary Training College for Men which Dryburgh and I launched here on Tuesday evening at 7 o'clock. That is my biggest venture, leaving GSEU, Glassiebarns etc completely in the shade. What we plan is to provide for the training of (a) Part time Lay Workers (b) Whole Time Lay Workers (c) Ministers by providing the whole of the practical training in our parishes under supervision and as much of the theoretical as practical and as men are not getting or would not get at Edinburgh University. We begin when the first student comes along.

Nothing much came of this venture apart from occasional lectures to individuals from DP's own youth groups, though it reveals a nascent interest in missiological education very much ahead of its time. Still, all in all, the experiments show Thomson's ambitious energy, his willingness to innovate, to see what good might come out of new ways of working. He was prepared to fail – to discover that what seemed a good idea did not in practice work, or needed to be modified in the light of experience. He was pushing the bounds of realism – the Training College went, disquietingly, well beyond those bounds – but some limits were recognised. He knew that he, personally, lacked the financial resources to attempt all he would have liked and he accepted this restraint. For DP these experiments were about discipleship, about going with his Master into the unknown – we may perhaps hear an echo of an ancient Celtic spirituality. Experimentation was also about modernity, about doing new things in a new world. Perhaps, also, we hear an after-echo, an ecclesial emulation, of the scientific minds of Dr Robert and Dr Christine Thomson?

In all these ways D. P. Thomson pursued his vocation while minister of Dunfermline: Gillespie Memorial. There were others who understood a call to a congregation entirely differently. Admittedly it was over 30 years later, but Hamish Mackenzie was to criticise as at best misguided and even perhaps exploitative ministers who initiated experiments and then, after a short time, left the parish. In his Warrack Lectures for 1963 Mackenzie set out a demanding and idealistic vision of the parish ministry: the call to be the preacher and pastor of a congregation for life, if God willed it; a call to be pursued as a pilgimage, without deviation – an utter commitment to the parish that, placing preaching above all else, excluded all other ambitions.[25] DP's ambitions for his ministry in Dunfermline, by contrast, from the beginning roved well beyond the Gillespie Memorial to Dunfermline town itself and, further, to West Fife. Moreover besides his non-parochial ventures he also made a number of changes in congregational procedures that he also ranked as 'experiments':

> Monday, 9th March [1931] . . . saw the latest Gillespie baby, Anne B., natal 9 days. Mother looking fine and baby 'A1', feeding contentedly at breast. Told them it must be the Church – will offer Easter Morning as an inducement . . . Yesterday we admitted Catechumens at the forenoon – an experiment which I hope will establish a precedent.

This entry describes two such changes. Leading ministers of the Kirk had recently emphasised that infant baptism was an act of the Church and not a mere domestic ceremony; in place of the previous practice of holding baptisms in private homes, it was argued that they ought to take place as part of ordinary Sunday worship. DP sought to put that teaching into effect, and clearly such an insistence was new to the Gillespie Memorial. So too was his innovation of admitting new members by requiring them to profess their faith before the whole Sunday morning congregation, rather than (as he himself had been admitted at Dundee) at the smaller Thursday evening Preparatory service for Communion. A life-long teetotaler, DP also moved his congregation from using their 'common cup' goblets at communion, replacing them with the sets of individual glasses that the use of non-alcoholic (and non-self-sterilizing) juice required. Six-plus years of experimentation – novelty – new ways for a new age – and then a move. Maybe there were those who thought that DP had been exploiting his congregation to further his own ambition? Mackenzie's misguided minister does have striking similarities to D. P. Thomson, who through his life tackled, simultaneously, more than enough for any one man. Their approaches diverging as early as 1931, the two friends were to drift apart in the later 1930s and 40s.[26]

Appointment as Evangelist of the Church

On a number of occasions DP became convinced that God was leading him into a change of course. By 1934 one of these turning points had been reached and he submitted his demission from Gillespie Memorial without having secured any final offer of a new position. How Christians receive guidance from God is a theme running through *The Road to Dunfermline* and on through DP's life. He retold in detail one particular incident in the chapter 'The Guiding Hand of God':

> On the evening of Tuesday, 5th February, 1918, I was discussing with a group of fellow students, at the Bible Training Institute in Glasgow, the

> question 'What constitutes Divine leading?' There were many different points of view expressed. Later in the week I happened to read of some remarkable instances of the Spirit's leading. Then, on a pouring wet Saturday evening, I set out for a full weekend's missionary deputation work in Greenock.
>
> On the way down in the train the conviction seized me that I had to speak somewhere that night for my Master.

What then happened was that DP dropped in, unexpected, at the beginning of a local mission's meeting and was invited to replace the main speaker, unaccountably absent. From contacts in the Hall that night came his invitation to act as locum at the congregation of Paisley: Wallneuk and 'It was that four month's experience which ultimately sent me into the ministry.' He concluded the chapter, 'I have not always had experiences of that kind, but I have had some clear indication of God's guidance at every decisive point in my life.'

What constituted such guidance for DP was the combination of a growing inward conviction allied to an apparent coincidence, a combination that took up an existing concern and resulted, perhaps in retrospect, in new openings. In 1943, for example:

> Tuesday, 28th December [1943] . . . My next call was to be Mrs Thomson. I never got there . . . On my way to my call on Mrs Thomson I bethought me of J. and I had a definite impulse to go there. I walked into stark tragedy. J.'s whole world was in ruins.

Some could disparage such stories as theatrical sentimentality but others, including ministers of note, DP's contemporaries, shared the same experience.[27] In maturity DP continued his youthful practice of searching for his Master's direct leading, guidance and intervention in his life. In his own devotions he continued to use the classic collation of Biblical texts, *Daily Light on the Daily Path*.[28]

If DP was prepared to see God's leading in daily events, he also saw his leading within the larger pattern of his life. His sense of his call to be an evangelist endured as part of his understanding of God's particular guidance to him. By 1931, when Glassiebarns was launched, DP noted in his diary: 'Sunday, 10th May . . . A week today I will be 35 – half-roads on the appointed journey.' The entry was suggestive of a certain restlessness, an awareness that he would have lived half of the Biblically-appointed 'three score years and ten'. Despite hints and rumours, no new call had come to him from any attractive evangelical congregation. By 1934 he had become convinced that the time had come for him to return to evangelism as his first priority. DP's development of his second residential centre, that of St Ninian's, Lassodie, provided the occasion for his departure from Gillespie Memorial. Glassiebarns was too small to cater for all the groups wishing to use it. New premises were found in the abandoned and redundant church, church-hall and manse at Lassodie, also in Fife, where the nearby homes of the miners of a disused coalmine were emptying. The derelict buildings were purchased for a small sum and the task of renovation begun by means of voluntary labour. DP became Warden. Joe Ritchie, the Sub-Warden, was also recruited from the Gillespie Memorial. One of DP's Gillespie converts, a Sunday School teacher and intimate, Joe was a student at Edinburgh University between 1929 and 1936; in 1932 he was 25. DP had encouraged him as a speaker, both within the congregation and as part of the Gillespie visiting team. At St Ninian's he offered ministry to those remaining residents of the village as well as leadership to groups visiting the Centre.

On a smaller scale this was a venture akin to, and pre-dating, George MacLeod's determination to rebuild Iona's monastery – though Lassodie Church was in no way such a historic site or important building as Iona! September 1932 had seen the celebration of the fifteen-hundredth anniversary of the death of St Ninian, whom DP honoured as 'Scotland's pioneer evangelist' and so (very typically) 'advantage was taken of the interest aroused' to launch a national appeal, 'sponsored by the Moderator and the heads of other Scottish Churches' to place the new centre on a viable footing. A mural picture of Ninian observing the construction of his 'Candida Casa' at Whithorn was commissioned for the dining room.

The aims of St Ninian's, Lassodie, were – as might be expected from DP – ambitious:[29]

> . . . not merely a place to which groups of all kinds could come for short periods of vital fellowship, study, prayer and meditation, along distinctively Christian lines, but also a base at which those who were anxious to attempt new methods of reaching the great non-church-going classes in our land might meet and plan out their ventures, and from which they might go forth to attempt them.

The Board of Management was chaired by a former Moderator of the General Assembly, Very Rev. H. R. Mackintosh; Toc H in Scotland and the Scottish YMCA were represented. Whereas Glassiebarns had had Oxford Group connections, Lassodie now sought to work with Toc H – Tubby Clayton's post-war organisation for fellowship and service, which lacked the problems perceived in 'Buchmanism,' and had also attracted George F. MacLeod. St Ninian's features were advertised as its cheapness, its privacy and 'the combination of a certain amount of manual and domestic work with prayer, meditation, discussion and fellowship'. In this pragmatic way the necessary renovation would continue, while 'a finer fellowship will be fostered than is attained where the common distinction between guests and staff prevails'. St Ninian's, Lassodie, owed much to the church-hall camping DP had experienced with the student campaigns; it also owed something to the Oxford Group Movement's egalitarianism and to his tours to England in 1923 and 1931. In *Life & Work*, November 1931, he offered an article on what Scotland might learn from the Anglo-Catholic monastery of Kelham and from Woodbrooke, an international Christian college of Quaker foundation:[30] 'Both aim at the cultivation of a much more intimate fellowship, and at the establishment of a quite different relationship between student and professor, than that to which we in Scotland are accustomed.' Something of this was being attempted on a small scale at Lassodie.

Such a centre, however, unlike Glassiebarns, clearly needed its Warden to be resident. Lassodie's buildings included an empty manse, purpose-built for a minister. DP could not pass by the opportunity to base himself there: at a non-parochial centre without the restriction of territorial boundaries and yet with a small village on its doorstep for practical Christian work; a centre that would allow him to extend his links with the evangelical student world and to bring his experience to bear in the quest for new methods of mission. Unlike the faith missions, however, he did not look solely to God to meet his financial needs. He also wished to retain his recognition as a minister active within the Church of Scotland. A public appeal had been made for donations for St Ninian's, Lassodie and DP now did two things more or less together. On the one hand he began the process of resignation from Gillespie Memorial (he announced his intention to his Kirk Session on Sunday 2nd September); and on the other he wrote to the Home Mission Committee of the Church of Scotland to offer his services, part-time, as an Evangelist – his letter was welcomed by a committee that met on 2 October 1934. The General Assembly's Home Mission Committee had previously appointed a full-time lay rural evangelist and a lay artist-evangelist for children's missions; they had appointed ministers for a month or two to lead particular campaigns or for seaside missions and were then seeking to form a 'Panel of Speakers for special evangelistic work throughout the country'. No longer-term post for an evangelist, however, had ever been advertised: DP simply chose his own time to write to offer his services. He would have seen this as, in its way, akin to Gideon in the Old Testament laying out a fleece before God, a testing that he had correctly understood God's leading.

On 6 December 1934 the Evangelism Sub-Committee of the Committee on Home Mission agreed the terms under which D. P. Thomson would serve as an Evangelist 'for not less than two-thirds of the year' and 'for not more than three years'. The Home Mission Committee, at its meeting on 19 December 1934, approved this recommendation of its Sub-Committee. DP had already demitted from Gilliespie Memorial on 6 November 1934 and, between his post as Warden of St Ninian's, Lassodie and his new duties to the Home Mission Committee, was committed for the next three years to be an Evangelist, effectively if not contractually full time, the only minister within the Church of Scotland at that time to hold such a post unconnected with a parish. In the next decade George F. MacLeod would follow in his footsteps. As DP came to write it later, his 'training' was completed. He was 38 years old and still, somewhat unwillingly, a bachelor.

ACCEPTANCE AND REJECTION, 1934-1940

> You are a remarkable man, Mr Thomson. Do you know that you are rapidly becoming one of the leaders of the Church – I am hearing your name in some connection or other nearly every day!
>
> Rev. J. W. Stevenson, Editor of *Life & Work*,
> as reported in D. P. Thomson, The Diary of My Life part 9.

D. P. Thomson was one among others promoting evangelism within the Church of Scotland during the 1930s. Developing the ethos inherited from the former United Free Church, the post-1929 Kirk sponsored first the 'Call to the Church' of the Forward Movement of 1932 and then the 'Recall to Religion' of 1937. The Home Mission Committee and then the Home Board of the Church of Scotland sought to promote a variety of evangelistic causes and brought the General Assembly to recognise a panel of evangelists, available to support local campaigns. DP was not one of this panel, and we will examine why this was so and why his two-thirds appointment with the Home Board lasted only three years, 1934-37, even though his work was well suited to the mood of the church. For this short time DP was to know a measure of official recognition as an evangelist, before he decided to follow a path that was personally fulfilling but that appeared to involve a permanent breach from the Board.

Post Union Evangelism: The Forward Movement

Two special national campaigns were undertaken by the newly united Kirk during the 1930s: the 'Missions of the Kingdom' of 1932, promoted by the Forward Movement to communicate their 'Call', and the 'Recall to Religion' National Mission of 1937-38. The first now needs attention, to see why the Home Mission Committee, for its part, was prepared to accept DP's offer of service in 1934.

Planning for the Forward Movement began in 1930. Intentionally inspirational, it was a deliberate attempt to 'forward' the missionary ambitions of the Union by heightening Christian commitment across the Church. It was the brain-child of Very Rev. Donald Fraser D.D., Moderator of the 1922 General Assembly of the United Free Church, a former UF foreign missionary and from 1925 the Home Administration Secretary of the Foreign Mission Committee of that Church. Originally ordained for service overseas in Livingstonia, Fraser had never served in a Scottish parish; the entire focus of his vocation had been foreign mission. His first conception was an Overseas Forward Movement, intended to assist and progress the coming together of the overseas work of the UF and Established Churches – viewed in retrospect, of awesome, global, extent. Processed by the various central committees, the Movement morphed into a general campaign promoting the whole work of the new Kirk, as the General Assembly of 1934 heard:

> The general idea of the Forward Movement is that a call to the whole Church should be prepared, setting forth the range of the Church's activities, the greatness of the responsibility which this day of opportunity has created, and the response which is necessary from each member and each congregation if the services which have been undertaken are to be adequately fulfilled.

The Forward Movement Executive led by Donald Fraser comprised 20 ministers, including D. P. Thomson, ten elders and ten women. The Movement was to consist of a major Church Congress, held in Glasgow in October 1931; its associated book, *The Call to the Church*; and the subsequent 'Missions of the Kingdom' as the message and 'Call' were taken to presbyteries and congregations across Scotland.

During the planning phase of the Movement DP invited Donald Fraser to Dunfermline to address a special Sunday evening meeting. He was much impressed, but his account of the weekend also suggests some of the complexities of the Movement:

> Saturday, 23rd May [1931] Donald Fraser is here, and has just gone to bed. He is a truly humble and shining Christian – it is something more than a tonic effect to be in his company . . .
>
> Monday, 25th May [1931] . . . Donald Fraser is a great soul and a real Christian. He has suffered much at the hands of the FM Comm. [*Foreign Mission Committee*], – is quite shelved so far as influence on policy is concerned and seconded to the Forward Movement to get him out of the road. Taylor, who is a pompous idiot, is now Sole Convener of the FM Comm. and rules policy in the field and McLachlan rules in the Offices with an iron hand, Fraser frequently being asked what business of his are matters of which he only, as a missionary statesman, really knows! . . . At 8pm we had 600/700 in Queen Anne for the Mass Meeting – a great address from the Doctor, full of charm and of inspirational power.

Fraser's own perception of the situation was thus that, as far as some of the Church of Scotland's influence-brokers were concerned, he had been 'got out of the road' to a Movement that explicitly did not lay down new policies and was not empowered to interfere with the centres of power in the Church. What success it might achieve would be by persuasion, by what inspiration it might bring to the grass-roots of the new Kirk. From the start there were questions and complaints. There were those who were cynical:[1] 'it is suspiciously like a 'business boost' in its crudest and most up to date form.' There were those who argued that ministers and congregations should be left alone to do their own proper work. One such who styled himself 'Inquirer' thus wrote:[2]

> Certainly we need a religious awakening or revival, but can such be 'engineered' by active propaganda such as is being undertaken in connection with the forthcoming campaign? I doubt it. Revival comes from within . . . Another point worth considering is this – all earnest and true-hearted and spiritually-minded ministers of the Church of Scotland are engaged in such work in the ordinary course of their ministerial or pastoral duties. Special preachers and evangelists cannot present the Gospel in any new or strange light.

Besides its opposition, Inquirer's letter also demonstrated one of the ambiguities of the Forward Movement. What, actually, was it? 'Many', an editorial said, 'candidly do not understand the object for which the Forward Movement is directed. Is it an Evangelical Campaign? Is it a Church "boost" on a nation-wide scale? Is it a drive for money?' That ministerial journalist concluded:[3]

> It would be worse than putting one's head in the sand to imagine that, either among the pulpit or the pew, the Forward Movement was a generally acceptable proposal. There are ministers who see no need for it. They profess to abhor 'stunts' and see the need at no time for anything more than the regular work of the ministry. There are others in pulpit and pew who proclaim that no revival can be organised, and certainly that no elaborate machinery will bring it about.

Still others took the opportunity to urge that, historically, revivals were associated with a fresh understanding of the Gospel and sought to find new light in the theology of Karl Barth, the German-speaking Swiss neo-Calvinist:[4]

> Every great divinely-guided Forward Movement in the Church has had at the heart of it a theology, a doctrine of God, and usually an emphasis on some neglected truth. The neglected truth which is crying out for utterance today, in my opinion, is the Biblical truth of a speaking God – a God who has spoken, Who speaks, and Who will speak.

Meanwhile the Editorial Secretary of the Movement (and Editor of *Life & Work*), Rev. J. W. Stevenson, argued that the Scottish Kirk needed to align itself with a resurgence of Scottish cultural and political nationalism, calling for a new evangelism for a new nation under the Forward banner.[5] At the very least the Forward Movement stirred debate about the real work of the Kirk, about the Gospel and its connection with wider society. At best, perhaps, the Forward Movement may be understood as the first national Stewardship Campaign, introducing the concept of offering heart and mind, time, talents and money to Christ. The Free Will Envelope system of regular Christian giving was promoted, and a call made for average giving to increase from 3d to 4d in the £1.

Despite its unplanned coincidences with a UK General Election in the aftermath of Britain abandoning the gold standard, and with widespread strikes and a naval mutiny at Invergordon, the Forward Movement succeeded in gathering 2,500 delegates from presbyteries to a national Church of Scotland Congress, held in Glasgow the last week of October 1931. *The Call to the Church* was published both to coincide with the Congress and to be the basis of study and discussion throughout the Church as the delegates returned home. Perhaps 20,000 copies were sold. The final sentence summed up the purpose of the movement:

> To every member of the Church is addressed the call to enter upon a more sincere and eager and wholehearted life and service, until all the resources of the Church are at God's disposal, and our faith claims His resources in all their plentitude for the service of His Son and of His Kingdom.

Its 'Call' issued, the Forward Movement now travelled across Scotland via a large number of local mission weeks as its leaders made themselves available to groups of members and elders for discussion. These 'Missions of the Kingdom' included a mobile exhibition with displays of the work of the General Assembly's Committees, including – of course – mission work overseas. By the time the Executive was wound up in 1934, 46 Presbyteries out of 66 had hosted missions and some 2,100 meetings had been held. The 1934 General Assembly was told: 'many in the membership of the Church have realised for the first time the greatness of the Church to which they belong.' As at Dunfermline in May 1931, warm feelings had been generated; but no real revival had broken out. No real inroads been made on those that *The Call to the Church* had publicised as unreached by the churches, the one and half million Scots out of a total of around five million:[6]

> Deducting those who are under the care of Sister-Churches there remain, of our own Scottish folk, and not taking into account the alien population,[7] some one and a half million souls who are as sheep without a shepherd.

As to Fraser's original concept of taking forward the work of Foreign Mission, presently this was given its own dedicated promotional programme: the Restoration Movement. Widely understood to have failed, in that no national revival transpired, the Forward Movement therefore left a legacy of a recognised but unrealised need for evangelism.

Summer Missions and other Campaigns

A sub-component of first the Committee on Home Mission of the General Assembly and then, after a 1936 restructuring, of its Home Board, the Evangelism Sub-Committee included among its members a leading evangelical minister of the former UF Church, Very Rev. Dr Harry Miller, co-convener with Very Rev. Dr John White of Home Mission immediately after the Union. Besides White's particular enthusiasm, Church Extension,

20: AT A SEASIDE MISSION, GIRVAN 1937: REHEARSAL GROUP FOR 'THE PARABLE OF THE TALENTS', WITH BANNER

Home Mission inherited all the specialist missionary and evangelistic work of both pre-union central committees among non-parochial special cases – variously young people, fisher-folk, lodging-house and hospital inmates, berry-pickers, tinkers, campers; missions to small mining and Highland communities. Through its Evangelism Sub-Committee it appointed the missionary staff for holiday makers at summer hutted camps and also continued the UF Church's central support for local evangelistic campaigns. The success of D. P. Thomson and his independent team of ministerial evangelists at Stirling were brought to its attention by the Presbytery of Stirling & Dunblane – and Home Mission, in turn, used Stirling as the model for a new policy that it brought to the General Assembly of 1931:

> 5: The General Assembly emphasise anew the call of the Church through the regular ministry and the work of its congregations to an active evangelism, express their appreciation of the measure in which congregations have combined in united missions, and commend the proposal of the Committee to invite ministers possessed of gifts for this work to place these for a period at the service of the Committee.

While the Forward Movement had the attention of the Church the Home Mission Committee held its fire on evangelism and nothing then came of its 1931 initiative. By December 1933, however, the way was clear for a new approach and a letter was sent out to all Presbyteries:

> The Home Mission Committee of the Church is desirous of drawing the attention of your Presbytery to the opportunities which this age offers for a sound and effective Evangelism in the interests of the population which is outside the Church. Consequent on the Forward Movement the Home Mission Committee has for the past two years held its hand in this matter, but it is anxious now to do all in its power to promote and further every effort along the lines of Missionary Campaigns and Special Missions. The Committee is prepared to give whatever guidance and counsel may be required by Presbyteries, by groups of ministers, or by individual ministers in the planning of Evangelistic Meetings. Suitable literature is available, and the names of suggested speakers will be submitted on request. Presbyteries are being urged to give renewed attention to the work of Evangelism, and to take all needful measures through ministers and congregations towards its furtherance.

Associated with the group responsible for such campaigns was another former Moderator of the UF Assembly, Very Rev. R. J. Drummond.

Together with this approach to Presbyteries was a further new initiative, by which Home Mission set aside £100 to support Church of Scotland missions at seaside resorts:

> It was reported that a conference had been held with ministers from the various seaside resorts. The conference emphasised the absolute need for the Home Mission Committee doing something towards assisting the local ministers during the height of the holiday season, and the Evangelism Sub-Committee puts forward a recommendation to the Home Mission Committee that for the year 1934 it should give assistance in three or four seaside districts and that it be remitted to the Evangelism Sub-Committee to come to a definite decision as to which require immediate attention. The Evangelism Sub-Committee further recommends that towards the carrying out of this scheme an expenditure up to £100 be authorised.

Gathering holiday-makers' children on beaches for Christian worship, teaching and organised play had a long, if perhaps obscure, history from well before 1934. The independent missionary society, the Children's Special Service Mission [CSSM], originating in England, had formed a Scottish committee by 1902 to promote beach missions and Bible-reading.[8] Social changes between the wars, however, presented new challenges to the denominations. The hutted-camp holiday movement began as families, exploiting new opportunities to travel (and free from the restraints of English laws of trespass), first erected tents and then wooden huts on otherwise unoccupied shorelines. Even when local authorities backed two major sites, Lunderston Bay on the Clyde and Port Seton on the Forth, the first religious efforts were rebuffed:[9] 'The early days of [Lunderston Bay] were indescribably pagan. Ministers who endeavoured to hold open-air services in the midst of the huts and tents had to compete, it must be confessed unsuccessfully, with jazz bands and dancing couples, gambling schools and rowdy gangsters.' Perseverance, official involvement of Home Mission from 1927, dedicated marquees and the offer of social and medical support had won a hearing by 1932 and the Committee was ready to tackle the larger problems of the coastal towns themselves. Sunday in the coastal resorts frequented by 'youth with post-war outlook and sense of freedom' was now 'often a busier and more frivolous day than any other day of the week':[10]

> In years gone by when the influx of summer visitors took place, the local churches were full to overflowing, and the larger congregations, with fresh and vigorous mentality, gave heart and encouragement to the ministers and office bearers, which carried them on from summer to summer. The position today is vastly altered . . . a Sunday in many of our seaside resorts today is a sad spectacle to the older natives and the more staid of our people. The modern conveniences of motor transport and

> Sunday trains, together with a less scrupulous regard for Sunday closing on the part of many of the smaller and alien shop-keepers, have contributed to a state of affairs which makes the Sunday often a busier and more frivolous day than any other day of the week. The shore is occupied not only by the youth with post-war outlook and sense of freedom, but also by old and tired-looking men and women, who appear as though they welcomed escape from the dismal colliery rows or the hot and dusty city streets. These people throng the town in their hundreds and thousands, and though the Churches be fuller than usual they seem to receive the consideration of only an insignificant proportion of the augmented population.

Whereas the mission to the hutted camps was to localised, if transient, gatherings, distinct from their surrounding area, holiday makers at, say, North Berwick or Troon, were intermingled with the host population. They would need to be attracted – gathered – the Kirk would have to recognise the legitimacy of the holiday-maker. It was thought, at least by the 'Auld Kirk' Joint-Head of the Home Department, Arthur Dunnett, that 'special ministerial missionaries' would be required:[11]

> The suggestion is thrown out for what it is worth that the Home Mission Committee might be ready to provide special ministerial missionaries, who, under the guidance and with the cooperation of the local ministers, would conduct short and attractive services on the sands and where the summer populations tend to congregate. It is neither fair, nor in many cases possible, to expect the local ministers to undertake such services in addition to those for which they are responsible in their Churches. It would require, of course, ministers with special aptitude for such services, and it would fail of its main purpose if it were thought that such special mission work could be adequately done by divinity students or lay missionaries. The Church must realise that in this it must give of its best and be worthily represented, or not at all. In anything that can be done by the Church, full recognition must be taken of the changed outlook of this and coming generations . . . Full weight in any scheme of the Church's devising must be given to the broader and saner, because healthier, outlook of modern life. The sense of God's presence and delight in the joys of the gleaming sands and the sparkling waves are in no sense incompatible. Human nature will no longer stand for the suggestion of evil in the full enjoyment of that life which God has given us to live.

The Church of Scotland central structures were, in fact, coming somewhat late to this work in the middle 1930s.[12] The pre-union United Free Church had employed G. C. M. Grieve as a Children's Evangelist, and he had undertaken beach missions.[13] D. P. Thomson had himself known involvement with beach work on the fringes of GSEU campaigns during his student days – it was by no means uncommon.

By 1934, then, the Evangelism Committee was delighted to receive DP's offer of service, made in terms of the deliverance accepted by the General Assembly of 1931, 'to invite ministers possessed of gifts for this work to place these for a period at the service of the Committee.' By appointing him they were able to pursue aspirations held since before the Union. By appointing him, they were able to call to their assistance a younger minister with considerable evangelistic experience who had tended to specialise in work with 'young people' (though not with children), an ex-member of the Forward Movement Central Executive, a liberal-evangelical evangelist with modernist leanings, prepared to try new things. Even by June 1935 it was reported that there were more requests for his services than could be met. By December he had conducted missions at New Lanark, New Stevenston, Millport (the traditional seaside mission) and at Invergordon. For its part, the Committee was willing to offer his services to the Presbytery of Glasgow for six months over the winter of 1936-37 to organise special missions, believing he could also manage to combine this with a request from Airdrie Churches' Council for a mission in September 1936. By 1936 the style of Home Mission's report to the General Assembly recalled those of its UF predecessors, with in its report a explicit subheading, 'Evangelistic Missions':

> For the past few years the Home Mission Committee has been anxious to devote much of its interest and support to the furtherance of definite evangelistic work in the belief that the need was great and the country ready to respond to the call for a deeper spiritual experience. The Missions of the Kingdom promoted by the Forward Movement, and the difficulty of creating a panel of speakers constrained the Committee reluctantly to hold its hand on this matter. The Committee readily accepted the offer of the Rev. D. P. Thomson to devote himself to evangelistic work for a period of three years, and he was appointed to organise and direct campaigns. The past year has been fully occupied in special missions in Coatbridge, Dingwall, Muir of Ord, Beauly, Millport, New Lanark, Invergordon, Elgin, Inverallochy, New Stevenston, Carfin, Peterhead, Rosewell, Maybole, Fort William, Aberdeen, Shetland and Flemington. As was to be expected, Mr. Thomson has in all cases been in close touch with ministers and office-bearers with a view to stimulating preparation towards the campaigns to be held and to outlining the plans of attack. The programme generally included meetings held with Church workers

> and members of the various congregational organisations, special meetings with different sections of the community, open-air meetings and gatherings at Auction Marts and Football Fields. Beyond the valuable assistance given by the local ministers the services of many ministers and students were made use of. The response in most of the missions was encouraging while in a few there was evidence of an indifference which the time set apart for the work was obviously too short to tackle adequately. The energy devoted by Mr. Thomson in encouraging the holding of such missions and the readiness of congregations to have them have made it apparent to the Committee that the employment of one evangelist is utterly inadequate to the opportunity. It has accordingly decided to appoint a second evangelist so soon as a suitable appointment can be made, and in the meantime it has appointed an assistant to Mr. Thomson.

Lacking any diary of DP's from this period, no account from him survives of these missions. In 1956, however, DP met a man in Dingwall who recognised him:

> . . . and spoke in glowing terms of the Missions of 1935 in Dingwall and Beauly and Inverness, all of which he had attended, and especially of the meeting at which I had addressed the farmers in the Auction Mart, speaking on the 'spare wheel' and the 'steering wheel.'

Paired with the Mart in DP's report were football fields, which recalled the trend of connecting the Gospel with sportsmen associated with Eric Liddell and picked up by the Oxford Group Movement. The 1931 Stirling Campaign had featured a 'Sportsmen's Rally' and minister-evangelists, correctly dressed in the deep clerical collars and broad-rimmed outdoor hats then worn by the clergy, had paraded with sandwich-boards at local football grounds.[14]

There were, of course, also the Seaside Missions. When DP offered his part-time services to the Home Mission Committee in October 1934, there had already been centrally-organised Church of Scotland beach missions at Millport and North Berwick.[15] Padres, medical students, Church Sisters were recruited to staff the church marquees provided for the hutted camps at Port Seton and Lunderston Bay. For the summer of 1936 he proposed seaside missions at Millport; North Berwick; Ayr, Prestwick and Troon; and Nairn, with himself as leader at Ayr, Prestwick and Troon throughout July and August. A survey of other possibilities on both the west and east coasts had been submitted. Presently Dundonald was added to summer camp activity. Seaside missions followed much the same pattern as campaigns and, indeed, students normally comprised their teams. Camping in church halls involved the teams in the same shared, intense fellowship and devotional life, and the seaside programme that also included children's games and parties, with specially adapted worship, Bible stories and choruses. It should not be thought that these were simply children's missions, for their purpose was to reach holiday-makers in general.[16] Photographs published in *Life & Work* show listening crowds that were largely adult. In his 1965 *The Church in the Open Air* DP summarised: 'Forenoons and afternoons being spent, for the most part, with the children and their parents; evenings with the adolescents and the adults.' If beach missions were open-air events, so too had the GSEU campaigns also accustomed their teams to open-air, and often extempore, speaking. To DP, summer seaside missions *were* campaigns that sought to go to wherever people might be found. An article in the *Scotsman* for 13 July 1935 – most likely contributed by DP – gave an account of the activities at Millport: open air services, a football competition, soloist singers. In 1936 further attractions were added to the Prestwick-based missions: both the Quarriers City Orphan Home Silver Band and the 4/5th Royal Scots Band would parade; and 'Parable Plays' would be performed by the children on the sands. Lantern lecture slides of these latter still survive.

#21: AT A SEASIDE MISSION, GIRVAN 1937, 'GOOD SAMARITAN' GROUP WITH AUDIENCE

DP's three-year remit engaged him as an active, generic evangelist under the direction of the Committee, albeit part-time, to conduct 'evangelistic missions on a congregational basis' in the winter, and to organise and conduct the 'Seaside Open-Air Work of the Church' in the summer. Both aspects required volunteers to staff them: younger ministers traditionally supported the Kirk's winter missions, while students from the universities ran the summer activities. A good proportion of DP's efforts was therefore

#22: At a seaside mission, a parable play on the sands at Ayr

#23: At a seaside mission, a parable play on the sands at Prestwick

spent in recruiting and training these volunteers. Such networking was a particular gift of his. Training in evangelism had been part of his vision for the GSEU, the Groups movement and residential fellowship. Over a hundred ministers and students were required for the programme for summer 1937, besides celebrities like Rt. Hon. James Brown MP, a former Ayrshire miner, the UK Labour government's appointee as Lord High Commissioner to the General Assemblies of 1924, 1930 and 1931, and a former open-air free-lance preacher in his youth. 1937 was the most ambitious programme yet, requiring a large team for the Ayrshire coast resourcing missions at Prestwick, Troon, Ayr and Girvan; and another for the Fife coast supporting missions at Leven, Largo, and Lundin Links. Teams were also recruited for Aberdeen, Arbroath, Carnoustie, North Berwick and Millport. William Fitch, minister of Loudoun East Church, Newmilns, led the Prestwick mission, and brought with him one of his congregation's young men, Tom Allan, then aged 21 – Allan would in time himself lead the Kirk's Seaside work.[17] DP certainly expanded this branch of home mission, so that the Board appointed first Rev. J. B. Merrilees and then Rev. Jack S. Malloch to be his assistant. Jack, an Edinburgh man then aged 25, a musician who was especially gifted in speaking to children, complementing DP's more general skills, began his appointment on 29 March 1937. These were years when DP found himself in the mainstream of a flowing evangelical tide.

The Home Mission Committee appear to have been pleased with the evangelists they had appointed and with their expanding portfolio of seaside missions. Sir James F. Simpson, one of the Kirk's leading evangelical elders, began his lengthy association with this work in the inter-war years. His article in *Life & Work* for October 1936[18] was concerned to show that these missions were supported not just by dubious extremists but by men brought up in the 'Auld Kirk'. George F. MacLeod and John White, 'well-kent' names of the younger and older generations spoke at seaside missions; so too did Rev. Dr James Black who occupied the famous Edinburgh pulpit of St George's West, and would be Moderator of the General Assembly in 1938. Sir Leon Levison – son of a Palestinian Jewish rabbi, a converted Christian, President of the International Hebrew Christian Alliance, knighted in 1919, evangelist to Scottish Jews – was a leading evangelical layman and publisher, known to DP from his Gillespie days. Further guest speakers included Sheriff J. Gordon Jamieson, of the Oxford Group. Bill P. Temple, who graduated from Glasgow University and Trinity College a few years after DP, had been involved with the Stirling Campaign and would continue as his colleague in evangelism until Temple left for a charge in New Zealand in 1948. D. C. Mitchell, who had been called instead of DP to St Mark's Lancefield, was a speaker at the coast in 1936, and Joe Ritchie, DP's protégé from Gillespie Memorial, by now minister at Armadale: East, was leader at Millport. The Church would hear more in the future of others involved with seaside missions in the mid-1930s: A. C. Craig M.C., M.A., Chaplain to Glasgow University, was part of a campaign team in 1937;[19] Andrew B. Doig shared the leadership at Prestwick with William Fitch and Bill Temple in 1936.[20] With such broad support from across the Kirk, Sir James' longer-term aspirations for further extension of the work were hardly unreasonable.

#24: AN EVENING 'OPEN AIR' AT PRESTWICK, 1937

Despite the success of his Seaside Mission work, D. P. Thomson faced personal problems. His mother Helena's illness forced him to cancel appointments in the summer of 1936. By now she was a widow: James Thomson had died in 1931 while he and his wife were resident in Durham, staying with their daughter Dr Christine Jane Thomson (known to DP as CJ), who was then attached to the university there. She had completed a medical research tour to India in 1930 and was to publish her report, *Still-Birth and Neo-natal Death in India: A preliminary enquiry* in 1931. While attending a family celebration in Durham in November 1930, DP had been made aware of his mother's increasing frailty:

> Friday, 28th November [1930] . . . It was a rather touching farewell at Durham. The poor dear Mater has reached an internal condition that looks like offering only two alternatives – a serious and grave operation or permanent invalidism. At a family conclave last night we faced all the issues and possibilities very calmly – even down to place and cost of burial. 'Peach' is wonderful and never turned a hair. We decided not to risk the operation unless the trouble proved malignant. She is prepared

> for the sofa if need be, even bed. I can't really write about it. I never thought or saw her more wonderful. She may never walk 100 yards again. [*Previously in the week*] . . . I left by car for Durham at 11.30. In good time for the luncheon the Mater was giving at the County Hotel – 22 in all sat down – many D.D.s and several College Principals. I was between Principal Walls of St John's – the Evangelical College – and Dr Grace Howie, CJ's chief – a daughter in law of the famous Dr Howie of Govan and mother of Christine's 'locum' while in India . . . Then on to 22a North Bailey. They stayed till 6 and we had a delightful time together. In the evening much love and a long family pow-wow! CJ finishes her Indian Report tonight.

His father, however, was first to die and is buried at Durham. DP himself, while at Gillespie, had had continued problems with his health. In 1931 in the midst of all his experiments he had a series of rectal injections designed to staunch bleeding from his bowel. Concerns for his family and for his own health were never far from his mind.

#25: DR CHRISTINE J. THOMSON (CJ)

Equally the overseas work of the church was never far from D. P. Thomson's mind. Missionary Days had been part of the Glassiebarns programme; now he recruited International Teams to support the seaside missions, often from the ranks of students at the universities or the BTI. An American post-graduate studying theology at New College wrote about his experience in the summer of 1938. The team had visited thirteen centres: seaside missions at Girvan, Ayr, Prestwick, Troon, Largs, North Berwick, Leven, Largo, Aberfeldy, Arbroath and Aberdeen; and the hut-camps at Meadowpark and Stevenston:[21]

> In each centre which it visited, the team conducted at least one meeting for adults and another for the children. At the meetings for adults, the 'Witness Box' played an important part. Each member of the team was cross-examined concerning his home land, his background, and his personal relation to Jesus Christ. This afforded opportunities to speak on many subjects which would have been difficult to deal with in a single address, and it also gave an opportunity for the men to tell what Christ meant to them, and what He would mean to every one who accepted Him as Saviour and Lord. In addition to the Witness Box, short talks and testimonies were given. At the children's meetings, one member of the team usually led in the singing of children's hymns and choruses. The children were very much interested in hearing about the various lands from which the men came, and on some occasions maps were used, to point out the locations of the nations represented. Missionary stories, tales concerning outstanding men and women of the faith, and anecdotes illustrative of the great truths of Scripture were told to the boys and girls. It might be added that usually more adults than boys and girls were present at the children's meetings . . . The members of the International Team count it a privilege to have had this opportunity to serve their Lord and to witness to His saving power; and their prayer is that the seed which they have sown will be blessed of God and that it will bring forth fruit.

A development of the soap-box approach to open-air meetings, but with the added dramatic interest of using interview technique, the Witness Box meeting may also have borrowed something from the Oxford Group's emphasis on personal testimony – it remained part of DP's repertoire after the Second World War.

Besides the romantic appeal of these students as representatives of the world church and its different cultures, we can speculate that those who had found the necessary funds for post-graduate study in Scotland may have had a higher than usual level of Christian commitment and hence were ideal for DP's evangelistic purpose. In 1937 he published a successful book telling the stories of the conversions of ten of these overseas men: *How I found Christ.* One of those who thus told his story was Nahum Levison, brother of Sir Leon: it was Sir Leon Levison's company, Marshall, Morgan and Scott, who were the publishers. The total list of contributors was impressive in itself, and also as testimony to DP's growing network of connections:

I Arabia – a sheikh Othman boy, by Ahmed S. Affara.
II China – a young engineering graduate from Hankow, by Y.T. Hu.
III Greece – a bank clerk from Athens, by Michael Kyriakakis
IV India – (a) an Anglo-Indian orphan, by John MacGilbert
(b) a Vaishnavite Brahman's son, by Paul Rangaramanujam
V Iran (Persia) – a Muslim landowner's son, by Reza G. Bourbour
VI Japan – a young artist from Kobe, by S. Segawa
VII Palestine – a Jewish Rabbi's son, by Nahum Levison
VII Portugal – a financier in prison, by Alves Reis
IX Russia – a Latvian pastor's son, by Robert Fetler
X Spain – a Franciscan scholar, by Juan Orts Gonzalez

#26: DP WITH AN INTERNATIONAL TEAM

As part of his work as Warden of St Ninian's, Lassodie – the one-third of his year for which he was not answerable to the Home Board – DP published other books during the 1930s, multi-tasking as usual. He created a new publishing company, the Lassodie Press, and the National Library of Scotland still retains three of its volumes. *The Romance of Blantyre: How Livingstone's Dream Came True*, by Alexander Hetherwick, was a missionary story. *The Worship Of The Scottish Reformed Church, 1550-1638* by William McMillan reflected another personal interest, Scottish church history. *The Scottish Churches' Handbook* sought to embody DP's catholicism – 'This Handbook is intended to be a definite contribution to inter-denominational understanding and fellowship, and a practical guide for busy men in every field of religious and social service' – and came out while he was still combining ministry at Gillespie Memorial with Lassodie. Joe Ritchie had helped with its collation. Hosting groups for conferences was, of course, the bulk of Lassodie's work. Thus DP led a three-day retreat for the Edinburgh Student Campaigners (president, Rev. George Gunn, of Edinburgh: Juniper Green) in June 1935, as part of preparations for an evangelistic campaign in Lochgelly, Fife. A conference of the Fife YMCA arrived as the students left. St Ninian's, Lassodie, also offered DP further opportunities to interact with the world church: temporarily on the staff in June 1935 was Rev. Aaron Gyenge of the Hungarian Reformed Church of Transylvania.[22]

To Jamaica

Two and half years into DP's remit as Evangelist of the Church of Scotland, an invitation arrived that was to change his life: a request that he conduct a campaign in the Caribbean island of Jamaica, then a Crown Colony in the British West Indies. He was to publish its story in *Two Scotsmen See Jamaica; An account of a three months' missionary and travel tour in the 'Isle of Beauty and Romance' in the Winter of 1937-8, in the form of letters to a correspondent at home*:

> In March, 1937, I received an official invitation from the Synod of the Presbyterian Church of Jamaica, sent by the Moderator, Rev. Henry Ward, asking me to conduct a series of evangelistic campaigns throughout the island, as part of a year's special preparation for the Centenary of Emancipation, which fell to be celebrated on 1st August 1938. The time suggested for my visit was the earlier part of the preceding winter. All expenses would be paid, including passage both ways, and I could be assured of the heartiest of welcomes, alike from Jamaican pastors and

> people and from the little band of Scottish missionaries. Full preparations would be made for my coming, the programme would cover almost the whole island, and the details would be worked out with the greatest care.
>
> What was I to say in response to this request? I knew a good deal about the island. Two of its twelve Presbyterian missionaries were personal friends of my own. I could recall having sat, as a very small boy, on the knee of a missionary's wife, and looking up into her face having promised solemnly that I would certainly come out one day and see her in Jamaica! On each of their missionary furloughs that missionary couple came to see us, and on every occasion the invitation and the promise were renewed. Was this now, at last, the opportunity of fulfilling my obligation? My mother's old friend was dead, but her husband was, I well knew, one of those who had heartily supported the proposal which had reached me from the Moderator's hand.
>
> When Mr Ward's invitation came I was nearing the end of a three years' appointment as a member of the Home Mission Staff of the Church of Scotland. Any renewal of my engagement, I felt, might well be made dependent on the necessary leave of absence being granted. Under these circumstances I had little difficulty in deciding to accept.

Aware as we are of DP's ambition to serve Christ overseas, part of his soul since his childhood, we can appreciate the irresistible nature of this invitation. The Jamaican church was English-speaking, the life of its presbyterian congregations founded and fostered by generations of Scots. Jamaican culture, though exotic to Scots, had had a seemingly comprehendible British layer imposed on both its indigenous and its imported, enslaved African and East Indian peoples since 1655. A visit to Jamaica would pose less of a risk to DP's uncertain health than a tour to, say, an African or Asian mission station. Christian work in Jamaica had been particularly honoured in his United Free Church. There were the existing personal contacts, clearly important to him. So he accepted the invitation, with only one condition:

> . . . that, providing the necessary funds were forthcoming in Scotland, I might be allowed to bring with me my Assistant in Evangelistic work, Rev. J. S. Malloch, B.D., B.L. He was an expert in children's work, and a soloist as well as a musician. These were gifts to which I could not possibly lay claim, and in work of this kind they would, I knew, be invaluable. We had grown to know and appreciate one another while working together in Scotland, and both of us realised that it was not for nothing that Christ sent out his disciples 'two by two.' What spiritual partnerships can achieve it is almost impossible to over-estimate . . . By the end of October we were ready to start, our kit packed, letters of introduction in our pockets,

> and much sound advice in our minds on which to ponder during the voyage.

Their friends having found the necessary funds, DP and Jack sailed from Liverpool on 8 November and arrived at Kingston on the 26 November 1937. Their stay was to last just under three months.

No full account survives of DP's mission in Jamaica. *Two Scotsmen* was based on letters home that were written to CJ:

> They give a visitor's impressions of the island as it was before the outbreak of the Second World War, and if they touch more on the lighter than on the serious side at times, it was because they were meant to afford some little amusement and relaxation for both of us. With many of the problems of Jamaican life, – obeah, pockomania, and illegitimacy – they do not deal at all. On many features of our work, and on some of our most memorable experiences, they hardly touch . . .

The 1929 Church Union had brought together two separate aspects of Christian work in Jamaica. Some congregations originated from Scotsmen engaged in colonial business or administration; others from the more radical missions of the nineteenth century Scottish Missionary Society to local people – abolitionist, the fruit of the movement for the emancipation of slaves. Called to the island as a prelude to the Emancipation centenary celebrations, DP honoured the work of the founding missionary, Scotsman George Blyth, whose congregation first celebrated the British Imperial Emancipation of Slaves by a Thanksgiving Service on 1 August 1834 - 'The Lord hath done great things for us, whereof we are glad' – and thereafter raised funds to promote mission in West Africa and to aid the cause of emancipation in the USA. Later, DP was also to note that his congregation at the Gillespie Memorial had been proud of their evangelical history of opposition to the slave trade.

DP's Jamaica mission followed the essential pattern of those conducted in Scotland: mid-week evening meetings; visits to schools and children's services; special Sunday services. The evangelists moved from one congregation to another, giving roughly a week to each: 'Today was the closing meeting of our week's gatherings in Savanna-la-Mar. Night by night the Church has been crowded to the doors, there not being even standing room round the porch on some occasions . . . It has been a very fruitful mission.' In his report, written on his return to Scotland in March 1938 to the friends who had sponsored the mission, DP recorded that they had delivered some 4-500 addresses between them, with perhaps the balance of the work being undertaken by Jack:

> In most of the larger centres, Mr Malloch conducted a series of children's meetings which made a deep impression on young and old alike, and during a large part of our stay in Jamaica he had the bulk of the country area, as well as assisting me at the big evening meetings in the larger centres wherever we went . . . We look back with great thankfulness to God, and real gratitude to all who helped to make it possible, on our visit to Jamaica, where we had the joy of knowing that hundreds were brought to a personal knowledge of Christ, and the Church quickened and stirred to new life and effort. One of the results of our work has been the inauguration of a scheme designed to bring Christian literature to the homes of the people throughout the island, and another the launching of open-air work in some of the bigger centres.

During 1938 the work of Jamaican church was to be severely tested. Soon after DP left the island the emancipation celebrations were destroyed in a wave of violent protest.

Whatever its local consequences, for D. P. Thomson personally his Jamaica Mission had two important results, the good and the questionable. As for the good, he wrote to his friends in March 1938, to their astonishment: 'I became engaged to Miss Mary Rothnie, the daughter of our senior missionary in Jamaica on the active list, just before sailing for home, and we hope to be married in September in Aberdeen.' On the other hand, his acceptance of the call to Jamaica led to a breach with the Home Board that jeopardised his longer-term influence within the Church of Scotland.

The first we hear of Mary, a domestic science teacher some seven years younger than DP, was when she brought him a chocolate cake 'which she had baked, having discovered how much I fancied it. She goes back to Carron Hall today, being on the staff of the Girls' School there.' DP's published letters actually tell us a great deal more of her father, the Rev. Douglas A. Rothnie M.A., from Aberdeenshire, brought up in the United Free Church and ordained by it to service in Jamaica in 1901. When DP asked for his daughter's hand, Douglas Rothnie was aged 65, missionary-minister at Lucea and a man of note:

> The Manse, Lucea, Hanover, Jamaica
>
> Friday 7th January 1938
>
> Our host is the Synod Clerk, and quite the most outstanding man we have met so far in Jamaica. An Aberdeenshire man born and bred, he came out here 37 years ago, and is now the senior Presbyterian missionary on the active list. Singularly youthful and active for his years, he is the very embodiment of vigour and efficiency, and is loved and honoured,

#27: REV. DOUGLAS ROTHNIE AND HIS DAUGHTER MARY, AT THE MANSE, LUCEA, JAMAICA

admired, feared, and respected throughout this whole section of Jamaica. A singularly devoted pastor, who is on the road before seven most mornings, a capable and far-sighted organiser, an outspoken and fearless preacher, and the leader not only of the community but of the whole district in any enterprise making for the social and spiritual welfare of the people, he comes as near to my ideal of a missionary as any man I have met. His brethren in ministry have long learned to turn to him for advice and guidance in their difficulties, his people worship him, and members and leaders of all denominations look up to him as the 'Bishop of Lucea' and the 'Father in God' of all the Churches of Christ in Hanover. It has been one of life's rich experiences to spend a week under his roof.

In marrying Mary, DP also acquired a man he was to know as 'Father,' a minister he was happy to look to with respect – perhaps Douglas Rothnie exemplified what DP would have liked to be, had the course of his life been different. But it was DP's love for Mary that mattered now. Though he was by no means so much the confirmed bachelor as friends perhaps thought, as far as DP was concerned this passion was something new for him, striking at first sight and overcoming all his previous uncertainties. Their whirlwind romance, besides frustrating Mary's former, local, suitor (he offered to fight DP for her!) and being met in Jamaica with 'amazement, incredulity, questioning' meant that DP travelled back to Scotland with Jack Malloch, as arranged, and that Mary and her father followed later in

1938 (her mother had died in 1928). Later she told DP that when it came to leaving Jamaica she had nearly had cold feet – but found the courage to go on:

> Monday 3rd April [1944] . . . Mary has told me . . . she wondered whether she ought to come at all the first time – well, well! On the way to the boat Father, who realised this, stopped half way to Kingston and said 'Well, what is it to be?' She hadn't the courage to turn back, so just went on to see it through! And here we are! Well, well!

DP himself could see, on reflection, God's leading in his decision to go to Jamaica:

> I was reflecting as I watched this morning on how wonderfully I had been led. Jamaica in my thoughts since childhood – the promise and the hope of going there. Destiny awaiting me in a way I could never have foreseen. When I think of the cold and the dark and the fog and all my darling gave up in that lovely tropical land for me, I am moved afresh by wonder, love and gratitude. How much I owe!

Rev. Dr Ian Doyle, who knew DP and Mary particularly well, wrote of her:[23]

> Mary Thomson was very different from her masterful husband, but complemented his work in a way that was quite remarkable to witness. Her graciousness, her modest ways, her friendly hospitality, the capacity for sheer hard work that seemed incredible in one of so small a frame, above all her complete loyalty to DP and the work he was called to do, made her a wonderful help-meet to him in the thirty-six years of life they shared.

DP and Mary Thomson set up their home at St Ninian's, Lassodie, in the autumn of 1938 and faced an uncertain future together. DP's decision to accept the invitation to conduct the mission in Jamaica had led also to a breach between himself and the Home Board of the Church of Scotland, a breach that threatened to become permanent. In dark moments during June 1943 he even wondered whether the whole Jamaican enterprise – and hence his marriage – had been a blunder:

> Last night as I walked the insistent question presented itself – had everything from my acceptance of the invitation to Jamaica been a mistake? Did I follow the Lassodie blunder by a greater blunder then? Was it better that like Archie Craig and George MacLeod I should remain as I was – unmarried? Would I have done better work for the Master thus?

To understand why – apart from his post as Warden of St Ninian's, Lassodie – D. P. Thomson was essentially unemployed in the autumn of 1938, we need to step back and consider the origins and progress of the 'Recall to Religion'.

Post Union Evangelism: The Recall to Religion

During 1937, just as DP was planning to be absent from Scotland, a national campaign of evangelism was being prepared. The movement took its name (if not its underlying roots) from England, from a December 1936 address by Cosmo G. Lang**,** Archbishop of Canterbury. Against the background of the Spanish Civil War, of Fascist riots on the streets of London and the abdication of King Edward VIII, the archbishop issued a very English, polite, well-mannered request, to 'return to religion'. Still, the initiative was well publicised. North of the Border the slogan rang many bells and quickly sparked a full-blown inter-denominational National Mission: 'The Recall to Religion'. Within the Church of Scotland the lead was taken by former UF Moderator, R. J. Drummond, convener of the Campaigns group of the Evangelism Committee of the Home Board. Drummond obtained the support of the Home Board at its meeting in February 1938, and John White's Board then gained approval from the subsequent General Assembly in May. Before the Union Drummond had been one of the foremost of the UF Church's public figures to advocate evangelism; he remained so within the Church of Scotland, and was supported by John Hall, senior joint-Secretary to the Home Board and formerly the sole Secretary to its UF predecessor.

Hall published in February 1933,[24] November 1936[25] and December 1938[26] articles in *Life & Work* that helped to sustain a mood supportive of evangelism. His 'Revival of Evangelism' article, that of November 1936, predated Cosmo Lang's address and is hence more typical of Scottish thought. Within the reunited Kirk an ambivalence persisted, Hall suggested: on the one hand a revulsion against a methodology associated with mass psychology, and yet a recognition that whether in Hitler's Europe, or at the apex of 20th century civilization, or in the decadent materialism of the age, the Christian Church's first duty was, winningly and passionately, to proclaim Christ. Hence Hall joined those who called for a 'new evangelism', not so much dependent on the old methods. Hall sought – as a senior executive of the united Church was bound to do – to bind together the 'Auld Kirk' and UF traditions; he sought to expand the concept of evangelism from the *ad hoc* special effort to encompass the ordinary ministry of the ordinary parish minister and of his congregation. Yet he also recognised that if this was to be effective, those ordinary ministers and congregations needed to be revived. The 'Recall' gathered behind it a coalition: those, largely from the former UF Church, who still longed to see the Union effectively mobilised for evangelism; those who sought an outlet for post-1919 ecumenism; those – often influenced by Karl Barth's theology of crisis – who sought to challenge what they perceived of the spirit of the times with Biblical theology; those who, like the Lord's Day Observance group of the Kirk's Church and Nation Committee (one of the official sponsors of the movement) sought to re-establish the social disciplines of the older Scotland; those who looked back to the revivalism of the 19th century and of D. L. Moody.

A new 'Call to the People of Scotland' was issued in March 1937 and explained in *Life & Work* in April 1937 by R. J. Drummond in his article 'God's Call to the People of Scotland: A Summons to His Church.'[27] The campaign was in some respects a re-run of The Forward Movement, but on a broader inter-denominational front. It sought first the renewal of spiritual life within the Churches, and then an evangelistic thrust into the wider community. Its structure, however, was very different. Reliance was placed primarily on local committees and not on central direction or resources. No attempt was made to promote the various denominations' central agencies – indeed, ecumenical partnership was strongly emphasised. Much was left to local initiative but after the initial stimulus in March a timetable was suggested that included both house to house visitation and more traditional if simultaneous campaigns that would begin in October 1937.

If there was thus much about the 'Recall' that was in continuity with the campaigns run by the GSEU or the SSCM, there was also much that was different. House to house visitation, whether by ministers or catechists, by elders or by Lay Missionaries, Church Sisters and volunteer Scripture Readers, had a long pedigree as part of evangelistic outreach in Scotland. Back in 1922 D. P. Thomson's early enthusiasm for the GSEU had committed his men to door to door work at Glasgow: Young Street. Yet the method was enjoying new favour in the 1930s as fashion turned against the mass rally with its Nazi, totalitarian connotations. Several other factors lay behind this, beyond a genteel dislike for religious emotionalism. There was a recognition that, because the non-Christian no longer attended Evangelistic Rallies, it was therefore inefficient to continue this use of an evangelist's time. This argument was attractive in the United States, with its business-like organised religion. In 1925 evangelist A. Earl Kernahan published *Visitation Evangelism: its methods and results*, with a critique of the mass meeting tradition in which he had been brought up. 96% of the audience at rallies, he argued, were evangelical Christians, come for a blessing; even those who were converted in such abnormal circumstances soon found that ordinary church life had few attractions and dropped out. On the other hand, as a US Army Chaplain during the First World War he had found personal contact had won enduring commitment. After the war Kernahan began an independent vocation as a consultant-evangelist specialising in enabling congregational mission based on house to house witness. Results-orientated, he claimed responsibility for some 10,000 converts through this method. Kernahan was (of course) an enthusiast: in promoting his technique as that of Jesus Christ and the early Church, he dismissed other, older, methods as both ineffective and inefficient. He also argued that enlisting the laity brought its own positive benefit by strengthening the faith both of the individuals involved and of the corporate life of the participating congregation. Besides declaring that the day of the professional evangelist as a solo preacher, a one-man-band, was over, his book was a strong affirmation of the missionary congregation.

Whatever effect stories of American practice might have had – and this effect should not be discounted, as professors, ministers and graduate students crossed the Atlantic in both directions as a matter of course – within Scotland there were other reasons for the revival of house to house visitation. The 1921 Articles Declaratory of the faith and constitution of the (established) Church of Scotland, on which the 1929 Union was part-based, declared the Kirk's 'distinctive call and duty to bring the ordinances of religion to the people in every parish in Scotland through a territorial ministry'. Once again it has to be remembered that the prime aim of the Union was to allow an effective mission of ministers and congregations across the whole territory – islands, cities, countryside – of Scotland, for the sake of the Gospel. John Hall's Established Church's pre-Union counterpart, post-1930 joint-Secretary to the Home Department, was Arthur Dunnett, who in 1934 wrote of mission and evangelism in his *The Church in Changing Scotland*:[28]

> We recognise that the function of the Church is to proclaim the Gospel of Jesus Christ and His redeeming love. The three thousand congregations spread over the whole country, while being fellowships of those who seek the way of life as it has been revealed in Christ, are also, in so far as they endeavour to work out the purpose of the Master, centres of evangelistic activity within the areas of their influence. Their charge is not merely their own inner prosperity and stability. They have, every one of them, the responsibility of bringing within the power of Christ all who are resident within their areas and not attached to any branch of His

> Church. This responsibility rests upon every Church member. Rivalries in the past made for duplication of effort in some areas and neglect in others. That day is now gone. Every congregation in Scotland will in a very short time have allocated to it a definite area which in almost every case ought to be perfectly workable. Within each of these areas it ought to be possible to know the religious circumstances of every individual and to keep trace of all who come and go. This will not be done without work. At the present moment the work of most of our congregations is being left to the two or three. The aim of the Church to-day is to bring to bear upon every one in the land the personal influence of those who form its membership. This cannot be done unless churches exist and congregations function within easy reach of the people.

Both joint-Secretaries of the Home Board were thus publicly committed to congregational evangelism – the evangelism of the ordinary church member, deliberately structured within congregations operating in defined areas, so that within the entire nation no single individual would be outside the knowledge, prayers and influence of a Christian. Like John Hall, Arthur Dunnett accepted but played down the role of the old fashioned revival, looking for something more permanent, more continuous, more regular:[29]

> The evangelistic work of the Church suggests to many people something along the lines of a revival, a more or less passionate effort to stir, within a neglectful community, the white-heat enthusiasm for repentance and regeneration. No one should belittle the value of many of the revivals which at odd times have spread over the country. The Church has still room for some such quickening. But this quickening must proceed from the very heart of our congregations, and it must not cease till it has permeated the lives of the entire community . . . The other evil is to work for a revival in fits and starts. The work of the Church is always revival, and it must always be in progress.

House to house visitation fitted very well into this vision for the national church, and following the Union we have seen DP and the elders of the Gillespie Memorial joining in what seems to have been a widespread practice of churches visiting and surveying their new 'delimited areas'.

There was also the vision of George F. MacLeod. Scion of a veritable dynasty of Established Church ministers, son of one of Glasgow's Members of Parliament, John MacLeod, 1st Baronet of Fuinary,[30] George was very much an 'Auld Kirk' man by family, upbringing and choice. Having moved from his prestigious first collegiate charge of Edinburgh: St Cuthbert's to Glasgow: Govan Old in 1930, MacLeod published in 1936 three *Life & Work* articles, entitled 'The Churchless Million' and on the theme of the territorial ministry of the Church, calling on his experience of parish mission in Govan Old.[31] Taking his cue from the Scottish Churches Council (1927) and the Forward Movement identification of a churchless million (give or take some hundreds of thousands), MacLeod called for a thorough-going return to a real parish system, so thorough-going as to require a radical new local loyalty and discipline from church members, who were used to criss-crossing towns and cities to attend their parents' church, or their preferred preacher's church, or to hear their favourite choir or for a host of other reasons.

In 1934 MacLeod organised a campaign (called a 'Message of Friendship' because his 'Auld Kirk' people associated missions or campaigns with 'those badly-ventilated halls' for the poor) that followed many of the traditional features that DP would have recognised. After a lengthy period of preparation volunteers visited the parish from house to house to survey the area, to discover religious allegiances and to invite residents to a special week of events: parades, stunts, services, question-times and other meetings. Results were published: over 200 children joined the Sunday School and over 100 lapsed adult members were restored. 200 more later joined the church by profession of faith after a ten-week instruction course, and over 80 adults were baptised. On the basis of this experiment, MacLeod blamed the existence of the 'churchless million' on the failure of the Kirk to operate a true parish system; and almost overnight he gained a reputation as an evangelist, being one of four keynote speakers on Evangelism at the Home Board's annual conference for younger ministers in 1937. His articles, expanded with a detailed supplement on his methodology, were also published as a booklet *Are Not the Churchless Million Partly the Church's Fault?* in 1936. Both house to house visitation and MacLeod's book were officially recommended by R. J. Drummond as an integral part of the 'Recall to Religion,' the timing of which was most fortuitous for George MacLeod. Not essentially original in concept but nevertheless strikingly presented, his system – his emphasis on the contribution of the congregation to evangelism, on collective witness and on house to house visiting to precede and supplement more traditional meetings – was before the church just as Cosmo Lang issued his 'Recall,' and as the Kirk sought 'a new evangelism' appropriate for the times. What Hall and Dunnett called for, MacLeod showed a way to achieve within patterns recognisable and acceptable to those from the formerly Established Church of Scotland.

The 'Recall to Religion' movement was thus a peak of the 'new evangelism' increasingly practised since the 1920s. T. Ralph Morton was to recognise four developments as its characteristics: that it related its message to the needs and problems of the day; that it involved inter-denominational co-operation; that its leaders were often 'ordinary' ministers and laymen, not big-name evangelists; and that it sought to work with the whole church.[32] Morton associated student campaigning, local missions and the Forward Movement as, together, responsible for developing this 'new' pattern. Never a supporter of the 'old evangelism', Morton perhaps underestimated real areas of overlap between 'old' and 'new' in each of his four characteristics. We have seen, however, that D. P. Thomson, an advocate for the new and modern after 1924, certainly believed in a relevant gospel, in co-operation, in the power of the witness of the ordinary Christian of both sexes, and in evangelism based in congregational life. DP would have added to Morton's analysis that the new evangelism had to take itself out of the pulpit and move into the open air: to the beach, to the street corner and the witness box.

But what of D. P. Thomson during the key period of the 'Recall to Religion', October 1937 to early 1938? What was the role of the Home Board's own ministerial evangelist? His friend John Kent was very much involved in the campaign in Glasgow. Without any Diary of DP's that covers this period, regrettably we have little idea of his activities beyond the reports of the continued growth of Seaside Missions over the summers of 1937 and 1938. The minutes of the Home Board, however, reveal a lengthy discussion of the issue as to whether his appointment was to continue at all beyond 31 December 1937. DP raised this question by letter as early as December 1936: he may have been provoked by an article by John Hall in November's *Life & Work*, which contained much that must have worried him. Was the joint-Head of the Home Department also speaking for the Home Board when he doubted the value of full time evangelists? In response to DP's request to know 'the Committee's intentions regarding his future', negotiations were arranged and by February 1937 apparently generous terms were proposed. What was now suggested was a full-time appointment, for a further three years, with a broad remit, secretarial assistance and a variety of expenses. The Board, however, instructed the Committee to discuss matters again with DP and to take on board any further ideas he might have – clearly, with the 'Recall' now in the offing, the Home Board was very keen to have available its own full-time evangelist to offer to the Church. At this stage, however, DP's mother,

Helena Thomson, died in London, and in March 1937 the committee suspended discussions for a month, owing to his recent bereavement. We are told little of DP's side of the debate, but he must have had two issues to consider. One was his Wardenship of St Ninian's, Lassodie. The Home Board wanted a full-time evangelist: but DP wanted both a base in the national Kirk's life as the official evangelist *and also* an element of freedom to pursue his own agenda, to nurse his own 'baby.' Besides, his mission to Jamaica was also in preparation. In May 1937 the Evangelism Committee came to a formal decision:

> Ultimately it was moved, seconded, and agreed that the terms of Mr Thomson's reply were a definite declinature to consider a full-time appointment. The Committee therefore recommends that his present engagement be allowed to expire according to agreement on 31st December 1937.

Yet talks did not end: DP had mooted part time employment and, in view of the success of the Seaside Missions, the Board was loath to lose all their ties with him. What in the end was agreed was that DP would be offered a final six months of service in 1938: two months to prepare for the summer, two months of summer missions, and then two months in the autumn for further evangelistic work. He was therefore officially unemployed during his visit to Jamaica, and the financial terms offered for the part time work were less generous, relatively, than had been contemplated. Having in June 1937 been forced to lose their senior evangelist over the winter of 1937-38, for just the time when the 'Recall' campaigns were scheduled, the Board now also lost their junior evangelist, and at only one month's notice instead of the three specified in Jack Malloch's contract:

> A letter was submitted from the Rev. J. S. Malloch, B.D., assistant evangelist, intimating that he had been invited to accompany the Rev. D. P. Thomson on his Mission in Jamaica, and asking if the Home Board would release him at the beginning of November. The terms of his agreement stipulate for three months' notice being given. The Evangelism Committee, while regretting Mr Malloch's resignation, recommends the Home Board to accept it, and at the same time expresses its appreciation of the excellent work done by Mr Malloch during his term of office as assistant evangelist.

DP, of course, was to blame; his decision to go to Jamaica and to take Jack with him had deprived the Home Board of both its minister-evangelists at a time when the attention of the Kirk was focussed on evangelism. And, also, we need to remember the authoritative presence of conveners of General Assembly Boards at this time, especially of this Convener, former Moderator John White. Given the set timetable of preparations for the General Assembly, DP's and Jack's departure gave the Home Board little time for manoeuvre before its Convener had to finalise a defendable Report for the 1938 Assembly. Further, the Home Board was used to directing its agents according to its own wishes – normally, the Board controlled and its staff obeyed. All except for D. P. Thomson! Seen from the Board's point of view, his actions might be simply self-indulgent: perhaps Thomson was not a man to be trusted?

'As Mr Malloch's resignation now leaves the Home Board without a full-time evangelist,' the minute of October 1937 recorded, a committee was set up urgently to consider what to do; and in December the Board decided to take the opportunity of broadening its evangelistic thrust by recommending that the General Assembly appoint a panel of 12 ministerial evangelists, 'drawn from the regular ministry'. Reports due to be considered by the General Assembly, which met in May, needed to be drafted, discussed and finalised early in the year – when, of course, D. P. Thomson was out of the country. In any case, given Hall's article of autumn 1936 and what may be suspected of John White's annoyance at DP's maverick refusal to obey the Church's clear call to home service, it is unlikely that even if he had been available to consult he would have been invited to join the list of ministers (which included Gaelic-fluent men) who were eventually recognised as the Church of Scotland's Ministerial Evangelists. Rev. G. C. M. Grieve (Aberdeen: John Knox) who was included had previously been the UF Church's full-time Children's Evangelist: perhaps his recognition was thought to obviate that of DP. The one man on the list neither an academic nor serving in a parish was George F. MacLeod who had been awarded his D.D. by the University of Glasgow in June 1937. The same May 1938 General Assembly that recognised George as an Evangelist was also the Assembly that spent some time debating whether or not to support MacLeod's new venture, the Iona Community and the rebuilding on Iona, for which he had demitted from Govan Old that April. George's biographer, Ron Ferguson, notes that the Assembly offered its support because MacLeod had the backing of John White: he was 'protected by the old boys'[33] in a way that DP never enjoyed.

When DP returned from Jamaica, it was therefore with the prospect of a six months' summer missions appointment ahead of him and the Wardenship of St Ninian's, Lassodie. He had, in effect, surrendered a possible role in the 'Recall' in exchange for a short overseas mission; he had embarrassed John White's Home Board – but he had met Mary! In the end he was unable to complete the 1938 appointment. Almost immediately on his return to Scotland he wrote to the Home Board with the news that he could not undertake work before or during the summer: he was expecting to go into hospital for an operation. Furthermore, 'owing to the uncertainty of his future arrangements, Mr Thomson indicated that he would not be able to engage himself for evangelistic work during October and November, and therefore it would be necessary to intimate accordingly to the Edinburgh Presbytery Committee, who desired his services.' The Home Board decided that the Seaside Missions convener, Sir James Simpson (supported by its own Secretariat), would have to make the necessary arrangements – whereupon Sir James resigned as convener. In the event one of the ministers who hosted seaside missions, Robert Miller of Leven, took up the convenership and oversaw the 1938 programme on DP's lines. As for DP, his operation over, Mary came from Jamaica mid-summer 1938, and her father married the couple in September. After a fortnight's honeymoon in the Highlands, they made St Ninian's, Lassodie, their home for the first months of their married life.

In March 1939, a year after his return from Jamaica, D. P. Thomson was inducted as minister to Cambuslang: Trinity, an urban parish in the Presbytery of Hamilton, adjacent to the City of Glasgow. He moved with Mary into the Manse there, which was to be their home during the Second World War. It was his second and final period of service as a parish minister. DP was not a war-time locum at Cambuslang: Trinity. He was regularly called and inducted to the vacant post of Colleague and Successor to William Gray by the full process then followed and had, indeed, allowed his name to be placed before at least one other vacant charge: that of Falkirk: St Andrews. March 1939 was, of course, some six months before Britain declared war on Germany: it was not until the end of that month that the Prime Minister finally pledged the nation to the defence of Poland. Reading between the lines, it seems that DP had come to realise that without his Home Board salary his post as Warden of St Ninian's offered neither a viable financial base nor a real home – perhaps especially so for a man then barely six months married. As international affairs worsened the Kirk also needed all its ministers and hence both financial necessity and professional duty led him to make himself available to be called to a parish. There was a sense of reluctance about this, however. In September 1940, hardly a year after his induction to Cambuslang, he wrote to the Convener

#28: MARY ROTHNIE

of the Home Board, still John White, offering himself again for service with the Board. He cited the letter in *Personal Encounters*:

> Happy as I am in my work here, and interesting and varied as this field is, I cannot dismiss from my mind the conviction that my best service to the Church could be given in a staff post of some kind rather than in the regular parish ministry. That being so, I felt that I ought to let you know,

> as Convener of the Home Board, that should any post eventuate in which I could serve the Church in the home area, I would be more than happy to consider it.

Though DP was called to an interview, nothing came of this application. The offer having been rejected, he was to remain at Cambuslang throughout the war. The fact remained that his heart was not wholly committed to his ministry there; and this, with other matters, contributed to the shadows across this period of his life. He certainly wondered what the future would hold, with – apparently – the door now closed to any renewed recognition by the national Kirk of his gifts as an evangelist. As he pursued his wartime ministry, he had to struggle against a sense of rejection.

***

What happened to St Ninian's, Lassodie? Though DP had committed funds of his own to the project, he had taken care to establish the Centre with a Board of Management so that it had a life independent of himself. He tendered his resignation as Warden to the Board once his election to Cambuslang was confirmed and new appointments were made: Miss Elizabeth Seth, Warden of the YMCA Hostel, Nicolson Square, Edinburgh, became Warden; two local ministers became Chaplains of the National Retreat and Conference Centre in West Fife; and Rev. J. Fraser McLusky (then SCM Liaison Secretary in Scotland and a member of the Home Mission Committee of the Home Board) joined the Board of Management.[34] In early 1942 DP got round to handing over to the Board the titles to the buildings. By then he was disenchanted with the entire project: 'How long will it be till I get quit of Lassodie for good? 10 years yet? An incubus about my neck: a fatal sidetracking? Lost years and money? Is the little it achieved any adequate return?' During September 1944 DP's Diary noted that 'I am moving now for the winding up of both the Lassodie Press and The West Fife Retreat and Conference Centres.' Neither survived the War. Little trace even of the village now survives.

PARISH MINISTER AND EVANGELIST:

II - At Cambuslang Trinity, 1939 - 1947

> Wednesday, 13th August [1941] . . . On my way to Greenock on Monday I came to the far-reaching decision to launch a new religious order – 'The Fellowship of St Ninian, the Evangelist' is the title I have long had in mind . . . At Iona I hope to thrash out the details of the scheme . . . The reasons which have impelled me to this are many. We are to have no children. My age, my marriage, my physical health, my times, my experience, my commitments are all against either a career as a lone evangelist or another HM [Home Mission] staff appointment.
>
> D. P. Thomson, The Diary of My Life part 10

D. P. Thomson's years at Cambuslang: Trinity are perhaps the least remembered period of his life. In his short biography Ian Doyle said nothing of this time apart from one sentence:[1] 'With the exception of the war years, 1939-1945, when he served as minister of Trinity Church, Cambuslang, evangelism was to be his total commitment to the day he died.' Yet DP's understanding of his calling as an evangelist was in no way diminished during the war. It was then that he, with others, founded the 'Church of Scotland Fellowship in Evangelism'. Even before it began to be possible to envisage victory over Germany, DP was becoming impatient with the parish ministry. He was under pressure from the war and from his own ill-health and that of both Mary and Christine. He was struggling with difficulties in Trinity's congregational life. He was still side-lined by the national church, a rejection he found hard to bear. At times he came near to despair. In fact the most fruitful period of his ministry was still to come. That the years of DP's national leadership did come, however, was a near-run thing, apparently turning – in an almost entirely opaque process – on a change of personnel among the small number of decision-makers within the committee-hierarchy of the Church of Scotland. In 1945 DP was once more very close indeed to being, yes, an evangelist, but not within the Kirk's structures. By 1947 he was at the forefront of the Kirk's outreach.

The early years at Cambuslang: Trinity

Cambuslang: Trinity was, like Dunfermline: Gillespie Memorial, a congregation that had entered the Church of Scotland from the side of the United Free Church. Both, indeed, had earlier entered the UF Church from one of its predecessors, the United Presbyterian Church. Both congregations, therefore, shared a constitution that committed their spiritual affairs to their elders with their elected minister as Moderator of the Kirk Session; and their financial and property matters to an elected Committee of Management, on which the minister did not sit. Often the church of choice of urban tradesmen, the UP denomination had had its own principles: from the start it had supported its work by voluntary giving. It had been an outward-looking missionary church, and a forward-looking church seeking greater Christian unity; it had been a church that sought to be free to obey its Lord, free from control by the state and also from the doctrinal formulations of the past; it had been a denomination for activists.[2] Both Trinity and Gillespie were therefore congregations in the evangelical tradition, newcomers to the Church of Scotland, unlike Dunfermline: Abbey and Cambuslang: Old with their large memberships – the traditional

#29: CAMBUSLANG: TRINITY CHURCH OF SCOTLAND IN 2010

parish kirks of the old towns. In each case, however, DP's congregations were the second largest of the several post-1929 Church of Scotland congregations within their respective burghs, Gillespie with some 700 communicant members; Trinity larger, with some 800 members and a fine red sandstone building, complete with sets of halls attached to its sanctuary.

DP therefore found himself in 1939 not the business but the spiritual leader of an active congregation with a number of regular organisations: some 30 men in the Kirk Session; a Woman's Guild of 175; the Women's 'Neighbourly' meeting; a Bible Class; a Scout Troop and a Cub Pack; Brownies and a Girls' Association; and a Sunday School with primary and senior divisions totalling 250 or so. As at Gillespie, he was committed on a Sunday to speak to the children and to preach at a morning service, to give an address to the afternoon Bible Class, and to preach at an evening service. There was also a midweek Prayer Meeting and a monthly Elders' Prayer Meeting; there were classes for intending new communicants every quarter, ahead of the Communion Sundays held in March, June, October and December. *Ad hoc* speaking engagements included pulpit exchanges, addresses to the local Office-Bearers Union and the Sunday School Teachers Union and – which DP particularly enjoyed – giving fund-raising lantern lectures to his own and other congregations on Jamaica or on his walking tours in Ireland, Wales, England and Scotland. Later in his Cambuslang ministry courses of lectures on evangelism were invited by the Glasgow Bible Training Institute. A considerable amount of time was given to taking funerals and visiting hospitals – the Royal, the Western, the Motherwell – as well as to visiting the sick and sharing in the visitation of districts. The Presbytery of Hamilton and its committees did not benefit from much of DP's time – he dropped in when the business interested him; if he went 'to town', he meant to Glasgow – but he did support the regular meetings of the Cambuslang Ministers' Fraternal. All this was the normal round of parish life.

But of course life was not normal: as DP began his Tenth Diary in January 1941, Great Britain had been at war with Hitler's Third Reich since 3 September 1939. The Army had been driven from France at Dunkirk in June 1940; Germany occupied the British Channel Islands in July. Some temporary success had been achieved against Mussolini's Italy in North Africa, but the u-boats were threatening to close the Atlantic and the Blitz had brought the war home to Britain's cities. Indeed, the Diary opened with an anxious reference to the bombing:

Friday, 3rd January 1941. I begin again, but will it be for long? We sat down to breakfast at 9 in the study, organ music on the wireless to cheer us. Mary had lit the fire while I shaved. Hot water pipes frozen and the frost so keen that even now at 10.30am I can see nothing through my study windows. What a boon we have electricity – this is the weather in which one feels for the men in camp, and the people in the bombed cities. So far we have been spared.

The Battle of the Atlantic was taking its toll: in January 1941 Mary had to make do with meat-paste sandwiches for the 'Neighbourly' New Year Party, as no meat pies, sausage rolls 'nor anything of that kind can be got – meat is so scarce.' Mary was also involved in helping with the Canteen for the troops at the Bothwell Street Christian Institute, supported in rota by neighbouring churches, and DP sometimes led late Sunday evening worship there if numbers of men had gathered. Both took their turn on a rota for fire-watching at the church: the authorities arranged for all prominent landmarks – all potential targets for bombing – to have teams on call overnight. Camp beds were set up in Trinity Church's committee rooms.

In the event DP and his Watchers were never called into action, though the violence of the Second World War certainly came closer to DP as a civilian than that of the First World War had done when he was in the ASC. Major Luftwaffe raids on Glasgow and Clydebank came over Cambuslang:

Saturday, 15th March [1941] I lag behind now with a vengeance! Truth to tell we are both thoroughly tired out after two nights of aerial warfare overhead . . . Thursday was our first night of the 'Blitz' on Clydeside. The Germans claimed to have 100 planes over. They were certainly going and coming all night long. The sirens went at 9.10pm – I was in Burnside and hurried home. Mary and I were on the go till 3 o'clock – got on our bunks for an hour or more then – and not to bath and bed till nearly 7 in the morning. We were quite worn out. We had a very experienced team on that night had anything happened locally. The nearest bombs fell on Oatlands and Tradeston – the West End, Scotstoun and Clydebank all got it badly especially Clydebank. The Manse shook all night beneath the gunfire and shrapnel hit the roof more than once. I had been unwell before it started – had to keep my bed till dinnertime yesterday then visited. Last night the sirens went at 8.30pm and already this afternoon they have gone twice. Last night Mary was thrown off her balance by a land mine and one side of the house shows a crack. It fell about one mile away and all the lights went out. There was heavy damage down Dalmarnock Road – other places I have yet to hear of. We got to bed for

> a spell after 2am, slept through the 'all clear' at 3 and were wakened by the sirens again at 4. Then at 6 we got finally to bed and lay till 10. Neither of us has felt up to much today and we can look for another night of it.

Together with much of the British population, the Thomsons listened to Prime Minister Winston Churchill's radio broadcasts: 'Monday, 10th February [1941]. Last night we had . . . the Fire Watchers over to hear the PM's broadcast. Churchill spoke a full 36 minutes.' That was the famous speech that included the plea to the United States: *'Give us the tools, and we will finish the job.'* Child of Empire though he was, DP was often pessimistic about the course of the war, his mood confirmed when he listened to the German propaganda radio programme with its announcer known as 'Lord Haw-Haw':

> Monday, 16th February [1942] Last night we got the news that Singapore had fallen – now we dread that Rangoon is in grave danger. What next? Ceylon – India – Australia – New Zealand? It will be their turn when Java and Sumatra fall, which looks like being this week or next. It looks like the end of white prestige in the East, I fear. Perhaps it is better so. Our superiority complex has created a resentment that is now flaming up!
>
> Sunday, 1st March [1942] This is Communion Sunday. I have a heavy cold and my heart is not too good but I have my message practically ready and that means much. I am preaching on 'The Redeemer's Kingdom'. 'My Kingdom is not of this world.' It cannot be identified with this world's causes. It cannot be judged by this world's standards. It cannot be defended by this world's weapons. It cannot be defeated by this world's powers. It is a great theme and as I have written it I have decided to rewrite it. It is a clear, cold day. We are just listening to the News – the Japs have now landed in Java, the last stronghold, I fear, Rangoon, has also fallen. We are in a bad way not only in the East.
>
> Tuesday 30th June [1942] . . . Almost midnight. We have been listening to Haw-Haw – diabolically clever and very depressing it was! Halfway across Egypt to Alexandria are the German legions already. By the end of the week Egypt may have fallen. What effect will it have on Churchill with his fatuous optimism? How near are we to the final crash of the mighty British Empire?

As he had at Gillespie Memorial, at Cambuslang: Trinity DP tried to focus his attention on the young adults, but as the war effort gathered strength more and more of this age group found themselves conscripted for war service. A pattern was established that those leaving paid a final call at the Manse. On Monday 21 April 1941, for example, 'had an hour each with Margaret Gibb, going off tomorrow to join the WAAFs and

Archie McIntosh, home on leave.' DP then kept in touch by letter, and his personal efforts expanded into a congregational Service Personnel Committee, in touch with some 200 individuals away from home. From the thousand or so letters that came back a book was finally published, as a record of what had been experienced and to reflect on hopes for the peace: *Letters to the Manse from members and adherents of Trinity Church, Cambuslang, on service with The Navy, The Army, The Air Forces, The WRNS, The ATS, The WAAF, The Mercantile Marine, The Land Army and The Nursing Services, 1939-1945*:

> A Service Personnel Committee was formed, before the war had entered its third year, to take the whole matter in hand . . . [*to be*] responsible for three things: (1) Keeping up to date the card index of addresses of those away on service; (2) Dispatching a monthly budget to each, consisting of two letters and some reading matter, when this last can be procured; and (3) Raising the funds necessary for this work, and for the sending of an annual Christmas gift to all away, in the name of the congregation. One of the two letters sent each month is from the Minister, and extends to two closely typed quarto pages – the other is from one of the organisations in the Church, these taking it in turn to write.

DP's wartime ministry was not marked by the experimentation he had initiated at the Gillespie Memorial, no doubt in part due to the pressures of wartime, but also perhaps because he did not have a longer-term vision for his ministry in Cambuslang:

> <u>Monday, 13th January [1941]</u> . . . The conviction came on me today more powerfully than ever that if I am spared to see the War through I return to evangelism.

Certainly – remembering the enduring lessons of the Oxford Group – he encouraged the witness and participation of the ordinary Christian. Brains Trust style meetings questioned mature Christians from a range of professions: congregational meetings heard reports not just from key office-bearers but from ordinary members. Young people were chosen to speak at meetings for young people. But these were one-off events, not the creation of new institutions.

Beyond his work at Trinity, DP engaged in only [!] two other major activities, 'the Fellowship and the ministry of the pen':

> <u>Wednesday 28th January [1942]</u> . . . A few weeks ago I noted a Colonial Vacancy at Demerara, New Guiana. Now I see one at Granada. Had I been a younger man I would have gone but my roots are here, my work outside Trinity with the Fellowship and the ministry of the pen.

'The ministry of the pen' sought to find new outlets for his bent for writing, continuing the work of Thomson & Cowan and the Lassodie Press. The professionally published book of personal testimonies from around the world he edited in 1937, *How I Found Christ*, had found an encouragingly good market. By January 1944 the second Brazilian edition had sold out: 'Thus can I reach lands I may never see!' DP enthused.[3] As he came to believe that his health was failing and that perhaps few years were left to him, DP's years at Cambuslang saw an intensified spell of research and writing, though not of publishing, for paper was in short supply during the war. A biography of the Rev. William Gray, the senior minister of Cambuslang Trinity who died in 1941, excited DP and was quickly researched but never printed. He worked, off and on, on a *Bibliography of Evangelism*, and on other titles:

> Had times been normal I could have looked forward to a busy year or two of editing and authorship, but as things are who knows what may emerge! I would like to finish William Gray, both for Trinity's sake and my own satisfaction, and I would like to get my 'magnum opus' done – *Women of the Scottish Kirk*. I am always busy at it and there is no question about the sale. *Ships of the Gospel* I am not so sure of. It is altogether a bigger task. *An Evangelist Looks Back* could be done at any time. *The Ministry of Evangelism* and *Personal Ministry* are both long overdue. How many will I live to see completed?

The Church of Scotland's youth magazine, *Young Scotland*, accepted a series of his articles on the adventures of ships associated with missionary work. After the war, Pickering & Inglis published the collection in two volumes, *Labrador to Savage Island: Stories of the Ships of Christ* and *Goodwin Sands To Solomon Islands*. *Women of the Scottish Church*, however, would be published only by DP's literary executor after his death, and – although some of the material gathered and written during the black-out and while fire-watching was eventually used – none of *An Evangelist Looks Back*, *The Ministry of Evangelism* or *Personal Ministry* saw the light of day under those titles.

Writing, however, did not have first priority in DP's scheme of things. In August 1941, by which time it seemed very clear that John White would never reappoint him to a post with the Home Board, DP resolved to re-engage with his first love – evangelism: 'I came to the far-reaching decision to launch a new religious order – The Fellowship of St Ninian, the Evangelist.' Beyond his rejected approach to the Home Board, a variety of factors had led to this decision. There was, of course, the previous experience of the GSEU and its FMF and SSCM spin-offs, and with the teams he had gathered around the Seaside Missions. But why was DP now thinking in terms, not of a society, but a 'religious order'? This, surely, was emulation of that other 'Evangelist of the Church of Scotland', George F. MacLeod and his increasingly significant Iona Community, created in 1938, whose members could in this period be described as 'Monks from Iona', and who were now engaged in rebuilding the monastery on Iona and conducting a series of experimental parish missions in cooperation with the Home Board. Just as DP had been interested in the Oxford Group Movement, now he explored the potential of this new missionary movement to arise within the Kirk.

Rev. George F. MacLeod, Evangelist of the Church of Scotland

During early summer 1939, George MacLeod wrote to the Home Board to offer the services of probationer-ministers attached to the Iona Community to enhance the mission of selected parishes. Essentially he envisaged a parish obtaining two Iona-trained probationers to work for two years as a team with the existing minister. After debates in the General Assembly, church-bureaucratic delays and issues to do with the funding of such posts and the correct relations with the local Presbytery, an arrangement was finally reached in negotiations February - March 1940. George MacLeod was appointed a part-time Evangelist under the Home Board on the understanding that, when parishes accepted a team from Iona, the package would include a 'Message of Friendship' programme such as that in Govan in 1934, introduced and led by himself in collaboration with the parish minister. The aim for such experiments was to find a way for missionary outreach to become permanent and normal within the life of a congregation. For over ten years from 1940 to 1950 and beyond, George led what came to be known as 'Iona Missions' on his own distinctive principles. He was a fanatic for the Church, believing in its life- and world-changing potential if it could only live up to its calling in Christ; if the totality of its ordinary members could somehow be rallied to fulfil their potential. In one aspect, the Iona Community was intended to train new ministers to live in fellowship, to grasp his vision; in its parish mission aspect, George / Iona led experiments to rouse entire congregations to witness to those surrounding them in their parish.

George MacLeod's surviving archives[4] contain a number of materials from these missions. There was the 'Message of Friendship' in Garrowhill, the parish of R. C. M. Mathers, held between February and May 1940. Autumn and winter 1941 saw the 'New Life Movement' at St John's, Perth, whose minister was W. A. Smellie. There was a Mission in the Canongate, Edinburgh, minister Ronald Selby Wright, in December 1942. Later came 'The Expansion Movement' in Edinburgh: Stenhouse (1946); the 'Message of Friendship' at Newmilns (1949) and others.[5] Although the details as well as the name of these operations differed from place to place, their first objective was to rally the congregation, often done by inviting men and women church members to a series of meetings with George himself. Volunteers were sought to visit within the congregation, to revive a sense of personal fellowship. Only when this was achieved was a visitation to the entire community organised, with invitations to a week of special meetings, at which George would be a guest preacher. Unlike D. P. Thomson, George MacLeod was not looking primarily for conversions.[6] Because he emphasised the mystic reality of the Church, he sought to raise awareness of Christian baptism. Most Scots were baptised; hence they *already were* members of Christ. What was needed was for them to acknowledge this and act on it. The best way to do that, he proclaimed, was the Gospel way – to share their faith with others. 'Then together we will get down to the task of deepening our Church life and at the same time we will go out to share it with others.'[7] There was a further conclusion to be drawn from George's sacramental understanding of baptism – it meant that Christ might be found both inside and outside existing church fellowships. Those visiting on behalf of the church thus did so not from any position of superiority but to share and, it might be, to learn.

Iona Missions were clearly in some respects in continuity with existing practice, being based on house to house visitation and often culminating in a week of special events. They also shared some of the techniques of the 'Religion and Life' weeks being held in English towns during the 1940s, whose aim was to engage with commerce and education, with civic and industrial leaders on a wide front. Together with the very existence of the Iona Community itself, the cumulative impact of Iona Missions and George's vision for team ministry meant that there were many ministers who, though they did not become members, still believed with Bill Smellie of St John's, Perth, that 'Iona' was crucial to the life of the Church of his day: perhaps the *only* vital current movement.[8] Certainly there were also those who, like John White, distrusted MacLeod's promotion of Christian pacifism in the midst of war; yet as DP noted, George was increasingly in demand as a speaker and as a guide to those seeking new ways of mission in Scotland, while in contrast his own acceptance at a national level was now just a memory:

> Saturday, 31st May [1941] . . . I must face the fact that outstanding pacifists like A. C. Craig and George MacLeod are being used freely for Conferences and Summer Schools as are friends and former colleagues of mine like Jim Munn and Roddie and John Kent and men like Alan Boyd Robson, whereas DP is no longer asked for any purpose of this kind by anyone. I think I know why! Nor need I worry. I have my memories. I have my work here and I have an abundant literary and study programme to keep me occupied for long enough. If I am spared and I am faithful, my hour will come again. I am forcing open no door: I am making no approach.

George MacLeod organised his own monthly meetings for ministers, the 'Cathedral Gatherings', which he hosted in Glasgow, Edinburgh and Perth. DP attended the Glasgow 'Gathering' when he was able. On 21 January 1941, he was present and: 'there must have been well over 180 ministers present – all types among them and a great many of our own lads – Joe, John Kent . . .' all gathered to hear about 'a new Catholic Movement originating in Belgium and with the aim of Christianising industry. Very arresting and thought provoking it was! Very radical and fundamental in its approach – very far reaching in scope.'

Yet another way in which George MacLeod offered leadership in the early 1940s was by holding Retreats on Iona, despite the fact that government clearance was required for the travel involved. DP was a participant in August 1941, though he travelled with Mary, stayed in a Guest House, and dropped in on George's programme as and if he chose. The Iona Retreats gathered, besides members of the Iona Community, substantial numbers of other ministers – interested, curious, sympathetic or supportive. In 1941 the list[9] of some 60 official participants included Mathers, Smellie and Selby Wright, besides D. M. Baillie and A. C. Craig – all men whom the Kirk would come to know, while yet another future Moderator, Leonard Small appears to have been participating while nominally on holiday on Iona.

The Church of Scotland Fellowship in Evangelism

D. P. Thomson's next experiment in evangelism was therefore announced first to George MacLeod on Iona, as the two 'Evangelists of the Church of Scotland' met by appointment:

> Thursday, 21st August [1941] On Tuesday before noon I saw George by appointment, gave him 10/- for the Community and told him of the Movement we proposed starting. He quite approved.

'The Fellowship of St Ninian, Evangelist' was conceived to achieve much the same ends as the GSEU had had, to undertake evangelistic campaigns under DP's direction:

> Wednesday, 13th August [1941] . . . On my way to Greenock on Monday I came to the far-reaching decision to launch a new religious order – 'The Fellowship of St Ninian, the Evangelist' is the title I have long had in mind. The objects would be the promotion of evangelism in and by the Church of Scotland and the bonding together for more effective service of those anxious to help in evangelistic work. We would strive to utilise all possible personnel and to meet all legitimate invitations. Ministers, students and laymen would be invited to join and we would begin with a HQ room, library and office in Glasgow . . . On the lines contemplated all my gifts will find outlet and if the work grows I can either remove to a smaller or more suitable parish or give my whole time to it. If it remains small I can direct it from here. The time has come when I must act or both lose my contacts and get rusty.

From the start DP saw the proposed Fellowship as a personal vehicle for his aspirations, as the Iona Community was for its 'Boss' George MacLeod. Another intended similarity with the Community was that, just as MacLeod offered training to candidates for the ministry, so too would the Fellowship offer students training in evangelism. On return from Iona, DP sent off a series of letters to friends he wished to attract to the Fellowship and also visited Trinity College to recruit for the cause. A meeting was held on Thursday 11 September 1941, but with mixed results:

> Friday, 12th September [1941]. The great meeting was definitely a disappointment. 19 men came but several were late. Less than half were really with us, others clearly wanted the evangelism without the Fellowship and perhaps my line of appeal lacked something . . . We go forward but will have to shed many of that group and attract others. It can be done.

The 'fellowship' aspect of the new group was important to DP: it was arranged that the Society (no more was heard of the original 'religious order' terminology and the reference to St Ninian was also officially, if not in DP's thoughts, dropped) would meet every week on a Monday – a heavy discipline and demand on the time of busy ministers and surely a reason why several withdrew their interest. Still, by March 1942 a viable working group had come into existence and formalised their relationship, recording the decision in a new Minute Book.[10]

15 names were subscribed that day, including that of DP. Three appear to have been laymen – the rest, Church of Scotland ministers. Eight were ministers subject to the Presbytery of Glasgow; DP himself and T. Gemmell Campbell were in the Presbytery of Hamilton, and the two remaining came from the Presbyteries of Paisley and Falkirk. None of these were then members of the Home Board or of its Evangelism Committee. Of those whose ages are known, the average in 1942 was 36: on the whole these were men in their first or second charges. Dan W. Montgomery (aged 56), who had previously worked with the Glasgow City Mission was, however, in his third charge: Glasgow Banton. His connection with DP dated back to their time at the Glasgow Bible Training Institute in 1917. T. Gemmell Campbell (aged 23) was as yet unordained, and while serving as *locum* at Cambuslang: Rosebank was a colleague and young friend of DP's. James Campbell was the lay Secretary to the Glasgow-based Mission to Mediterranean Garrisons. James E. Duncan, minister of the Church Extension Charge of Glasgow: St Paul's Provanmill, and to be one of the more active members of the Fellowship, had already hosted an Iona-resourced team ministry. Vincent Ross, newly married and ordained to his first charge of Glasgow: Rutherglen Greenhill, was a close neighbour and younger colleague of DP's. At the heart of the FiE, however, were Jack Malloch and Joe Haldane, then DP's two closest and longest ministerial friends. Of these two men, Jack was the younger. Having shared with DP in the Jamaica campaign, soon after their return he was ordained and inducted to his first charge, Glasgow: Thornliebank – Spiersbridge. Joe was an older man, born in 1887, who like DP had studied at the BTI and the UF College, and had served in H.M. forces in the First World War. A GSEU member, he was ordained to the ministry of the UF Church in 1924 – in his case, to be a foreign missionary at Madras. Returning to Scotland to Glasgow: Plantation, Cornwall Street in 1934, by 1942 he was in his second actual parish, that of Paisley: Canal Street.

By 1944, DP was able to list Jack and Joe as among the 'big five' of the Fellowship:

> . . . the 'big five', Joe, Jack, Bill, myself and Jim Munn foregathered at Bothwell for a council of war and high tea.

'Bill' was Bill Temple, then minister of Glasgow: Rutherford, one of the select number of ministers designated as 'Evangelists' by the General Assembly. DP had met Bill during the Stirling Campaign and involved him with Seaside Missions in the 1930s; since then they had become close friends. When Temple married in 1941, it was DP who conducted the service. 'Jim' was James Munn, (aged 38), again a former UF minister and former GSEU campaigner, then at Dundee: St Paul's, who though not at the founding meeting of the FiE was by those present invited both to join and to be a Council member. To DP's regret neither John Kent nor Hamish Mackenzie, his close friends during his time at Dunfermline: Gillespie, joined the Fellowship, preferring George MacLeod's approach.

The formal Constitution agreed on 23 March 1942 was detailed and ambitious, envisaging a structure whereby a nation-wide federation of area groups, each with their own local programmes, should be governed by a General Council (with both executive and honorary office-bearers) and subject to an AGM – and this at a time when membership was confined to 15 men meeting in or near Glasgow. Still, the Iona Community had begun with only 16 members beside the 'Boss'! Section II ('Aims and Basis') and Section III ('Terms of Membership') of the Constitution made it clear that participation was intended to be active, with a shared mutual responsibility – 'Members of the Fellowship will be required to share in its activities and to undertake responsibility for its financial commitments.' Entrance was if necessary via an interview to be conducted by DP, as Secretary. Like the GSEU the Fellowship did not require subscription to a formal doctrinal Basis of Faith. It is also significant that the aims were stated *both* in terms of benefit to the Church (by offering the service of FiE members) *and* in terms of the 'spiritual discipline, growth and enrichment of its members': indeed, this latter goal was listed first. Consistent through DP's career was his insight into the importance of Christian fellowship in generating spiritual growth. The campaigns run under FiE auspices clearly sought to win people for Christ, while the experience of running them enabled the FiE members to hone their skills and gifts, to develop as Christian leaders. In its final form the parallels with Iona were watered down: the Fellowship was never in a position to offer training to students in quite the collegiate way DP had first envisaged, but 'junior members' were recruited, to whom training by involvement was offered. And the Fellowship was certainly a vehicle whereby DP as its volunteer Organising Secretary could continue his pre-1938 work as organiser of summer missions and leader of local campaigns.

On one level, acting as a purely local fraternal, the Fellowship organised and led joint Saturday rambles for the young people of their congregations:

> Sunday, 12th April [1942] . . . Yesterday the Fellowship held its first Young Peoples Ramble to Cathkin Braes. Willie Wood was in charge and Jamie

> Duncan acted as Games Leader. There were 60 present including seven ministers and three minister's wives. Wallace was there and voted it a great success. Next week we go to Milngavie. I couldn't get. I was at Bellshill addressing the Annual Conference of the Lanarkshire YMCA on 'The Church and the Troops.' My address was well received.

From his diary, it seems that DP 'couldn't get' fairly frequently. Nevertheless his young men and women of Bible Class age, and those of his colleagues, seem to have enjoyed the programme of walk, games, tea and devotions. Some asked if the evening could be extended by involvement with street evangelism, so training for open-air work was offered. The industrial west of Scotland had a lively street culture and open air meetings were held by a large number of religious and political movements:

> Monday, 20th October 1947 . . . I worked at . . . correspondence to 7.30, then went to town, posted my mail and surveyed the open air meetings. (1) A Gospel meeting with a mere handful near the Cross. (2) 1000/1200 at Brunswick Street, divided between Marxists, Infidels and unknown. (3) 200 at BTI, Miller Street. (4) A handful at next corner – Gospel. (5) Our Bible Reading friend, standing alone at Maxwell Street. Wouldn't shake hands: no sanction in the Bible for that, so I offered him a kiss. He had to take it but didn't seem too pleased. (5 [*sic*]) Communists at West Regent Street – about 200. (6) Scottish Socialist party at Wellington Street, 2-250.

Presently the ramblers volunteered to accompany the senior members on Seaside Mission in the summer and the 'training' aspect of the Fellowship blossomed with enthusiastic Christians of all varieties and both sexes.

The early pages of the FiE Minute Book demonstrate that the original members were closely involved in the Church of Scotland Seaside Missions programme. Indeed, the Home Board had already agreed a grant for a team trained by DP to conduct the Missions at Prestwick and Troon. So having agreed their new Constitution on 23 March 1942, the members turned to their current responsibilities:

> Seaside Mission work: decided to concentrate on Ayr, Prestwick and Troon unless more personnel were available than these three centres could absorb. It was suggested that there should be a big central Seaside Mission Rally in Glasgow in the last week of June as a send off for the summer's work.

Next week, Monday 30 March, it was determined that the first AGM would be in Edinburgh, '18 May 1942 at 5pm, to be followed by an Evening Meeting at 7.30pm at which Seaside Lantern and Cinema to be shown' and then after lunch together they got down to their local, practical business – the forthcoming Seaside Mission at Prestwick, Troon and Ayr, to which they were already committed. Cutting the story short, the Fellowship supported Seaside Missions, in varying numbers of locations, in 1942 and 1943, cooperating again with Sir James Simpson. Indeed, Sir James had chaired the first AGM of the Fellowship in Edinburgh in 1942, and he sought – at that time unsuccessfully – to bring DP back into the work of the Home Board. The Church of Scotland Seaside Mission tradition thus struggled through the middle years of the war, at least on the west coast. DP sought to adjust the programme to suit a nation at war. Besides Witness Boxes and Brains Trusts, 'Our Allied Nations Day was the feature of the first week.' He went to much trouble to book the Ayr Bandstand and obtain official consent for the use of the 'Union Jack, Stars & Stripes and Allied emblems', including that of Greece. Then:

> Saturday 25th July [1942] . . . On Thursday we had our first Soldiers Night – at Prestwick – when three from the Army and two each from Navy, Air Force spoke, the Senior Padre for the area giving the closing word. Jimmy Wood was one of the Army speakers. I gave a short message on my tie – my engagement to be a soldier of the King; my light grey suit – my engagement to be married; and my Commitment card, my engagement to be Christ's. On Friday we tried out a literature night at Ayr – it went well.

It appears, however, that neither the Fellowship nor the Board were able to undertake or sponsor summer activities in 1944 or 1945, unless it was associates of FiE at Aberdeen that, with Sir James, organised activities on Aberdeen beach during the summer of 1945.[11]

One particular way in which the Fellowship reflected DP's own enthusiasms was its support – from all the overseas causes then looking for support – of the Greek Evangelical Church. Michael Kyriakakis, a bank clerk from Athens, had trained for the ministry of his Church at New College after 1934 and had supported DP's international contribution to Seaside Missions before taking up a call to the 1st Evangelical Church of Athens. During the war they kept in touch by Red Cross letters. Meanwhile the pastor of the 2nd Evangelical Church of Athens, Rev. George A. Hadjiantoniou, a former lawyer, had been stranded in Britain by the outbreak of war. He, too, was invited to join in the Fellowship's Summer Missions programme and also to speak at Cambuslang: Trinity's 'Sunday Night at Eight' outreach services. The Fellowship created, besides a Seaside Mission Fund, a Greek Evangelical Church Fund. In DP's mind, evangelical work at home and abroad were always closely related. He consistently sought to keep the international, world-church aspect to mission at the forefront of his own presentations of Christ's call.

The Fellowship struck a welcome note. Other ministers rapidly joined, including – as might be expected – numbers of DP's friends. By November 1943 membership had risen to 67, of which 12 were laymen and 55 were ministers. Eight members were foreign missionaries and eight more were away on service as Chaplains to the Forces or working at the Church's canteens ('Huts') for the Forces. Of the total, 31 were associated with the Glasgow area weekly meeting: clusters also existed in Dundee, Aberdeen, Edinburgh and Dunfermline, though not all were formally constituted or meeting regularly. Among those who joined FiE after March 1942 were Merricks Arnott of Aberdeen: Ferryhill South, who became a leading exponent of the use of the cinema for Christian purposes, and John E. Brown, minister at Dunoon St Cuthbert's and Govan: St Mary's during the war years, whose son Gordon was later to be the Prime Minister of the United Kingdom. J. W. Meiklejohn of the C.S.S.M./Scripture Union was a member of the Fellowship, as was R. J. Watson Mathewson, then Field Organiser of the Youth Committee of the Church of Scotland. Joe S. Ritchie was a corresponding member while serving as a Chaplain to the Forces throughout the war, as was James W. Hood both as a student and then while in the R.A.F. (1942-45). Several of these men remained involved with DP after 1945. The possibility of inviting women to join the Fellowship had been discussed and shelved, though girls were welcome among the junior members, on the rambles and on mission.

Besides the Seaside Missions, the Fellowship was involved in a number of district and parish campaigns during the war years. DP had celebrated the beginning of his new venture in evangelism with a mission to the Hamilton Army Barracks in 1941, and once the Fellowship was formally constituted, Jack Malloch was supported in a summer 1943 Children's Mission in Carnwadric by both junior and senior members, with two divinity students from Edinburgh's New College and two members of their own Youth Groups in residence at Thornliebank Church Hall. Other missions followed. A parish mission was held at Glasgow: Ibrox Church in 1943. Then, after consultations with the Glasgow United Evangelistic Campaign the Fellowship at first agreed to be responsible for 'only one mission in that series, namely at Dennistoun to be held in Rutherford Church' in the autumn of 1943, together with a week's experimental mission for children at Mount Florida Church. DP later reported that he had met a crisis request from the GUEC's organiser, for support at Gorbals-Govanhill, booking nine Fellowship speakers at 'a 5 guineas weekly fee to Fellowship funds and not individually, preserving their normal basis of work.' Early in 1944 missions were held at Pollockshaws and Dennistoun, where Bill Temple was the leader. Thereafter followed Dumbarton in September 1944 and invitations from St Paul's, Cambuslang and St Nicholas, Larkhall, for the spring of 1945. An invitation that brought some debate came in October 1944 from the city centre church of Glasgow: St George's Tron, for the Fellowship to lead the weekly midday meeting there and/or a series of evangelical meetings. Some members thought it could be useful to have such a centre to which to bring outstanding men, others that the invitation should be an opportunity for their own members, while others thought it doubtful whether the Fellowship should consider the proposal at all. In the end nothing came of this. Nevertheless for a group of ministers, fully involved in their own parishes, to support even the number of commitments that they did was no mean achievement. The fact the invitations continued to arrive also demonstrates that the Fellowship had some measure of recognition and acceptance.

The final years at Cambuslang: Trinity

It took time for D. P. Thomson personally to regain credibility in the circles of those who ran the central agencies of the Church of Scotland. The outbreak of war, if it curtailed the Home Board's evangelistic programmes, had sharpened high-level discussions about evangelism and its relation to Christian doctrine and practice – and DP was sidelined from these discussions. Until well into the 21st century the Church of Scotland's system of making appointments to its central bodies was deliberately opaque: by invitation only, applications positively forbidden. Those in power and in the know chose those they thought suitable – so selection depended on networks and connections, patronage and rumour. The word in 1944 was that D. P. Thomson was unreliable. He was not appointed to the General Assembly's Commission on post-war mission or to that sponsored by the Home Board to discuss the future of evangelism:

> Friday, 25th February, [1944] . . . Joe Haldane has been asked to join a Special Commission on Evangelism which the Home Board are setting up. They are not asking me. I have to watch that the iron does not enter into my soul – the church makes so little use of me – has so little place for me – and I have so very much to give. No one knows more about Evangelism than I do but they don't want me!

> Saturday, 11th March 1944, I was dumped yesterday when Joe told me that Vincent Alexander had said to him that I had not been asked to go on the Commission on Evangelism because I didn't team well. Now, that is just not true. I have led and directed more teams than any other minister in the country, and the men who are most closely associated with me today are the men who have been associated with me longest and most intimately – Jack and Joe. So be it! No Assembly Committee wants me. No Assembly Commission wants me. The Home Board doesn't want me. The BBC doesn't want me. At 48 is my day done? And yet . . . I know my subject as few men if any but Bryan Green know it. I can still proclaim the Gospel so as to alert and quicken. There are 'seals' of ministry there, though few appear in Trinity. George Knight has 50 young communicants this Communion. I have had almost none in the past year! What ails me? What ails me?

These extracts only marginally overstated the situation. A month earlier DP had had a most gratifying reception to a speech to students at Trinity College, and he had been invited to a Conference on Evangelism held by the Home Board in February 1944. Later in the year Bill Temple's influence was sufficient, if at the last minute, to gain DP an invitation to speak at the Conference on Evangelism organised as a Summer School by St Andrew's University.

The hurt and exclusion DP was feeling in 1944 can be sensed in his question 'At 48 is my day done?' His years at Cambuslang: Trinity were indeed difficult years. Though DP and Mary Thomson were spared any serious physical damage from the German bombing of the Clyde to themselves, their Manse or Trinity Church, nevertheless living in 'this very bombable house' was a constant strain. The realisation that, after only three and half years of marriage, they would be unable to have any children of their own was a severe blow. Mary suffered an early-term miscarriage in January 1941 and by April, after a further operation, it was clear that 'We are to have no children'. DP nearly broke down when baptising a baby one Sunday in Church. The loss was heightened by unexpected contact with a lady whom he might, perhaps, have married, and her two children, 'that might have been mine'. There was the pressure of his responsibility for Mary, for having brought her from the seeming security of Jamaica to wartime Scotland. This pressure was increased when, without giving them any prior warning, Mary's father announced he had remarried, to her very great distress. Though their relationship with Douglas Rothnie was soon restored to its former level, at the time DP's concern on Mary's behalf was considerable. Then there was his responsibility for his sister, Dr

Christine Thomson. Living alone since the death of their mother, and based in the early years of the war in a hospital near London, she suffered 'a dark and deep depression' in July 1941, so that DP went south to visit in August and November. In December her condition became so bad that she was compulsorily – forceably – hospitalised and DP had to take her affairs into his legal administration, necessitating a further urgent and hurried journey south. She lost her post and her home, eventually coming to stay for a time in the Manse before, at least partially restored to health, in April 1942 she obtained a suitable residential post at the Crighton Royal Hospital, Dumfries. Encouraged by this, she applied for and was appointed to the Assistant Superintendentship of the Murray Royal Hospital, Perth, in January 1944, only to learn that the head of the hospital distrusted women doctors – 'I could see that he would have no use for CJ if men were available,' DP noted. A further breakdown followed – a further stay with DP and Mary – a return to Dumfries on a greatly reduced salary. 'Poor, dear CJ – she is so distressed at the realisation that she may never really be fit for fulltime work again.'

DP's own health had, of course, been damaged during the First World War. He suffered what he described as a heart attack in March 1943 and was off work for three weeks. In May further internal pain, described as a 'rupture', forced him to accept that an operation would be needed. His consultant agreed and arranged for admission to the Church of Scotland's Deaconess Hospital, Edinburgh, on 22 June 1943. DP's Diary entries for that month show mounting anxiety, a real suspicion that he would not survive the operation. Arrangements for his funeral were discussed; he made a point of saying good-bye to Christine at the station as she journeyed back to Dumfries – he had parted finally with both Robert and James at railway stations. He stored in the safe last letters to family and friends and said goodbye to both his Kirk Session and the Fellowship, fretting that neither group appeared to respond as he would have wished. He even misinterpreted Mary's refusal to accept that the end had possibly come as lack of concern, so black was his mood. Questions about God's providence and guidance recurred, together with assessments of what had been achieved, sometimes gloomy, sometimes resigned. He found it significant that he reached the final page of the Tenth Diary on 22 June itself, and – with light beginning to shine in the darkness – he completed it before departing for the hospital:

> Tuesday, 22nd June [1943] My last entry! Is it the end of the road – or the beginning of a new chapter? I don't really feel equal to this operation; but all may go well. I have had five wonderful years – far beyond my hopes or dreams of what married life and love would be. I grieve for my darling – should I be taken, but there is no prospect of her getting back to Jamaica for many a day I fear. I have had a full and very happy life, and have been able to do much. But there is much I still had hoped to do – I would like liked to have harvested my reading and experiences in the books on Evangelism I had planned; would like to have finished my own 'Reminiscences,' to have written on 'The Women Of The Scottish Kirk' and to have had a few more games of croquet. We had three grand ones yesterday. 'Be Thou My Great Deliverer Still, Thou Lord of Life and Death' is my prayer.

As we now know, of course, his Master had vastly more in store for D. P. Thomson than he could yet imagine. He returned home after a routine operation.

Between August 1944 and September 1945, DP and Mary opened their home to two girls separated from their parents and evacuated, ahead of the German occupation, in 1940 from the Channel Islands at the ages of 12½ and five. The Thomsons were to remain to touch with Peggy and Margaret Rose Lovell and, post-war, travelled to Guernsey for Peggy's wedding. This was a particularly happy period in which, uniquely, he shared with Mary the responsibilities of family life. Yet, though life in the Manse was rewarding, DP often felt himself somewhat adrift from Cambuslang: Trinity. His ministry there had its highlights – the Service Personnel Committee, the success of the 'Sunday Night at Eight' series with guest choirs and speakers, and the congregation's contribution to the Canteen for the Forces – but DP often wondered whether he really had the full support and sympathy of the congregation's leadership and members. In particular he had a lengthy and frequently anxious dispute (which began in January 1942 and continued until the end of his tenure) with the Scout-Masters about the overall control, conduct and policy of Trinity's Scout Troop, which enjoyed very considerable parental and congregational support. His pastoral support of the sick and dying was diligent but attendances at both ordinary Sunday worship and at Communion frequently disappointed him. Certainly there were individuals who welcomed his spiritual leadership. New members of the congregation trickled in, but its membership stagnated or declined so that DP could not perceive any great blessing by God on his ministry. Indeed in 1943 he was able to look forward to little more than a 'period of discipline and suffering':

> Sunday, 6th June [1943] 25 years ago today I began my ministry in Wallneuk Church, Paisley, taking charge of a congregation of nearly 700 while Samuel George, the minister, was in France with the YMCA Huts. The circumstances leading up to my going there were more striking than almost anything that has happened to me since then. Those four months yielded fruit such as I have not seen in my four years here. Is the difference primarily in me, in the times, the place, or the people? Is it I who have lost the first fervour – the first, fine careless rapture? Is this period of discipline and suffering on which I may be entering designed to prepare me for a new beginning – or is it a Judgement Day of God?

Even his 'ministry of the pen' was frustrating:

> Monday, 5th March [1945] . . . And of my vast reading in preparation for the literary work practically nothing made yet. I keep on starting books I may never be spared to finish: I fail to finish those almost completed!

By September 1944 he was concluding that he needed to move on:

> Tuesday, 29th August [1944] I am going back to Evangelism – it may be very soon now. Already I am making my plans, and looking at my library with a very different eye from what I did.

The difficulty, of course, was: to what was he to move? Another congregational ministry was not attractive. He seemed as unwelcome as ever to those in power in the Kirk:

> Monday, 5th March [1945] Within a few weeks I will enter, if spared, on my 50th year. It is a sobering thought! I had not expected to travel so far. I had not anticipated experiencing such frustration. In the councils of the Church I count for nothing – all my accumulated states of knowledge, theoretical and practical, thrown away so far as '121' is concerned!

Why were the doors to the Kirk's headquarters so firmly shut? We can only speculate. Perhaps DP and his Fellowship in Evangelism represented too much of the 'old evangelism' for those whose vision was for the post-war world? Or perhaps his brief investigation into the influence of Freemasonry on patronage within the Kirk had offended; or perhaps the opinion that he didn't 'team' well still recalled his apparent unreliability in 1937-38? There was, however, a new Head of the Home Department: Rev. Robert Mackintosh had replaced Arthur Dunnett. The Fellowship therefore made approaches about co-operation on Summer Missions, but it seemed that the conveners of the Home Board had no wish to resume Seaside Missions – either in the closing months of the War or in the coming Peace that was clearly just over the horizon in the spring of 1945:

Wednesday, 14th March [1945] . . . A letter from Robert Mackintosh today to say there is no opening for Seaside Mission work. So that's that!

Tuesday, 20th March [1945] . . . A letter also from Mackintosh of the Home Board, from which it would appear as though there were little prospect of a resumption, after the War, of Seaside Mission work as we knew it during its great days – and indeed on any scale at all!

On the other hand, some doors appeared to be opening. Despite some expressed doubts about his theological 'soundness', and though his attitudes towards keeping the Sabbath, dancing and visiting the cinema were not among the strictest, DP's connections to the more conservative wings of the evangelical movement were strengthening:

Monday, 26th March [1945] . . . Another IVF request. Strange I should have so become 'persona grata' there, when unwanted by 121!

Glasgow's Bible Training Institute commissioned two series of lectures, on Open Air Evangelism and on Personal Work. May 1945 saw him addressing a branch of 'Crusaders', the independent Sunday School movement. The Church of Scotland Fellowship in Evangelism remained in an ambiguous position. Already with some non-Church of Scotland members, perhaps it should develop into a full-blown, independent Society? Rooms of its own had been secured at 139 St Vincent Street, Glasgow in September 1944, a move that some observers viewed with suspicion:

Thursday, 14th September [1944] . . . A great step has been taken – the Fellowship now has an office and headquarters of its own at 139 St Vincent Street . . . I hope it will be the first of many such – Edinburgh, Dundee and Aberdeen to follow!

Thursday, 21st September [1944] . . . I caught the 8.8 to town and the 8.35 to Edinburgh. I had phoned Bill [Temple] and ascertained that Sir James Simpson could see me at once. I went to the Overseas Club and had a full half-hour with him – nearly an hour. He is much concerned lest we break away altogether from Home Board control.

Thursday, 28th September [1944] I have had a difficult day. I went early to town and got through a good deal. I called on Sir John Craig and asked him for a fiver for the Fellowship. He fired out a broadside on me – against the whole idea of the Fellowship, against separate societies and premises – we should meet in the Church Offices! The furniture arrived just before one and I got it all installed.

Perhaps the 70+ member-strong Fellowship might now acquire a full-time organiser – just as George F. MacLeod was the Leader of the

150-strong Iona Community? Perhaps the opportunity DP sought could come via the Fellowship? He had had that idea in mind since May 1944:

> Future Policy: A lengthy discussion took place on the future policy of the Fellowship. Had the time come to consider expansion on a big scale, to make the bold experiment of appointing a whole time organiser?

Opinion, even among his close colleagues, was and remained divided on this:

> Saturday, 1st September [1945] . . . I went early to town yesterday and met Merricks Arnott for lunch. He is not at all keen on the plan for my being a full-time secretary of the Fellowship.

By the end of the summer of 1945, though, no better light had shone to guide him. Perhaps it was of this period that he was thinking when he wrote, in *New Testament Christianity: 60 Short Studies*, about 'guidance by frustration', the experience of wondering about and seeking to plan for the future, only to find that doors did not open as expected – that all courses were blocked – apart from the one that had not been seen but that God had chosen.

The Second World War ended – the Cold War began. Friends from overseas could now leave: Joe Ritchie and other friends in the Forces were coming home. The Manse wartime family was breaking up: Peggy and Margaret Rose Lovell, the two girl refugees from the Channel Islands whom 'Uncle David and Aunt Mary' had to their great joy fostered, left in September 1945. After May 1945 DP had gained attention (both considerable and favourable) as the originator and chief organiser of the Eric Liddell Memorial Fund and the Eric Liddell Memorial Services in Edinburgh and Glasgow, supported by the great and good of both the Kirk and the world of Scottish sport as the news spread of Eric's death in a Japanese internment camp. Suddenly two doors opened, more or less together: the metaphorical door of the Home Board was unlocked, and a very physical key to the door of a flat as a new home was offered as an opportunity that if not taken would be lost. So, once again, DP burnt his boats: just as he had demitted from Dunfermline: Gillespie before securing his Home Mission post in 1934, now in 1945 he demitted from Cambuslang: Trinity before even applying for any new position. After the best part of seven years he felt the time was right to go. He signed the missives for 32 Leven Street, Glasgow: it wasn't a flat he took to at first – but no matter. Would he be an independent evangelist, full time organiser of the Fellowship? Or would Robert Mackintosh's hints bear fruit? It seemed that White Anderson, John White's successor as Convener of the Home Board, might be more flexible, even if he appeared to like DP not much more, despite their serving together on the Eric Liddell Committee:

> Wednesday, 9th May [1945] This is what is called VE Day +1 – yesterday being VE Day. There has been some confusion. The Russians are still fighting and have not yet celebrated it. The German radio station is still giving out anti-Soviet propaganda 24 hours after they have announced the surrender . . . In Edinburgh I had an appointment with [*the new Convener, Rev.*] White Anderson for 3.30 and there I repaired. He was quite frank – the Home Board contained many who didn't want me and wouldn't have me, but he agreed to a conference with Mackintosh, Vincent Alexander, himself and myself on the whole matter. That may come before or after the General Assembly. He thoroughly approved my idea of an Eric Liddell Memorial Committee and agreed to act on it if formed.
>
> Wednesday, 4th September [1945] . . . I then caught the 1.52 Edinburgh, phoned White Anderson, to whom I had been on the phone the previous night and made an appointment with 2.30 that day . . . The interview lasted 45 minutes. I formed the definite impression that he doesn't want me, but wants less that I should be working outside Home Board auspices. He had not realised how deeply committed the Home Board was to the resumption of seaside work and I came away feeling that he might recommend my employment with that!

With further encouraging hints from Robert Mackintosh and having announced his departure, destination unknown, to his congregation, DP now followed through with his demission to his Presbytery and wrote a letter offering his services to the Home Board. He also accepted an invitation to lecture to the Edinburgh Medical Missionary Society, another to run a week's Conference on Evangelism for the Church of Scotland Presbytery of Melrose and two more invitations to lead Evangelistic Campaigns in Northern Ireland in November 1945. Further, he was commissioned by the University of St Andrews to write a pamphlet on the Scottish Reformer George Wishart and to join their Committee for the celebration of the Quarter-Centenary of Wishart's martyrdom.

DP's rehabilitation was gathering pace, though he was not awarded the D.D. from St Andrews University that he was quarter-promised at this time. Meanwhile in '121' what appears to have happened was a *coup* by Mackintosh, who managed, as Head of Department, by issuing a Handbook soliciting congregational donations which contained a commitment to restart the Seaside Missions, to pledge the new Convener to an area of work that John White had blocked. Robert Mackintosh clearly realized that, post-war, the Kirk would expect his central Board to be involved with evangelism within Scotland and that experienced staff would be needed. Further, there was undoubted pressure to re-engage with Seaside Mission, the major route by which, before the war, Home Mission had maintained the pre-union United Free tradition of direct evangelism. Things hung in the balance for some weeks yet, but when DP came back from his first sally to Ireland matters came to a conclusion:

> Sunday, 2nd December [1945] Belfast. It is 10 days since anything was chronicled here! I left Randeltown just after the last entry . . . On Tuesday I left early for Edinburgh and after a coffee I went straight to 121. Mackintosh was closeted with the Moderator Designate but he came out to see me and told me that he, Sir James and White Anderson had met and decided to put my appointment through. The Special Committee would meet on Thursday.
>
> Sunday, 2nd December [1945] [*continued*] . . . I journeyed home via Edinburgh and in the evening phoned Mackintosh from Waverley and learned that the Special Committee of the Home Board had that day unanimously decided to recommend my appointment as Organiser of Seaside Missions and Summer Camps at a salary of £500 per annum, plus £50 house allowance and personal travelling expenses. Mary was greatly relieved when I got home to tell her and together we gave thanks.
>
> Thursday, 20th December [1945] On Tuesday Mary and I left at 9.55 for Edinburgh, coming off the train at Princes Street . . . I went to the offices and saw Mackintosh, getting some information and all of it very satisfactory about my appointment. We lunched with Tom Torrance, whom I encountered coming out of the Foreign Mission Committee Meeting . . . After lunch Mary went to the Temples [*ie Rev. Bill Temple's Manse*], while I got Sir James Simpson at the offices and learned more about the proposed appointment. At 3.15, I met Drs White Anderson and R. J. Drummond, Robert Mackintosh and Sir James to discuss it and we continued in session for one and a half hours. It was a completely satisfactory interview, I think I may say under the circumstances. I am to get the use of room number 9 at 232 St Vincent Street and to engage secretarial help. I am to be called 'Organiser for Seaside Missions & Summer Camps' but am to be free to lead and direct campaigns, to carry on Eric Liddell & George Wishart and to lecture at the BTI. I am to have £500 a year, with £50 house allowance and personal and travelling expenses and the appointment is to take effect from 1st January. How Mary and I rejoiced! After the meeting Sir James and I went out to the Temples to join Mary and we had afternoon tea . . . Late in the evening Tinto came up to hear the great news. Jack and Joe Haldane I had phoned . . . Today I meet Mackintosh at three to see over Room 9 at 232.

The appointment went ahead: though there were further crises in their relationship, DP was to remain with the Home Board for the remainder of his working life.

DP was asked to return to preach at Cambuslang: Trinity on Sunday 10 February 1957. He noted afterwards that, between them, Mary and himself had recognised perhaps half the congregation and also:

> It was a very happy weekend, warming both our hearts with the knowledge that we had been and done more than we had realised in those crowded war years and that we were more loved and appreciated than we knew.

***

While visiting Cambuslang: Trinity in 2010 in order to take the picture that heads this chapter, I met one of its current members, Robert, who was tidying the gardens and who had been in the Sunday School there during the Second War. Yes, certainly, he was pleased to remember Mr Thomson. 'He was a big man!'

THE NEW EVANGELISM, 1945-1950

> Wednesday, 3rd May [1950] . . . The last 4½ years have seen an influence on the Church beyond anything I achieved in the previous 25 – not so vital an influence on individuals but rather on the whole policy and outlook of the Church in evangelism – and not only the Church in Scotland.
>
> D. P. Thomson, The Diary of My Life part 17

Although much was made of the discovery of a 'new evangelism' in Scotland after the Second World War, there was at first much continuity from before 1939. Out of the campaigns and debates of the post-1945 period would in time develop, however, a sharp dispute about what evangelism might be, about how it might be properly undertaken; what, indeed, the church meant by the word itself and how it understood its calling to mission. The desire for discontinuity, for a new start, was growing and within the Iona Community had influential advocates. This chapter explores the first stages of D. P. Thomson's post-war practice having first examined what others in Scotland were attempting, to seek to clarify just what was 'new'. This was the period when his gifts were again recognised as consonant with the needs of the Kirk.

Making Contact with a New World

In May 1940 the Church of Scotland, intrepidly, had begun the prophetic task of how best to plan for a new world, after victory had been obtained.[1] The General Assembly set up a special 'Commission For the Interpretation of God's Will in the Present Crisis'. Chaired by the Rev. Professor John Baillie, the Commission's work was to guide the thinking of the Church through the war and into the eventual peace.[2] Against the violence and divisions of global war, the Commission presented the vision of a 'world-wide Christian fellowship' and identified two new priorities: a new ecumenical emphasis and a 'progressive and zealous evangelism', repenting of any pre-war slacking in missionary impetus. From these wartime roots can be traced much of the new evangelism of the Church of Scotland, post-1945, with its emphasis on the 'essential of a living Church' whose entire membership, not just the ordained, actively participated in a spiritual, missionary fellowship.

The Baillie Commission's vision for the post-war church reemphasised the importance of the parish as the basic Christian unit. A firmly worded section of its 1943 report echoed a call from the World Council of Churches for the renewal of parish life and confessed to a very real breakdown of Scotland's geographically-based parish system. There were the unresolved tensions arising from the 1929 Union of the United Free and Established Churches, whereby all local congregations participating in the Union, no matter how close to each other were their sanctuaries, were allocated exclusive, if nominal, areas of responsibility. The Commission acknowledged that these areas were too often determined by the need to provide a parish for each minister rather than by any overall vision of how best to offer spiritual care to a population. To the inefficient distribution of the ministry was added the problem of the personal loyalties of church members. Where families had a choice of church (as was the case in all urban and many rural areas), loyalties to a particular minister or to the church building and particular pews associated with parents or grandparents, or to liturgical or theological traditions, all resulted in disconnection between worshippers and the population surrounding their church building. In this, the Commission was restating arguments heard before the war from one of its members, George F. MacLeod. Now, however, the growing claims of communal responsibility, of modern efficiency and of evangelistic urgency combined to reassert the mission of minister, elders and congregation to their local area or parish.

The Committee on Survey of the Parochial System, a spin-off from the Baillie Commission, highlighted, again and again, the need for the membership of the churches, for ordinary Christians, to carry a due share of the burden of ministry. Effective contact had to be made with those outside church and congregational life. Remarkably but perhaps realistically, the Committee did not expect that the ordinary Sunday worship of a congregation would be, in itself, attractive to unbelievers. District visiting was essential – the formulations could differ, but the idea was the same: 'All congregations should be educated to a true sense of their parochial responsibility,' 'There should be in every congregation a body of voluntary workers to visit the people in their homes, and use every means that Christian fellowship can suggest to bring them into living fellowship with the Church,' 'There is a need for a carefully selected and well-trained team of visitors in each congregation whose special task would be parochial visitation. Elders should give help in parochial visitation.'[3]

The Baillie Commission also saw a need for Christian teaching beyond the pulpit: 'The radio and the use of films afford other methods of approach to many who seldom enter our Churches' and, moreover, new people and methods as well as new technologies would be required to speak for Christ.[4] In these, as in many of its more practical suggestions about evangelism, the Commission gave the impression of throwing out ideas to see where they might fall. What was vital was that methods relevant to the times and the situation should be employed and that Christ's 'great commission' should be fulfilled. In the final paragraphs of its final report (1945), the Commission – above everything else it had said – chose to select the importance of the ministry of the laity. Because its vision for the future encompassed such a range of issues, clearly implementation could not depend simply on the ministers of the Church: 'Our Report of 1942 contained the italicised sentence: *On nothing does the future health of our society more depend than on the initiative of our Christian laity.* Of all that we have said during the past five years, there is nothing that we are now more anxious to repeat.'

The work of the Baillie Commission led to the General Assembly appointing yet another special committee, the Joint Committee on Evangelism, in which representatives of the Commission joined with those of the Home Board's Evangelism Committee and other co-opted members to produce the definitive manual on evangelism requested during the earlier consultations. Uncompleted when the Baillie Commission reported finally in 1945, *Into All the World: A Statement on Evangelism*, was published at Easter 1946 as a self-standing booklet. It ran to 64 pages and concluded with a summary of 30 principles and recommendations. Basic to its analysis was the perception that, despite the opportunities of the time, a great gulf divided the church from the un-churched masses.[5] 'The problem of contact' was therefore the primary question that evangelism faced. *Into All The World* refined, and somewhat narrowed, the approach outlined by the Baillie Commission. Belief that the traditional evangelistic meeting was as time passed increasingly less successful in bridging the gulf – in that the unchurched were increasingly less likely to attend such rallies – led to a renewed emphasis on the 'indirect evangelism' of 'parochial visitation'. To the 'training of lay people for evangelism', was added understanding of the 'influence of social environment' in differing communities, and hence of the need for 'different types of evangelistic approach'. 'We recommend,' the Joint Committee wrote, echoing the Commission's

1943 report, 'that much greater use should be made of suitably gifted men and women in conducting evangelistic services and missions.' Greater use of broadcasting, of the press, of film and drama, of special chaplaincies and of open air missions all found a place in *Into All The World* which also restated the essence of the Gospel and of the importance of personal decision to follow Christ. Beyond or alongside the Sunday School and Bible Class, congregations were recommended to sponsor Youth Groups which should combine regular worship and Bible study with 'some form of service to the community': 'Youth best understands Christianity in action.' Each congregation should also have its own 'group or cell of people who have the concern for evangelism deeply at heart, and are prepared to give time and effort to it.' While the Baillie Commission's understanding of evangelism had been broad and interwoven with the everyday witness of the ordinary Christian, *Into All the World* tended to concentrate rather more on the communication of Christ's call to commitment. Finally the Joint Committee strongly recommended 'that the Church of Scotland should consider making a full-time appointment of someone competent to organise and further its work in the sphere of evangelism.'

The 1946 General Assembly instructed the Home Board to do more to promote the call to evangelism, and during 1947 four pamphlets were published under the general title, *The New Evangelism*, in an attempt further to popularise ideas from *Into All The World*.[6] The concept of the congregational group for evangelism, one of *Into All the World*'s detailed recommendations, resurfaced in one of these, *The Parish Church*:

> It is also valuable to have special 'cells' or groups of men and women within a congregation who feel themselves especially called to the work of evangelism, and are prepared to consecrate themselves to it and train themselves for it. It is to be hoped that such a policy may be more carefully and prayerfully developed in the future.

The Home Board faced something of a quandary. The 'new evangelism' it sought was intended to be the work of the laity: but the Board did not normally interact with the laity, but rather with the parish ministers of the Church and their Presbyteries. At that time, no Board of the General Assembly had a general remit to promote adult Christian education: the ordained ministry of Word and Sacrament *was* the teaching arm of the Kirk, operating in each parish. Central sponsorship of locally based short term campaigns, however, was a recognised procedure and so, beyond the pamphlets, what was proposed to the 1947 Assembly was the appointment of a further two men, described, variously, as evangelists or 'Special Missioners' or 'Emissaries of the Church.' What was envisaged was:

> . . . to be directed not so much to making new Christians, at least not directly, as to making existing Christians into evangelists.
>
> This was considered to be a most valuable and significant decision and one which may very definitely determine a line of policy for our New Evangelism for some time to come. It will mean the first objective will be to make a witnessing Church a witnessing membership. What is in view is a nation-wide campaign, lasting it may be for several years, to create an evangelistic spirit in every member of the Church.

Such sentences were easily written, but the objective as stated was much less easy to tackle or even to define more closely. The Baillie Commission had, with some success, sought to widen the concept of evangelism to encompass the witness of the Christ-filled and socially involved life of the ordinary Christian. It is worth reflecting how very much broader a concept this 'new evangelism' was than the specialism in preaching and personal counselling discussed by Ray Price and D. P. Thomson in Salonica in 1916. How to direct outwards the spirituality of the entire membership of the Kirk was the issue in 1947; and if, as experience appeared to show, the regular ordinances of religion in 2,410 parishes were failing to achieve this, what might two emissaries achieve? Perhaps this gulf between task and tool was why no such appointments were ever made.

The 'new evangelism' of the late 1940s was driven, not so much by any especially new doctrinal insights (though these would come), as by the belief that the Church – once again! – faced a new world. In its statement of the content of the gospel, *Into All the World* used an outline – 'Faith in God', 'The Truth about Man', 'God's Intervention', 'The Holy Spirit', 'Conversion and the Christian Life', 'The Church and the Sacraments', 'The Future Life', 'The Consummation of History' – that was intended as an expression of protestant Christian orthodoxy. The leaflet thus began with a chapter heading 'The Unchanged Message'. Its 'Foreword', however, recognised that:

> There are, however, special periods of social change and crisis when it becomes peculiarly necessary for the Church to review and reconsider the whole task and technique of evangelistic enterprise. We are living at present through such a period of transition. It could not be otherwise, after the upheaval created by two world wars within the compass of half a century, and the resultant physical suffering, economic chaos, intellectual confusion, and moral bewilderment. The changes in the social

> environment, outlook, and manner of life of the people in this country are so vast that some of the older methods of religious work have been inevitably outmoded, while others call for careful re-adaptation to new conditions. The eternal Gospel remains itself unchanged, but it requires to be proclaimed in a new idiom, and presented new ways and through fresh channels.

A thoughtful analysis of this need to engage with a changed Scotland was expressed by the Deputy Leader of the Iona Community, T. Ralph Morton, in a pamphlet *Evangelism in Scotland Today* (1953), based on work he had led for the World Council of Churches, where his friend Robert Mackie was now Associate Secretary with responsibility for evangelism.[7]

Rejecting any conception of an ideal world of the past when 'most people went to church', Morton argued three things. If Scotland had once been a Christian country in the sense that, accepted or not, the faith had no rivals, this was so no longer; the wars, global communications and a global economy had broken down that 'insular exclusiveness'. The challenge to the Church was thus not simply to explicate what people partially understood, or to reclaim the lapsed and indifferent, but increasingly to commend the faith from scratch to those altogether outside. Then there had been massive changes in the 'ordinary affairs of life'. The home was no longer as central to the daily life of most Scots. Quite apart from the massive re-housing caused by the parallel trends of industrialisation and the de-population of the countryside, which had severed historical family ties, for most adults – and Morton was explicitly considering both women and men – daily life now centred round work in 'a factory, an office or a shop'. Moreover these adults were now voters in a democracy, members of Trade Unions or of professional associations, consumers of the mass entertainment of the radio and at the cinema. Yet the historical outreach of the church, in Morton's analysis, had been tied to the home and was often entirely unrelated to the world of work or to the citizen. *Evangelism in Scotland Today* therefore continued the perception of both the Baillie Commission and *Into All the World* that the key task of the Church's evangelism was to *connect*; to connect in new areas and with altered concerns. It was, Morton claimed, towards such a missionary attitude that the Scottish churches had been moving since the war. 'There is a new evangelism in the Church' he asserted, that saw the life of the Christian congregation as the key to connection.

After the war George MacLeod and his Community were leading advocates for mission in Scotland. MacLeod was convinced that the modern world could not be won by an outmoded church. Instinctively, he resisted both theologies and techniques that seemed to look backwards and not to the future. Yet one of his key principles was in fact ancient: the responsibility of a local church for its own neighbourhood. In 1944 what D. P. Thomson described as the 'manifesto' of the Iona Community, *We shall Rebuild*, was published, repeating some of the arguments already heard in the pre-war, *Are Not the Churchless Million Partly the Church's Fault?* 'Iona Missions' based on systematic visitation continued post-war in the parishes of ministers who were connected with the Community. In its occasional magazine, *Coracle*, January 1951, one of the sponsors of the Community, Rev. Professor Donald Baillie, spelt out Iona's contribution to post-war evangelism: he commended what he called the new Iona principle of reliance on the congregation, contrasting it with the former practice of importing a special evangelist.[8]

To place responsibility for mission on the members of a local congregation required a revolution in the established practice of Scottish churches. In his 1944 pamphlet *Missionary Principles for the Home Front*, Ralph Morton sought to express the typical Scottish church member's understanding of Christian mission: essentially a Cinderella-role, confined to the kitchen of foreign work, or as a stand-alone optional extra, beyond the routine life and worship of a congregation; out-sourced to enthusiasts.[9] This view of home mission had a long history in Scotland, associated with the movement's origins in filling theological, social or geographical gaps in the parish system. It had been concerned with the marginal. MacLeod's recommended pattern of mission therefore began with winning the consent of the Kirk Session and proceeded via a (possibly extended) period of education of the existing congregation.[10] The dominant theme of Iona Missions was one of welcome and friendship. MacLeod wrote not so much of converting outsiders as about re-engaging with the mass of the population – the confused, alienated and lapsed. MacLeod was somewhat more optimistic about the underlying spiritual state of Scotland than Morton, his Deputy, who was more prepared to accept that there were those entirely outside the faith – the Iona Community was not composed of MacLeod clones!

Acceptance of 'new' methods of evangelism, in fact, might or might not also imply rejection of older techniques, and in particular that of the mass meeting, the great evangelistic rally or crusade. Many accepted Ralph Morton's view that, post-war, the technique of summoning crowds to an evangelistic meeting had had its day.[11] The case was made that those who attended rallies were mainly already committed; that in any case those outside the churches were sufficiently ignorant of the Christian lexicon that no single address could reach them. The indirect approach was therefore advocated: not the direct preaching of the professional evangelist or minister, but rather the witness of the ordinary Christian; not simply home-based morality but rather ways to demonstrate the relevance of the faith in the worlds of work and public life; not so much the church-based sermon but, rather, faith, spreading like a virus, person to person, in the daily life of home, work and club. The methodology of the youth club established in 1942 at Church House, Bridgeton, Glasgow, by Arthur Gray, minister of St Francis-in-the-East, was thus for a church-based adult leadership to engage in sports and games with young people coming into the club for an evening's activity, with some form of corporate prayers towards the end. No direct evangelism was undertaken, but the aspiration was for the faith of the leadership to rub off on to the members. This and other similar clubs were supported by the Iona Youth Trust and the Community's Experimental Parishes Committee.[12]

As Tom Allan was to come to see, however, it was one thing to recognise that a method was inadequate in itself and another to abandon it altogether. And, in fact, many did not abandon the older methods. There were those for whom the traditional evangelical campaign was by no means dead: for whom a well-publicised rally with an invited speaker and well-chosen music was the gospel method. Allan was to name the Brethren and the Baptist denominations in particular as traditionalists in this sense, along with Rev. Prof. James S. Stewart and the Church of Scotland minister of Glasgow: Springburn Hill, William Fitch.[13] Other congregations of the Church of Scotland, the UF and Congregational denominations could no doubt also have been named. John Highet's 1960 survey listed the Scottish Evangelistic Council, the Scottish Colportage Society, the Scottish branch of the Worldwide Evangelisation Crusade, the Faith Mission and a variety of local coalitions as maintaining regular evangelistic activities of the more conventional kind; he might have added the Glasgow Bible Training Institute.[14] And, indeed, Tom Allan himself, along with D. P. Thomson and others of their mutual friends, worked with Bill Fitch on his committee for Youth Rallies in 1948.

Rev. William Still's autobiography describes his period of supporting such rallies and campaigns 1945-47, the first two years of his ministry in Aberdeen, when he was involved with Alan Redpath and Billy Graham's early campaigns with Youth for Christ rallies each Saturday night combining

Redemption Hymnal singing with evangelistic sermons in his own Aberdeen: Gilcomston South church.[15] Nevertheless, Still, whom no-one could ever describe as other than a Conservative Evangelical, also came to believe that such old-style rallies were obsolete in the post-war world. He soon abandoned his apparently successful because well-attended rallies in favour of a Saturday evening prayer meeting and a life-time of expository preaching. Still shared the view that new – in his case 'reformed' would be a more appropriate word – methods were needed: that pre-war evangelistic techniques no longer made connections in 1950. He also drew a conclusion from this analysis similar to that of others at that time: that the key need was a revitalised church. It was in his perception of the channel by which God might renew his blessing of his Church that Still's distinctive contribution lay.

Outside the refined world composed of the General Assembly Commissions and the theologically acute, Scotland's traditional evangelical constituencies continued well-established practices: the 'new evangelism' was initially something of a project of an elite. Thus *Stedfast*, the magazine of the United Free Church, in March 1956 reported a campaign organised jointly by the Sauchie & Fishcross UF congregation, the Hillfoot churches and Sauchie Church of Scotland. During February there had been a month of special 'After Church' evening rallies, led by a Message of Life Gospel Team from Glasgow, supported by the gospel-singer, tenor David McNee, then a detective in the Glasgow police. In order to bring the people in, a loudspeaker van toured the area on Saturday and Sunday afternoons.[16] Apart from this use of 20th century technology, the concept was a straightforward local adaptation of the methods of Moody and Sankey in 1871. There were still many in Scotland for whom this was what it meant to run an evangelical campaign. Alternatively, 'traditional' campaigns might run alongside the new. In 1951, for example, the Church of Scotland's Presbytery of Edinburgh unanimously agreed to offer support to an old-style preaching campaign led by the London Evangelist Tom Rees, in co-operation with the Edinburgh Churches' Committee and the Evangelistic Union. Evangelism Convener Rev. Dr George S. Gunn of St George's West recognised that indirect visitation and congregational efforts could be especially beneficial, but nevertheless he successfully moved that Presbytery welcome the Tom Rees Mission and commend it to the city.[17] Thinkers, writers and missiologists might proclaim that the day of mass evangelism was over, but there were many in the post-war church who never heard them.

Beyond all these special evangelistic efforts, new and old, there were those – and there were also many and more of them – for whom the normal ordinances of religion were still the way forward, continuing as they had done over the years in the parishes and congregations of the land. The Baillie Commission had indeed spoken for many when against the horrors of the Second World War it called for a recovery of faith in the Christian Gospel: many ministers in the post-war period had served in the war, whether as chaplains or in the armed forces, and shared the Commission's perception of the alienation from the church of so many of their wartime acquaintances. Among the ministry were still many whose lives had similarly been shaped by both the First War and the subsequent disillusionment of the Depression. The years after 1945 offered an opportunity finally to realise the hopes that had driven the 1929 Union of the Established Church with the United Free Church. As the population was re-housed after the war, several Scottish denominations therefore gave much effort to church extension: the erection of new church buildings for the new housing estates, the appointment of ministers and the creation of new congregations, so that the churches and their regular ministries should indeed be within reach of the people. The work of that generation of Church Extension ministers, often supported by Lay Missionaries and Deaconesses, was certainly grass-roots evangelism of the most arduous type: by no means an 'in-and-out' campaign but ministry rooted in community.

Others remembered the large, broad-based campaigns of the pre-war era – the Forward Movement and the Recall to Religion Campaigns – movements led from the heights of the denominations, respectable, orthodox, designed to galvanise the churches. Among the new types of campaign in post-war Scotland were the 'Commando' Campaigns in Edinburgh (1947) and Glasgow (1950) which featured simultaneous 'assaults' by teams of (mainly) ministers on places outside the home where people gathered – offices, factories, football matches, pubs etc. Military commando units had gained prestige during the war as Britain's specially selected elite strike or raiding troops: and they had trained in Scotland. The term first used of evangelistic tactics by the Methodist Church in England, it had a vogue in Scotland in the immediate post-war years. President of the Glasgow Churches Campaign was perhaps the Kirk's most influential minister of that time, John White; also speaking in support of the mission was Most Rev. J. C. How, Primus of the Scottish Episcopal Church. Many of the proposed themes of *Into All the World* were attempted by the Campaign: plans to 'go out' to where people were, at work and at leisure; the use of new media – drama, cinema; the inter-church shared responsibility and common action; the targeting of particular groups; ministers and laymen cooperating in a 'combined operation.' What was also new was the sheer scope and ambition of the campaign, its simultaneous nature, and its deliberate attempt to focus not so much on seeking to attract the public to church services and rallies (though mass rallies were held) as to concentrate at a local level on congregational mission and at a city level on the 1,500 or so individual raids or assignments, when team members led by Johnstone R. McKay spoke at leisure-locations and at work-place visits throughout the 'Gospel City'.[18]

If the Press highlighted the 'Commando' aspects of Glasgow 1950, its planning also included a substantial congregational aspect, run by a committee under the convenership of Tom Allan, managed broadly on Iona lines with first an inward and then an outward aspect. From the Campaign's Bulletin no. 2, February 1950:[19]

> The main emphasis of the Campaign has now settled on the Congregational Missions, including both the missions in the congregations in the Spring and the missions by the congregations in the City in the Autumn . . . The general aim of the congregational missions in the Spring should be to awaken the churches again to the message of total salvation to which they witness and secondly to rouse them to a lively sense of their power and obligations to pass on that message to the community in word and act . . .
>
> Success of the mission in the Autumn – both the congregational house to house visitations and the commando invasions of the factories, offices, places of entertainment – will certainly stand or fall by the effectiveness of the missions in the churches in the Spring.

Both George MacLeod and D. P. Thomson were asked to support preparations for the mission: George by addressing a meeting of ministers, and DP by addressing a meeting of office-bearers, both in January 1950. (DP had, indeed, been invited to lead the 1947 Edinburgh Campaign, but the invitation was sent so late that it proved impossible for him to accept it.)

A note of his address to the Glasgow ministers is retained in George MacLeod's archives and it reveals the way his thinking had developed over ten years of conducting missions.[20] He was, in fact, in two minds about supporting the venture at all, for his experience had taught him how very far from being missionary-minded most congregations were. His suspicion was that Glasgow 1950 was too broad-brush an approach and that it might be counter-productive, encouraging a regression to the 'old' evangelism. George was, nevertheless, essentially an activist, and he preferred on this occasion to offer support. Choosing not to offer his audience a rehash of the techniques already outlined in his publications, he gave a typically provocative assessment of the situation facing the church, the reasons for 'the crisis in mission today'. In the 19th century, he suggested, there had been a fruitful relationship, a shared faith, between the evangelical activists and the mass of church members. By the mid-20th century, however, he argued that evangelists simply did their thing but were disconnected from congregations whose spiritual life had no corporate vitality, depending solely on their minister's conduct of Sunday worship. It was the consequent inability of spiritually-somnolent congregations to absorb or care for converts that he most feared as the consequence of importing external evangelists.

Ten years of 'Iona Missions' had convinced George MacLeod that even his model of parish mission barely scratched the surface of congregational life. The gap between his vision of the Church of Christ as she was meant to be and the life of an ordinary Church of Scotland had widened to such an extent that he believed that almost any attempt at a single campaign, a quick-fix, was bound to fail, counter-productively. What he was still sure of, however, was his doctrine of the Church: 'I roundly claim that the congregation or the eldership, as it is, *is* the ecclesia that God has given us.' Ministers should therefore be prepared to work with their elders as they were, the 'Marvellous', the 'Mediocre', even with 'the Morose'. His practice advice for 1950 was therefore that everyone had to be involved: 'Don't run a mission simply on the devout – you will be sectional at the start and no more ready to receive the outsider . . . So design the Rally for everyone: songs and dances and real industrial issues and games and a gospel address at the close of every evening so the devout can make their appeal.' The overall impression given by the paper is that the prescription carried less conviction than the diagnosis. George MacLeod was, seemingly, not too optimistic about the prospects for Glasgow 1950. Later, professional sociologist and active church member John Highet was to offer a more positive assessment of the Glasgow Campaign in an article in *The Third Statistical Account: The City of Glasgow*. His research led him to report that there had indeed been conversions and increased attendances at worship. Moreover, some 31 factories had asked that industrial chaplains be appointed – industrial chaplaincy was then one of the 'new channels' beyond parish ministry that was being developed by the Church of Scotland.[21]

The 1950 Glasgow Churches Campaign coincided with another new form of post-war mission: the Radio Missions of 1950 and 1952, of which the BBC's Rev. Ronald Falconer was the prime mover.[22] In post-war Britain the BBC's Scottish region had considerable freedom to devise its own schedules: it was also assumed that the BBC as a public body could quite properly support the work of the Christian Church, both partners being integral to the fabric that held society together. Evangelism on the radio-waves was attempted by an autonomous agency of the British state, organised by ministers of the Church of Scotland as BBC employees, with as their stated aims: 'To challenge the careless, to reclaim the lapsed, and to strengthen the faithful.' George F. MacLeod of Iona; Tom Allan of North Kelvinside; Prof. James S. Stewart; the ecumenist A. C. Craig; Edinburgh University Chaplain David Read and pastoral expert Hugh Douglas led the 1950 Mission. Falconer gave to the mission the best resources available to him: for six weeks a wide range of speakers offered some 60 programmes, ranging from broadcast services and hymn-singing to Christian drama and discussion. All ministers of the participating denominations were circularised to advise them of the mission and to suggest that they send volunteers around the homes of their parish to contact any whose interest had been stirred. Presbyteries were requested to appoint BBC Liaison representatives. Falconer found the overall experience disheartening, however: he heard of only 24 local campaigns and of rather more where the programmes had, certainly, been publicised but the clergy were disappointed when no newcomers arrived. One lesson from the 1950 Radio Mission was that the vast bulk of the ministers of Scotland had little conception of how to connect with those outside their congregations. The heart might be willing, but ordinary parish life did not lend itself to evangelism and in any case no-one had experience of cooperating with broadcasters.

For the Radio Mission of Lent (March-April) 1952, more was done by way of preparation. In the small county towns of Ayr and Forfar, the Clydeside industrial town of Greenock and in Glasgow's Partick district, the BBC's ministers worked with the churches in planning local Churches' Campaigns that synchronised with the broadcasts. Preparatory programmes, under the guidance of Tom Allan, again a leading missioner, set out how participating congregations (whether or not in the four selected areas) might form 'Volunteer Action Groups': 'Form a Group, listen to the broadcasts, discuss them and take the action that your situation demands.'[23] Greater priority was given to the aim, 'strengthen the faithful'.

Once the campaign proper began, its publicity suggested inviting neighbours round for the evening and listening to the special broadcasts with them; or making the programmes talking-points at work or with friends. There was certainly a variety of options: for seven Sundays that March and April, the morning [9.30am], evening [7.45pm] and Children's Hour [5.00pm] services on the Scottish Home Service were themed to the mission, as were the 'People's Services' [11.00am] and 'Sunday Half Hour' [8.30pm] on the Scottish Light Programme and Saturday's 'Family Prayers' [10.45am, Scottish Home Service]. Every week-day on the Scottish Home Service, the short 7.50am 'Lift up your hearts' continued the theme, as did each Wednesday's 'Children's Hour Prayers' [5.50pm] and the Thursday evening dramatic / experimental programmes, 'Make up your minds' [7.35pm]. The 90 or so broadcasts included special outside programmes from the four centres; contributions from the Moderator of the General Assembly; from the bishop of Edinburgh, the Rt. Rev. Dr Kenneth Warner and the Very Rev. Provost M.P.G. Leonard of St Mary's Episcopal Cathedral, Glasgow; from the North East Coast Fishermen's and other Choirs; from such ministerial academics as Dr A. C. Craig and Dr William Barclay, both of Glasgow University. Once again, however, results were mixed, so that 'fair to disappointing' might have been written on a notional report-card.

The Radio Missions showed, as the Scottish Controller for the BBC concluded, that the ordinary life of the churches was itself a major barrier to missionary success.[24] It was to remain the major barrier. Nevertheless, taken all in all, the special and the ordinary, the new and the old, the post-war years saw evangelistic activities that John Highet believed to be unprecedented in both quantity and variety in the history of the Scottish Church.[25] Many had come back from the War shocked to the core by its revelation of humanity's capacities and determined to rebuild on the basis of the Gospel of Jesus Christ.

Seaside Services Organiser, 1946-1948

In 1 January 1946 D. P. Thomson began again the work with the Home Board of the Church of Scotland that had engaged him before the war, as the Organiser for Seaside Services and Summer Camp Work. This title somewhat understated what the post actually involved. It had been agreed that a resumption of his pre-war wider duties was in view: he was to 'be free to lead and direct campaigns, to carry on *Eric Liddell* & *George Wishart* and to lecture at the BTI.' DP was later to record in *Personal Encounters* that:

> I returned to the staff at the end of the war, in 1945 [*sic*], to begin what proved to be the busiest, the happiest, the most exciting, and probably in the long run, the most fruitful, 21 years of my life.

His bold decision to leave Cambuslang: Trinity had been justified. Almost immediately he found himself invited to lead a campaign in the Borders countryside around Galashiels and Melrose: planning began in January 1946. By July he was able to submit an interim report to the Evangelism Committee, and the Committee 'expressed its appreciation that Mr Thomson had been able to accomplish so much in face of the initial difficulties of resuming this work after the war years.'

DP's work now took wings. From the first months of 1946 he toured the universities, addressed the students, recruited a new generation of mission teams, developed Summer Mission lantern lecture presentations. Consistent with his previous practice DP maintained links with both the IVF and the SCM student groups in the Scottish Universities, despite the theological differences between the two groups, and he continued to be a guest lecturer at Glasgow's BTI. It was at the very beginning of his appointment that he first met Ian B. Doyle, some thirty years later to be Secretary of the Home Board and DP's literary executor. DP employed Ian as his Summer Missions adjutant over the summer of 1946. In 1947 it was the 17-year old Bill Shannon's turn to join DP's 'staff':

> Sunday, 1st June 1947, 9am . . . Bill Shannon and his mother coming for a cup of tea. Bill starts a week on Tuesday on my staff at £2 a week plus keep.

When in 2008 Bill Shannon was asked who else was on DP's 'staff', his reply proved illuminating:

> . . . I was 17. Earlier that year DP and Tom Allan conducted a Mission in my home town of Bellshill, Lanarkshire, and, as part of it, did several sessions at my school. Their communication was arresting. So much so that I attended other meetings of theirs at the local YMCA . . . DP had his eye on me for two reasons. He well understood that I had set out on a new road of Christian Faith and Commitment. He wanted to nurture that, so how better than to recruit me to work with him. It was an invitation for my sake and, of course, any kind of payment was very much needed by my widowed mother and I. But equally it was in DP's interest too because he needed some youthful energy and muscle to be at his behest for ANY job needing done. You ask what the remit was. There certainly

> wasn't any recorded anywhere . . . He needed availability plus that energy and brawn to get the considerable amounts of necessary equipment allocated, sorted, transported and delivered to the various resorts round Scotland. The reverse had to take place at the end of the 2 month summer period. This equipment was stored, extracted and finally returned to a massive company building in central Glasgow. I worked a lot in its gloomy depths! But once out it went to so many of the most wonderful places in the land none of which had ever had a visit from this Shannon. Also it put me in first contact with Churches all round the country. DP took a great risk here. He hired a rookie. I entered into a very steep learning curve indeed, and so did he. I laughed a bit at that phrase 'my staff'. As far as I know I was the only one paid and kept. All others, of whom there were many, were volunteers helping short term; leading or participating in the Mission projects.

Both Ian Doyle and Bill Shannon were thus appointed by DP personally to be successively his aides-de-camp, the arrangement, at least in Bill's case, displaying admirably DP's combination of the pragmatic, the practical and the pastoral. Both men would prove to be missionary leaders of the post-war generation. We should also notice that DP had been campaigning with Tom Allan earlier in 1947 – indeed, Allan had been the first to arrive at DP's first training session in January 1946. This, too, was to prove a long and fruitful collaboration. The Rev. Tom Allan was called to his first charge of Glasgow: North Kelvinside in 1946 having also already joined the Seaside Mission teams.

The other key member of DP's 'staff' was of course Mary Thomson, who now also found herself undertaking a ministry of her own as hostess for mission teams:

> Wednesday, 23rd July [1947] Just into the boat train from Stranraer to Glasgow. It is 20 minutes late. Mary down to see me off – we won't meet again for a week or more. She comes up tomorrow night as I come down; she will be at the flat tomorrow night, I at Ayr. She there also on Friday and I, alas, at Millport. Only once this summer, I think, have we slept together at number 32 nor will or can we hope to yet awhile!

Running the expanding suite of Summer Missions meant for both Mary and DP a constant shuttling between the various centres: addressing meetings, leading worship, greeting and 'farewell-ing' leaders, crossing the country again and again from east coast to west coast, and meanwhile handling all the correspondence involved with forward planning. The whole experience he found rewarding, but exhausting. There was also the consideration that D. P. Thomson had never really learnt to drive; of the two of them, only Mary was a confident driver. In all his travelling, DP mainly used public transport: the Glasgow trams, the buses or the trains, or else found himself a driver.

During August the pattern continued, with the addition that DP was himself leading the one team that shuttled between the two resorts of Ayr and Girvan. He had, besides Mary, also enlisted his parents-in-law, Douglas and Kathie Rothnie, then visiting Scotland on leave from Jamaica. Besides the standard summer campaign fare of Open Air and Children's services and Witness Box presentations, Girvan also had a 'Jamaica Day':

> Thursday, 7th August [1947] I am at Girvan Station, in the train, leaving for Glasgow. It is the Jamaica Day here, and we got £5 10/ - of a collection for Jamaica this morning. Father, Kathie and Miss McTear all spoke. I made the announcements and the appeal. They are having an exhibition this afternoon and an evening meeting.

'Commando Raiding' was a further new activity for these post-1945 summer teams:

> Monday, 4th August [1947] Father, Kathie, Miss Gardiner and Charlie Taylor just in from the 1st Camp Commando Raid with the Van. They had a great reception, met with interesting experiences, and sold over two pounds worth of literature, which was good going! Tonight we leave about 7.30 on the 2nd Raid, going inland and then north. Mary will drive, and I will be in command. So here's to it!

'Commando' raiding being the newest tactic available, DP of course incorporated it into his programme, running unplanned tours by a vanful of leaders, who dropped in without appointment on camp sites and pubs with Christian literature and Christian witness.

In order to provide the 200 or so people needed for the seaside centres from Millport to Aberdeen in operation in summers 1947 and 1948, D. P. Thomson had to look beyond the universities and young ministers seeking a charge. Whereas in the pre-war situation DP had mainly called upon men with some form of theological training, whether formal or informal, now the men and women comprising some 50% of his teams came from backgrounds other than academic. Viewed one way, this was simply an extension of his wartime practice, the involvement of the junior members of the FiE in summer mission and evangelistic work. Viewed another way, in longer retrospect, as DP was to write in *Harnessing the Lay Forces of the Church*, this decision was 'one of the most far-reaching of a lifetime' – it led directly into his work of the 1950s and 1960s. At the time the changing mission personnel, while gratifying, had its implications. Students at the traditional universities had particularly long summer vacations; but these new recruits had at most two weeks of *annual* paid holiday. As DP wrote in 1967, 'Their holiday period was of the shortest and they were intending to give half or all of it to the work. How then were they to be trained, and where could this training be carried out?'

Training, of course, and of the more Spartan residential variety, was an old enthusiasm of his. Week-night evening training classes began in January 1946 within days of taking up his post. Presently, in order to train his new recruits for the summer missions programme, DP began residential training schools, based in congregations on the fringes of the cities, so that his teams might devote their evenings to preparation, while not leaving their day-jobs:

> We would ask them to leave home, but not their work, for a period of a week or a fortnight at a time during the months of May and June. We would take over new housing areas on the outskirts of the four big cities as training grounds, and church halls there and in immediately adjacent areas as training centres and billets. The young people would come straight from their work. They would be in residence for a week or a fortnight, returning each morning to their daily duties, while the Woman's Guilds of the churches in nearby districts would undertake the necessary catering and cooking.

Glasgow: High Carntyne thus hosted some 40 trainees in June 1947, together with the Dedication Service for the Summer Mission season. Two schools, at Dundee and Aberdeen, were held May - June 1948. These pre-summer mission training schools did not consist solely of prayers, Bible studies and lectures – they were in effect mini-campaigns in their own right with all the nitty-gritty of Christian street work: door to door visiting, speaking on street-corners, leading children's games and running meetings for adults.

The demands of DP's work were considerable and recognition of his gifts grew. George F. MacLeod, while trying to find a way through the difficult relationship between himself, Iona and the Home Board, at one point suggested that experimental missionary work be authorised: that in parishes under himself, and all extra-parochial work under D. P. Thomson.[26] There was, perhaps, something of a pre-emptive strike in this suggestion! As early as January 1946 DP had begun again to plan parish and local area campaigns on his own, old lines. Campaigns that spring with churches in the Borders were the first of his new series. Requests again mounted. By the time the Board's report to the 1948 Assembly came to be approved the next April, not only were momentous future developments foreshadowed, but a mission of considerable significance had taken place:

> The Organiser of Seaside Mission Work, the Rev. D. P. Thomson, M.A., has directed this interesting and rewarding work with unflagging energy, and with characteristic thoroughness and enthusiasm . . . The effect of this work extends far beyond the services in the immediate localities concerned. During the winter and at other times Mr Thomson is able to call upon the services of trained personnel not only of ministers but of others, young and old, from various walks of life and with these he has been outstandingly successful in carrying through Presbytery Campaigns, and such notable efforts in congregational evangelism as was accomplished by a thorough-going system of visitation in the parish of North Kelvinside, Glasgow. The Committee is fortunate in having the gifts of Mr Thomson in these enterprises put so ungrudgingly at its disposal.

Here was an acknowledgement that under DP's guidance even such a limited programme as Seaside Missions had had widespread consequences and diffused benefits for the church, through its by-product of 'trained personnel', 'young and old, from various walks of life', increasingly available to support campaigns even in locations that lacked a beach.

The congregational mission at Glasgow: North Kelvinside of September 1947 was in time to become the best known of all local missions in the second half of the 20th century, just as George MacLeod's experiment at Govan: Old had been in the first half. Its minister's account of it, Tom Allan's *The Face of My Parish*, became a best-seller. It was a mission that arose out of the enthusiasm and the frustration of the new generation of seaside mission workers that DP had trained. In passing, it is worth noticing that involvement in mission had an addictive quality: perhaps like service in the wartime forces for others, it had such a heightened quality of fellowship and such a spiritual reality that in comparison ordinary congregational life could pall. To renew and sustain the experience, another mission was required. DP's own, no doubt simplified, account of its origins in *Personal Encounters*, ran as follows:

> It was at the end of the second summer, in the early autumn of 1947, that a group of these young people came to me, asking if there was nothing of the same kind they could do for us in the winter, like the open air evangelism in which they had been so profitably engaged during the months of July and August . . . That night when I got home I put through a telephone call to Tom Allan, one of our young Seaside Mission leaders, then recently settled in his first charge, at North Kelvinside in the Maryhill district of Glasgow. 'Tom,' I said, 'do you think we could borrow your

> parish for a fortnight, send these young folk out with literature and see what kind of a job they make of it?' 'Well,' was the answer, 'it's worth thinking about. Suppose we meet for a coffee to-morrow morning and discuss it?' We agreed to do so.

In his own November 1947 pamphlet *Visitation Evangelism or Tackling the Parochial Problem: A Report of the North Kelvinside (Glasgow) Experiment*, DP recorded that the eventual two week campaign was conducted by two teams. The initial visiting of the 1,854 homes in the parish was undertaken by his volunteers: some fifty men and women, of whom five were ministers, twelve were divinity students, thirteen were students of other faculties, and the remainder [c.20] young men and women from business and industry. Their aims were fivefold and would not have been unfamiliar to the Lay Missionaries and Colporteurs of the 19th century:

> (i) To carry the greetings of the Church to every home in the parish, irrespective of congregational or denominational tie. (ii) To gather as much information as possible about the family and church connection in each home. (iii) To bring something of the wealth and variety of the Church's literature to those who never had either the time or the opportunity to see it. (iv) Where no vital church connection existed (and only in such cases) to extend an invitation to the parish church, and to suggest that a follow-up visit might be made by a representative of that church. (v) To make a natural witness for Christ, and do such personal work as circumstances might permit or suggest.

On one night DP himself, with Mary, Douglas and Kathie Rothnie were all out visiting. From these weekday evening visits, during which arithmetic suggests the teams (operating singly or in pairs) must have averaged some 5-7 households a night, a database of the religious affiliation of homes was compiled. Where a follow-up was requested, details were handed to the second, smaller, team of North Kelvinside volunteers who then began rounds of their own. The mission functioned from the church hall, beginning with prayers at 5.30pm and supper at 6.00pm; the teams set off at 7pm and generally returned about 9pm to report; communal prayers concluded each day. This was parish visitation cut down to the bare bones: it had nothing of the variety of related meetings and open air events that MacLeod had included at Govan: Old or that DP would use subsequently. When Allan wrote that this was 'not the working out of a carefully prepared plan of campaign', what he meant was that there was little if any pre-campaign training or publicity. DP did his own normal planning – the preparation of maps and lists, the gathering of equipment – about a week before. No special preacher was featured, other than DP, speaking (he thought himself rather below par) at the normal congregational worship of the first Sunday and at the opening meeting of the Youth Group on the second Sunday evening.

From what were at first very short visits, within three months some 50 people were to join the congregation by profession of faith and another 50 by resuscitation of previous but lapsed membership of the church. The Sunday School doubled; Sunday attendance improved markedly. In his 17th Diary DP was able to record one particular letter of thanks: it was directed not so much to himself as to his father-in-law:

> I wanted to quote a letter received to be taken out by Mary to Father from the old couple he and Kathie visited in the North Kelvinside Campaign.
>
> 'Dear Sir, May I ask you to forward this note to Jamaica. I tried to get the address at Christmas to send my very best wishes, but better late than never. Mr Black called today with it. They were the third callers during the house-to-house campaign and I am very pleased to tell them we liked Mr Allan and all his elders very much. Mr Allan is so enlightening, so we became members and I also in the Guild. I am now a member of the Old Folks Club and enjoy ourselves every Tuesday at a concert. I do hope you will remember your visit to us and the kind thoughts you left in our memories. Perhaps next Christmas I will get an answer to my note. With good wishes to you and yours for all time. We remain, [*name and address removed*] '
>
> That old couple in their 70s were filthy, evil tongued, gambling and drinking and disreputable. Their home was appalling. Father and Kathie were shocked. Their visit was the beginning of a complete transformation. They have never missed a Sunday at Church since that day. I know that Father will be greatly moved and cheered.

Besides such individual cases, Tom Allan also reckoned as substantial gains the actual knowledge of the parish that the survey gave him as minister, and – very particularly – the spiritual growth and confidence that came to those of his own members involved in the follow up. Less welcome was the actual hostility towards the mission shown by others of his church members, and the way that the dynamics of relationships within his congregation worked to make the assimilation of the newcomers so problematic in the longer term. All in all, the North Kelvinside mission gave Tom Allan a great deal to think about, the fruits of which he was, famously, to share with the church in *The Face of My Parish*, and through the articles in the *British Weekly* that preceded the book. Widespread interest in the mission was encouraged when the BBC in Scotland featured it twice in a new series of programmes on 'The Church at Work'. Such publicity for the mission opened the door of the BBC to Tom Allan. In a very short time he found himself one of Scotland's leading religious broadcasters as well as an acknowledged thinker and practitioner of mission.

The lessons DP learned from North Kelvinside were also far-reaching. 'As for me,' he reflected in *Personal Encounters*, 'it set the pattern for the remaining 20 years of my active service, leading to new methods of lay training, area and regional, as well as parish missions in every part of Scotland.' The negative effects of the mission were in the nature of things less obvious to him: they were to unravel over time, when he was long gone. Indeed DP was dismayed when, five years later, Tom Allan first began publishing his considered account:

> Sunday, 14th December [1952] Tom Allan's *British Weekly* article of last week has given me seriously to think. He as much as says the fruits of both Visitation Campaigns have more or less vanished. More case than ever for the fullest possible investigation on my part.

In 1947 what DP saw were, *almost* wholly, the positives. From his personal point of view, leading such a team offered an opportunity for extending his outreach at a time when his own preaching seemed less fruitful. He realised that his team – and particularly those who were the 'young men and women from business and industry' – had been able to thrive on their task and more than that, to bring their own qualities to its successful completion, with a bare minimum of prior experience. The short, on-the-job training offered to this class of volunteers was clearly transferable from seaside missions to the vastly wider world of parish mission. Both at North Kelvinside and at the pre-summer schools, these young, less formally educated people recruited from the world of work had something to teach the more theologically sophisticated: they had something to give to evangelism beyond youthful enthusiasm, as he wrote in *Harnessing the Lay Forces*:

> And wherever they went we ministers who had charge of them found they had something supremely worthwhile to contribute – a simpler, a more natural and a more realistic approach than that of the divinity student, and a witness for Christ which had behind it a rich variety of experience in the rough and tumble of daily life in the world.

This, then, was a real discovery, not the least of the aspects of which was that DP accepted women volunteers on an equal basis with men. The

Church of Scotland at that time did not ordain either women ministers or women elders, though (depending on the history and constitution of each parish) they could be eligible to be elected to bodies managing the financial, property and business sides of congregational life. The Woman's Guild offered its own parallel, separate and ultimately unequal route to participate in local and presbyterial church life. Insofar as Church of Scotland congregations engaged in visiting, unless there was a deaconess on the staff this was a function of the minister and the eldership – and elders could only be male. Increasingly, however, women would be equally represented on DP's visitation evangelism campaigns, not just serving the meals but being encouraged 'to make a natural witness for Christ' in the households they visited and in speaking at church meetings associated with the campaigns. He was a significant advocate of the ministry of women.

Following the apparent success of North Kelvinside came further Visitation Evangelism Campaigns at Glasgow: Mount Florida where John R. Ramsay, a founder-member of the FiE, was minister (March 1948), and Glasgow: Martyrs (November 1948) besides more ambitious missions at St Mary's, Motherwell in the autumn of 1948 and at Edinburgh: McDonald Road in February 1949. It was at Ian Doyle's Motherwell parish that DP began what he described as 'the three-fold simultaneous approach' – in effect the combination of a commando-style campaign with intensive visiting. DP recognised that just visiting homes as at North Kelvinside left the wider world untouched, so he planned in the Motherwell Campaign to take his teams throughout the parish. Supported by visiting ministers and students as well as by his young people, a team (including local supporters) of approaching 100, DP arranged for visits to the schools, factories, warehouses and hospitals of the parish – and to the pubs, billiard saloons, the greyhound track and the cinema. As he put it in *We Saw The Church In Action!*: 'At the greyhound track, bookies stopped shouting the odds and punters stood in silence while homilies were delivered between the races. And last night, during a break in the programme, patrons of the New Cinema heard a Gospel Address.' Including a programme of systematic visiting of the parish's 1,250 households, the 'Three-Fold Approach' therefore sought to make contact in all three of the worlds of home, work and leisure. Following the practice of his earlier student campaigns DP also offered meetings in the church each evening, reportedly to large congregations. Indeed the St Mary's Motherwell Campaign was in direct continuity with DP's student missions of the 1920s in its reliance on preaching, though now in a wider range of locations and as part of a deliberately comprehensive approach. Yet it also combined both the 'new' commando and the visitation evangelism styles of its immediate predecessors, and to an extent embodied at least some of the recommendations of the Baillie Commission, attempting new, informal opportunities for preaching, the cultivation of special techniques and of the gifts of lay people.

Rev. Joe Ritchie's Edinburgh: McDonald Road Campaign quickly followed that at Motherwell. The parish covered an industrial area and DP calculated that most of the seven to eight thousand people working there lived outside its bounds. The February 1949 campaign therefore emphasised assignments to places of work yet more strongly, and highlighted the parish itself through an exhibition mounted in the Church Hall and by a pamphlet, *By the Water of Leith: The Life of a North Edinburgh Parish*, intended to be distributed during the visitations and based on a survey of streets, factories, leisure and retail facilities. The Church of Scotland monthly magazine, *Life & Work* April 1949, reported:

> The church hall became microcosm of the daily work of the parish. Models of the highly-mechanised steering-gear of the great ships of the Clyde stood alongside examples of the finest modern printing and book-binding; samples of a well-known make of chocolates were there, beside an equally well-known brand of coffee essence. Cakes from a famous firm were iced and decorated in public view during the days of the exhibition. Tobacco-importers, rope-makers, carton-makers, tea merchants (and the Army) were among those represented. The school also had its own exhibit. 'We never knew there was all this in the parish,' many said.

George MacLeod, the Baillie Commission and *Into All the World* had sought to recover a sense of the parish as the locus of Christian witness: press reports cited by DP certainly agreed that the campaign had raised the profile of McDonald Road. He himself was less confident of the result of the visitation aspect of the campaign:

> Saturday, 19th February [1949] . . . The Exhibition was a great success – very striking and much commented on – as 'The Water of Leith' has been likewise. If the house-to-house visitation had been as encouraging, all would have been well.

Although the programmes offered by these three campaigns of DP's may not have been too dissimilar from those Iona Missions being conducted in the same period, there was a rift between DP's focus on outreach to a parish and Iona's focus on the mission of a congregation that would widen over the years as Scottish theology also polarised. Indeed, a growing factional divide can be identified around this time. The Community's membership and influence was increasing in the years immediately after the war, despite the problems George personally had with the courts of the Church of Scotland when he tried unsuccessfully to combine Leadership with acceptance of a call to return to be parish minister at Govan: Old. DP was distressed to find his 1946 annual Report censored by the Convener of the Home Board in favour of a commendation of Iona Missions:

> Tuesday, 22nd May [1947] . . . I heard White Anderson move the deliverance and make the Home Mission Report. He went out on his way to eulogise the Iona Missions and made no reference to any others. In paying tribute to me for my Seaside Mission work he made no reference to my other missions. I then got hold of the Blue Book and found that all I had written in my Report on campaigns had been erased and only what I had written on the Summer Work left in. So now we know just what we are up against! Then came the report on the work of the Iona Community . . . When the sederunt was thrown open for discussion George MacLeod at once came forward. He made a very brilliant speech and claimed that the Community could now speak in the name of the Church. I was never more profoundly disturbed. This is a situation in which we may have to fight and fight desperately. I had a very long talk on the phone with Tom Allan and with Jack Malloch. Tom is as disturbed as I am. Jack was prepared for even worse.

Was the Iona Community seeking so to own the outreach of the Church as to exclude DP and those of his mind? Public controversy did not erupt at this stage, partly because George had his own difficulties, partly because 1947 was White Anderson's last year as Home Board Convener. DP was also aware of the problems that might follow from disputes between those leading the mission of the Church. A generous acceptance of the ministry of others, and not aggression, was near the heart of his faith:

> Sunday, 14th September [1947] . . . It has been for me a seminal forenoon such as I have not had for long. Among the things that came to me were these (1) I must see A. C. Craig and attempt a 'Bridge Building' ere a clash comes with the Iona Community to the delight of the ungodly . . .

At and after North Kelvinside, however, DP very publicly came into territory previously occupied by George. Aggravating divisions was not his intention, but that seems to have been one of the results:

> Wednesday, 26th November [1947] . . . I had a long talk on the phone with George Docherty – he thinks the church is being split into a D. P. Thomson & a George MacLeod party! He is very much concerned about the whole thing! I am grieved about this.

In part the problem came because both George and DP sought to recruit in the Divinity Colleges. Basic to the Iona Community's practice was recruiting men from the Colleges to participate in Iona-supported probationary training. Equally basic to DP's mode of operations since the 1920s, however, had been his leadership of student campaigning: his 1946 Home Board appointment now gave him new access to the Colleges. Divinity students, though, more than most within the Church, were conscious of theological issues and were at the stage of determining their own approach, of defining themselves and developing their own networks. Divisions grew:

> Saturday, 13th December [1947] . . . At 12 noon I addressed St Mary's College – only 20 out of the 50 students came . . . I got on well with the students – the MacLeodites boycotted the meeting.

In 1947 these theological and factional issues between those gathering behind George MacLeod and D. P. Thomson were still a small cloud on the horizon, embryonic or inchoate as far as the wider Kirk was concerned; but they were taking shape.

At this stage George F. MacLeod and D. P. Thomson in fact had many things in common. Both were orators, equally well at home on the soap box in the street as in the pulpit. Both shared a similar vision for the fruitfulness of Christian fellowship, both had a loyalty to the Church of Scotland that did not exclude a wider catholicism; both were prepared to take personal risks to experiment (as they both called it) in order to find channels for new spiritual life. Both were heirs of liberal-evangelicalism, both evangelical in theology, believing profoundly in a God who was, as George's biographer Ronald Ferguson put it, 'both *out there* and *in here*,' yet not too rigorously tied to doctrinal formulations.[27] In 1937 George had publicly welcomed DP's collection of sermons, *Men Christ Wants*, and during the war had on occasions called for tea at Trinity's Manse, enjoying a relationship of mutual respect with DP.[28] On his side, D. P. Thomson could very well have penned what George MacLeod published in *Coracle* in June 1942:[29]

> For Christ is a Person to be trusted, not a principle to be tested. The Church is a Movement, not a meeting house. The Faith is an experience, not an exposition. Christians are Explorers, not map makers.

Indeed, he *already had*, in *Men Christ Wants*, published something very similar!

> Christianity is not a programme to be adopted. It is a life to be lived. It is not a handful of panaceas for the solution of human ills. It is a fellowship of men and women who are pledged to a life of redemptive service in the world by a living faith in a living God . . .

Both men, increasingly influential in the outreach of the Kirk, were committed to making contact with the post-war world.

Home Board Evangelist, 1949

By November 1948 D. P. Thomson had written to the Board announcing that it was time for a change. On his own initiative he expressed an opinion he had been privately pondering since the summer, that attempting to run both Summer Missions and parochial campaigns 'involved a burden of work beyond the strength of one man to carry'. At first the Seaside Convener, Sir James Simpson, was horrified and even angry: there was a chance that DP's letter would be taken as a resignation, a repeat of his departure of 1937-38. This time wiser counsels prevailed and D. P. Thomson remained with the Home Board. How close he came to returning to the wilderness, no-one now will ever know. Evangelism was, after all, what the churches were seeking to do, and Robert Mackintosh was a listening and facilitating General Secretary of the Home Board. The Board's budget still allowed for the engagement of the emissary-evangelists who had not been found. DP offered training to the laity within the model of the Board's existing support for local parishes and Presbyteries. His work could now be presented as contributing to the 'new' evangelism for which the Baillie Commission had called. Moreover in Tom Allan a new, young, gifted enthusiast for mission had emerged. Allan was asked if he would take over the Seaside Services work *per se*, allowing DP to devote himself to campaigns. After discussions it was agreed that Allan would simply take on the next season's work on a part-time basis, seconded from his parish, the Home Board funding his locum at North Kelvinside. D. P. Thomson was then free to be recognised and reappointed as an Evangelist under the Home Board as from 1 January 1949 – it was typical of his edgy relations with the Board that the conditions of his appointment took a year to negotiate. Though not without administrative constraints, his new full time five-year remit was wide-ranging. His primary task was now to be engaged in 'active evangelism' – the old UF term was again used – and to explore throughout Scotland all possibilities for success in the work. The Home Board was to present his appointment as a key part of its response to a rising Communist threat – to the aggressive 'Marxian dialectic materialism directed by the resuscitated Cominform'. The Cold War and the atomic age had replaced the war against Nazi Germany as the background to the call to evangelise for Christ's Kingdom.

The change from Seaside Services Organiser to Evangelist of the Church of Scotland was welcomed by DP, but it also had consequences for his pattern of work. During both 1947 and 1948 he had held mission training schools in the late spring, run seaside missions in the summer and moved on to his experiments in visitation evangelism in the autumn, thus considerably extending the active year for his summer volunteers. With Tom Allan taking over the seaside work from 1 April 1949, however, DP's link with those teams was less direct. After a campaign in Dalmuir Church, Clydebank (March-April 1949) he therefore organised a joint Summer Training School and Campaign by securing an invitation to parishes within the Presbytery of Kintyre. This was akin to shaking a kaleidoscope: a new pattern emerged from the same elements. Pre-summer training events had already offered involvement in evangelistic activities; now a School would undertake a full campaign of its own, attempting to visit all homes in the entire rural peninsula, and yet remain a School in Evangelism. Perhaps a desire to offer his young people an opportunity to spend their holiday campaigning in an attractive, country area of Scotland was part of his choice of location – the adventure of the thing was also a draw. Perhaps, too, DP was attracted to Kintyre by its historical associations, including those with St Ninian, his own personal 'patron saint'.

From Kintyre in 1949 came two of DP's pamphlets based on the romanticism of local church history, *In Happened in Kintyre!* and *Kintyre Through the Centuries*, part of a series of such pamphlets that he enjoyed researching and writing, and that were sold to publicise and (ideally) to help to finance his campaigns. His best account of the Kintyre Training School was given as the last chapter of *Kintyre Through the Centuries*, 'The Invasion of Largie Castle':

> To Largie Castle in the middle of August, 1949 – by motor-bicycle, by special bus and shooting-brake, and on foot, to the number of about fifty – came the members of the Church of Scotland Summer Training School in Kintyre, a very miscellaneous company. Down in the entrance hall of the castle, which served as refectory and office, they mingled and talked – ministers, divinity and other students, day-school teachers and landed proprietors, young men and women from office and bank, from shop and factory; some from as far away as Aberdeenshire and the Solway, and even from Italy and Africa, others from Kintyre itself.
>
> A quite unusual type of Summer School this was – capable of being mounted on a seven-ton lorry and completely mobile, so far as its equipment was concerned; staffed, both in kitchen and classroom, entirely by voluntary workers who shared to the full in the life of the fellowship;

> combining in the most realistic way possible theoretical and practical training; and making its facilities available both for those on holiday and for those who were at their daily work in Campbeltown, some eighteen miles away . . .
>
> Within the castle itself was activity and variety in abundance. On the floors of the upstairs rooms were stretched palliasses which had once been intended for the needs of air-raid victims, serving – with a handful of army blankets and a pillow to each – as beds for the trainees. In the cosy dining room gathered for study each forenoon and evening those whose period it was indoors (next day they might be out visiting) while down in the kitchen went forward a schedule which provided for the manifold needs of this company from '1st Breakfast' at 6.45 (for those beginning work in Campbeltown at 8) to 'last Supper,' for those coming in from late visitation, just before midnight.
>
> An unforgettable experience this was, destined to leave its mark on many lives. Already from that Summer School with its fun and its fellowship, its deep commerce of mind with mind and heart with heart, its open air and indoor meetings, and its visitation of home, farm and tourist hotel, have gone three young men to whom the call came in August, to begin their preparation for the ministry; while others have returned to their homes and daily work with a new vision of possibilities, a new sense of loyalty to Christ and His Church, and a new realisation of the meaning of Christian discipleship.

DP believed not just in open air preaching but also in open door hospitality. His schools were open to any who wished to attend, for a session or for the entire course, whether residential or on a daily basis. The Kintyre teams were therefore composed not just of those coming on from that summer's seaside missions, young people and students: one reporter reckoned that while when he visited 52 were in residence, another 80-100 were coming on from their work to the evening sessions. *Life & Work's* reporter believed that those who gained most were the foot-soldiers of the campaign, those who came from Kintyre's own congregations. The School was of course made welcome by the local ministers. Clerk to both the Presbytery of Kintyre and the Synod of Argyll, Angus MacVicar led the initial welcome service at St Columba's Church, Southend; the Moderator of Presbytery, John R. H. Cormack, hosted the welcome when the School moved to Carradale. In the nature of things, however, the School had its own corporate (if shifting) fellowship and so its own forceful initiator and leader was yet more in the driving seat during the Kintyre Campaign in relation to the individual parish ministers than DP had been at North Kelvinside, St Mary's or at McDonald Road. It was DP who preached at the open-air service in the ruins of Saddell Abbey; his guest, Prof. David Cairns of Aberdeen University, led the praise while the parish minister was simply one of the congregation.

The McDonald Road Campaign and the Kintyre Training School were not the only missions that DP led during 1949, though they were the only ones to feature in his subsequent booklets. The Report of the Home Board to the 1950 General Assembly offered an account of its new Evangelist's first year, described as comprising campaigns largely 'of an experimental nature', conducted also in Aberdeenshire, South Ayrshire, Campbeltown and Dalreoch Parish, Dumbarton. In time this word 'experiment,' which both George F. MacLeod and DP used so often, was to become suspect.[30] There was a growing reluctance to use terminology that suggested that Christian mission could be conducted with laboratory-style detachment or as a sort of spiritual physics, so that one learnt to do *this* and expect *that*. But DP was simply accepting the logic of the day and of his Board. The post-war consensus of the home missionary elite was that the old methods had had their day – they did not work. So, what did work? If the 'old evangelism' had indeed lost its impact, by what means could the Churches contact the people of the post-war world in the name of Christ? It was a natural question, and one that DP sought to answer. Appointed to investigate 'the possibilities of successful evangelism in any part of the country', during 1946-1949 DP tried new combinations and new approaches; he recruited new classes of people to his teams and he initiated new training methods.

Not all the experiments were equally successful: indeed, doubts were raised during 1949 about the evangelistic effectiveness of visitation itself. In his General Assembly report DP summarised the results of his School in Kintyre: 'While the meetings were largely attended and very valuable work was done among the trainees themselves, the results of house to house visitation in this case were rather less than had been hoped for.' Much the same was said of his Easter 1949 campaign based between Inverurie and Alford, conducted with a team drawn from the city of Aberdeen that included ministers, students, school teachers and senior schoolboys. House to house visiting with literature was tackled in three rural parishes spanning the Presbyteries of Garioch and Alford and the reception varied somewhat from district to district. Reading between the lines, the teams had reasonable sales for their literature but made no further impact on the people of Aberdeenshire, who may well have considered that they had no need to be evangelised, appearing reluctant to talk about matters of the faith. DP recommended that on a future occasion older and stronger methods be used: 'The next campaign of this kind held in a rural area should take a somewhat different line, house to house visitation being followed by a week of special meetings.' What spiritual impression had been made had come through direct contact with the environment of the team's central fellowship: 'In Inverurie itself a very real impact was made on the young life of the town, particularly through the medium of the common table in the campaign billet.'

By contrast the miners of South Ayrshire were certainly prepared to talk and to debate with the team, but not to respond further in any of the ways expected during campaigns. Compared to the taciturn people of the countryside, 'the miners were much more ready to discuss personal religion and to raise problems in the field of applied Christian ethics, but much less ready to respond in the way of attending meetings of any kind or to purchase literature.' A campaign similar to Inverurie and North Kelvinside had been attempted, essentially of colportage, house to house visitation with literature, from the central base of Patna. What was recommended for the future was, again, based on what was known to gather an audience: children's work, as practised at seaside missions.

Campbeltown itself had been deliberately excluded from the visitations carried out by the Kintyre Summer School, though activists from its congregations had attended for preparatory training. Learning the lesson of Inverurie, visitation was not in itself the campaign but only preparatory to a special week: 'a crowded week during which an appeal was made to the community through the medium of cinema, drama and exhibitions, one of which featured the spiritual heritage of the area, while the other sought to present the challenge of the present national and world situation.' DP was pleased with the response to the exhibitions and also that inter-denominational cooperation had enabled the visitors to compile a complete survey of church-going and Sunday school attendance. Little was claimed in terms of growing membership for the Church of Scotland congregations in Campbeltown, though their numbers were increasing in this period. Indeed, of the six 1949 campaigns, only for those at McDonald Road (where some 50 new members were acknowledged) and at Dalreoch Parish, Dumbarton was 'an immediate harvest in the shape of new members and fresh homes linked up with the church' claimed. Dalreoch was a campaign in a single parish, conducted on established summer mission lines and with summer mission teams, well supported by the local young people.

Volunteers from the parish had previously gained experience by participating in the team for the Glasgow: Martyrs Campaign. DP rejoiced at the news of three post-meeting conversions.

One conclusion, then, might have been drawn from these experiments: that Scotland's rural communities reacted to visitation in ways entirely different from the estates and suburbs of the cities. The rural kirk was, in fact, to remain largely resistant to special evangelism of any kind throughout the 1950s. The success of North Kelvinside and the other estate and suburban campaigns may have benefited from the desire of their post-war populations for the stability of belonging; at any rate to social as well as to spiritual factors. The old couple in North Kelvinside so assisted by Douglas Rothnie appreciated *as a package* spiritual enlightenment from Tom Allan, the Woman's Guild, the Old Folks Club and the weekly concert. There is some evidence that the new estates or housing schemes on the outskirts of Edinburgh and Glasgow had lower rates of connection to the churches than elsewhere in Scotland. There, therefore, was also the scope for greater growth.[31] Another conclusion was also possible from DP's immediate post-war work: the most rewarding in terms of increasing church attendance and membership were indeed the most local campaigns, those relating to individual parishes, though even these were not invariably successful. Something of the importance of locality he did understand. Though his focus in 1950 was to be the truly massive Mid-Century Campaign in Paisley, intended to be a comprehensive mission in a major urban setting, a decision was taken to use only the people of Paisley's churches:

> This, in point of fact, represented one of the most important decisions we had come to in our thinking and in our planning; that if the 'Threefold Simultaneous Approach' was to achieve its maximum impact, then the Campaign Team must be drawn wholly from local congregations.

This conclusion, however, contained in his retrospective *Aspects of Evangelism*, was hardly reflected in DP's own practice of the later 1950s – nor was it even scrupulously followed at Paisley itself. A key dilemma for the church of this time was just how to relate successful outreach with the need to stimulate spiritual growth within the existing congregations. DP was both an evangelist and increasingly a pastor of a dispersed flock: the balance of his own efforts was to alter over time.

D. P. THOMSON, EVANGELIST

'It is not *what* I believe that matters in the end of the day; it is in *Whom* I have put my trust; it is to *Whom* I have committed my life.'

D. P. Thomson, *When Christ Calls*

Where in DP's practice did the balance lie between new and old, between direct and indirect evangelism? Certainly he became especially associated with visitation evangelism, the 'new' method that Tom Allan particularly contrasted with that of the 'great public meeting'.[1] Yet, as they developed over the years, DP's campaigns were hybrid creatures, with substantial continuity from the past. By 1949 DP had been engaged in evangelism for over 30 years; it can be fairly said that, though he remained open to new techniques, his underlying theological thinking was mature. Before we reach the busiest period of his life, a short summary may be helpful.

Considered as an evangelist, six characteristics can be identified of D. P. Thomson at the age of 53. First, he was indeed an evangelist: since 1917 he had become experienced, when addressing congregations, to appeal for commitment to Jesus Christ and to look for conversions. On many occasions he had been asked to front campaigns in Scotland and overseas as the key speaker. Unlike other such evangelists, however, DP was not exclusively an evangelistic preacher. When, post-war, he preached *ad hoc* around the country as a guest preacher, his sermons – while direct and challenging – were not so explicitly demanding an immediate decision as those of his 1920s missions; he had a teaching ministry both in and outside the pulpit, as, indeed, he had had at both his own congregations. Moreover he consistently placed an emphasis on working with teams, often in a residential setting. With this came an emphasis on learning by doing. He increasingly understood the value of his work not only in terms of any who might be converted but also in terms of the growth in Christian usefulness and maturity of those who comprised the teams themselves. This is very clear in *The Road to Dunfermline* where he listed, among the 'fruits of the work' of the student campaigns, a selection of eminent ministers, professors and missionaries: 'Men like these would be the first to confess how much they owed to both the training and the fellowship they enjoyed in the ranks of the Student Campaign Movement.' When

DP recommenced the Summer Mission work of the Church of Scotland after the war, it was entirely consistent with his track-record that he should hold residential training schools for his team members, now drawn from a broader spectrum of society.

In his own way DP was thus, secondly, a pastor: keen to see those who were already Christian go on in Christ, though his calling was not primarily to the parish ministry. In *Men Christ Wants* he identified from the Gospels (and presumably from autobiographical insight) a pattern of vocational progression from 'fisherman' to 'shepherd', from evangelist to pastor. Perhaps his reputation suffered from this lack of an identifiable single focus; but he had a big-picture mind, seeing connections and always trying to learn from others. It was consonant with this breadth of mind that the third aspect of his evangelical churchmanship was his catholicity, a preparedness to work with and learn from others: the Episcopal, Methodist and other denominations; the Oxford Group Movement; the Iona Community. This life-long willingness was closely related to his third characteristic, his internationalism, derived from his youthful and lasting commitment to foreign mission in the era following Edinburgh 1910. Belief in an inclusive church was also an integral part of the liberal-evangelicism of Henry Sloane Coffin, to whom DP acknowledged an intellectual debt. Certainly his own catholicity was a function of his commitment to Christ and His Church, and detracted neither from his evangelical faith nor from his loyalty to the Church of Scotland, which we may list as the fourth and fifth aspects of his mature vocation as an evangelist.

D. P. Thomson did not think of himself as a fundamentalist in theology: but even those then leading the definitively conservative IVF distinguished themselves from American fundamentalism.[2] As regards DP's approach to Scripture, he was willing in *Why I Believe* to admit that, during his college education for the ministry, he had moved from 'a more rigidly fundamentalist' view of Biblical inspiration held in his youth. Yet respect for Scripture as his authority for faith and conduct, taking the plain sense of the words within their context, lies behind all his work and is especially evident in *Men Christ Wants*. DP wrote, certainly, in *Aspects of Evangelism*, of the need to separate the 'kernel from the husk in the application of Christian truth'. By this he meant the need (long recognised in the field of foreign mission) for the proclamation of Christ to be understandable in terms of the culture and vocabulary of the hearers. DP called for a contextual, relevant and appropriate evangelism suitable to the needs of the time and place but always based on what God had revealed in Christ.

He had no doubt at all that the Bible is the revealed and reliable record of the person and work of Jesus Christ, through which the Spirit still speaks to the heart. See, for example, his *Beginning the Christian Life, a First Month's Daily Bible Readings from the New Testament for Young People*:

> Every day, however crowded, you must make time for the study of the Bible. You will discover it to be more and more a source of instruction and of inspiration, as you advance in the Christian life.

It is also true that DP did not focus on the doctrinal issue then central to the conservative evangelical position, the substitutionary atonement, but that did not mean that it was not present in his thinking. He wrote in *Aspects of Evangelism* that making a 'moral decision' to follow Christ 'is not enough'. Pardon for sin was an essential part of the Gospel he preached, but not the sole part: 'It is the evangelist's joy to tell men of a Saviour who not merely delivers and pardons, but who empowers for conflict and for service.' He believed that the decision to accept or reject Christ was one between salvation and 'the outer darkness' but he was not one to seek to frighten by speaking of the reality of hell: he preferred an appeal that summoned to service and eternal life.[3] The Holy Spirit's work of conversion and sanctification was an essential part of DP's Trinitarian faith. But DP preferred not to pack the Spirit into a theological box. He was conscious of his own human weaknesses, and those of others: in *The Road to Dunfermline* he portrayed the Christian life as a life-long pilgrimage in devotion and obedience:

> Suffice it to say that I have long since learned from my study of history and biography, from my own clinical work, and, above all, in the personal experience of life – that it is not by one cataclysmic experience of conversion, nor by a second of entire sanctification, but more often by a series of definite crises, or discernable landmarks, spread over the whole of our earthly pilgrimage, and each taking us at once 'further ben with God,' and higher up the hill, that we progress in the spiritual life.

When asked in 1942 to clarify the position he took on some theological issues, DP had declined to satisfy his questioner: 'Jock Troup tackled me before the Noon Meeting – about my beliefs – demanding my positions on certain points. I quite failed to satisfy him.' DP was very clear in *When Christ Calls*, when speaking about Christian commitment, that 'It is not *what* I believe that matters in the end of the day; it is in *Whom* I have put my trust.' On another occasion, after hearing a speaker at an IVF conference, DP wrote:

> Saturday, 24th May [1947] . . . He was very legalistic and dogmatic in his address on the Cross – [*but it is*] not my theology [*that finally counts*], but my Crucified Lord, let me never forget – my Jesus as well as his, and he ever my brother in Christ.

Not an academic theologian, DP empathised with ministerial academics like J. S. Stewart and, of the next generation, with Tom Torrrace, but he himself simply refused to dogmatise, beyond a few essentials, on the mechanisms of the relationship between frail humans and the Almighty. From *The Road to Dunfermline* again:

> *I know that I am saved,* that Christ has redeemed me with His own precious blood. *I know that I am being saved* – that His Spirit is at work in my life, both in ways I can appreciate and in ways of which I am at least dimly aware. *And I know that one day I will be saved* – that the weakness and frailty of the flesh will be transmuted into an instrument through which I can serve Him as I really ought. But just how and when it all comes about is a matter on which I am no longer prepared to dogmatise.

Within the Bible he was most at home in the Gospels and Acts rather than in Romans or the other epistles. Perhaps the clearest systematic account of the essentials of his faith may be implied from his tractate *Pocket Guide for Personal Workers*, reprinted in *Aspects of Evangelism,* where redemption through 'the precious blood of Christ', 'the complete transformation of heart and life which a real experience of Christ brings', 'the limitless possibilities of the new life in Christ', all take their place among the other doctrines.[4] DP preached Jesus in a holistic way that emphasised the Resurrection:

> I must strive to present Christ in all His fulness – the whole Christ to meet the needs of the whole man; not merely his Saviourhood, but Christ as Lord and Master, as Teacher and Friend, as Satisfier and Sanctifier; as the One who begins His work of grace in us at the moment of trust and committal, and will carry it on till finally completed, not here but hereafter.

He indeed displayed that Christ-centred-ness that Oliver Barclay saw as the final evangelical characteristic.[5]

By nature and personality a warm-hearted but sometimes lonely man who stood apart from the various factions within the ministry, D. P. Thomson was not considered a conservative evangelical in the terms that the largely English leaders of the IVF of the 1950s and 1960s understood. He was not one of them – his catholicism, indeed, separated him from them. Neither did he belong to the somewhat later and distinctively Scottish version of conservative evangelicalism, the 'Crieff Fraternal' of friends of William Still, dedicated to (besides a Calvinistic approach to theology) the systematic exposition of Scripture. While DP sought to follow his call to be an evangelist, he also accepted the advice of W. M. Clow and chose the path of the ordained ministry of Word and Sacrament within a national denomination rather than a life's work with 'County Christian Unions and the Mission Halls'. Because D. P. Thomson was a Bible-believing person and a gospel preacher, he was also a churchman,[6] proud to be a minister of what he described in *Through Sixteen Centuries*: 'the strongest, freest, richest, most warmly evangelical and at the same time truly catholic, Established Church to be found anywhere in the world today.' More than this, he knew that Christ had called him into the fellowship and discipline of His visible Church. If membership and ministry within the Church of Scotland as part of Christ's Church meant working with – meant fellowship with – those who did not fully share his formulation of his faith, DP was prepared to live with that as part of his calling. He did not operate on a factional basis; his services were available to all Christian congregations in Scotland.

D. P. Thomson as an evangelist was, finally, special in the degree to which he multi-tasked. A compulsive worker, besides everything else he was normally engaged in some aspect of 'the ministry of the pen' – the purchasing of books, his eclectic reading (systematically card-indexed); whatever writing project was on the go. Sometimes these projects resulted in booklets that supported his current campaigns; more often, it has to be said, they did not. Multi-tasking also meant that he was a great traveller. Provided he was present for the addresses and meetings for which he was booked, DP was well able to spend much of a week in which he was leading a campaign actually miles away from the location – preparing future plans, attending other committees, honouring previous engagements. It would be easy to say that this manner of working was built into the remit of the Organiser of Seaside Missions – and of course it was, he had oversight of simultaneous missions at numerous sites on both coasts – but, in fact, this tendency was obvious from the very first of the GSEU campaigns back at Greenock in 1922. Ever since his ASC war service he had been an organiser: planning, recruiting, delegating, and now trusting God for the outcome. This manner of working was to be a requirement of the 1950s visiting campaigns, for the leadership of which his gifts and experience particularly qualified him.

One entry in D. P. Thomson's 17th Diary serves to illustrate much of this analysis of his characteristics as he approached his climatic years:

> Sunday, 21st November [1948] . . . Within the last few days I have had two invitations that have given me a great deal of food for thought. One was to be a speaker at the 1st Post-War Strathpeffer Convention in October: the other was a renewed invitation from the Londonderry Churches – a city in which I have never opened my lips for Christ – to conduct a United Mission there. To the first I said a regretful but unhesitating 'No'. I realise that I am not a Convention speaker – neither my life, my doctrine nor my experience qualify me. I tried once in early days at Bangor – then I had the qualifications – in embryo at least and then I succeeded but I have come to doubt the emphasis I then put and the experience I then desiderated. 30 years went by and I tried again – at Dumfries. I failed, quite conspicuously – and I was the only speaker. I failed. I will need some clearer compulsion than the Strathpeffer invitation to try again. Londonderry is another matter. It is the second city of Northern Ireland – big, but not too big. It presents a tremendous challenge. It bristles with problems and it may afford the chance of a very far-reaching experiment. God has undoubtedly opened doors to me in Ulster and has given me my place in the heart of Irish Presbyterianism. There are two things I would count it a joy to do – to make some contribution to the breaking down the barriers between Protestant and Catholic, and to the sweetening of the atmosphere: and to help (as I believe I already have done in some small measure) to a new and worthier conception of evangelism than dear W. P. Nicholson and his like have done. I am writing to make certain proposals to them.

DP had been one of the speakers at the Faith Mission Convention at Bangor in April 1919 at a time when his emphasis was very much a dispensational approach to the Second Coming of Christ and when he looked for decisive and public experiences of conversion and sanctification. By 1948 he was clear that he no longer held these doctrinal positions nor did he insist on such an immediate, clear-cut response to the Gospel. He was not, in fact, a preacher of doctrine so much as of Christ and, after offering a series compiled from his existing addresses to a June 1947 local Bible Convention at Dumfries, he had come – no doubt correctly – to see himself as unqualified to give the sort of devotional, systematic and detailed unpacking of a Biblical passage that the Scottish Northern or 'Strathpeffer' Convention, a off-shoot of Keswick, expected. That these invitations were issued still showed how respected and accepted DP was, not only 'in the heart of Irish Presbyterianism' but also by constituencies within the more traditional wing of Scottish evangelicalism. That he could envisage – *in 1948!* – working to break down the barriers between Protestant and Roman Catholic in Northern Ireland shows without doubt his breadth of view and the irenic trajectory of his mature faith. He valued as a brother in Christ W. P. Nicholson, an Irish presbyterian evangelist with a worldwide ministry, a man very much in the older tradition of issuing an appeal and demanding a response; yet DP himself sought 'a new and worthier conception of evangelism' suitable for the post-war world. He was not, in fact, to go to Londonderry.

DP's own thoughts on a 'new evangelism' had been developing for 20 years:

> Saturday 12th August [1950] . . . I am at work at last in deadly earnest on the book I have promised myself for 20 years to write on Evangelism. I have completed two of the seven chapters. Here it is –
>
> A NEW APPROACH TO EVANGELISM
>
> 1. A New Approach To Evangelism
> 2. Beginning With The Ministry
> 3. The Evangelisation Of The Parish
> 4. The Training Of The Lay Forces
> 5. The Way Of The Incarnation
> 6. The Gospel In The Open Air
> 7. At Grips With The Individual.

Regrettably, this was another book DP was not to finish; not, at least, in the form outlined in 1950. *Beginning with the Ministry* and *The Way of the Incarnation* did, however, appear as separate pamphlets and *Aspects of Evangelism* (1968) undoubtedly contained much on which he had pondered since the late 1920s. The essence of his thought was that evangelism was the task, not just of the 'professional peripatetic' but of the whole church: of the ordained ministry and also of the congregation, corporately and individually. Yes, *Beginning with the Ministry* so that the call to Christ found its place in all the normal round of parish life, but extending outwards to the enabling of 'The Lay Forces' in circles of real and vital Christian fellowship. Evangelism, moreover, was to be liberated from the pulpit and taken out into the Open Air, to wherever people gathered for work and leisure, the beach and the factory, the whist drive, the pub, the Masonic meeting and the young people's dance. The 'new and worthier conception of evangelism' that DP harboured was evangelism at home in the ordinary life of the church, and that life turned outwards to engagement with wider society. At its simplest, it meant Christians visiting and witnessing to their neighbours.

In an address DP gave to members of the Rotary Club in Forfar in 1953, during his Strathmore Campaign, he compared the Kirk's current methods with those of old time revivals. In the future, the Church of Scotland had decided, DP said, that mission was to be based upon the parish, as the minister and his workers made contact with the people around them.[7] This was, of course, the party line: though described as 'new,' DP was in fact reiterating – with the Baillie Commission – with George F. MacLeod – what had been the objective of the 1929 Union, that the Church's life and outreach should be based around an effective working of the parish system. What he summarised as the new technique was in direct continuity with home mission policy as enunciated by Arthur Dunnett in 1934. Visiting homes, mounting exhibitions, the use of cinema and drama, speaking assignments at places of work, literature distribution and sales; rallies, special meetings and children's work: the balance between possible activities differed from place to place. Certainly no campaign now took place without a substantial element of systematic visiting, whether as the principal element of outreach or to draw up a survey preliminary to more focused pastoral work. This was one of the new elements within the church's practice and one particularly associated with DP. By contrast with the 'old' evangelism, with its appeal publicly to stand to signify decision or to come for counselling there and then, the 'new' fed those it attracted into the normal patterns of congregational life, to the route to church membership via classes for new communicants. 'Results' were measured not so much in conversions as by congregational growth. The increasing length and intensity of campaigns was another new feature as a new car-based mobility, card-index managerial techniques, and the media of newsprint and radio broadcast were all exploited to achieve maximum saturation. New to DP in the post-war years was also his understanding of those on whom the outreach of the Church would depend. Whereas in his earlier years he had worked with students, and during the war with ministers, now he often bypassed the ordained (whether ministers or elders) and increasingly placed his trust in the men and in the women he found, not in Scotland's universities, but in its pews.

FAMILY MATTERS AND PAISLEY MID-CENTURY, 1949-1951

> Friday, 23rd December [1949] . . . I asked my Lord for five years to do the work of an evangelist when I left Cambuslang. On that reckoning and basis I can only count on one more – may it be in every way the best of all – and may I be given the strength to gather up the threads and put all in order before my time comes to go.
>
> D. P. Thomson, The Diary of My Life part 17

Towards the end of 1949 D. P. Thomson had again felt himself to be at a turning point – indeed, he had been wondering whether the world might not be at a turning point. More than ever he had sensed that he might not have long left to live. His vision of the future was clouded and New Year 1950 was a time of anxiety and loneliness. One measure of a man is how he copes with such times. In retrospect, we now know that DP was about to begin a series of major regional campaigns of visitation evangelism, the campaigns that would result in the 1966 General Assembly declaring him 'one of the outstanding leaders of the Church in this generation'. A number of his publications contain his own accounts and summaries of these campaigns. The objectives of these booklets were threefold: hortatory, to encourage others to follow the same patterns; apologetic, to defend and justify the path he had taken; and devotional, to give thanks to God for his guidance and power. DP thus sought to show the continuity that lay behind his ministry of the 1950s. Now, over 50 years later, we can also look at the challenges he faced, giving an account of his work in the contexts both of his personal life and that of the overall outreach of the Kirk in Scotland. It was by no means a smooth path that he trod and it took strength to walk it.

Family Matters

Even for a devout Christian it is not easy to be told that your health has been seriously damaged and that your life-expectancy is short. In 1921 D. P. Thomson had written in his 6th Diary:

Sunday, 27th November [1921] Here I am at Kilmacolm again, another year having nearly run its course. Looking back I praise God for his goodness in the 4 years that have elapsed since I got my discharge from the Army. Told then that I would be a semi-invalid all my days, I can look back on 4 years during which I have not had 3 days in bed at any time and not 10 altogether.

By November 1949 he had lived with that 'at best a semi-invalid' diagnosis for over thirty years in an age before either the inauguration of the National Health Service (July 1948) or the widespread use of X-rays, CT and now MRI scans, non-invasively to investigate internal conditions. During his time at Cambuslang he had grown increasingly concerned about his health, in his diaries recording the various symptoms he perceived in his heart, appendix, stomach (ulcers), bowels and lower organs in general, besides rupture, possible migraine, a more general rheumatism and considerable dental problems. By 1942 he was writing:

Friday, 29th May [1942] I have been very unwell in the past few days . . . the moments are not few when I feel that my days are numbered. I would like to see the Fellowship on its feet and to get my books written but I fear that is too much to hope now.

His operation of June 1943 eased his mind, but from January 1944 his concerns were again growing:

Saturday, 1st January 1944 Yesterday . . . I felt my wound get very sore – and realised that my operation had not succeeded. I hope they may not have burst – but it limits me more than ever. Taken with my heart murmur I suddenly realised that all thought of an itinerant evangelism abroad must go – if I am to leave Trinity it will be for a lighter sphere now.

Saturday, 10th May [1947] A week today, if I am spared, I will be 51. I never thought to see that day – or this! Bodily infirmity is increasing upon me. There is deep seated rheumatism (at least, so I judge it to be) coming out now through my hands and down my legs. No manifest swelling yet but considerable pressure pain and in parts sore to the touch. It is just a question now how long I will be able to carry on, and what I will manage to get through this summer!

Death, in itself, was not the issue. DP believed firmly in both the Resurrection of Christ and of the promise of the eternal Kingdom of Heaven for Christians: he thus wrote of death, both of his family and of his own, as 'going home'. Because DP believed in the providence of God, in the personal oversight by his Master of his life, he was inclined to over-interpret events as signs for his guidance. It is hardly surprising that during those years of the 1940s when he was excluded from national affairs, when his parish ministry seemed unfruitful, after they had learnt that Mary would be unable to conceive, that DP interpreted as all of a piece with these what he guessed to be symptoms of impending internal organ failure and drew the conclusion that his earthly life, already extended well beyond the expert prognosis of 1916, was nearly over.

In this context D. P. Thomson's decision to leave Cambuslang can be understood as a prayer: a request to complete his work, to complete his life by returning to the beginnings of his ministry, to evangelism. That, indeed, had been his prayer, and he believed it had been answered. If DP's approach to work, to life, seemed pragmatic, about doing what came to hand; if it often seemed hyper-active, we should remember that for years he was unable to take a long-term view: very simply, in his heart of hearts, he did not believe he had a long-term future in this world, and so he made the very most of the time lent to him.

Thus understanding D. P. Thomson's underlying perception of his health and available time, we can also understand how devastated he was when in the autumn of 1949 Mary Thomson determined to make a previously postponed visit to Jamaica. Mary Rothnie had had, of course, very little time back in 1938 to adjust to her engagement to the evangelist from Scotland or to the thought of leaving employment and her father's home. She had in fact returned to Jamaica for a brief period in 1940, two years into their marriage, and the time of parting had been hard for both herself and her husband. Not unnaturally Douglas Rothnie remained dear to his daughter; and, indeed, he was much respected by DP. Besides a constant flow of letters, the Thomsons supported his ministry from afar by talks and lectures. During the Woman's Guild 1944-45 season, for example, DP gave his Jamaican lantern-lecture to Woman's Guild branches at Bridge of Weir (October), Tollcross-Victoria (November), Netherlee congregation and Stonelaw Church, Rutherglen (February), MacGregor Memorial Church, Govan, and Springburn Hill Woman's Guild (March). Mary also accepted invitations to speak on her 'Blessed Isle'. Hospitality was given to Jamaicans visiting Scotland: servicemen during the war, and girls in training or 'in service' thereafter. A 'Jamaica Tea' was held annually in Edinburgh while the General Assembly was meeting and, even if DP himself was elsewhere, Mary made a point of attending.

In 1947 Douglas Rothnie and Kathie themselves visited Scotland on furlough:

> Tuesday, 7th May [1947] . . . Mary is all excited with preparations for Father's coming. He should be here at the weekend if all goes well . . .
>
> Friday, 9th May [1947] . . . Wire today to say that Father comes on Sunday at eight . . .

Saturday, 10th May [1947] . . . Father will have landed . . .

Monday, 12th May [1947] Father is not long away to bed! Kathie went much earlier. They arrived on Sunday at nine and what a load of stuff they had with them – three sacks of bananas, three cases of fruit, trunks etc. . . . Father is looking amazingly well – I was, if anything, holding back the tears when his train drew in at the platform. A great man – a truly great man.

The Rothnies returned to Jamaica at the end of October 1947 after an extended stay that included his presentation to the Moderator of the General Assembly, participation in summer mission, preaching, visits to his native Aberdeenshire and general touring, accompanied during June by Mary, sometimes to DP's suppressed jealousy:

Tuesday, 22nd May [1947] This is Foreign Mission Day at the General Assembly. Mary will be there and tonight she will see Father welcomed by the Moderator from the Moderator's Gallery, for which I have managed to get her a ticket. Dear Lass, she is so happy to be able to have her dear father in her own home and to be able to make him happy and comfortable and to see him at his ease at last.

Tuesday, 3rd June [1947] I hurried eagerly home from Ayrshire, but it looks as if I am not particularly wanted and were indeed rather in the way. I am an upsetting influence to the orderly household plans. And so I have no desire to stay.

Thursday, 5th June [1947] I am sitting in the upstairs lounge of Winston Private Hotel in Dumfries, at the writing desk . . . Later I phoned Mary. There are twin beds in my room and I am alone at a little table. It seems providential – yet she may not feel she can come . . . [*Later*] No word from Mary. I fear she is not coming. Perhaps it was too much to hope. We may never holiday together again.

Although DP took the opportunity of Douglas Rothnie's availability to obtain from him materials for two projected books, one on the church history of Jamaica, and one a biography *Rothnie of Lucea,* neither book was to be completed. By the end of the Rothnies' stay, however, it had been agreed that the Thomsons would pay a return visit to the West Indies:

Wednesday, 29th October [1947] At eight o'clock on Monday, after a quiet and happy Sunday evening in the drawing room, we sat down to our last meal at number 32. Will the next be in Jamaica – or will it be the 'Marriage Supper of the Lamb'? They left on the 10 train and are due to embark and sail on the *Jamaican Producer* tomorrow from West India Dock, London. In 14 months time we should sail, if we are ever to go! I wonder – I wonder greatly!!!

On 4 December 1949 Douglas Rothnie was 76: he was not, in fact, to retire until 1958, having been in Jamaica since 1901. Over the period the island had undergone profound change and periodic civil unrest, an influx of American troops during the War and a recession accompanied by widespread poverty following the peace. Mary was no doubt concerned for his health, his ministry and their people; she had committed herself to a visit in early 1949 but agreed to abandon their plans when, just at the critical moment, DP was appointed Evangelist of the Church. Perhaps, however, she felt more disappointed than DP's account of cancellation of their tickets suggests he felt:

> Tuesday, 30th November [1948] I have been on to Tom Allan on the phone and have told him what I forgot to record overleaf – namely that I learnt from Mackintosh . . . on the phone yesterday that the Evangelism Subcommittee had approved of the scheme whereby I am appointed Evangelist of the Church & Tom Allan becomes my Deputy for Seaside Work . . . 8pm . . . I worked at home to 3.30 and then went to town. I booked my sleeper to London, cancelled our passages for Jamaica, bought three books for Father and Christine, picked up two excellent little books on Edinburgh, went through the Edinburgh telephone directory to check information for the McDonald Road campaign and tried on new boots.

A further year on and Mary felt that circumstances were now right for her to go, if necessary alone. She played an active part in DP's work, especially in seaside missions: but he was no longer Seaside Mission Organiser and he had no campaigns planned for early 1950 apart from an unaccompanied visit to Ireland. She had saved up funds in an account of her own and could afford her own ticket. And so . . .

> Friday, 9th December [1949] Mary is away getting her hair permed. She has made up her mind to go to Jamaica, though she knows that I am against it. My heart and my judgement alike refuse to acquiesce in this decision. I feel it is the ending of more than a chapter in our lives – it is a veritable parting of the ways and we will never resume on the same footing again, if resume we do. However Mary is convinced that the way has opened for her going and in my opposition I find myself in a minority of one! . . . She has made up our mind to go and three weeks today, unless something drastic supervenes, she will be on the sea. After that – what? I don't know . . . I may be far away from 32 Leven Street when the little lass comes back, if she ever does, which I gravely doubt. No, it is the parting of the ways – after 10 unforgettable years with many hours of unalloyed bliss amid their ups and downs! Jamaica – the Isle of beauty – you gave me a wife and now you are robbing me of one. With one

hand you gave – with the other you take! . . . My poor old heart is fair done – truth to tell – and whiles I weary for Home!

Christmas Day! Sunday, 25th December [1949] . . . This is our last precious Sunday together – the last, perhaps, that we will ever have. I am feeling very far through, my strength is spent, my heart weak and tired and I have this queer feeling in my head – always at the one spot, where there seems to me to be a slight swelling. Only three more nights together now and then three precious days before my darling leaves me. I hope the winds and waves will be kind to her as she journeys away from me into the warmth and sunshine of the tropics, to the great and loving welcome that awaits in the dear home of her childhood by the sea . . .

Wednesday, 28th December [1949] . . . This is our last day together – dark and cold and wet it is outside . . . And now the sadness of farewell. The dear lass has no realisation of how weak and how far through I feel. I lay in bed this morning wondering if I could stand up and if the shock of her going would itself finish me. Sometimes when I wake in the early morning hours I feel very near to 'Journey's End.' . . . And now to the overseas correspondence again, while dear Mary packs for her long trip and big adventure. Oh, that it should come to this! 10.40 pm My darling has gone! At half past eight, we were alone and we sat quietly weeping, she on my knee, holding tight. We dried our tears and read and talked a little and then I made the supper. We had tea and a biscuit each. I had intended reading and writing now awhile and having another tea, but have no more notion of that. After we had supper we knelt together by the fireside, arms around one another as we always do, and we each prayed, I first, then we made quietly ready and there was no hurry when the taxi came. A nice car and a friendly man, a quick and easy run in and we were there. I bought for her a magazine and an evening paper and meanwhile, in pouring rain, she found her sleeper and got her luggage in. I stayed in the corridor till after 10, then we had our last loving 'Goodbye' and I made quietly for home . . .

Monday, 6th February [1950] Two letters from Mary this morning, both of them written last Sunday at Lucea. She did not write from Kingston as she had intended doing. She now talks of perhaps not coming home til June. Her father wants her to stay, that is as I anticipated – she repeatedly asserted that it would be three months and three months only and that nothing would induce her to stay longer, but I felt it would be very otherwise once she got there – and so it is, I felt it in my bones when she decided to go that the chances were we would not meet again here – I think so even more today. However one must just face the situation and adjust one's life accordingly.

What do we make of this? DP's love for Mary drives the anguish of the narrative: a love that recognised her capacity to make her own decisions, to untangle her own responsibilities and to follow the guidance that she believed she had from God. Her decision made, he followed it through and tried not to resort to emotional blackmail, revealing quite how ill he felt only in his diary.

Of course, it turned out that he was wrong: not only was he not anything like as ill as he thought, but Mary left Jamaica on 23 April and returned safely to 32 Leven Street on Wednesday 10 May 1950 and they were again together. Perhaps her view of his health, more objective and less prone to swings of mood, had in part underpinned her original decision. DP was a mixture of both the romantic and the realist: his romanticism, rooted in a rich imagination, could mutate into tragic mode, expressed in diary paragraphs heavy with emotion. Meanwhile, as to his daily and working life, 'one must just face the situation', using the time he had been given as best he could. The strength of the man shines in his weakness.

DP took a similar attitude to world affairs. He listened to the night-time BBC radio news; he read his morning papers. In March 1948, he commented, 'World affairs are looking very black – it might be war with Russia at any time. There is great tension in and around Berlin.' This tension resulted from the widening gulf between the Soviet Union and the western Allies over the post-war treatment of Germany: the USA, Britain and France were moving towards the creation of a new federal state comprising their zones of occupation, to which the Soviet response was a land blockade of the Western-occupied sections of Berlin. War between east and west seemed possible, and the atom-bomb was now part of the western armoury. Once again, DP's response was practical: prayerful concern allied to a determination to persevere with his own calling. He wrote: 'Anything may happen any time there and the consequences may be quite overwhelming and catastrophic, that seems clear. What can we do but pray and work quietly on?' He did, of course, also attempt to understand world events through the eye of faith and, in view of his youthful interest in prophecy about the Second Coming of Christ, it is hardly surprising that strands of this speculation recur in his thought. The defeat of US and UN forces in Korea in autumn 1950 again raised the possibility of atomic Armageddon; while 1948 had seen, besides the Berlin Airlift and threatened conflict with the Soviet Union, the creation of the State of Israel:

> Wednesday, 29th December [1948] I have just heard on the wireless the astounding announcement that the Army of Israel has invaded Egypt. Who would have credited that even six months ago? Years ago I remember the scorn with which the idea of prophecy being fulfilled in the return of an unbelieving Israel to their own land was received by liberals and modernists of all kinds. Now Israel is a strong state, warding off attacks by all the Arab states combined. Astonishing beyond words! Is one now to anticipate the Lord's Return and the Battle of Armageddon? Are we indeed near the end? All the signs are – and if ever there was an Antichrist it is Stalin! How remarkably prophecy has been fulfilled these last months and years!

To live and work while expecting the imminent return of the Lord is, of course, a thoroughly New Testament attitude. To the end of his life DP taught that Christ will come again in salvation and judgment: in his *New Testament Christianity*, for example:

> This Christ is coming again, as He Himself foretold. This time He comes as Judge as well as Liberator. Men will have to take Him as He is then – they will have no choice. They will have to take Him, and they will have to reckon with Him, as the final arbiter of destiny, as the one from whom nothing can be hid; as the one before whose judgment-seat, and in the blinding light of whose presence, each one of them must stand.

DP also held strongly to one of his earliest theological principles, that Christ's Kingdom is not of this world. War, that extension of politics by other means, was not for him the way to establish the rule of God. The basic principles of his Redeemer's Kingdom were spiritual, as men and women responded to the love of God in faith and service.

Paisley Mid-Century

Despite DP's concerns about his own health and his speculations about the End, both he and Mary Thomson were in fact to live to 1974. 1950 saw neither a secular nor a spiritual Armageddon, nor his death, but a major regional visitation evangelism campaign, the Paisley Mid-Century Campaign. News that he was to be invited to organise and lead Paisley's answer to neighbouring Glasgow's 1950 Commando Campaign arrived less than a month after Mary had left for Jamaica:

> Friday, 21st January, 1950 . . . 12.30 am News of the first rank in importance as I described it to Tom Allan on the phone a few minutes ago. Paisley Churches Council, at their meeting tonight, unanimously agreed to the proposed United Campaign for the town, to be led by me, and Joe Haldane was empowered to go ahead with the arrangements.

From the beginning it was clear that the Paisley Campaign had all the potential to answer DP's prayer, that the fifth year of his return to evangelism would be 'in every way the best of all'. The invitation brought by Joe Haldane, one of his oldest and closest friends, was to lead a campaign to an urban population of just under 100,000, nominally on behalf of all the protestant denominations. The Paisley Council of Churches, however, the sponsor of the campaign, was a very recent creation of some of the town's ministers and was not considered an 'official' body: it had few structures of its own and bypassed the regular decision-making courts and committees of the denominations. The Church of Scotland Presbytery of Paisley was to approve the campaign a mere 14 days before it began. DP was thus free to devise his own organisation and to follow the visitation methods he had developed since 1947.

Out of a time of anxiety and uncertainly had come clarity. His Master had brought him to this point and he had a real job to do for Christ, even if it proved to be his last:

> Sunday, 26th February [1950] . . . The more I contemplate Paisley, the more do I see how wonderfully everything has been overruled – the Aberdeen Chair, Fetteresso, Campbeltown, the Glasgow Campaign. And the more do I feel that this may well prove to be the grand finale – after 30 years of evangelism.
>
> Sunday, 19th March [1950] Over the top today on the greatest adventure on which I have ever embarked. Quite clear the leading. Paisley was not my choice but became very evidently the place appointed.

In passing it is worth adding that among the cul-de-sacs explored by DP had been an application he had submitted for the vacant Chair of Practical Theology at Aberdeen University. He had, however, been given to understand that a younger and quieter man was wanted, so that the tempting 'greater ease and security and prestige' offered by a professorship were not for him. Although he was a member of the central Committee of the Glasgow Commando Campaign and helped to shape its overall plan and while its full-time Organiser often consulted him, DP had not been appointed to convene any of the 16 executive committees. He himself had had to decline the invitation to lead the Edinburgh Commando Campaign. Paisley, however, now offered virtually a free hand: his would be the controlling voice; the prospect was for an engagement far beyond what involvement with any number of *ad hoc* Glasgow events could have offered.

The Mid-Century Campaign was to occupy DP until April 1951, a full fifteen months. Unlike its Glasgow counterpart its primary thrust was planned to be visitation, and visitation as it had never been planned before. Months in the preliminary stage were spent simply gathering information. Collating the statutory Electoral Registers with congregational Communion and other membership records, teams of voluntary typists sought to produce thousands of card index records that listed any known religious allegiance in every household. Surveys were conducted that identified every factory, public house and place of entertainment in each of seven areas. Each area had its own planning committee, so that the Campaign moved in stages from area to area, with visitation, exhibitions, work-place assignments, rallies and services in each area: the 'three-fold' home, work and leisure procedure of the St Mary's Motherwell Campaign serially multiplied from one parish to an entire industrial town. Contemporary observers were much impressed by this thoroughness, though as Ronnie Falconer (to DP's annoyance) remarked, there was nothing essentially new about the programme. Starting with the genuine innovation of a local council-authorised Flag Day and house-to-house collection as a publicity-enhancing appeal for funds, the whole concluded with a week of rallies in the Town Hall.

At first things proved sticky:

> Thursday, 18th May [1950] I am very tired – my head and heart are both troubling me – the head dull & heavy with that pressure feeling on the left, the heart throbbing in a curiously disturbing way. We are due to go together to Paisley today to see about the Highland Show with the YMCA representative from Edinburgh and I have asked the various ministers' subcommittees to meet me from 3.30 to 6 p.m. It remains to be seen how many of them will actually turn up. Last night I opened my heart to the handful who turned up for the Campaign Committee meeting and told them how disappointed I felt with the lack of response and interest in Paisley. The office work is well ahead so far as the card index is concerned but hopelessly behind so far as the survey is concerned.

Pressure of work led DP to abandon his projected historical booklet, *It happened in Paisley*, despite having bought many relevant books as source material and spent (wasted?) much time on reading and research. By June, however, he was feeling more positive. Volunteers were coming in; support from such as Rev. Nelson Gray of Parkhead Congregational Church was generous; the Campaign's local version of the Saturday night Youth Rallies Tom Allan organised in Glasgow proved a draw; attendance at Training Classes was improving:

Saturday, 10th June [1950] . . . On Tuesday we journeyed to Polmont to Jim Hood's Induction to which his friends travelled in very large numbers. I was back in time to lecture in The Methodist Central Halls, Paisley, at the second last of our Training Classes on Visitation Evangelism. Crowded to the doors. With the Youth Rally of last Saturday it would seem that the tides had definitely turned. We have never looked back since then. On Wednesday the Campaign General Committee met: on Thursday Joe Ritchie had a packed house for the closing Training Class of the series.

A summary account of the Paisley Campaign was prepared for the General Assembly of 1951, no doubt originally by DP himself:

The Paisley Campaign began with several months of preparatory work, during which the whole town was surveyed and card-indexed, both the Electoral Roll and the Congregational and Sunday School Rolls of the Churches being used for this purpose. Training classes for prospective workers and visitors were also held over an extended period, and these were supplemented by two Summer Training Schools, both partly residential, in the course of which a complete visitation of two large parishes was made as part of the practical training.

The Campaign proper began in September 1950, the town having been divided for the purpose into seven areas, to be taken consecutively, the forces of all the churches to be engaged successively in each.

In each area there has been a threefold visitation – home, work and leisure time activities being the points of contact. The complete visitation of one large mill involved as many as forty-seven separate meetings in order that all the employees might be covered.

Over 1,000 workers have been engaged in the house-to-house visitation alone, and the experience they have gained has in itself been a great enrichment to the life of the churches. Fully 1,000 more have been employed in office work or in catering, tea and supper having been provided throughout the campaign for all taking part, the various church halls in the town being used for this purpose in turn.

The visitation of factories, works, shops, offices and public institutions such as schools, hospitals, and training centres, and of cinemas, dance halls, public houses, clubs and places of recreation and amusement, has been done through the day by the local ministers and in the evenings partly by them and partly by the young people of the churches, for whom the campaign has brought at once a great challenge and a great opportunity. Many of them have been called on to speak in the churches of other areas, following a campaign in their own district, and many have become articulate for the first time so far as their faith and witness were concerned.

> Each area has been left free to plan its own programme of meetings, demonstrations, or exhibitions – sometimes a combination of two or more of these, and in presenting pictorially and from the platform what the churches of their area have to offer to the people of the area, hundreds of boys and girls, as well as of older folk have found their opportunity of helping in the work of the campaign. Sunday evening rallies, held in each area during the 16 days of intensive missioning, have been very largely attended, and at the close of the whole visitation it is intended to hold a short series of mass meetings in the Town Hall, which is one of the largest and best equipped in the country.
>
> Throughout the town generally increased church attendances have been reported right from the start of the campaign, and there have been very many accessions to membership – by profession, by certificate and by restoration. New avenues of regular Christian service for the community have opened out to old and young alike, and thousands who never attend public worship have been reached with the message and challenge of the Gospel, numerous lives and homes having been really changed.
>
> Mr. Thomson's work in Paisley will conclude with a Summer Mission in the open spaces of the new housing areas of the town, in which further visitation will be carried out.

The pressure of work was enormous: it took much time simply to get the organisational and administrational structure in place, dependent as it was on volunteers. DP found himself purchasing the stationery, interviewing local company directors and the Secretaries of local Paisley Trusts to solicit grants to fund the work, interviewing the Director of Education and the Medical Officer of Health, visiting up to 20 congregations in a week, speaking to Woman's Guilds and Boys Brigade Company Captains, moving his local headquarters from church hall to church hall on a weekly basis, touring housing estates:

> I worked steadily all morning and early afternoon on the compilation of (a) a card index of Paisley ministers; (b) a telephone book of Paisley numbers I already need to use; (c) a Paisley address book for my own use and (d) the marking of Joe Haldane's copy of the Paisley Telephone Directory for extracts and especially for the compilation of a business directory. The first three I had finished by 2.45, so I gulped down my post-luncheon cup of tea and left for Paisley. My first call was on the Campaign Treasurer, with whom I left £1, the first donation (my own) wherewith to open the campaign account . . . Over a coffee I had addressed my Paisley envelopes and back to the YMCA, with stamps on them, I found the circulars ready and proceeded to envelope them . . .

and on the way had made an extensive purchase of ledgers, cashbooks, jotters, posters and telephone books and writing pads.

Although the Campaign as a whole ran for well over a year, each of the Area segments was restricted to 16 days, a fortnight with three weekends, and was in essence a series of special events ending with a United Service. Each area planned their own programme to coincide with their local household, factory and leisure-place visitations. Events for Area 4 (three parishes of the Church of Scotland: St John's, Mossvale and North; St James Street Methodist and Holy Trinity Episcopal Church) ran as follows, as far as the Holy Trinity congregation were concerned:[1]

Date	Event	Place
Sun. 7th Jan.	Sunday School Rally 3pm	St James Methodist Church
	Evensong, 6.30-7.15pm	Holy Trinity
	Opening Rally, 7.30pm	St John's, School Wynd
Mon. 8th Jan.	St John's Sunday School: Tableau by Teachers; Film Show, 7.30pm	Mossvale Hall
	St James and St John's Mission Sunday School: Demo., 7.30pm	Muir Memorial Hall
Tues. 9th Jan.	Women's Rally, 7.30pm	St John's Hall
Wed. 10th Jan.	Sunday School Beginners Demonstration, 3.30pm	St James' Hall
	Men's Clubs At Home, 7.30	Muir Memorial Hall
Thur. 11th Jan.	Youth Rally - speaker, Rev. Tom Allan, 'well known broadcaster', 7.30pm	St John's Hall
Sun. 14th Jan.	Annual General Meeting, 6.30pm	Holy Trinity
Mon. 15th Jan.	Holy Trinity Kindergarten, Demonstration and Filmstrip	Muir Memorial Hall
	Demos. by Mossvale Junior and Senior Sunday Schools	Mossvale Hall
Tues. 16th Jan.	Women's Rally, 2.30	Mossvale Hall
Wed. 17th Jan.	Men's Clubs At Home, 7.30pm	St James' Hall
Thur. 18th Jan.	Youth Rally: Bible Quiz & Brains Trust, 7.30pm	Mossvale Hall
	Joint Choir Practice, 8pm	North Church
Fri. 19th Jan.	Uniformed Organisations Display, 7.30pm	Muir Memorial Hall
Sun. 21st Jan.	United Service of Praise, 7.30pm (after Evensong)	North Church

The most obviously outward-looking of these meetings was the Youth Rally to be led by Tom Allan; the others appear to be rather less challenging joint meetings of the usual Women's, Men's, children's and uniformed organisations round which much of congregational life revolved.

Both June and August 1950 saw residentially-based Training Schools, one at Eastwood, led by Joe Ritchie and held jointly with the Summer Mission teams, and the other at Kilmacolm, led by DP in person with Mary as hostess: both schools also undertook house-by-house visiting, the Kilmacolm school in the near-by Woodhall area. The sequence of Area campaigns began in September and initially things progressed slowly and disappointingly. By April 1951 DP's health had in fact collapsed and the final stages of the Campaign he had to leave to others and especially to Tom Allan.

DP's own active role in the Campaign, besides its overall planning, organisation and publicity, was concentrated on the 'assignments' – the visiting of factories, shops, pubs and other places of work and leisure. The 'commando' pattern was followed, with teams of ministers arriving (with or without prior arrangement) to visit canteens and to speak about the Campaign and for Christ. The programme was non-stop:

> Friday, 27th October [1950] . . . Yesterday I went down at 7.15am and addressed Van Boys and Men of Bell's Laundry in the packing shed, the management had fixed the canteen and only four men came. I left Sim and Balfour of Penilee to address them and went off with one of the managers to where the boys were. They listened well. After that Balfour and I had breakfast with two of the 'big chiefs', who had come in specially early for that purpose. A very good breakfast it was! Then I went to the East School Paisley to join Willie Muir and Nelson Gray and we went in first to the Nursery School where it was very fascinating to see the children in their coloured smocks – green for girls and blue for boys. Then I addressed the Seniors and Juniors successively and after that we went, all three, for a coffee. Then to Thom, Lamont & Co., Pump Makers, Hawkhead Road, where we got a very good reception – a 100% attendance, greatly to the surprise of Mr Thom and the Manager, and a splendid hearing – all men. After that to Bell's Laundry and Dye Works, where, in the Canteen, Sim, Nelson Gray and myself addressed some 2-300 of the workers, mostly women. After that we had a very good luncheon at three tables – four at each, with the management. I think we managed to make some impression on them. From there I went to shop-visiting again and then, at 3.15, I addressed to a Teachers Meeting in the East School Paisley, where I got a very good hearing. Then on to the BAS Department Depot in Mill Street, which struck me as a fairly tough

> assignment. There would be about 60, mostly men. After tea I went to the Paisley Grammar School Evening Classes where I addressed to some 2-300 in the main hall of the School before they went to their classes, and after that I was so done that I had to be motored home. So ended a full and busy and worthwhile day in Paisley.
>
> Saturday, 28th October [1950] Let me continue my narrative. I write in brilliant sunshine after a delightful Saturday dinner. Yesterday I left at 8.35am but was late for my Williamsburgh School Service in Paisley, Burns of the Middle Church presiding. Afterwards I spoke in the Infant Room then on to MacNabs Thread Works in Lacy Street, where I found the owner (an eccentric Abbey choirman), his forewoman, also in the choir, a boy and two girls. He gave me one pound after I had addressed them and drank tea with them. Then home and back at one o'clock to Reid's Engineering Works, Thread Street, where we got what I reckoned one of the best hearings of the week. Home after that and down again to address the Paisley Grammar School Teachers at 3.30pm. Here, I just never got off my mark – that Rector intimidates me! My next assignment was the Paisley Ice Rink, Lions v. Pirates match, where I spoke on the microphone at the interval to about 5000. Then I addressed the Oldhall Scout Troop on 'the Race of Life' and later spoke in the Kelburne Cinema just before the big picture. Then to the Kelburne Cricket Club Whist Drive where I got three minutes with 40-50. Then, finally, to the British Legion Dance. Mary was out visiting and we came home together.
>
> Sunday, 29th October [1950] . . . Last night I went down to the Freemason's Young People's Dance in the Masonic Hall, Penilee Road, Ralston. Gilbert George was waiting for me at the end of the road. We went in together and asked for Mr R, the Welfare Officer at the Rolls-Royce who runs the dance. He came at once, and immediately began telling us his own story. A man who wanted to be a church member but didn't feel fit to sit down at the Communion table. Then one or two other leading Masons came in, including the Master of the Lodge, with whom I arranged to address the Masons on Wednesday at 10 at the close of their regular meeting. Then, after a cup of tea, we went in to address the dancers. We got rather a noisy hearing, chiefly due to the fact that I started off on the wrong foot. But they were friendly and one young rebellious Catholic kept us hotly engaged for quite a while. Gilbert and I felt it had been very worthwhile evening.

With mornings, afternoons and evenings all taken up, DP found himself travelling to and from Paisley sometimes three times a day.

The pace speeded up [!] towards Christmas, when a party for the teams was held, additional publicity and posters for Christmas and New Year services were distributed throughout the town, and DP led elite commando teams on Saturday evening raids:

> Sunday, 17th December [1950] . . . At 6.40pm I left for Paisley for our first Paisley Saturday Evening Commando Raid. I found waiting for me Bill Shannon, Jim Carson, Jim Beckett, Ann Beckett, Walter Barbour and Jack Gisby. After prayer and consultation, we split into two parties – I took Jack Gisby and Jim Beckett and the Abbey side of Glasgow Road; Bill Shannon taking the remainder up the other side. First assignments were fish and chip shops. We did a little there. Then we tackled the Burgh Bar and Harvies Bar and in both we made good contacts and did good publicity. After that we made for the Territorial Hall, but the dance there had not begun nor had it in the Co-Operative Hall in Bank Street, which we had visited earlier. We then made for the Kelburne Cinema Café, which was full, and after doing the tables sat down to 3/- worth of tea and biscuits, plain and chocolate. This was our rendezvous and after we had been there a little the other party joined us. Next we tackled the Ice Rink, first in the café, then the sides of the rink and the lounge bar, which was crowded with a well-to-do heavy drinking crowd. Here we got the best contacts of all. I sat next to a youngish married woman who wanted to talk to me, and later she exchanged with her husband. I have made a date to visit them this week at their house in Renfrew. I left Jim and Ann Beckett busy among the dancers in the Territorial Hall while I mounted the bus for home with Bill Shannon.

What, then, were the results of Paisley's Mid-Century Campaign? Apart from his contemporary campaign newsletters and later compilations of testimony and methodology, D. P. Thomson was to produce three publications that included considered accounts of Paisley 1950-51.[2] Consistently in these, besides a generalised assertion of 'results' in terms of both conversions and increased church membership, DP chose to emphasise the less tangible gains of ecumenical cooperation, of interaction with the community, of the creation of a climate of interest. These were exactly the goals of the 'new evangelism' aim of *making contact*, that had so often eluded the 'old evangelism.' From *Aspects of Evangelism*, for example:

> So far as I know, not one home was left unvisited; only one place of business refused admission to the campaign team, and only one place of leisure-time resort. Never before had the Church gained access to so many places – never had she had such opportunities of proclaiming the Gospel to the people.
>
> Apart altogether from personal conversions and commitments, and from restorations to Church fellowship, of all of which there were many, a campaign of this kind had certain notable achievements to its credit. It brought together the rank and file of the churches in a completely new way.

> It built innumerable bridges across denominational and congregational barriers, and across the yawning gulfs created by class distinction and contrasted social and educational backgrounds. It brought the ministers of the local churches for the first time into the closest possible touch with every field of business and industry in the community, and with the extraordinarily variegated pattern of leisure-time interests and pursuits. It made the Church aware of the community in a totally new way, and the community aware of the Church. It gave the man in the street a new respect for, as well as a fresh interest in, parson and church folk alike. It afforded opportunities by the hundred and by the thousand for personal witness and personal work, for open confession, for friendly conversation and debate, and for the asking and answering of questions about the deeper things of life.
>
> It made religion a talking point everywhere, and *the* talking point in some of the most unexpected places. Above all, it created a climate of interest, of awareness, of expectancy, and of goodwill, by means of which all sorts of things became possible which had not been practicable before.

Among these gains was the tremendous spiritual benefit that being involved in such an effort brought to many of Paisley's ordinary Christians. As with the GSEU, as with the FiE and as with Summer Mission teams, DP always looked for the spiritual growth that being part of an evangelistic team could encourage. If Summer Missions had particularly appealed to the younger generations of the 16-30 age group, Visitation Evangelism, because it offered new opportunities for existing congregational office-bearers, enabled what he described as 'the spiritual movement among the middle-aged', the 30-55 (and older) age group:

> It was at Paisley, during the Mid-Century Campaign of 1950-51, that we saw the beginnings of this movement. That Campaign was the most comprehensive ever undertaken in this country, involving as it did the training of over 1,000 local workers and the visitation of every home, every place of work, and every club, association and fellowship of whatsoever type, in a community of just under 100,000 souls. The Campaign lasted for a whole year, and the fifty Protestant Churches of the town were all actively engaged in it, although not all, of course, at the same level or depth.
>
> There came a day on which two elders of the Church approached me during the early stages of the Campaign, when 'The Fellowship of the Common Table' had already begun to reveal what a potent instrument it was going to prove in the breaking down of barriers, in the bridging of gulfs of every kind, in the fostering of fellowship, and in that communion of mind with mind and heart with heart which lies at the very root of an effort of this kind.

> 'Mr. Thomson,' said one of them, 'we have a confession to make to you! We have sat on the same Kirk Session for 16 years, but we have got to know one another better in the course of this week than we have done in all these sixteen years.'
>
> Instinctively I knew what they meant! It was not merely that coming from completely different backgrounds of life – in home, in daily work, and in leisure time interests and pursuits they had never really got to know one another until then. It was that 'breaking bread' day by day together – sharing the fellowship of a tea-table at which barriers went down so easily and bonds were forged so quickly – each had come in a completely new way to appreciate both the actual and potential contribution of the other to the life, work and fellowship of the Church.
>
> That was the kind of thing we were to see happen – not in scores or even hundreds, but in literally thousands of cases – the breaking down and disappearance of generation-old prejudices, of those barriers of class and custom, of tradition and vocation, which may, and do, separate so completely from one another, even within the one Christian congregation – say the working miner and the business executive, the lady of leisure and the factory hand. It was not just that they understood one another in an altogether new way; it was that they came to see how indispensable each was to the other, spiritually even more than economically.

DP's accounts need to be read with an element of caution: they were hardly objective and rarely described difficulties encountered. On the figures made public (1,000 visitors from some 50 congregations) an average of around 20 visitors – both men and women – per congregation is a number sufficiently small that it is clear that large numbers of the existing male-only office-bearers were not involved. The 28 Church of Scotland congregations based in Paisley had on average 20 elders each: five had Kirk Sessions of over 60 men. Sydney Still, minister of St James, one of these five, after two previous appeals for visitors had the names of only 20 volunteers by December 1950: he wrote in his newsletter that the work was crying out to be done and he turned to the women of his congregation to do it.[3] Originating from the ambitions of Joe Haldane's group of ministers via the Council of Churches, the Campaign had a life of its own irrespective of the Kirk Sessions involved. While this gave DP considerable freedom to implement his vision, the downside was that it was not necessarily strongly rooted in the localities. Connections with the non-ministerial leadership of some of Paisley's congregations appear to have been tenuous at best, despite DP's claim that the fifty Protestant Churches of the town were all actively involved. He did, in fairness, add that they did not all engage at the same level or depth. The Church of Scotland Abbey Close congregation, for example, which hosted the Campaign in its halls for an extended period, despite an encouraging start provided the fewest visitors of its group and its Kirk Session only discussed the Campaign on one occasion: to apologise to its Woman's Guild that the let of its halls for the Campaign headquarters had meant the cancellation of a Guild meeting. The Orr Street Kirk Session, meeting nine times during the period of the Campaign, mentioned it not at all.

Given the size of Paisley's protestant community (the Church of Scotland alone had over 25,000 communicant members in the town), an attendance of 60-80 at the Summer Training Schools can hardly be said to have even scratched the surface; nor was an attendance of 600 to hear Tom Allan at the Friday Mass Meeting of the final week especially large. The opening meetings for the parallel Glasgow Campaign had been mainly supported by those that DP described as working class: the same may have been true of Paisley, where the congregation that he felt most supportive, at least initially, was the independent Hope Mission Hall. By contrast, Tom Allan was attracting not 60 but 300 to his Training Classes for the Glasgow Commando Campaign. Because, however, unlike Glasgow, the Paisley Campaign moved over time from area to area, it was possible for DP's band of activists also to move to supplement local deficiencies. Indeed, this moving army was essential as DP recognised when rejecting Tom Allan's advice to switch to the Glasgow pattern:

> Monday, 9th October [1950] . . . Tom Allan . . . thinks we should abandon our area by area plan in Paisley: do numbers 3-7 at once. Quite impossible say I, and quite unwise also!

Provided a minimum number from any of the congregations of an area came forward, then visitation was viable even if others of the group were barely involved. By December, for example, DP calculated:

> Friday, 1st December [1950] . . . I went through the three area lists [*ie areas 1, 2 and 3*] and discovered 26 people had visited in all three areas, 52 in two.

The expected mix of people involved – locals to the area, some from the other Paisley groups, and some from outwith the town – was made clear by the minister of St James in his *Quarterly Review*:[4]

> You will be 'briefed' by Mr Thomson, the leader of the Campaign, out of a long and varied experience, and we can hope for better results than we had in our last venture of this sort. St James's people will not be sent out to visit St James's parish: the four parishes are one unit and will be

treated as such: we are campaigning, not for our own congregation, but for the Church of God. We shall have helpers from the other districts in the town (some have been helping in all the district campaigns held up to now) and from outside Paisley too. It will be a real experience of fellowship in Christian service and should result in the enrichment of the life, not only of the Church, but also of those taking part in the work.

The facility to bring in volunteers from elsewhere, portrayed by Rev. Sydney Still as an opportunity for fellowship, was also the basis of near-contemporary criticism of the Paisley Campaign as superficial, despite its tremendous organisation:[5]

> In the town 'mission' it is possible to be impressed by the gathering together of those interested from over a wide area and to forget what is left untouched. It's the selected few of a number of churches that have come together and seem to form quite an army. It is easy to forget how unrepresentative they are. Such superficiality is harder in a [*mission restricted to a single*] parish.

Among the opinions gathered by Ralph Morton in preparation for the World Council of Churches study, *Ecumenical Studies: Evangelism in Scotland*, were the conclusions of some ministers who had supported the Paisley Mid-Century Campaign. These tended to support DP's own reports, while still casting doubt on the underlying methodology in favour of Iona's preference for working with single parishes:[6]

> a) All houses were visited and undoubtedly good work was done among Church members who were on the verge of lapsing. It was found that among the Churchless not many were hostile. Some were indifferent and the majority were careless or just needed encouragement to come to Church.
>
> b) The quality of visitor was uneven. Some of the work was poorly done, some of it brilliantly. To my mind the area was too big. This work can best be done by a minister and congregation in their own parish. The minister knows the quality of the visitors. Training, which is essential, was provided but not taken advantage of.
>
> c) It roused the Church membership. It increased Church attendances. It made people think out their own faith before visiting those who had none. Above all it gave my congregation a sense of mission. They realised this was their job as well as the minister's. A very deep impression was made in factories and public houses. In them we really got somewhere with the folk we were after. And I think many a house is now at least open to the Church where formerly it was closed.
>
> d) For myself it was a great and exciting experience but I feel that the results would be more definite if each parish church organised its own effort.

Assessments of evangelism, of course, depend in part on what was anticipated in the first place, and as radical change in congregational life was not then an objective DP shared, it is hardly surprising that for some the results were 'superficial'.

Evangelism in Scotland also argued that there was little evidence of lasting influence from the Campaign on the 'unchurched'. Beyond the published anecdotal reports, only limited help in verifying this can be gained from statistics, given the scarcity of publicly available local church records from the 1950s and the problems of interpreting national denominational membership figures. The Church of Scotland's tables of communicant members, given year by year, presbytery by presbytery and parish by parish, show net gains or losses. The minister who could be expected to support DP's campaigns might also, however, be the sort of minister actively to remove from his roll those members who took no part in congregational life. Large accessions to membership could easily be obscured by vigorous pruning. The Orr Square congregation thus admitted 68 new members, adding 5% to its roll by profession of faith during 1950,[7] yet its overall reported membership declined from 1,308 to 1,307. Analysis of these net figures for all Paisley's Church of Scotland congregations suggests that between the end of 1949 and the end of 1951 total membership shrank by less than 1%, roughly in line with the trend of the Scottish population, at a time when nationally membership rose by less than 1%. These figures do not seem especially significant: clearly the Campaign did not lift Paisley's Church of Scotland congregational membership beyond any national trend. The tables of gains and losses collated at a Presbytery level by the national Committee on General Administration show adult baptisms within the entire area during 1950, 1951 and 1952 as, respectively 141, 158 and 144; an increase but not a dramatic increase over the immediate post-war years' [1947-1949] average of 121. In terms of professions of faith these years were in line with the previous three years: the figures of 1,392, 1,457 and 1,362 were reported, as against 1,348, 1,605 and 1,334 for 1947-49.

This is not, of course, to deny what DP reported – that numerous lives had been changed and hearts opened to Christ that might not otherwise have been reached. Space allows for only one example, that of a young officer who made a strong impression on DP:

> In the evening I visited the Exhibition, saw the largely attended Women's Guild Pageant for a little, and went with Stuart McMillan to the Territorial [Army] Hall, next door to the Allison Halls, where I addressed the RE [Royal Engineers]. I made a definite appeal to the officers and men sitting

> in the canteen and said I was there for recruits. After me Stuart, then a young officer stepped forward and said 'Here is your first recruit.' I asked him if he meant it and he said yes, certainly he did. I have a date with him on Sunday evening. He is a young married man living close to here with a little boy of 3½, and he had told his parents in law that he would take a stand when the Church came to the people and not till then. He said to me 'The Church has come to the people – and here I am.' I was deeply moved, and could not but feel that we often leave these meetings too much up in the air.

What can also be said is that the creation of new congregational organisations was part of the spin-off of the Campaign, and that a few congregations reported fairly strong net growth in these years: Lylesland, Martyrs' Memorial, St George's East, and the Priesthill, St Ninian's and Penilee Church Extension congregations. These latter three, being relatively newly formed, presumably had fewer annual losses to counter-balance their growth.

The Paisley Council of Churches had selected Joe Haldane's old friend to run and lead their mission because they believed D. P. Thomson was best fitted to lead the campaign; despite mid-term blues, at the end they did not regret their choice:[8]

> As the Campaign progressed it became increasingly evident how right was the Council of Churches in seeking the leadership of D. P. Thomson. His vision, initiative, and passion for evangelism, combined with his remarkable organising genius, largely account for the effectiveness of this effort.

DP, of course, involved others in the campaign and especially in its training classes and schools. Bill Shannon continued to offer his services as DP's personal aide-de-camp throughout the Campaign when his studies allowed. There was close coordination with both Tom Allan and Joe Ritchie, the latter having succeeded Allan as the Home Board's Summer Missions Organiser, being seconded for six months from McDonald Road. Ritchie ran the Eastwood Training School (10 - 20 June 1950) and booked as lecturers DP, Tom Allan, Rev. Dr Charles Duthie and Guy Ramsay of Hillhead Baptist Church and John R. Ramsay of Mount Florida Parish Church. With Duthie DP had been acquainted since 1931, when while a student at Aberdeen University he had been a leader in the Student Campaigning Movement. He was a Past-President of the FMF, and had been appointed Principal of the Scottish Congregational College in 1944, from which base he was to organise his own student mission teams.

At DP's own Kilmacolm Training School, for the morning series of lectures he chose to speak himself on 'In Scotland Today: The Church and Its Task' and 'The New Approach to Evangelism' and he engaged Tom Allan for 'Evangelistic Work among Children', the BBC's Ronnie Falconer on 'Religious Broadcasting', an academic Dr James Kelly on 'The Church in the World Today' and James W. Hood on 'In the Ministry Today - Some First Experiences, Impressions and Discoveries'. Jim Hood had joined the FiE, aged 19, in March 1942 – his talk in August 1950 was very much about 'first experiences' as he had been ordained and inducted to Polmont South the previous June! The evening lectures had a definitely international theme, with speakers from the Gold Coast (Rev. F. W. K. Akuffo), Northern Rhodesia (Rev. Fergus Macpherson), West Africa (Rev. Dugald Davidson), and Rev. Dr Hans Bolewski, a German padre in Scotland and for 'five years a prisoner in Russia'. Davidson, originally from Jamaica, had trained for the ministry in Scotland and was ordained in Jamaica for service there before transferring to the YMCA in West Africa; he was sufficiently close to both the Thomsons that, when DP had thought himself on the verge of death, he had pondered whether Mary might some day marry Dugald!

D. P. Thomson's appointment as Home Board Evangelist gave him a certain credibility. It offered him at least a hearing from presbyteries, ministers and congregations, besides making available an office, off-season use of useful summer mission equipment (soap-boxes and pulpits for open air preaching; banners; palliasses and cooking equipment for the billets in schools and church halls) and occasional availability of a shooting-brake for transporting it all. For personal support and prayer he looked to his own networks of friends and colleagues in evangelism, built up over the years. Certainly he was as free from commitments to a Presbytery as any Church of Scotland minister could be. On leaving Cambuslang: Trinity and moving first to Glasgow and then to Crieff, DP had retained his membership of the Presbytery of Hamilton; he received its mailings and avoided its meetings, thus keeping himself entirely outside the formal structures of ministerial interaction. This remoteness brought both gains and losses: gains in terms of his ability to follow his own course; losses in terms of disconnection from currents of church life and perhaps through suspicion raised among those who followed conventional paths.

By 1950 D. P. Thomson's own network was no longer the formally constituted Fellowship in Evangelism of his Cambuslang days. In its adult form the Fellowship, in which he had invested so much time and hope, had not for long survived his reappointment to the Home Board in 1947. Perhaps curiously, no entry in DP's diaries chronicles its demise, the last references occurring in Diary 17. Back in May 1947 the Fellowship had ceased to maintain their own Headquarters and DP had split his office between his flat and the room made available to him at the Church of Scotland's Glasgow offices. Though the junior branch, the Youth Fellowship in Evangelism, continued to support the work of Summer Missions, and by 1955 was still sponsoring meetings and talks, somewhere in the months between February 1948 and April 1949 the parent, adult, Fellowship ceased to be an active fraternal. By the end of 1950 DP thus felt the urge to devise the constitution for a new endeavour: 'The Order of the Burning Bush'. He appreciated formality– he was the son of a solicitor – and perhaps the growing success of the Iona Community as the contemporary 'religious order' nagged. The concept may also have been born from his continuing uncertainly about his future. Of all DP's initiatives, 'The Order of the Burning Bush' achieved least: no further record of it survives. Yet its name remains as a testimony to his commitment to the Church of Scotland, whose emblem features Moses' ever-burning and never consumed bush.

Perhaps DP's desire for a more formal grouping of his friends and associates sprang from continued unease about his relationship with the Home Board. A minor crisis had blown up in September 1950 when Sir James Simpson, whose loyalties remained firmly with the Seaside Missions, sought to recruit Joe Ritchie as a full-time member of the Board's staff. Such an arrangement might have ended the existing partnership between DP as the full-time Evangelist and the part-time Seaside Organisers, who worked as an informal team sharing equipment and personnel. Tom Allan suspected that other, more political objectives might lie behind the move: 'Tom thinks they mean to squeeze me out!' Ritchie did not in fact accept the post and the crisis passed, but the episode illustrates the sense that DP and Tom Allan shared, that while his relations with the Home Board's General Secretary were friendly (despite DP's inveterate inability to complete the accounts and paperwork for one mission before he began the next), DP held his post without committed support from the leading members of Board. A further crisis followed in January 1951 when a delegation of the Evangelism Sub-Committee (of which Tom Allan was a member) made arrangements to see the Paisley Campaign Committee without DP being present. He interpreted this as a loss of confidence in his leadership. Actually, it was simply an attempt to ensure that the Paisley

Campaign did not simply run and run: the Committee sought DP's leadership for other, rural, areas of Scotland.

The Mid-Century Campaign at Paisley thus came to an end in April 1951, 'Today I enter on the final month of the Paisley Campaign, to which I have given myself now for over a year, and in many ways it will be a great relief to be quit.' By then the Thomsons – DP, Mary and also Dr Christine – had made what DP liked to call a 'far-reaching' decision about their future. In the midst of DP's illness and the final weeks of the Campaign, they had decided, between 31 March and 19 April 1951, to move together to share a house, Barnoak, in Crieff.

More Family Matters: the Move to Crieff

Dr Christine Thomson's reappointment to the Crighton Royal Hospital, Dumfries in June 1944, albeit at only £50 a year with her keep, had lasted until another attack of depression over the summer of 1947 led to her departure and admission for further residential treatment at a hospital in northern England. Her consultants then believed she would never work again, but sometime after August 1948 she was discharged and by November had obtained the part-time post of acting Deputy Superintendent at the Dykebar Hospital, Renfrewshire, a former Asylum newly admitted to the NHS as a mental hospital. Living in a tied hospital flat of her own, CJ was now only an hour's travel from DP and Mary's own home. Regular, Christmas and birthday visits were exchanged – CJ was 56 on 25 July 1949. Despite occasional scares Dr Christine retained her post at Dykebar, being given additional responsibilities, enjoying both her duties and a higher standard of living. In March 1951, however, DP broached with her the question of her longer-term future: she really should not count on having tied accommodation provided for her. This question of housing escalated to involve all three of them:

> Wednesday, 28th March [1951] I am facing a series of crises and big, far-reaching decisions . . . In the early afternoon Mary and I . . . caught the 3.15 bus out to Christine's. We had a very happy and restful 2 hours with the dear girl, to whom I mooted the proposal that the time had come for her to buy a property and thereby ensure a home for herself if and when she had to give up. She has taken up the idea with avidity, the more so as Barnoak, Mary Burn-Forsyth's house, is on the market and she has plans to go through to Crieff today to examine it afresh. We have both stayed there – CJ often – and know the house well. Taking everything into consideration I think the idea is a sound one. It would provide for us

both if anything happened, as it is already divided into two flats. I think to consult Mr Russell and Mr Donaldson today and unless they persuade us, to go through tomorrow, Mary and I, and examine it with CJ . . .

1.10pm I am back from town – John Russell and Donaldson both approve and Mary and I are minded to move in May and make our home in Crieff. We plan to go through tomorrow to see the house . . .

4.10pm Drama heightens and excitement grows! CJ came in at 2.40 and she and Mary left at 3.25 to get the four o'clock train to Crieff, where they are spending the night. Then I hope to join Mary in the morning. The journey may be quite abortive for Mary Burn-Forsyth has already given a first offer of the house to a family coming from India.

A quick series of visits to Crieff ensued, with Mary and CJ increasingly convinced about the prospective move, which would involve DP renting half of Barnoak from CJ. The plan having originated in order to provide a retirement home for CJ, DP grasped its potential also to be a home for himself, should (as, of course, he rather expected) his own health fail. CJ's lawyers submitted her offer on Saturday 31 March and an outline contract had been agreed by Tuesday 3 April.

DP now – somewhat irresponsibly and no doubt exasperatingly – threw the whole question up in the air by raising issues that should have been sorted before: which rooms were, in fact, he and Mary to rent? What would the Building Society offer as loans? Was this really a wise move considering his health? How would he manage to fit his library into the available space? What would Mary's father think of the plan? Douglas Rothnie, in fact, was inclined to disapprove. CJ rejected DP's first ultimatum, and it was primarily her money and not his that was at stake. The move was on – and then off – and then on again:

Saturday, 7th April [1951] . . . On Thursday I travelled by the 10 o'clock train to Gleneagles, and got a lift in the post van to Crieff. I looked round Barnoak before meeting CJ for lunch at a very nice restaurant in Burrell St. run by Watsons of Dundee. We then went together by way of the MacRostie & Taylor Parks to the house, which really has a very fine situation. We went all over it, and I became quite clear that we would go if, and only if, CJ were prepared to rent us the front half of the house as it stands, for which we would give her £80 per annum. She ruled that out on Thursday, then appeared to change her mind, and now has changed it again, so that we don't know where we stand. Mary had set her heart on going, and is naturally very disappointed.

Monday, 9th April [1951] It looks as if we are going to Crieff after all. Christine is going to take the bottom two rooms of the front half of the

> house and give us the kitchen and the upper floor. We will move in on May 30th. Mary went out today to see her . . .
>
> Wednesday, 11th April [1951] Christine was here last night and we have got Crieff all fixed up unless the Building Society creates any difficulties. We plan to go next month, and Duncan Campbell is coming here this morning to see our flat.
>
> Wednesday, 18th April [1951] . . . Mary has been writing her father – her mind and heart are clearly set on Crieff – mine are not yet! I cannot but feel that there are 3 factors still to be weighed – Father's opinion, the Drs. verdict and that of the Building Society. CJ and Mary take it as all fixed – but I don't by any means yet. What to get rid of before we leave (if Crieff it be) is a very real problem!

While DP was swithering (after his initial unhappiness with the flat at Leven Street he had come to enjoy it), CJ went on holiday to France and Spain, visiting their brother JP's war-grave at the military cemetery at Warloy-Baillon en route, – '*I am bringing home a handful of earth from the dear grave for our Crieff garden, so that we will always feel that a little memorial of JP is there'* – and by the evening of Thursday 19 April DP was able to finish his 18th Diary with the conclusion: 'We are for CRIEFF – Mary's heart is clearly set on it, I can see.' What family heirlooms DP still possessed were sold to fund their costs of the removal, the eminent heart specialist Olav Kerr brushed off DP's concerns about his heart ('rest and recuperation I needed' – DP didn't take his advice), and he and Mary moved on Thursday 24 May 1951, not quite a month since the idea was first discussed. Having arrived, DP understood what Mary and CJ had seen before, what a treasure the stone-built, self-standing town-house 'Barnoak' was:

> Thursday, 24th May [1951] The second van is just arriving! We were up at 7 and it has rained nearly all the time since then. The neighbours are all most helpful and all very distressed at our going . . .
>
> Monday, 28th May [1951] AT BARNOAK, CRIEFF I am sitting at my study table in the new home looking out on the green fields, the woods beyond, the near tree-clad hills and the distant mountains . . . What a lovely home we have got! I have never had anything remotely like it!

Moving house is a very stressful experience. The move to Crieff was not without temporary downsides, particular for Mary and Christine. DP attempted to move house without much interruption to his work; and his work was pretty well all he had made time for since he and Mary had had a week of holiday in the English Lake District in July 1950. Running the Paisley Campaign had meant working mornings, afternoons and evenings seven days a week, month after month, though 'work' was understood to include time to trawl second-hand bookstalls and for his reading. Indeed, DP wrote 'I have spent a small fortune on books this past year – but they have been my substitute for holidays!' Before Paisley ended – well before the move to Crieff was even thought about – the next visitation campaigns, those at West Fife and Kirkcaldy, were being discussed and prepared. During the first two weeks of May – amazingly – DP was away on the island of Arran conducting a traditional preaching mission. So during the summer of 1951 the most that DP and Mary had of time off together were occasional walks or bus runs in the Crieff area: 'This afternoon Mary and I are planning an expedition to Loch Earn, just now she is at the coffee morning in the South Church Hall. I am going down now for my coffee!' Much of the work of getting Barnoak into shape fell to Mary, and she threw herself into it. But of course the house was not in fact theirs but CJ's, and she had her own renovation plans, which unexpectedly turned out to be both substantial and disruptive:

> Saturday, 16th June [1951] . . . The joiners are in, still busy at CJ's work. What a lot she has had done!

> Thursday, 22nd July [1951] . . . Yesterday . . . all day there were tradesmen in. The whole house is being upturned to get Christine's alterations done and all the labour Mary has put in getting it cleaned and ready has gone for nothing.

It is hardly surprising that DP thought Mary looked stressed: 'Mary is looking quite washed out, obviously she is taking far too much out of herself over the house.'

The situation was not an easy one: the remaining man of the family, DP liked to be in control, and it was he and Mary who were in permanent residence at Barnoak while CJ on the whole remained at her flat at Dykebar. This conflict of interests between herself and her remaining younger brother no doubt aggravated Christine's next depression, which hit in September 1951. By November she never wanted to see the house in Crieff again. Christine Thomson spent Christmas 1951 at Dykebar, though partially recovered. By March 1952, however, she was again instructing change at Barnoak and DP found himself outvoted:

> Saturday, 1st March [1952] . . . I was home for a night on Wednesday – I had to be in Edinburgh that afternoon for a Home Board Evangelism Subcommittee Meeting and I caught the 4.25 at Princes Street and went right through to Crieff. Then I found CJ had re-mapped out the garden and digging operations had begun: plants and shrubs to break the line

> between the gate and the lovely stretch of lawn. I much regret this and feel that a unique feature has been spoiled. Mary, however, has acquiesced, if not actually approved, so I fear I can do nothing about it.

Ill again during 1952 – so ill by the winter that DP thought he might lose her – CJ had to leave her post at Dykebar in January 1953 and she returned to stay at Barnoak. In March, however, she secured a flat of her own in Gilgal House, part of a Perth hospital, where she could retain her independence from her brother while sharing in the life at Barnoak when it suited, obtain occasional employment when fit, and also receive necessary counselling and support. The arrangement was to work well for all concerned.

And what of Mary Thomson? The pressures of DP's endless working pattern, of moving and getting her new home into order, of mediating between her husband and her sister in law, and finally of finding herself largely alone in Barnoak while DP ran the Kirkcaldy Campaign from bachelor's digs in the 'Lang Toun' over the winter of 1951-52 were too much:

> Saturday, 15th March [1952] . . . Back at Lady Nairn Avenue, [*Kirkcaldy*], after a cold weary journey. . . . My wee lass was in tears when we parted – poor girlie, she is feeling it lonely at times.

Mary Thomson was very much a home-maker, and her marriage has been rightly been called a happy partnership. Yet just as DP knew times of 'discipline and suffering', Mary too had her own physical and spiritual difficulties and her choices to make, to which DP was not always fully sensitive. The Keswick tradition could ask of evangelicals that they place their obedience to the call of God even before their marriage, as indeed the C. T. Studds had done. DP's underlying assumption was that his wife's overriding priority, even before home-making, was to support the ministry into which he had been called many years before their marriage. He and Mary could and did annoy each other in private, exchanging cross words or angry looks. Occasions when one or the other was in tears can be found in DP's diaries – as well as many more occasions when they were in each other's arms, lovers in every sense. It hardly needs to be said that their marriage also took its strength from their shared faith. A short morning time of prayer and Bible study typically began the day. During this period they found the Bible speaking with fresh insight through J. B. Phillips' *Letters to Young Churches: a Translation of the New Testament Epistles.* And at Barnoak they came to enjoy the competition of the croquet lawn, both becoming adept as through the game DP learnt to give Mary more of his time and attention:

> Sunday, 27th April [1952] . . . Yesterday Mary and I had our first game of croquet for 6½ years – a dingdong battle which I just succeeded in drawing.

There were to be many more such 'dingdong' battles and, indeed, a lengthy 'Barnoak Championship'!

#30: MARY WITH HER FATHER, 1953

THE WEST FIFE, KIRKCALDY AND STRATHMORE CAMPAIGNS, 1951-53

> We who decided to work in the Campaign found that it wasn't limited to visiting people in their homes but if we were willing could be extended to other places. We visited public-houses, factories, pitheads, gambling schools – in fact, wherever men and women were to be found the message of the Church was taken to them.
>
> Testimony cited in: D. P. Thomson, *Harnessing the Lay Forces of the Church*

By the time that the Paisley Mid-Century Campaign ended in April 1951, D. P. Thomson had been actively planning for the West Fife and Kirkcaldy Campaigns for several months. By the time Kirkcaldy closed in April 1952, he was already 'on the eve of the big adventure in Angus and Perthshire!' – the collection of campaigns under the umbrella title of Strathmore that lasted until the end of 1953. The mining villages of the Fife coalfield, the farming parishes of Angus and its small market towns all presented their own particular challenges to the Kirk's outreach and especially to new-style visitation evangelism. DP's move to Crieff, un-thought of when Fife and Kirkcaldy were approved, at least facilitated his travel by bringing his home to the doorstep of these mission fields. Not that these areas were new to him. The Training Schools for West Fife were based in Dunfermline, of which he had happy memories from his ministry at Gillespie Memorial and before that, from his first days as an itinerant evangelist, participating in the outreach of Dunfermline's James Street Hall to the mining villages. He had – unsuccessfully – argued for a 'push in West Fife' back in 1917.

The campaigns of these years, 1951-1954, mark a high point in D. P. Thomson's vocation. By 1951 he had settled into a model of mission that, crucially, had broad support across the presbyteries of the Church. During the campaigns described in this chapter DP was (local opinion apart) free to direct and plan as he wished. They represent the flowering of his personal brand of 'new evangelism' before the reawakening of mass evangelism in 1955 and the controversies surrounding the advent of Dr Billy Graham in Scotland. In these years DP was operating under his own 'brand', not that of the inter-denomination *Tell Scotland* Movement with which he was later associated. But the 'new evangelism' was not an unqualified success story. To understand the more general problems faced by the Churches in Scotland with regard to evangelistic policy before and after 1960, it is important to recognise that D. P. Thomson faced considerable difficulties in these first years of the decade. We therefore follow his doings in these years in some detail.

The Dunfermline Training Schools, 1951

Under pressure from the Evangelism Committee of the Home Board to spread his availability across the country, 'I might be needed in any part of Scotland', the balance of DP's time up to 1959 was spent away from Scotland's major cities, though he was heavily involved in Edinburgh 1954-55 and led the Central Glasgow Churches Campaign of 1958. His pattern of working was to hold short pre-campaign Training Schools based in larger towns or cities, and then to run a series of local missions in outlying areas, each generally of two weeks, within an overall regional campaign structure of several months. Following Paisley's precedent, these campaigns were inter-denominational but, from West Fife onwards, with rather more attention being paid to obtaining the support and sanction of the relevant Church of Scotland authorities. Crucially, his work was not that of an independent, itinerant evangelist, but promoted by a Board of the General Assembly with the backing of local Presbyteries and Kirk Sessions. Evangelism was on the Kirk's agenda in these years, and D. P. Thomson was a high profile enabler of campaigns.

The Parliamentary constituency of West Fife, from the General Election of 1935 to that of 1950, returned to Westminster the leading British Communist, Willie Gallacher MP who as a Trade Union leader had been part of the labour unrest in Glasgow in 1919; he had served a short period of imprisonment for inciting riot. In 1950 the seat had been won for the Labour Party by Willie Hamilton MP, the son of miner and noted for anti-monarchist views. The political heartland of this consciously working-class electorate lay in the mining villages of the West Fife coalfield, which in 1952 supported 29 working pits, nationalised under the National Coal Board after 1946. The Fife coalfield had seen rapid growth between 1890 and the end of the First World War. Typically, mining villages were originally built by the private company that had sunk or owned the mine, with terraces of houses clustered around the shaft and spoil-heap; industrial complexes surrounded by agriculture, neither urban nor traditional countryside. By the 1950s they had their own traditions: the Working Men's Clubs, the gala days, the banners and symbols of the National Union of Mineworkers, *For Safer Industry – For Peace And Socialism.* Such mining villages, in some ways quite separate from the rest of the country, were thought to pose problems to the Church. Between the wars, the Church of Scotland often provided ministry to the miners via Lay Missionaries rather than by ministers of Word and Sacrament.[1]

In a class-conscious community with bitter memories of industrial strife in the 1920s and 1930s, the Kirk had suffered from its former association with the colliery-owners and managers, who had often provided grants for the establishment of the missions in their villages. These villages had gathered together new populations that did not fit the distribution of the ministry in rural parishes; they lacked the culture of deference still expected by ministers; they could be pilloried by senior churchmen as nurturing hard-bitten communists.[2] In the *Third Statistical Account*, ministers wrote in condemnation of the gambling, grey-hound racing and indifference to religion they believed to be common among the mining communities. West Fife, then, was seen by D. P. Thomson as a suitable area for 'the biggest ever all-in and all-out attack!'

DP was well abreast of the Kirk's concern to understand and counter communism in this new era of Cold War. Back in his days at Gillespie Memorial, one acquaintance had been Jimmy Watt, a converted ex-communist and Oxford Group speaker. Another friend of DP's Dunfermline days, George M. Dryburgh, was the convener of the General Assembly's Committee on Communism. Established after the report 'The Challenge of Communism' which Dryburgh edited for the Youth Commission in 1948, this offered the Assemblies of 1950-1954 lengthy assessments of the global impact, philosophy and politics of communism, with suggested responses by the churches. Of particular concern to Dryburgh's Committee was the need for more effective Christian education for adults, which was explicitly related to the 'new evangelism' of the laity central to DP's remit: 'We have to learn to give to the laity their proper place in the life and witness of the Church. The proper agent for evangelism is nothing less than the whole body of the faithful.'[3] Early in the Second War, his overseas contacts had convinced DP that the Soviet Union was as despotic as Nazi Germany: 'If ever there was an Antichrist it is Stalin!' he had written in December 1948. His passion for open air, street corner witness and preaching had brought acquaintance with Glasgow's politically radical orators. DP had given lectures on 'Christianity and Communism' at the Kilmacolm / Woodhall School of 1950. His reading at that time included Lex Miller's *The Christian Significance of Karl Marx*. He also purchased extensively on this theme, including copies of Karl Marx's *Das Capital* and the Dryburgh Commission's 1952 book *The Challenge of Communism*, and he wrote in his diary:

> Friday, 2nd February [1951] . . . I have been typing extracts on Communism . . . Nothing must have priority now over an intensive study of that fascinating and diabolical system. The biggest thing by far that Christianity has ever been up against.

'The Challenge of World Communism' was the title of one of the sessions at the Dunfermline Training Schools, and DP waxed eloquent on the theme:[4]

> Communism is capturing millions of the youth of the world . . . because it seems to have enthusiasm, and offers them unselfish social passion – the opportunity to clean up whole swamps of human life which the Church has failed to clear up. The Church seems to be content to be a little pharisaic sect singing itself blissfully into blindness to the hideous glaring evil that it ought to be rolling up its sleeves to tackle. Nine-tenths of the clergy and nine-tenths of the laity are just playing at religion . . . The time has come when we have to set our own house in order or the whole fabric of what we call Christian civilization will disappear and will deserve to disappear as a monstrous blasphemy in the face of God and man.

Despite the strength of this rhetoric, D. P. Thomson should not be thought of as socially radical. He had once been an embryonic businessman; his wider family had been in business and he looked to local businesses to support his campaigns. Apart from an opposition to communism that he shared with George F. MacLeod, he – unlike George – took care not to be involved in party politics.

The West Fife and Kirkcaldy Campaigns owed their origin to two sources. There was DP's desire to work again in Dunfermline and Fife. There were also local fraternals of ministers happy to invite him and with evangelical ambitions of their own, groups eventually embodied as the inter-denominational Campaign Committees of the Lochgelly Churches, the Cowdenbeath Churches, the Kirkcaldy Churches, and 'the Campaign Committees responsible for the forthcoming Missions in the Halbeath, Crossgates, Hill of Beath, Crombie, Glencraig, Crosshill, Lochore and Ballingry areas'. First promoted by these small clusters, the campaigns had gained the consent of the two local Presbyteries, Dunfermline & Kinross, and Kirkcaldy, by the first week of March 1951. A number of ministers also sought the approval of their Kirk Sessions for what was proposed. During June and July DP oversaw the various local groups of workers as the by-now usual work of card-indexing the populations was undertaken. Everything went as smoothly as could be expected, with good cooperation. DP then spent the whole of August – with a single day at home for Mary's birthday party – camping in church halls at the two successive Dunfermline Training Schools, 'the busiest and most rewarding month of my life', as he wrote enthusiastically on 1 September 1951. The timetable advertised for Dunfermline, West Fife and Kirkcaldy ran:[5]

The Training Schools:	
Dunfermline [1]	3 - 13 Aug. 1951
Dunfermline [2]	17 - 27 Aug. 1951
The Campaigns:	
Lochgelly	13-30 Sept. 1951
Glencraig, Crosshill, Lochore & Ballingry	30 Sept. - 14 Oct.
Halbeath, Mossgreen, Crossgates & Hill of Beath	28 Oct. - 11 Nov.
Crombie area	18 - 25 Nov.
Cowdenbeath	25 Nov. - 9 Dec.
Kirkcaldy, ward 4	6 - 20 Jan. 1952
Kirkcaldy, ward 3	27 Jan. - 10 Feb.
Kirkcaldy, ward 2	17 Feb. - 2 Mar.
Kirkcaldy, ward 1	16 - 30 Mar.

DP was to describe Dunfermline 1951 in his *Harnessing the Lay Forces* as 'the most ambitious, and in many ways the most significant, of our Residential Summer Training Schools.' Unsurprisingly he dedicated a good number of pages in that booklet to describing the principles embodied at Dunfermline, its staffing, programme and results. They were principles that he had been developing since his first ministry at Dunfermline and the experiment at Glassiebarns: training occasions that were egalitarian, international, ecumenical, open, holistic, communal; visionary *and* down-to-earth; theoretical *and* practical. Such Schools were intended to train lay workers and were not themselves primarily evangelical campaigns.

What distinguished the Training Schools of this period from the residential centres of DP's earlier and later periods was the fact that they were located 'on the job'. The school came to where mission work was to be done so that 'Theoretical and practical training must be completely integrated'. DP's hope was that the ladies of the Woman's Guild who came to do the catering, or even any casually interested visitors, might find themselves swept up in the atmosphere and themselves engage in active witness in door to door visitation. Once again the School acted as the centre for a mini-campaign – indeed for more than one, as two discrete mining villages, were (with some success) visited: Blairhall and Oakley. 'In both of these districts every home was visited, local members and workers being encouraged to go out paired with trainees from further afield.' There was an emphasis on 'open air' activities – services on the sands of Aberdour, a children's open air service on the Blairhall green, a Conventicle at the Hill of Beath: 'The Lochgelly and Cowdenbeath Town Bands will lead the praise, together with a United Choir of the West Fife Churches; in the barn of Mains of Beath Farm if wet.' The promotion of Christian literature always featured in DP's work, so a travelling bookshop was borrowed and 'trainees discovered both problems and possibilities in colportage work'.

If the outreach programme was demanding, so too the lectures offered were of high quality. Charles Duthie, by now the Chairman-Elect of the Congregational Union of Scotland, spoke on 'The Gospel for Today' and 'The Basis of Group Fellowship in Church and Campaign'. Tom Allan spoke on 'The Church in the Open Air', 'The Church and the Child', 'Personal Problems of Christian Discipleship' and 'What it means to be a Christian'. DP was able to offer to these schools the services of specialists such as Ronnie Falconer of the BBC and William Macintyre, Organiser for Industrial Chaplaincies in Scotland. Representatives of the Overseas Churches were Andrew B. Doig, Nyasaland; Donald MacFarlan, Old Calabar, West Africa; Kenneth Mackenzie, Central Africa; David Spowart, India; and Stalios Kaleterakis, Greece. Emeritus Principal Hugh Watt, D.D., LL.D., New College, Edinburgh, Moderator of the General Assembly of 1950, spoke at the opening Rally and the Convener of the Home Board, T. B. Stewart Thomson (a Chaplain to the King) led the final Thanksgiving and Dedication Rally in Dunfermline Abbey, after which the School closed with a midnight communion in Dunfermline: Erskine Church. As DP wrote, defensively, in 1958: 'There is nothing narrow or individualistic about a Training School of this kind.'

How did it all go? Over the month of August 1951 some 1,000 men and women attended Training School sessions at some stage, with between 140 and 200 in residence for at least part of the time. This was sufficient to provide a good nucleus of workers for the subsequent West Fife Campaign and it also included individuals who were to associate with DP's work for many years. Willie Frame, for example, in 1974 attributed his conversion and his subsequent vocation as a Lay Missionary and then a minister of the Church of Scotland to his attendance at the Dunfermline Training School.[6] DP himself cited a number of testimonies to both conversion and deeper consecration flowing from Dunfermline in *Harnessing the Lay Forces* and, though these were given anonymously, those of Frame and Roy Copeland, both originally miners, can be identified. He was delighted to record, at the service at the close of the Schools:

> . . . a great gathering in Dunfermline Abbey on the final Sunday evening, at which for the first time in history the voice of a working miner rang down the nave, as trainees told of what these memorable weeks had meant to them.

DP had discovered that the Fife coalfield might, certainly, be home to committed communists; it could also be home to equally committed Christian men and women, waiting for their gifts to be used by the Kirk.

West Fife, 1951

On average, the dozen Church of Scotland congregations in West Fife that D. P. Thomson sought to organise for his 1951-52 campaigns had perhaps 240 attending communion, out of memberships of around 500. These generalities naturally conceal differences. St Andrews, the former Established Church at Lochgelly, had a membership of almost 1,000 whereas Cowdenbeath: Guthrie struggled to reach 300 and Cairneyhill, 200. At Lochcraig on occasion nearly 60% of the membership attended communion; Guthrie was fortunate to manage 30%. Besides Sunday worship, other formal activities were the children's and youth work universal throughout Scotland: Sunday Schools junior and senior and, hardly less common, Bible Classes. Branches of the uniformed organisations – Scouts, Cubs, Brownies, Girl Guides, Boys' Brigade – could be found. Woman's Guilds were also standard, in whose programmes the support of the foreign mission work of the Church often featured, besides sales and social evenings and guest speakers.

Beyond these, different congregations were attempting new ways to make contact or promote spiritual growth. New organisations were created: a midweek Bible Study and a Men's Social Club (Lumphinnans); a Mixed Youth Club (Lochgelly: Churchmount), a Badminton Club (Cowdenbeath Guthrie Memorial). Cinema films and concerts by a local Choral Union were offered in Cowdenbeath West Church Hall on Sunday evenings in the winter, and their Youth Fellowship ran an Easter midweek service. At Lochcraig there was community singing using the *Redemption Hymnal* before evening services, again in the winter. The area certainly had ministers with energy and vision: besides Alastair McTavish of Lochgelly: Churchmount (a member of the Home Board's Evangelism Committee), Bill Morris of Lochcraig was also being head-hunted by Sir James F. Simpson to lead Summer Missions. J. Monaghan of Lumphinnans, while a young National Serviceman in the navy during the Second War, had had the initiative to found a fleet-based branch of Christian Endeavour - 'CE Afloat'. These three ministers were in their first parishes and had arrived in Fife since 1947. Indeed, of the dozen ministers potentially involved with the West Fife Campaign only two had been in place for over five years. As to their Kirk Sessions, of the eight records available for study, six contain minutes of support: Cowdenbeath: Cairns; Cowdenbeath: West; Lochcraig; Lochgelly: Churchmount; Lochgelly: St Andrews and Lumphinnans. The working-class congregations of the coalfield had known 'old-style' evangelism in DP's youth; now, invited to participate in a 'new-style' campaign backed by the General Assembly's Home Board and led by a nationally-accredited evangelist, they offered their approval.

The Lochgelly Campaign began two weeks after the Dunfermline Training Schools concluded. Further evening training classes were in the interim arranged at the village of Crossgates. In the meantime DP's sister Dr Christine Thomson was again ill. Concern for Christine and the need to visit her in hospital in Edinburgh remained a pressure through September and October. During these weeks DP was also finishing *The Road to Dunfermline*, the first part of his projected autobiography. Pressure of work meant that he had to cut it short; it was published in October 1951. Pressure of work also had its usual impact on DP's health and his attendance at Lochgelly was less than he had hoped. Still, the campaign began well and it ended well with a Rally at a packed-out Town Hall, and it brought DP new experiences:

> Monday, 8th October [1951] . . . I had assignments that were quite new to me, like Trades Union Meetings and Coal Pits. I also addressed Social Clubs, Lodge Minto of the Freemasons and the Lochgelly Town Council & spoke at many Clubs.

The two week Lochgelly campaign contained the now-usual mix of styles of evangelism: visitation of some 3,000 homes by both locals and volunteers recruited at the Training Schools; 'commando' visits to places of work including the Nellie, Jenny Gray and Minto pits, and also at least one evangelistic meeting with an 'after meeting' offered for counselling. DP had been preaching on 'Counting the Cost' since his Glasgow: Central Campaign of 1921 and probably earlier! The three Church of Scotland

(St Andrew's, Churchmount and Macainsh) and the Lochgelly Episcopal (St Finnian's) and Baptist ministers supported the mission and they all spoke at a question-and-answer meeting at the Town Hall. Besides the collieries, assignments included open air meetings, speaking at the interval in the local cinemas and at half-time to football crowds; and a bookstall was run from borrowed space in a Main Street shop. The local paper, the *Lochgelly Times*, finally printed a congratulatory report under the headline 'Lochgelly Churches' Campaign: A Great Revival of Interest' with the broad conclusions (no doubt fed to their editor by DP who reprinted them in *We Saw the Church in Action!*) that they had seen how well different denominations could work together, that the people of the town had given the campaign a sympathetic hearing, and that many were returning to worship in the local churches.

Space does not allow for individual accounts of all the separate West Fife campaigns that continued to December 1951, though they did not run entirely as advertised before the Training School. No campaign took place in the Cairneyhill / Crombie area, the Church of Scotland minister there declining to be involved. DP spent the allocated time in refining preparations for Cowdenbeath and Kirkcaldy. The three areas that did follow Lochgelly, however, used the same pattern. Glencraig and Ballingry, the first two weeks in October, built on the growing interest, so the visitation there was more thorough, besides being supported by a number of ministry students of the Scottish Episcopal Church. A UK General Election being called for 25 October, the Churches' Campaign also coincided with political campaigning and DP was pleased that the Christian meetings were reported to be better attended than those of the Communists. He felt under the weather again, however, recovering briefly to preach at the concluding Rally:

> Wednesday, 17th October [1951] . . . Last Sunday I attended Ballingry Parish Church in the morning and preached in it at night. It was crowded as I have rarely seen a church crowded – every available form and chair carried in.

For health reasons, DP tried to take things as easily as he could while at the Mossgreen / Crossgates campaign at the beginning of November and this may have contributed to a sense of hanging fire as things began slowly. That the mother of one of the ministers involved was dying and that all DP's powers of persuasion were needed to get the minister of Beath to offer even nominal support cannot have helped either. Finally both DP's fitness and local interest improved for the Cowdenbeath and Lumphinnans Campaign in the last week of November and the first of December. The opening Workers' Rally attracted 70 volunteers – and 100 were at the Closing Workers' Rally: 'We covered some 1,300 homes the first four nights and had as many as 37 couples out one night.' Here, DP credited progress to the active support of the ministers concerned: 'The local ministers went out on assignments. They covered a lot of ground and interest has grown steadily.'

Featured at Lumphinnans was a form of service that DP was to use again and again in the next years, 'The Voice of the Pew':

> The popularity of the 'Voice of the Pew' service held in Lumphinnans Church on Sunday evening was reflected in the capacity congregation. Even with the provision of extra seating many had to remain standing throughout the service. Another feature was the large number of non-church members present. No clergyman took part. The service was conducted by Mr W. T. Gilchrist, local manager of the Gas Board, who also spoke as a business man. Mrs W. Hunter, Foulford Road, gave the viewpoint of the housewife; Miss Jean Honeyman, of the Town Council staff, spoke as a typist; Mr R. Dalgliesh, of the staff of Beath High School, spoke as a teacher; and Messrs. W. Frame and R. Copeland testified on behalf of the local miners. All stressed how the application of Christianity had helped them in their various spheres of life.

A variety of the 'Witness Box' that featured extempore speaking about the reality of the faith, the 'Voice of the Pew' was more structured and allowed its participants time for preparation. Personal testimony to the living practicality of the Christian life was what was intended; that both women as well as men spoke was significant. The other special service that featured in the advertising for the Cowdenbeath & Lumphinnans area was the 'Heckling Meeting for Men Only', held in the Cowdenbeath Miners' Welfare Institute on Wednesday 5 December. The title somewhat over-hyped what was in effect a 'Brains Trust' style event, with questions from the floor coming, without preparation, to a ministerial panel. Besides questioning the level of support some of the ministers gave to the Cowdenbeath football team, topics raised included world peace and whether the institutional Church could bring about the brotherhood of man? Was there anything wrong with the man who took a pint of beer on a Saturday and went to church on a Sunday?[7]

In an article in the religious newspaper, *The British Weekly*, Tom Allan summarised the findings of the West Fife Campaigns.[8] The coalfield had certainly posed problems for the churches: in one area, more than a third of homes visited had no contact with the Church and wanted none. Allan commented that, in this respect, West Fife was different from elsewhere: it provided a warning against the complacent assumption that Britain was a Christian country. Beyond general affirmations that church attendance had increased, and noting that between 300-500 adults were baptised as a result of the West Fife and Kirkcaldy Campaigns as a whole, DP made few claims for 'results' of the outreach of these 1951 campaigns beyond that they met his three general objectives, later explained in *Aspects of Evangelism,* as (1) to make 'effective personal contact in the interest of the Gospel, with every man, woman and child in a community;' (2) 'to put religion on the map, to bring it in from the circumference of public interest to the centre;' and (3) to open up new opportunities for local Christians and congregations.

T. Ralph Morton suggested that the nationalisation of the mines having freed the church from its perceived alliance with management, miners might be prepared to give the Church a hearing where before class solidarity had kept them away.[9] There were certainly those for whom West Fife was a spiritual awakening. One miner's testimony is worth recalling, for in miniature it encapsulates the type of spiritual benefit DP's ministry brought to individuals and through them to the Scottish churches. The man concerned was 'a Boys Brigade Officer, a Life Boy Leader, and a Deacon' and his story was reported in *Harnessing the Lay Forces of the Church*:

> In the course of the Campaign, I, like others, learned many lessons and made not a few discoveries; for example, during talks with people in their homes and pubs, and other places visited, I found out how much was expected from our ministers, and I realised that it was impossible for one man to fulfil all these duties. I also saw unlimited scope for the laity of the Church, jobs which can sometimes be done better by a layman than by a man with a clerical collar, such as visitation of aged and sick people, work within the organisations of the Church, and, what is most important, actual witnessing in our everyday lives as to what Christ meant to us, and proving by our actions that He is alive and working in the world to-day. This was brought home to me very forcibly. I discovered during this period of work that something had been happening to me. Jesus Christ had become a real person to me, living in me, and working through me. It would have been impossible to have knocked at strange doors, or to go out in the name of the Church to wherever men and women were to be found, without the power and strength that only He can give through the Holy Spirit.

And if this sort of thing was a discovery for the volunteers, their discipline and strength was a discovery for D. P. Thomson:[10]

> The miner wants to attach himself to the Church with the enthusiasm of a football fan – no distance is too great for him to travel and no

> sacrifice too big for him to make once he gets cracking. I have seen nothing . . . to touch the self-denial and sacrifice of the miners in our team – two of them I think of especially, out night by night on the job till after ten, then home to be in the pit by five in the morning to begin their shift. I have a new vision of what the Church might do once it has harnessed the proletariat! And they are waiting to be got if we really mean business.

The best part of 100 Christian workers recruited in West Fife also volunteered for the Kirkcaldy campaign of January to March 1952, and this influx of activists was for DP by no means the least of the results of his work.

What followed the one or two weeks of special activity was always a problem for campaign evangelism, whether old or new style, and visitation evangelism posed questions of its own to the congregations involved. DP's system produced a multitude of record cards, reporting the results of visits to homes and indicating households where there were problems, or children to invite to Sunday School, or adults wanting to know more of the faith, or . . . the possibilities could be extended. But his teams of external volunteers had moved on, and – at best – it fell to the local minister and his elders to deal, unsupported, with this information. And there might be other issues to deal with if the Campaign had not gone as expected. The West Fife Kirk Session minutes give some indication of what happened. Not all households were in fact visited in Cowdenbeath: some areas not at all, while at some addresses the single attempt to call had found no-one at home. There was therefore remedial work to be done by teams of volunteers from the Cairns Session and congregation. At least that Session was able to create teams led by its own membership. This could not be taken for granted. At Cowdenbeath: West, a new congregational group was formed to do the work, one the minister hoped some elders might join. At Lumphinnans, James Monaghan was an enthusiast for the December 1951 campaign. He began his attempt at follow up in January but volunteers were not easy to find and by May nothing much seemed to have happened. Lochcraig offered its own variant on this theme. Its campaign with DP had been in October 1951. Follow up was not immediate but, working at its own pace, the Session agreed on a further 'Visitation Campaign' timed for October 1952 and successfully carried this through. It is, however, at least interesting that this 'Campaign' was confined to their own congregation: it thus took special effort to arrange for elders to visit the households of their own congregation. Still, the Lochcraig Session believed that its follow up campaign had been successful, measured in the terms it was used to: at their October 1952 Communion the attendance of 341 exceeded the previous best, that of 335 in October 1951.

There is evidence from West Fife to substantiate claims for the sort of results that were expected of visitation evangelism. The numbers joining Lochcraig Church by profession of faith showed a marked increase, from the five or seven typical before previous communions, to 32 in October 1951, 27 in February and 23 in June 1952. Moreover the minutes also recorded that 18 of those joining in October 1951 and 16 of those in February 1952 had first to be baptised as adults, showing that they had been raised by parents who had not followed the normal presbyterian practice of infant baptism. Similarly Lumphinnans recorded 13 new members at its first Communion following its campaign, when three to five had been more typical before. Cowdenbeath: Cairns raised its attendance at communion from 377 in February 1951 to 515 at February 1952, and those joining there by profession of faith rose from seven to 37. The other available minutes record further, if not such dramatic, gains. Within the Presbytery of Dunfermline & Kinross as a whole, a total of 45 charges including 11 in Dunfermline alone, adult baptisms rose from 190 in 1950 (January to December) to 265 in 1951 and 315 in 1952, the last two successively each the highest since the war. Professions of faith were also high in these years, though not at a record level. The testimonies already given show how important to the individuals concerned such decisions could be.

Kirkcaldy, 1952

If (by June 1952) the Dunfermline Training Schools were 'the most ambitious, and in many ways the most significant' DP had run, and the West Fife Campaigns particular challenging, the subsequent Kirkcaldy Campaign was, he believed, his most successful to date. Beginning early in January 1952, the mission had four subdivisions which ran as planned and concluded at the end of March. Its preparation appears to have been very thorough, having been conceived by the town's ministers' fraternal a year earlier: H. R. Ferrie of Kirkcaldy: Old, Presbytery Home Mission Convener, sat on both the Home Board and its Seaside Missions subcommittee. Sixteen Church of Scotland charges in Kirkcaldy, with the two congregations of adjacent Dysart, were involved to some degree, in spite of the fact that Raith was then without a minister. Support came from ministers ordained less than 10 years, a group of six including M. W. Cooper [Abbotshall], as well as from those ordained before the Union, another group of six including A. Renshaw Mackay [Bethelfield]. As in West Fife the average size of all these congregations was just under 500, though five were over 1,000 and two under 400. As far as is known attendance at communion was about 50%. In his diaries DP also mentioned the participation of the West End Congregational, the Sinclairtown Church of Christ, the Whyte's Causeway Baptist, Normand Road United Free, Kirkcaldy Methodist and Pathhead Evangelical Union Churches.

All the usual apparatus was engaged: bookstalls offered Christian literature; visits were paid to clubs and pubs and to a Raith Rovers football match and to the Annual Show of the Kirkcaldy Domestic Rabbit Society; more 5am pit-head meetings were held and over 100 visits to the huge linoleum factory of Sir Michael Nairn & Co. In February there was 'an impressive Open Air at the Quayside – dockers, sailors, office workers etc to the number of 60-70'. Speakers went to the hospitals and schools; to bowling clubs; to the County Council, the Public Library, the Ice Rink, the bus depot and the Tudor Dance Hall. DP spoke personally to 'the Marks & Spencer girls . . . the Police, the Prudential Inspectors and other groups'. An 'International Trio' – Salvatore Carco of Sicily, N. Kodara of Japan and David Newquist of California – added their witness. There was a Special Campaign Parade of the Boys Brigade and other uniformed organisations at St Brycedale. All the while teams of local volunteers, supported by the activists from West Fife, visited the households of Kirkcaldy, many of them coming straight from work to tea at headquarters before commencing their rounds. Certainly there were lulls: during February DP reported to the Home Board that the main impact of the campaign had been to rally Kirkcaldy's ministers and office-bearers, a very limited if useful effect. Still, by 26 June 1952 he found himself satisfied: 'Kirkcaldy certainly stands out as perhaps the most the successful effort we have had.'

Lacking all but four of Kirkcaldy's Kirk Session records from this period, it is difficult to investigate this claim beyond looking at the officially published statistics, which suggest a small net loss for the Kirkcaldy churches between 1948 and 1953, and that the total numbers of both professions of faith and of adult baptisms across the Presbytery were less in 1952 than they had been in 1951. 1952 does, however, appear significant in the *Year-Book* figures for Gallatown, where net growth was 74. Yet even this does not tell the full story. The Kirk Session records show the growth came from 57 new members joining by profession of faith, 40 joining by transfer from elsewhere and 8 more added as the Session agreed to restore lapsed members to full communion. These gains more than compensated for the nine deaths and the 22 members who asked for their 'lines' so they might join some other congregation. Perhaps Gallatown congregation's gains would have appeared larger if better harmony had prevailed: there were grievances in the congregation over plans to modernise the sanctuary of the church. Bill Cooper's Abbotshall congregation had also gained 60 new members by profession of faith and, indeed, the *Year-Book* shows an even larger net gain of 91 for Abbotshall between December 1951 and December 1952, against 39 and 34 in the first two years of his ministry there. The Abbotsrood congregation was also growing in this period even if not especially strongly in 1952. Figures showing a net growth out of pattern with the previous few years were declared by the congregations of Bethelfield, Gallatown, Pathhead East, Pathhead West, St James', St John's and Sinclairtown even if, as in the cases of Bethelfield and Sinclairtown, seemingly small gains in 1952 have to be set against a pattern of decline. Some seven of the 18 charges in Kirkcaldy/Dysart were in general decline in this period, and the Presbytery's Union and Readjustment Committee was actively seeking adjustments to realign their charges with new patterns of population. Although there were numerous personal decisions behind all the reported professions of faith and restorations to the communion rolls, the success of the 1952 Kirkcaldy Campaign may have been to staunch a tide flowing somewhat against the church.

Besides the recruitment of campaign workers, preparation for these campaigns required soliciting the backing of people in positions of power and influence. Three forms of support were asked from local businesses: direct donations to the funds; paid advertisements in newsletters and programmes; and authority for work-place meetings. DP believed in the direct approach, and thus at Kirkcaldy he sought interviews with Sir Michael and Sir Robert Spencer Nairn, the linoleum manufacturers. The founder of the company, the first Sir Michael Nairn, having been a pillar of the Free Church and behind the building of its city-centre St Brycedale Church, DP featured him in the second of his two booklets of biographical studies published to coincide with the Kirkcaldy Campaign, *Born in Kirkcaldy* and *Raith and Kirkcaldy*. DP appears to have met little resistance to his arrangements for evangelism in the workplace, whether from private-sector industrialists or public-sector managers of the National Coal Board. At

West Fife and Kirkcaldy there seems to have been no repetition of the clearly unusual occurrence at one Paisley works, where the staff had been asked to vote in advance whether or not to give the campaign a hearing. Schools, too, were open to the visiting ministers. It all took a great deal of organisation, but it also depended on an acceptance that all these doors could be legitimately opened to the campaign by their keepers. Perhaps, for some, this reinforced the old perception that the Church belonged 'to the world of the managers, the bankers, the teachers'.

Some criticism surfaced at the 'Heckling Meeting' held at the Dysart Miners' Institute.[11] The panel were asked why Kirkcaldy was being singled out as in need of the Gospel? Was this some sort of reflection on the 'Lang Toon'? Was the message too political – was the campaign anti-Communist? Conversely, why did the Church not speak out clearly to oppose the atomic bomb, which on 26 February 1952 the Prime Minister, Winston Churchill, was to reveal that the United Kingdom was developing? Why, the ministerial panel were also asked, had the Church lost touch with the great mass of the people in Scotland, and especially with those in industry? Nevertheless, some at least of the congregations were assisted to grow. T. Ralph Morton's correspondents, too, were (in moderate tones) positive in their reports.[12] That there were no large-scale evangelistic meetings was welcomed, as was the training offered for the volunteer visitors and the opportunities the workplace assignments gave the ministers: 'We did no street-corner preaching. We simply went after people where they were. Nor did we ask for decisions.' Nevertheless:

> People have become interested. I had a Communicants class of about fifty as did another church. Quite a few were restored to Church membership. I think I would otherwise have had about twenty. . . . Attendances have gone up in most churches . . . We have also set up a Christian Council in the town where Christians can come to findings on any particular issue and speak with one voice. The worrying point is: are we going to hold on to those incomers? Are we going to be able to fulfil our promises to them?

The criticisms thus published in *Evangelism in Scotland* were once more that they would have preferred greater emphasis on their individual congregations: more time spent training workers – 'Many put both feet in, through lack of knowledge and inexperience. Certain types of visitors proved more harmful almost than good' – and more time helping the congregations to be more open, welcoming and understanding. Hence, 'I still think a parish effort could be more effective than this wider one.' Still, even if a little grudgingly, there seemed to be a general acceptance that the Kirkcaldy Campaign did what it had set out to do.

Perhaps there was something about the pressure and sense of a building climax to the Kirkcaldy Campaign that once more brought D. P. Thomson to wonder if his death was imminent. The image chosen for posters was a Cross, standing stark on a hill – 'in the night watches' he saw this as his tombstone. Concerns for symptoms of illness were never far from his mind. Nevertheless during March 1952 other new prospects appeared on DP's horizon that helped to shake him out of this mood. In 1948 his close friend Bill Temple had been called across the world from Edinburgh: Barclay to St John's Presbyterian Church, Wellington, New Zealand, where he quickly became involved in radio ministry and his new denomination's 'New Life Movement'. Now he sought DP's assistance:

> Wednesday, 19th March [1952] This is for me a day of destiny. A long airmail letter – four quarto pages – from Bill Temple in the course of which he says: – '*I am to ask you what are the possibilities of your coming out? The idea would not to be so much that you should run the mission on Bryan Green lines, or even on the lines you have been exploring more recently, but that you might inform the church as to how the whole business of evangelism can be tackled in terms of the modern situation. The first thing to be decided is what prospects are there of your coming and when. If you find it quite off the map to project the trip would you be willing to recommend someone for the job. We should accept your recommendation without hesitation.*' That is the invitation for which I have been waiting for 30 years. It is the one trip I had wanted to make before my work was done – and I had almost given up hope of. Ray Price has passed off – Don and Brian and Vic getting old now. I had almost given up hope of seeing them here. Now it looks as though, perhaps, I might! I called Bill today asking for a firm invitation to be sent to Edinburgh by cable or overseas letter. Strange, but just these last few weeks I should have felt that my work in Scotland was done. If the new lands want me I am ready to go, even if it means resigning my job to do so.

DP's immediate reaction to this was – understandably – precipitate. What would such a call have meant for Mary? His request for an explicit invitation, however, was more than the New Zealand authorities were ready for. Bill had to write to throw cold water on DP's enthusiasm. Yet Thomson's reaction to that anticlimax was remarkable: setting aside any sense of disappointment, he focused on the new work calling for his enthusiasm, energy and experience, the Strathmore Campaign:

> Thursday, 3rd April 1952] . . . Yesterday I went to Edinburgh for an interview with Macintosh & Sawyer about New Zealand. It appears that the Committee will let me go for a year as from April next. On top of that comes a letter from Bill Temple today saying it is all off! So where are we? – – we are on the eve of the big adventure in Angus and Perthshire! Meanwhile I must finish my packing here in Kirkcaldy!

That the Presbyterian Church of New Zealand even contemplated an invitation to D. P. Thomson to become their Adviser in Evangelism shows how far the value of his work was now recognised. A similar invitation soon followed from Canada. Both possibilities remained on his agenda for some time, but in the end he had too much on his plate in Scotland to leave.

In Strathmore, 1952-53

The Strathmore Campaign began with a Training School in June 1952 and was not wound up until its Closing Rally on 2 November 1953. DP used 'Strathmore' as loose shorthand for the largely rural areas of Tayside, Angus and the Mearns, lying south of Aberdeen, north and east of Dundee and Perth; an ancient agricultural area that comprised the hills and mountains of the glens of the Grampians to the west; traditional rural parishes, market towns and small North Sea ports. Some 100 Church of Scotland parishes were potentially involved, within the jurisdictions of the six Presbyteries of Brechin & Fordoun, Forfar, Meigle, Arbroath, Dundee and Perth. Under the overall umbrella of the Strathmore Churches Campaign Committee some nine distinct phases were planned, with three training schools, three training weekends and weekday evening classes.

DP was to report to the Evangelism Committee (5 November 1952) that 'he had discovered more deep-seated opposition in Strathmore to the whole idea of such a campaign than he had ever done in any other part of the country', and in his diaries he often expressed frustration and disappointment at the attitudes of ministers and kirk sessions. Volunteers for visiting did not come easily and as a response to this he relied increasingly on an elite team, gathered from across the region. Out of this came his most enduring movement, 'Work & Witness – A Movement Designed to Help In The Training & Utilisation of Lay Workers in the Services of the Scottish Churches, particularly in United Action.'

Its account spread out over three of DP's own Diaries, its story retold in some detail in *We Saw the Church in Action!*, an outline of the Strathmore Campaign may now assist.

The Strathmore Churches Campaign 1952-1953

1952	**Event**	**Base**
Apr. 17, 1952	Strathmore Churches Campaign Committee constituted	Meigle
	Training Classes	Montrose
June 13-16	Training School	Gannochy Lodge, Edzell
August 8-19	Training School	Dundee
Sept. 5-8	1st Training Weekend	Cardean House, Meigle
Sept. 12-15	2nd Training Weekend	Forfar
Sept. 10 on	Central Area Training Classes	Blairgowrie & Forfar
Sept. 19-22	3rd Training Weekend	St Cyrus
Sept. 23-25	Campaign Prayer meetings	Montrose
Sept. 28 - Oct. 24	Montrose Churches Campaign	Montrose
Nov. 2-13	Mearns Campaign (1)	St Cyrus
Nov. 14-30	Mearns Campaign (2)	Inverbervie
1953		
January 3	New Year Rally	Perth
Feb. 1-16	Coupar Angus Campaign	
Feb. 25 to Mar. 10	Burrelton and Area Campaign	
March 15-26	Newtyle and Area Campaign	
April 2-20	Grampian Glens Campaign	Cray Manse, Glenshee
June 15-30	Training School and Glens Campaign	Kirriemuir
Sept. 20 - Oct. 11	Forfar Campaign	
Oct. 21 to Nov. 1	Glamis Campaign	
Nov. 1, 1953	Closing Rally of Strathmore Churches Campaign	

From this table can be seen both the scope and the limitations of 'Strathmore'. The substantial area under the authority of the Presbytery of Arbroath was not effectively involved. Nor were the cities of Perth or Dundee, apart from hosting a Rally and a Training School. No campaign specifically targeted the cathedral town of Brechin, or the Grampian upland parishes of the Mearns. Still DP and his teams did travel up the Angus glens to locations that surely no other such campaign ever attempted, and the market towns of central Strathmore came into focus by turn, in so far as they chose to invite his presence.

On 12 February 1952, William Eadie, minister of Aberluthnott, persuaded the Presbytery of Brechin & Fordoun to issue a general invitation to D. P. Thomson, one that the Home Board encouraged him to accept. Further invitations arrived: from the neighbouring Presbytery of Meigle for a local, denominational campaign and from the inter-denominational Montrose Ministers Fraternal. In March 1952 DP took the initiative in mooting his plans for a phased regional campaign to Bill Eadie's Home Mission committee and its counterpart in the Presbytery of Meigle, to office-bearers of the Presbyteries of Fordyce and Forfar, to the Montrose Ministers Fraternal and to individuals he knew in the Presbytery of Perth. From this beginning a string of authorisations followed, between April and June, from the Presbyteries of Forfar, Meigle, Brechin & Fordoun, Perth and Arbroath. The bishops of Brechin and St Andrews also approved the campaign on behalf of the Episcopal Church of Scotland. All these decisions, of course, committed no-one to actual action: these permissions were general, leaving it up to each congregation to decide whether to join in. Thomson had in fact met with some resistance during private meetings in Forfar, and friends were both pleased and surprised at the unanimity of support offered by Meigle Presbytery. Events now moved rapidly. The overall Campaign Committee had already been constituted on 17 April, co-chaired by David C. Mitchell, minister at Burrelton in the Presbytery of Perth, DP's old acquaintance. Frederick Kennedy of Montrose: Old represented the northern half of the area as the other co-chair.

Ecumenical agreement to a Montrose campaign having already been locally secured, the first phase for Strathmore was planned to open there in September. But before Montrose began, there was an extended period of training events: two formal 'Schools' on the Dunfermline pattern followed by three training weekends and one-off meetings in local centres. Such events in advance of his campaigns were by now a hallmark of DP's procedure and the scattered nature of Strathmore meant that these had to be arranged in a variety of locations. Empowering the ordinary Christian for outreach was now at least as important to him as the immediate missionary impact of what he organised, or so he reported to the Evangelism Committee: '[Mr Thomson's] chief aim was not merely to recall the lapsed and to awaken the careless as to discover and train teams which themselves could carry on evangelistic and visitation work in their own area.' Two full Schools of a fortnight each were held in 1952, the first based at a shooting lodge, Gannochy, near Edzell in the north of Angus, and the second operating from the Dundee YMCA. Each included experience in visitation, the one in Glenesk and the other in the parish of Downfield-Strathmartine. Meanwhile, after a Montrose Preparatory Rally, members of the West Fife and Kirkcaldy teams spoke encouragingly to the congregations of Montrose, and George Irving with young people from Gallatown offered meetings for familiarisation with the concept of visitation.

The Gannochy School, certainly, built up as it went on. Beginning with only one retired minister in residence besides DP, Mary and four overseas guests, its concluding Rally had to be moved to Edzell Parish Church to fit in the 300 who came. The Congregational Board of the parish of Newtyle agreed to hire a bus to take their people up to Gannochy. The real draw, to ministers from a wide area and increasingly to local people, was the International Team: Rev. Howard Goddard from California; Dr Ahmed Affara from Arabia; Hans-Ulrich Herrmann from Switzerland and Ulrich Mauser from Germany; the Sicilian, Salvatore Carco; and a Miss Wong, a Chinese American. Added to these were, besides DP himself, lecturers Prof. David Cairns from Aberdeen; Fraser McLusky the 'Parachute Padre' (then at Broughty Ferry); and Jim McEwen of Invergowrie, soon to be appointed Lecturer in Church History at New College. In addition to those at the Lodge itself, meetings were held in Edzell, Brechin, Montrose, Logie-Pert and Bervie; the primary schools of Edzell and Tarfside were visited; 200 attended the Glenesk Conventicle in the Lochlee Churchyard on 15 June, and the Moderator of the General Assembly came to call. In the end DP was able to record Gannochy as 'a grand success'.

Thereafter, however, the various training events struggled. Even before it began, DP could see that Dundee was not going attract 'Strathmorians' as he had first hoped:

> Thursday, 7th August [1952] . . . I am apprehensive about this Training School – perhaps unduly so! Bookings from outside Strathmore are good, especially on the women's side, but not half a dozen Strathmorians instead of the 50 there ought to be. I can see that there are three things very much against us – the mentality of the area, much slower to respond than Fife; the scattered nature of the terrain; the unsuitability of August for this area as compared with Fife. Something of real value will, I am sure, emerge but I know not what.

In the event sufficient folk attended, if from all over Scotland, to enable the School to proceed and for the minister of Downfield-Strathmartine, to be pleased with the support he had received: he credited the visitation with 100 new members and a more-than-doubling of his Sunday School.

For those who came the School was worthwhile, but it failed to take forward the Strathmore Campaign in the way that Dunfermline had helped inspired West Fife:

> Wednesday, 20th August [1952] . . . We have had a very strenuous but very worthwhile fortnight in Dundee, beginning with a crowded Opening Rally and ending with a crowded Closing one . . . the numbers attending came far short of our expectations – the catering being badly overestimated. The total number in residence was about 78 – the smallest for the last few years I think, unless Kintyre fell below that figure. Dunfermline and Kilmacolm certainly didn't. The Bible Study, I would judge, was the best ever and spirit throughout was very fine. We never had a finer bunch of girls but were less well served on the male side.

Similar difficulties beset two of the three training weekends that followed the Schools. 'These weekends will take some planning and the apathy and opposition of the ministry some breaking through!' The event at Cardean House, Meigle, was Dundee in miniature: really too few, and from too far. There were only seven in residence for the Training Weekend in Forfar besides DP, Mary and his new assistant ('Adjutant'), Rev. E. Forter Hall. That at St Cyrus in the Mearns was somewhat better attended: 'We opened that evening with a goodly crowd.' DP was already concluding that volunteers would be fewer in Strathmore than had come forward in Fife, but that those who did break the barrier of reticence would have much to offer.

The first months of Strathmore presented other difficulties as well as some encouragements. The Kirk Session of Meigle listened politely to DP but in the end contracted out of participation. The Kirk Session of Logie-Pert, however, were 'for full co-operation', while Mhair Watson of Glamis, 'an Iona fan' and with a mission programme of his own, 'all drawn up on the George MacLeod plan', was prepared to work within the larger framework. One of Watson's elders, farmer Willie Bruce, would become one of the voices of Strathmore. Indeed, Mhair Watson and five of his eight elders were to travel north to support the visiting teams in Montrose. Other ministers were keen supporters: Graham Hardy (Alyth: Barony), G. H. McBride (Newtyle Parish), Harry Cumming (Forfar: Lowson Memorial) and Ewen Traill (Rattray Parish) – the last two both being members of the Home Board. A Campaign Rally at St Andrews, Blairgowrie, attracted about 80, of whom 15 enrolled for visitation, 'eight of these being men. Tonight we had about the same number in Barony Church Hall, Alyth, but more young people.' Only seven people in all, however – four ministers, one of them accompanied by his wife, child and an elder – turned up for the Preliminary midweek Rally in Kirriemuir in late September. Until DP recruited 30 senior pupils from Blairgowrie High School insufficient volunteers had reported to the Campaign Office in Blairgowrie to process the Voting and Communion rolls, yet the attendance at the Opening Rally at Forfar was sufficient to create a sense of occasion and to pave the way for the trainings based there: 'We had full 60 there, including eight ministers and the Sheriff. Bell of the Old Kirk brought down his Kirk Session. Quite a few enrolments.' Forfar was not new to post-war campaigning for it had very recently been one of the centres for the 1952 Radio Mission: yet of this, too, there had been mixed experiences and DP met at least one of Forfar's ministers who had been disillusioned by the Radio Mission.

After the build-up of the summer months, the Montrose Churches Campaign ran between September and October, 1952. This mission benefited from a number of factors: apart from the Roman Catholic priest, it had the support of all the town's ministers. DP personally was still fresh; the town of some 11-12,000 people was a compact but socially varied community with some 4,000 Church of Scotland members and a near-universal claim to church ties of some sort. Well before the visitation started the existence since May of the local Campaign Office, busy card-indexing the population, had stirred up correspondence in the Montrose press, thus fulfilling one of DP's objectives, to 'bring religion from the circumference to the centre', to create a climate of interest. Taking his cue from the speech of Alan Fraser at his 26 May induction to Montrose: St John's, in which Fraser denied that anyone could be a 'good Christian' apart from active Church membership, 'Dandelion', a pseudonymous correspondent to the *Montrose Review and Angus & Kincardineshire Advertiser*, took up the challenge. Practical Christianity, he argued, honest goodness and neighbourly support, was abundant in the working-classes who never went near a Church. Christ never taught that his followers should sit in pews! And conversely, far too many pew-sitters did nothing to help anyone. Real, Biblical Christianity, 'Dandelion' thus argued, was about practical service and was hindered rather than enabled by the institutional church. The correspondence continued through June into July, with the Montrose Baptist pastor entering the fray.[13] The letters were part of the wider debates of the time to which the campaign contributed: if being a Christian wasn't synonymous with being British, what was a Christian? Was there a minimum level of doctrinal content to the faith? Had the doctrine of hell and the institution of the church both outlived their plausibility? How was the Bible to be interpreted and by whom? Hans-Ulrich Herrmann, one of DP's International Team, offered a campaigner's perspective in St John's Church Hall Montrose on 12 June to a packed meeting. What struck him, he said, about the Scottish churches was both the variety of social activities they offered and their inward-looking nature, too often too middle-class and unable to recognise the gifts of the ordinary worker. In place of a mere habit of attendance, he called for a living, out-reaching missionary fellowship. To DP's dismay the Scottish page's editor of the *British Weekly* reported this speech under the headline: 'Class Distinction in Scots Churches.'

DP camped in the vestry of Montrose Congregational Church for the campaign in the town, being joined on occasions by Mary. Many days, however, he spent away in the Mearns to the north, making final arrangements for the next phase, with bases at both St Cyrus and Inverbervie. The complex, rolling nature of Strathmore meant that after the Gannochy School he rarely concentrated on one locality alone. He looked for – demanded – leadership from the Montrose ministers: 'I had to issue an ultimatum . . . If the Montrose men didn't pile in within 24 hours I was going home and not coming back. They piled in!' By 8 October progress was being made, but he was still not satisfied: 'The Campaign is going moderately well – the ministers are not fully hot as yet and Montrose is not pulling its weight at all. 220 visits only and, out of 4,300, less than a third for half the time which won't do, I fear!' The congregations of Montrose never did produce sufficient volunteers for the visiting: the campaign had to be extended by a week in order to complete the programme with assistance from activists travelling from Alyth and elsewhere outside not just Montrose but also beyond the bounds of the Presbytery. The spin DP put on this was that 'the people of Montrose have been so friendly that they won't let our visitors away', but Bill Eadie was more forthright in his Presbytery report: local participation had been most disappointing. Yet by November 1954 DP's perspective had changed. During the visitation of Edinburgh's Fountainbridge district he recorded that: 'We had 25 couples out. The total number of people out visiting was 102 for the 3 nights, the largest number of local people in any area since Montrose.' Recruiting local people to visit locally was never easy.

The weekend of 11-12 October was when DP made his own particular contributions to the assignments, but even then he was away to Kincardineshire on the Sunday morning preaching in Arbuthnott Parish Church before taking a team to Montrose Royal Infirmary and at night speaking at a Variety Entertainment in the Beach Pavilion. Opinions in the local press on all this activity were mixed. A correspondent wrote to say that the issues of concern to the workers were material and could only be solved by political and material means, by getting rid of the capitalist society and its so-called spiritual values.[14] One elder wrote to say that he, personally, had been met by campaigners paying visits and speaking at the cinema and the theatre, at his office and at his club: it was the most efficient mission he had ever encountered and it deserved success.[15] Against this, the pseudonymous 'Backslider' responded that he, too, had heard the presentations – 'sandwiched between a comic and a cartoon film on the first occasion, and between two acts of a farce in the second' – and while he gave points for sincerity, the message was not convincing. Come back to Church? But why? For what? 'It would, perhaps, be too harsh to say that *the mountain has laboured and brought forth a mouse*.'[16]

In the end the ministers of Montrose expressed themselves in public as very satisfied with the campaign that concluded, as Kirkcaldy had, with a BBC Scottish Home Service radio broadcast service on Sunday 19 October. Sunday 26 October was for most of the town's congregations a Communion Sunday and on the next Tuesday DP recorded: 'Very good news from Montrose – all churches reporting big attendances on Sunday – St John's a record Communion!' Frederick Kennedy rejoiced in the largest communion in his five-year ministry at Montrose: Old. Valentine Fletcher reported that there were twice as many in his Episcopal Church than when he first came to the town; other spokesmen said similar positive things to the local press that DP republished in *We Saw the Church in Action!*[17] 'A considerable measure of success' was the *Montrose Review's* conclusion, with a caution that, out of the whole population, a 35% attendance was not a wholesale 'back to church' movement.[18] In un-attributed comments made to T. Ralph Morton, one observer applauded the training offered and welcomed the assignments as at least beginning to get ministers out of their pulpits to meet working men, but was critical of the traditional piety in which the language of the campaign had been cast and of the standardised arrangements. The objection was clearly that such superficial encounters were inadequate, in themselves, to reach the working population.[19] DP saw the same facts differently. In a newspaper interview after Montrose[20] he said that those who were dubious of such a campaign took too short term a view, looking for too quick returns. Again and again he emphasised that his campaigns aimed to bring new life and purpose to the local churches, equipping their members with new vision and new skills, and that the results of the work would therefore come to fruition in the years to come. Nevertheless between 1950 and 1954 aggregate membership of the Church of Scotland congregations in Montrose declined from 4,544 to 3,773.

DP was later to claim that a new discovery had resulted from the necessity that, to complete Montrose, he had had to bring in 'lay workers of both sexes and of all ages from a very wide area – from Alyth and Blairgowrie, from Brechin and Forfar, from Coupar Angus and Newtyle, from the foothills of the Grampians and the farmlands of the Mearns.' Setting a local campaign in a broader context – and the increasing availability of private cars to offer transport – had enabled Christians across Strathmore to break out of the confines of rural parish life and to contribute their witness on a regional scale in partnership with the Montrose congregations. Against George MacLeod's emphasis on the single parish, D. P. Thomson suggested (in his pragmatic way) the advantages of regional evangelism. Local people might be awkward about visiting locally – but they could find it easier to do a parish or two away.

Moving north of Montrose to the Mearns for the next phase, a campaign running the whole of November from bases in St Cyrus and Inverbervie, required yet more mobility. Local volunteers were once again in very short supply as visiting began at Inverbervie:

> Friday, 14th November [1952] I am sitting in the Church Hall at Inverbervie, on the first night of the Campaign in this area. Only three couples are out so far – all girls except for Mr Ross from Gourdon [*Home Board Lay Missionary at Gourdon, within Bervie Parish*]. I can see quite clearly that unless I had laid on special buses for next week we would have had nobody here.

To run the campaign at all DP had once more called in his mobile elite from across Strathmore. Each evening after work they gathered at a designed farm, where local people provided supper. Paired with guides offered by the congregation they then set out by car on the visitation. Meanwhile DP and the ministers went on the usual assignments to farms and shops and schools, and his growing number of activists spoke in 'Voice of the Pew' services. 'Last Sunday's attendances were phenomenal at St Cyrus,' DP wrote as he began at Inverbervie, and 'in the evening we had good rallies.' By the end of the month, preparing to return to Barnoak, he was able to write:

> I was out for half an hour and spoke for a little with a group of men in the turnip fields. It is a hard black coast, but not without its own beauty in the winter sunshine. I am sorry to go – very sorry, for I have enjoyed this work and have benefited by it in health also.

December was now given over to preparations: to meetings with ministers in Newtyle and Forfar, Coupar Angus and Blairgowrie; a broadcast service, a joint Mearns and Montrose Rally, a Preliminary Sidlaws Rally in Newtyle Church. The Strathmore Churches Campaign had certainly been difficult during 1952, but he had completed what he had set out to do.

Strathmore having got into the swing of operating visiting teams on a regional basis, its seven local campaigns in 1953 were staffed in the main by the travelling activists and met with some success. The year began with a New Year Rally and Reunion, held in St John's Church, Perth on Saturday 3 January, to which 107 came for tea and speeches. DP thought that the minister of St John's, Bill Smellie (the old friend of George MacLeod and now Convener of the Home Mission Committee of the Home Board) was most impressed. Not impressed at all was David C. Mitchell, co-chair of the Strathmore Campaign, who entirely disapproved of the Rally and asked for its cancellation – presumably because DP was gathering these key men and women leaders without the consent or presence of their own ministers. DP sent back 'a letter to Mitchell that blusters and burns – I will be deeply interested to see how he reacts – I didn't pull my punches!' The incident was typical of how DP was now handling liaison with ministers and campaign volunteers: once invited to lead, he determined policy; and the personal, group and pastoral relationship he increasingly established with the volunteers tended to supersede their congregational ties. Later in the year he would give this relationship institutional form.

During 1953 the Brechin Ministers Fraternal and two key Kirk Sessions within the Presbytery of Meigle decided not to participate in the Strathmore Campaign and thereby prevented their towns from doing so, to DP's immense frustration. The parishes of Meigle, Ardler and Bendochy had already withdrawn. The Session of the Presbytery Clerk's parish, J. Sibbald Clark of Alyth: High, finally decided not to take part in January 1953. They, fairly, gave DP a final chance to persuade them and he took along a strong team: farmer James Cochrane, the Dunnichen Session Clerk; another farmer, Willie Bruce, Presbytery elder for the Parish of Glamis; and a further Glamis elder, Norman Ewan, the Roundyhill School Headteacher and a local preacher. The Alyth: High elders, however, decided that they were sufficiently busy visiting their own members to explain the new Freewill Offering Scheme of donating to the church; they would not take part. Both the rector of St Ninian's Episcopal Church, Alyth, and the other Church of Scotland minister in the small town, the noted evangelical Gordon Hardy of Alyth: Barony, had already taken a very active role in producing volunteers for Montrose and the Mearns. These now held what DP referred to as 'an indignation meeting', to protest that they were being forbidden to campaign in their own town – he had to calm things down. Similarly a campaign in the town of Blairgowrie was vetoed by the Kirk Session of the Parish of Rattray where the elders declined to follow the lead given by their minister, Ewen Traill. This was a substantial embarrassment, for Traill was a key spokesman for Strathmore, a close collaborator with DP. He had put it to his Session that rejection would mean the end of his ministry there but still, by a margin of one, to DP's great dismay they voted no.

What was it about the Strathmore Campaign that alienated the elders of these Kirk Sessions? At Rattray's neighbouring parish of Blairgowrie: St Mary's the elders had decided that, if their local campaign did go ahead, the congregation would support it but on condition that they would not assist with the visitation. This was a congregation where, for the local Memorial Service held to commemorate King George VI, it was agreed the elders would wear mourning dress and black ties, and that the pulpit would be draped in black. The men who were elders in these Angus and Perthshire market towns might well be involved in social, municipal, political or Masonic circles, they might teach in the Sunday School or run a Boys Brigade, but going round the doors to speak about their faith outside the regular institutional structures was not, on the whole, for them. Two elders and a Woman's Guild member explained in DP's later pamphlet *You Are Going Out Visiting? Let us tell you about it!* the mental hurdles they had had to overcome:

> [*An elder*] . . . probably you feel that this is not the sort of work for you; you think that visitation should be left to those who find talking easy on matters of religion or who are accustomed to dealing with strangers, or who have had Iong experience of active church work and know all the answers.
>
> [*A Woman's Guild member*] When the Campaign started in our town I was most reluctant to help in the house-to-house visiting. I felt that to intrude upon strangers in their homes was an invasion of their privacy which they might justifiably resent. I was quite wrong!
>
> [*An elder*] On the first doorstep I looked at my partner and said 'What will we say to these people?' At no time before in my 50 odd years of life had I felt so helpless and inadequate for a task.

Reticence, doctrinal uncertainty or ignorance, a sense of inadequacy in spiritual matters combined with, perhaps, a status-informed sense of what was appropriate, kept both men and women back from DP's style of campaigning. Not so many were prepared 'to go beyond convention in the service of Jesus'. The new evangelism's reliance on the laity was at once a strength and a major weakness.

The Sidlaw Campaigns, run in two phases at Coupar Angus and Kettins, and Burrelton, Balbeggie, Collace and Cargill, respectively 1-16 February and 25 February to 10 March, ran much as expected but DP was to meet further problems when the focus of activity moved to the rural parishes of Auchterhouse, Newtyle and Eassie in March. In the first phase of 1953 he was working with congenial ministers who were in some cases enthusiastic – though local volunteer support was no more forthcoming. At Kettins, R. K. Goodfellow was certainly cooperative, while at Coupar Angus both J. B. Logan of the Abbey and Neil Gordon Kerr of St Anne's Episcopal Church were enthusiasts, 'experienced campaigners' that DP was happy to leave to run some outdoor and early morning meetings while he worked in the office. He did, however, speak at the Coupar Angus Dance to celebrate the Coronation of Queen Elizabeth, a football match, the Pigeon Club, to the employees of local printers and builders, and to the residents at Belmont Castle, the Church of Scotland Eventide Home. The Opening Rally was led by the Bishop of St Andrews. The minister at the United Free Church of Balbeggie also supported the campaign, himself coming out to visit and hosting a 'Voice of the Pew' service. Burrelton was David C. Mitchell's own parish and J. A. Honey and R. Robertson, of Cargill and Collace, were his colleagues in the Presbytery of Perth and in the campaign. With the Robertsons, DP had an excellent relationship: their student son, Tom, now became his personal driver, shuttling him across Strathmore and back and forward to Barnoak at all hours. House to house visiting was conducted from Collace Manse by teams gathered from across the region. The same names thus recur again and again in DP's diaries of the Strathmore Churches Campaign, members of a team that he was pleased to record [*We Saw the Church in Action*] included:

> . . . at least ten farmers and many secondary school teachers. The village blacksmith and the village cobbler, the shepherd and the scavenger, the fisherman and the fruit salesman, the architect and the artisan, the electrician and the engineer the shopkeeper and the railway surfaceman, the lawyer, the dentist, the doctor, the banker, the headmaster, the managing director, the shop girl, the masseuse, the nurse (of both sexes) – all these and a score of other types I could name are already in the Campaign team.

In his printed 1958 account of the Strathmore Churches Campaign, DP gave little or no attention to its 1953 phases: the Glens, Kirriemuir, Forfar and Glamis. Each nevertheless had their own story. DP and Mary enjoyed the romance of camping in the vacant Cray Manse to coordinate the events and visitation of the scattered crofts, farms and lodges of Glenshee and his diaries contain fascinating accounts of his uninvited calls on the landed and industrial gentry in their country retreats, soliciting funds and making spiritual enquiries. The Kirriemuir phase was run as a Summer Training School with Mary again as hostess, a substantial International Team and other volunteers camping in the Church Hall of Kirriemuir: Barony. Visitation was confined to the rural parishes of Glen Prosen, Clova, Cortachy and Memus. During that period DP felt himself unwell, did not keep a diary and was content to allow the bulk of the work to be carried by others. The School closed with a 'Voice of the Pew' service. May, part of June and August 1953 D. P. Thomson spent at home – he was exhausted; he had a writing project on, the biography eventually published as *David Inglis Cowan: Man and Minister*. Already he was planning new enterprises and reunion meetings took place in Montrose, West Fife and Kirkcaldy. A suggested 'commando' tour of Shooting Lodges during the grouse season was abandoned. The Glamis campaign he almost wholly skipped, leaving the on-the-spot organisation to his current assistant, Ken Mathers, paying a few visits to the team and preaching at the final Communion Thanksgiving on 1 November, which doubled as the Closing Rally of the entire Strathmore Churches Campaign.

The Forfar Campaign, however, the last but one, was a major effort, in the largest of the Angus towns, the County centre. The campaign there began with a 'Preliminary Meeting of Town and District Leaders of Community and Public Life in Forfar', held in the Town & County Hall. Perhaps added interest was gained by the demission during the period of the campaign of Harry Cumming of Forfar: Lowson Memorial to take up a call to Edinburgh: Barclay. DP spoke at his Farewell Social. Friends and supporters were called in to assist at Forfar from across Scotland. As usual in Angus the bulk of the local eldership stayed away, but the ministers worked hard and congregations flocked to the services. At the end DP was delighted with what had been achieved. He wrote of the final Sunday with its morning worship and Closing Rally:

> Tuesday, 13th October]1953] I am home at last! I arrived at 9 last night. I preached on Sunday in Forfar Old Parish Church to almost 400 at the Forenoon Service on 'Counting the Cost'. I had liberty and I felt real

> power. There was rapt attention and quite obvious impression. In the evening I encountered Sheriff Mackinnon in the Old Kirkyard, and he spoke feelingly of the impression made in the morning. 'It must have gone home to some,' he said, 'it certainly went home to me.' In the afternoon I conducted the service at Whitehills Tuberculosis Hospital preaching in Ward 2 and by loudspeaker to all other wards. In the evening we had 1,200 at the Forfar Churches Campaign Closing Rally in the Old Parish Church – the largest congregation William Bernard, the organist, told me he had seen in his 21 years there. Bell [*The Church of Scotland: Forfar: Old*] presided and all the other ministers spoke, D. O. Noble [*of St John the Evangelist Episcopal Church of Scotland*] last and most effectively of all. It was a great gathering – bigger than any closing rally since the War and recalling the great days of the GSEU in the 1920s – and in Forfar of all towns, with cinemas open on either side! It was a fitting close to my 33 years as a Campaign Leader.

There was more than a hint of the 'old evangelism' in DP's reactions to the close of the Forfar Campaign, though it lacked any after-meeting or enumeration of converts. It was not often in the post-war years that he used the terminology of his student days – 'liberty and power' – about his preaching. The Strathmore Churches Campaign, though all its phases placed a solid emphasis on visiting all homes in a designated area, also placed a greater emphasis on special services, on rallies, than had been acceptable at Kirkcaldy. The 'Voice of the Pew' services, at which representatives from the team of visitors spoke of their own faith, were an important part of the package in each phase, to which congregations came in large numbers. At Kirriemuir, for example, the participants were asked to speak on 'What Christ and His Church mean to me'. Fitting easily into the pattern of public meeting then popular, the point of such testimony was twofold. It was of course intended to proclaim the living power of Christ and the spiritual reality and practicality of the Christian life. More than that, however, its appeal came from the fact that the speakers were not professional ministers but farmers or miners or housewives, speaking of how their religion became real in lives and homes no different from those of their hearers. Beyond the words that were said, the people were being offered as role-models. And, given the reluctance demonstrated by the elders of Angus to speak about the faith or to go out visiting on its behalf, the 'Voice of the Pew' services were intended to demonstrate that 'our lay folk can become articulate, and how arresting and compelling their witness can be'.

In his *The Scottish Churches*, John Highet identified the way in which results from campaigns were conventionally described: some new enthusiasm, better attendances, some of the lapsed restored and some new members brought in. This cool assessment came from his coverage of the Paisley Mid-Century Campaign. In truth, though the guarded statements of the time, 'It is too early yet to say much about the results' may irritate, the nature of historical evidence for individual or community levels of Christian faith still prohibits much by way of scientific or precise accounting. Without an adequate supply of Kirk Session minutes, the sort of detail about adult baptisms and new professions of faith that illuminated the West Fife Campaign is unavailable for Strathmore. Perhaps significantly, DP's own account (provided to the General Assembly via the Home Board) only singled out Dundee: Downfield-Strathmartine as markedly benefiting from this sort of growth. In his report to the Home Board, he claimed, rather, that 'already new vision and incentive have come to many, and not a few churches and parishes have experienced a real spiritual quickening.'

There were those for whom this sort of vagueness was unsatisfactory. DP's visitation campaigns could be portrayed as a soft form of evangelism, a mixture of old and new styles that seemed more concerned with recruitment for the institution than with the conversion of individuals. He, personally, still believed – and always would believe – in the possibility of conversion; but, compared with his early years as an evangelist, clear differences can be seen. He was no longer often personally engaged in counselling; he recognised that he was no longer regularly bringing people to Christ in private conversation and prayer. Nor were campaign meetings arranged so as to call for those moved by the preaching to come forward, publicly, for counselling. This new evangelism fed, as it was intended to do, the ordinary denominational processes whereby those who wished now to be Christians 'joined the church'. DP had a moment of introspection brought on in March 1953 by reports of an address to the College of the Free Church of Scotland, a bastion of traditional theology, that contained explicit and implied criticisms:

> Saturday, 28th March [1953] . . . These are the remarks made by Principal P. W. Miller in his closing address for the current session of the Free Church College in Edinburgh – Close examination of many of the campaigns which have been organised up and down the country seems to confirm the suspicion that the permanent results are not

> quite comparable to the effort or even to the hopes of the campaigners. Dr Miller asks the questions (1) Has the message, the Gospel, been understood? (2) Has the Church, the Christian community, been over stressed? (3) Is the spiritual life of the evangelists sufficiently sound and healthy? Any group to whom the idea of campaign appeals must ask themselves those questions, especially the last one! Now Tom Allan and I are the only two men doing the type of campaign indicated on a big scale and I have no right to pass the buck to Tom Allan!

The challenge that the 'permanent results' did not seem to measure up to the effort and expense involved in campaigns was one that would be asked again and more loudly as the 1950s progressed. The questioning would also lead to further examination of just what was the nature of 'the Church, the Christian community' which new converts were invited to join? In the meantime D. P. Thomson was satisfied that both men and women had indeed been converted as a result of the campaigns that he organised – Roy Copeland was prepared to be cited in the press as a specific example – and also that what was done did assist congregational life. Yet against the optimistic gloss that DP gave to his accounts of the missions of this period, it is important to remember that, from Paisley to Strathmore (as, earlier, at North Kelvinside) congregationally-based outreach needed high levels of energy to overcome a fairly common hostility or suspicion from within the Kirk that restricted its scope and limited its longer-term results.

The question was: 'Where, next?' for the activists that had gathered to DP's side during his months in West Fife and Strathmore. Just as the young people involved in summer mission found participation addictive, so now the adults DP had recruited for visiting and speaking on a regional basis sought new opportunities to continue in a form of Christian service and in a fellowship that had become important to them.

The Birth of Work & Witness

During the winter of 1952-53 D. P. Thomson had, once again, found himself pondering: 'Myself, I am often asking how long I will be able to carry on!' More and more he began to wonder about what came next. One March night, while Thomson was in his bath, a new evangelistic organisation to embody his work took shape in his mind:

> Friday, 13th March [1953] . . . on Wednesday . . . afternoon I met with Tom Allan, who ran me out in his car to see Sutherland of Eassie and we colloqued about Tom's future. We agreed that it is time for Tom to leave North Kelvinside now and he is to offer his services to the Home Board . . . On the way to Glasgow my own future clarified – I came to the great decision as we crossed the Machany River which was for me the crossing of the Rubicon. I can see clearly that the time has come to launch a new Movement, into which the fruits and experience of the work we have done these last few years can be gathered . . . Last night in my bath the name came to me: 'WORK & WITNESS – A Movement Designed to Help In The Training & Utilisation of Lay Workers in the Services of the Scottish Churches, particularly in United Action.' I am going to launch immediately – a steering committee at once and a provisional fund, provisional enrolments now and pledges, inaugural meeting 3rd Saturday of April, Dedication Service on 1st Sunday of May in the Barony Church, Alyth at 8pm.

Its first formal meeting actually occurring on 11 July 1953, Work & Witness did do much to extend DP's work of enabling the outreach of the laity, besides providing both him and its membership with strong mutual fellowship. In retrospect, of course, we can see that it did not spring to mind entirely out of nothing, out of the waters of his bath! Retrospect also allows us to understand quite how committed DP was to Work & Witness. At one stage he expected that his position as its Director would be incompatible with his post under the Home Board.

D. P. Thomson was happiest in his ministry when leading teams: students on mission, the Gillespie Oxford Group, Summer Mission teams, Visitation Campaign teams. From his youth he had created movements around himself in the old 19th century tradition of the Home Mission society: soldiers, students, ministers; his residential centres. He was not of course alone in this. Tom Allan had created 'United Christian Witness' [UCW] in March 1951 to draw together a group of ministers and lay men and women, based mainly in western Scotland, who supported his Youth Rallies, the Seaside Missions and the work of Christian Highway, their inland, youth-hostel based counterpart for which Bill Shannon was the Home Board's Organiser. The aims of UCW were training in evangelism, study of the implications of Christian discipleship and support for united evangelistic action. It met monthly in association with the rallies held on Saturday evenings at North Kelvinside. Allan sent D. P. Thomson a sample membership card in October, and then invited him to speak at the Service of Dedication – Thomson was unable to accept. UCW's committee comprised both ministers (including Rev. Prof. J. S. Stewart) and unordained Christians; whether Tom Allan was currently president or not, it looked to him to leadership. Allan had very quickly become a recognised leader among active evangelicals in the Glasgow area and beyond. After his six months of secondment to Summer Missions he combined ministry at North Kelvinside with a continuing executive role in Summer Missions, shared with Joe Ritchie; with leading regular youth rallies and with regular broadcasting; with a countrywide guest preaching and evangelistic ministry, sometimes in support of D. P. Thomson; with membership of the Evangelism Committee of the Home Board (from May 1950). He had had the key responsibility of leading the congregational aspects of the Glasgow Commando Campaign. By the January 1952 UCW Training School, membership of the movement had reached 113.[21] D. P. Thomson would have been well aware of the growth of UCW. Secure in his faith but often insecure in his position in the church, he tended to assess his influence by comparison with that of George MacLeod and Tom Allan. Just as the Fellowship in Evangelism had begun with the Iona Community in mind, so Work & Witness bore some imprint of UCW.

Both Work & Witness and UCW described themselves as 'movements' and Tom Allan's definition of a movement is to be found in the UCW Minutebook:

> An organisation is created by men: a movement is guided and led by the Holy Spirit in spite of its members – not because of them.

In other words, both groupings had come into existence as their members had engaged in active Christian work: they first found themselves to be in fellowship and then sought to define their communal rule. Both bodies were inter-denominational in theory while in practice deriving from the life of the Church of Scotland. Both bodies specified that loyalty to existing congregations was a prerequisite of membership; they sought to offer the churches 'a task force' [UCW], 'a mobile force of workers' [Work & Witness]; the one for 'united evangelistic action', the other for less specified extra-congregational service and witness. Tom Allan's creation was a straight sign-on-the-line evangelical movement, its membership required to promise 'Personal obedience to Jesus Christ as Saviour and Lord', 'readiness to serve Christ to the point of sacrifice' and 'willingness to submit to a rule of discipline in private and personal devotions'. D. P. Thomson's movement, however, was very simply open to any in communicant membership of their own denomination that he (and, nominally, the committee) thought suitable for 'a fellowship and enterprise of this nature'. He had never liked specific theological tests. Unlike his previous organisations however, Work & Witness was essentially a lay movement. It did not by its constitution exclude ministers, but the service it recruited for was that of lay evangelism, the service that the visitation evangelism campaigns needed: door to door work, speaking at meetings, 'Voice of the Pew' rallies. Finally, while Tom Allan's was only one voice – certainly a strong voice – within UCW, D. P. Thomson was Director of Work & Witness, its founder and (at least at first) only minister; its CEO in the first years of the movement, though a Chairman and Secretary of the national Committee, with regional secretaries, were duly elected at the launch:

> Saturday, 11th July [1953] The great day is over! We gathered to the number of 36 in all – 38 have joined so far – 17 women and 21 men. Mr Lawson of Brechin becomes Chairman of Committee – Rowland Dalgleish, Secretary and Mr Husband, Mrs Ritchie Smith of Alyth [*members of committee*]. Mrs Grant becomes Regional Secretary for Strathmore and Mamie Oram and Barbara Guild Secretary for Alyth and Coupar Angus.

In founding Work & Witness on his own initiative and with no consultation wider than his teams of lay activists from Strathmore and Fife, D. P. Thomson recognised that he was 'throwing down the gauntlet' to the hierarchy of the Church and to his institutional manager, the Home Board. In the 1930s he had briefly combined his part-time appointment as Evangelist with being Warden of his foundation, St Ninian's Lassodie: and the Home Board even then had wanted him full-time. As before, in the 1930s, he wanted to have his cake and eat it: to retain a stipend from the Board and also to pursue his own agenda. Besides, there were aspects of Work & Witness that were controversial. The fellowship DP was creating was giving members and elders of congregations new regional loyalties under his leadership, well outside any presbyterian oversight. What he was doing might have been construed as an uninvited intrusion into parish ministers' pastoral relations. Even James Monaghan of Lumphinnans with whom he had worked well, Roy Copeland's minister, was 'in fundamental disagreement' with Work & Witness. DP knew that the Home Board might be, too, and his appointment was due to expire at the end of December 1953. Was it to be renewed?

In the event DP had a friendly interview with Robert Mackintosh on 6 September, and disaster was averted when he met a delegation of the Board on 18 September. The interview was chaired by the Board's Convener; among others also present was Sir James F. Simpson, veteran of previous clashes between the Board's regularities and DP's impetuousness. The Board's institutional concern about Work & Witness was that it would conflict with the newly formed Scottish Churches Industrial Order [SCIO], a child of its own Church and Industry Committee. Since 1919 many had believed that the Church was far too remote from 'industrial man'.[22] Experiments in placing ministers in the industrial workplace had attracted attention since the Second War – the Rev. Ian Fraser began his ministry working in a factory before induction to the Naval Dockyard parish of Rosyth. The Home Board reported to the General Assembly of 1953 that it sought to sponsor a body that, operating nationally and in local workplace branches, might unite Christian workers with Christian managers 'to advance the knowledge and understanding of the Christian Faith and its practice; to promote the best human relations in industry on the basis of that Faith; and to further the application of its principles throughout industrial life and society' and to counteract subversive communism. June 1952 had seen the national launch of SCIO and the next year was given to recruiting for local branches. D. P. Thomson's friend and former GSEU campaigner, William Macintyre, the Church and Industry Committee's full-time member of staff, had been organising meetings to promote SCIO in Fife as DP's campaigns there came to an end. Now the Home Board's own Evangelist was creating a parallel or even competing organisation for laymen on no-one's authority but his own.

Sufficient calm prevailed for it to be seen that Work & Witness sought to operate in a different sphere and with fewer resources than SCIO. When, eventually, D. P. Thomson's appointment was renewed, care was taken to enforce this separation of spheres of interest. His position as Director of Work & Witness was accepted and he was to remain with the Home Board, though not without yet further crises in the relationship.

Work & Witness also offers an insight into his relationship with George MacLeod. DP called at George's home to ask him to become a Chaplain of his new baby – and was introduced to George's own 'babies', a boy and a girl! DP's invitation never developed into anything of substance. DP greatly respected George but their paths were their own, as one of DP's diary entries for 1954 demonstrates:

> Wednesday 24th February 1954 . . . last night . . . to Ness Bank Church, Inverness, for Inverness Presbytery Elders & Officebearers' Union Meeting at which I got 5 minutes before George MacLeod started on Iona. George told the Chairman he would give 1/- to Church funds if I kept to 5 minutes and he flashed down his shilling and used it as his introduction when I sat down at 4½ minutes. I think I got something across – perhaps more than on Sunday . . . More than ever was I impressed by the fact that Iona has nothing to offer the layman but becoming a Friend or a donor and joining a political party; spelling-binding oratory but it led nowhere!

Work & Witness, however, was not the only new evangelistic movement to be created in Scotland in this period. While D. P. Thomson had been so engrossed in the Strathmore Campaign, the beginnings of a new major, national, missionary enterprise slipped under his radar. The *Tell Scotland* Movement had began quietly in October 1952, the fruit of a somewhat minor committee meeting in Edinburgh.[23] The personal stories of D. P. Thomson, George F. MacLeod and Tom Allan now became inextricably interwoven with the success, failure and tragedy of *Tell Scotland.*

Yet before telling that story, again it is important to hold in mind the very real difficulties DP had faced in West Fife, Kirkcaldy and Strathmore. Were the 'results' actually proportionate to the massive effort and disruption of a campaign? There was the opposition or apathy of some ministers; the reticence, doctrinal ignorance, and spiritual inadequacy so often impeding contribution by the lay leadership of congregations; and, beyond the churches, a rising questioning of both the truth of traditional Christian doctrine and the social and/or spiritual utility of traditional Christian institutions. Come back to the Kirk? But why?

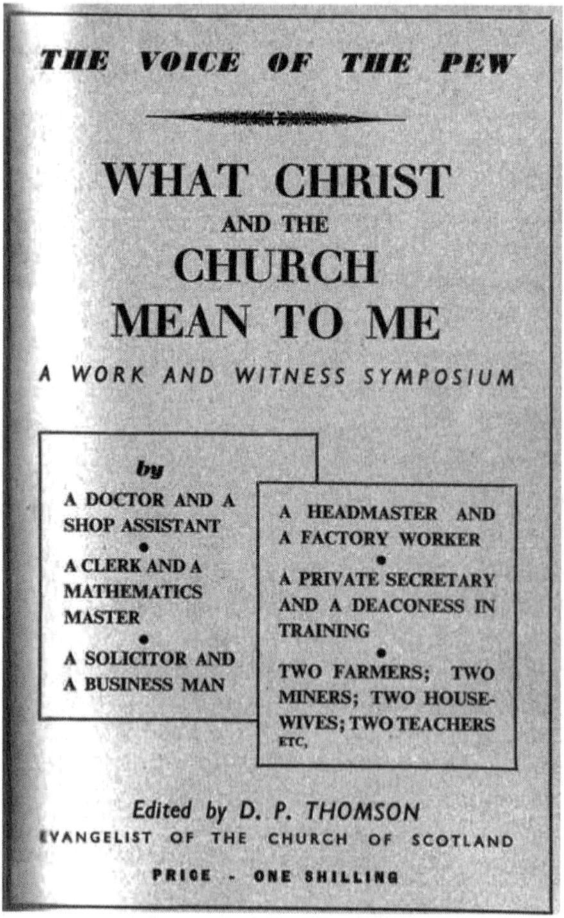
THE VOICE OF THE PEW

WHAT CHRIST AND THE CHURCH MEAN TO ME

A WORK AND WITNESS SYMPOSIUM

by

A DOCTOR AND A SHOP ASSISTANT

A CLERK AND A MATHEMATICS MASTER

A SOLICITOR AND A BUSINESS MAN

A HEADMASTER AND A FACTORY WORKER

A PRIVATE SECRETARY AND A DEACONESS IN TRAINING

TWO FARMERS; TWO MINERS; TWO HOUSE-WIVES; TWO TEACHERS ETC,

Edited by D. P. THOMSON

EVANGELIST OF THE CHURCH OF SCOTLAND

PRICE - ONE SHILLING

31: Cover page: *The Voice of the Pew*

D. P. THOMSON AND *TELL SCOTLAND* – MOVEMENT AND CRUSADE, 1952-60

Tell Scotland that Christ is the answer,
The Way and the Life and the Truth;
Tell Scotland that He holds the secret
Of joyful, victorious youth:
Send out the message, live for your Lord,
Loving and serving, embody this word;
Tell Scotland that Christ is the answer,
That Jesus is Lord.

Ian B. Doyle, 'Tell Scotland', dedicated to Rev. Tom Allan[1]

By the early 1950s Scotland was recovering from the immediate post-war crisis. Rationing ended. The relative stability of the decade offered an opportunity for a coalition of missionary forces to apply the new thinking and methods of the 1940s. The 1950s saw the Church of Scotland seeking, unhindered by economic depression or war, to utilise the strengths flowing from the 1929 Union.[2] The *Tell Scotland* Movement was to be ecumenical, sponsored at the highest levels of the protestant denominations; seeking to mobilise not just the ministry but the whole church for the task of mission. Coalitions, however, last only as long as all their participants remain convinced that their distinctive interests are being served. Born in late 1952, by 1954 the Movement had hardly reached its vital phase of winning grass-root support when the advent of Dr Billy Graham, the American evangelist, re-awakened existing differences. The undoubted power and apparent success of Graham's All-Scotland Crusade of 1955 strengthened centrifugal tendencies as, quite separately, gulfs between strands of Christian theology also widened. By 1960 the *Tell Scotland* coalition had in effect dispersed.[3] Both the Movement and the Crusade, however, in their own ways and for a time generated widespread interest, gained momentum and achieved successes. For those involved in their leadership, seeking a principled way forward, the period was one of tension that put relationships under strain. DP was no exception to this trend, though his energies were in no way lessened and his work with *Tell Scotland* was personally most fulfilling.

The role of D. P. Thomson in these events – momentous events as they were experienced at the time – was from our point of view both disappointing and interesting. DP was not part of the inner circle of leadership of either *Tell Scotland* or the All-Scotland Crusade: indeed, at times he was grieved that the decision-makers of both inter-related bodies, his colleagues and friends, side-lined him, so that in theatrical terms his part in each was a restricted cameo and not as a principal. Nevertheless DP did play a significant public role in both enterprises. He brought his own energies and his own methodology to each; from the enthusiastic support that each generated, his own work developed in new ways – ways he found stimulating and exciting. His ambivalent relationships with the inter-related Movement and Crusade serve to illustrate both the tensions and the successes of the period.

D. P. Thomson and the Genesis of *Tell Scotland*

32: ONE OF THE LETTER-HEADS DEVELOPED FOR THE *TELL SCOTLAND* MOVEMENT

Although the *Tell Scotland* Movement drew on many precedents, its immediate origins lay in the BBC Scotland Radio Missions of 1950 and 1952. Ronnie Falconer, Religious Broadcasting Organiser for the BBC in Scotland, had originated these Missions, bringing together a team of radio missioners on the basis of their records with this medium and in their own spheres. Part of the post-war quest for new modes of evangelism, the BBC missions offered lessons on what was, and was not, effective outreach: the greatest need was a renewed church.[4] They also brought together a nucleus of leaders willing to go further on the quest.

A joint Church of Scotland Home Board / BBC Scotland conference was held in late October 1952 to find a way forward: D. P. Thomson was invited but was unable, through pressure of work, to attend. From this conference an executive, the Steering Panel, was established, chaired by Bill Smellie, convener of the Home Mission Committee of the Home Board; Tom Allan was a key member of the Steering Panel. November's Panel chose the name *Tell Scotland* for the new mission. As initiative switched from the BBC to the churches, the originating *ad hoc* conference was reconstituted as the *Tell Scotland* Parent Committee and expanded to include ecumenical representatives and other broadcasters and practitioners of mission. DP was a member of this, the *Tell Scotland* sponsoring body, along with George F. MacLeod and T. Ralph Morton, Leader and Deputy Leader of the Iona Community; the Conveners of the Evangelism Committees of the Congregational Union of Scotland, the United Free Church of Scotland and the Baptist Union of Scotland; the Bishops of Glasgow and Edinburgh and Rev. Charles Anderson from Scottish Episcopal Church; Rev. Edward Page from the Methodist Synod in Scotland and Principal Charles Duthie of the Scottish Congregational College. The Churches of Christ and the United Original Secession denominations had joined *Tell Scotland* by autumn 1954.[5] (The Roman Catholic Church in Scotland did not participate formally in ecumenical bodies until the formation in 1990 of Action of Churches Together in Scotland.)

In line of development from the Forward Movement, the 'Recall to Religion' and the Baillie Commission, *Tell Scotland* sought to emphasise the witness of the ordinary Christian in evangelism as in work and leisure. This emphasis derived from critiques, shared by its first leaders, of the 'old evangelism' and of Scottish church life in general. Bill Smellie, Horace Walker, Principal Duthie, Tom Allan and Ronnie Falconer convened a Press Conference in September 1953 as a public launch and in answer to the question, 'Why is this being done?' a briefing paper replied:[6]

> Because Mission must be the constant activity of the Church in love and obedience to her Lord. The urgency of the Church's missionary task is being brought home to us in several ways: (i) We are recognising the inadequacy of traditional methods of evangelism. (ii) We are conscious of the apparent failure of the conventional life of the Church to respond in compassion to the needs of the world. (iii) We are convinced that the only word for a bankrupt world is the Word of the Church's Lord.

This confession of failure, both of the 'conventional life of the Church' and also of traditional evangelism, was as much a challenge to the Kirk as to those outside. *Tell Scotland* called on ministers and congregations not simply to attempt new campaigning methods but, much more radically, to renew their common life, structures and programmes. In particular, Tom Allan shared George F. MacLeod's analysis of ordinary congregational life as far too centred on the single minister.[7]

After its official launch in September 1953, *Tell Scotland* planned to move from motivation (mission to ministers and office-bearers: September 1953-June 1954), to recruitment and training of the laity (mission to congregations: September 1954-June 1955) and thence to 'the outgoing mission to the community,' 'Beginning September 1955.' Its uniting principles, as stated in the Home Board's report to the 1954 General Assembly, were that 'effective evangelism' required not only one-off events (though these were not disavowed) but continual engagement with the whole of society; that the whole church was called to mission in 'word, fellowship and deed' and, as the role of the laity must thus be decisive, 'every effort must be made to encourage the layman to recognise his calling to the apostolate and to train him for the task of witness.' *Tell Scotland* was presented as a new and open-ended movement of the Spirit to renew the church in Scotland as 'a missionary community involved in a ceaseless engagement with the world.' It embodied ideas then current across the English-speaking world.[8] In Tom Allan the new evangelism of *Tell Scotland* found a powerful advocate,[9] and he now left Glasgow: North Kelvinside to become its full-time Field Organiser (September 1953-September 1955).[10] He recommended the Movement at many Church of Scotland and other denominational occasions and also as an established religious broadcaster: direct, open, persuasive, with a very large listening audience.

It was, however, the Steering Panel as a whole that served as an executive for *Tell Scotland* and, while it included Tom Allan and Charlie Duthie, men who were DP's friends, it also included his critic T. Ralph Morton. As by the autumn of 1953 it was clear that *Tell Scotland* was not going to be simply another Radio Mission, but *the* focus of Church of Scotland and inter-denominational activity for the foreseeable future, Allan requested that D. P. Thomson should now join the Steering Panel – the request was refused. DP was not therefore part of the small circle, so warmly recollected by Ronnie Falconer in his autobiography, that met fortnightly at the BBC studio in Edinburgh with himself as secretary and Bill Smellie in the chair.[11] *Tell Scotland* had life and leaders apart from Tom Allan.

Why was D. P. Thomson excluded from the *Tell Scotland* Steering Panel? A number of reasons suggest themselves. DP was never at his best as a member of someone else's committee. The old accusation that he 'didn't team well' always had a good element of truth in it; certainly he was not one easily to follow another's lead. He seldom attended decision-making meetings unless he had determined the agenda or otherwise arranged for proposals to be made, sometimes even hijacking the meeting. Neither was the dynamic of DP's relationship to Tom Allan straightforward. Allan's rise to national leadership had been meteoric: although he had been thinking of the ministry before the war, he dated his walk with the living Christ to a Good Friday service he attended in 1945 while serving with the RAF in France. As a divinity student at Glasgow after the war he very quickly joined D. P. Thomson's circle, taking part in the April 1946 campaign in the Borders and thereafter joining the Summer Missions leadership so that DP could describe him [in *Personal Encounters*, my emphasis] as 'one of *our* young Seaside Leaders'. Once ordained, although he continued to support DP by lecturing at his Training Schools, collaborating with broadcasts and joining him at frequent meetings for coffee, he was clearly his own man, no mere *protégé*. As *Tell Scotland* grew in significance DP grew increasingly irritated at Allan's failure to consult with him and, indeed, it had to be made clear to him that Tom Allan was now, in institutional terms, the senior Home Board evangelist. DP's *Personal Encounter*'s description of Tom Allan's 1953 appointment – 'it brought him to my side as additional Church of Scotland Evangelist' – was disingenuous. Tom Allan was Field Organiser of the *Tell Scotland* Movement, and D. P. Thomson was instructed by his new appointment, finally agreed in June 1954, to offer the closest cooperation to *Tell Scotland*, linking his work with it wherever possible, and subordinating his own Work & Witness to the wider Movement.

Beyond the undoubted convenience in terms of personal relations of retaining DP on the *Tell Scotland* Parent Committee, at arm's length from its real directors in the Steering Panel, there was also some divergence between DP's style of regional visitation evangelism and the principles advocated by the Movement. This was discussed at the Steering Panel and the Parent Committee in November 1954:

> Friday, 26th November [1954] . . . In the afternoon I attended the TELL SCOTLAND COMMITTEE MEETING at 2.30 at 121 George Street. It was a perturbing meeting. Smellie said there had been a long and anxious discussion about my Training Schools in the Steering Panel – doubt being expressed about two questions: the use of people outside our own area and the question of whether they were making that a way out of their

> local responsibilities. The whole tone of the discussion disquieted me – Tom could so easily have dissipated the impression.

The complaint of 'the use of people outside our own area' was a restatement of the difference between D. P. Thomson and the pattern of Iona Missions. George F. MacLeod sought a revival of congregational life and he was not alone in believing that this was best achieved by involving the congregation in active mission and service. Gently disparaging comments had been made of DP's Paisley and Kirkcaldy area campaigns to the effect that 'This work can best be done by a minister and congregation in their own parish.' Work & Witness, in contrast, explicitly existed to mobilise enthusiasts for evangelism *outside* their own parish. DP was angered by the reflections on his work contained in the World Council of Churches' 1954 publication *Evangelism in Scotland*, and successfully blocked its re-publication by the Church of Scotland. Nevertheless *Tell Scotland* did publish and recommend Ralph Morton's much shorter *Evangelism in Scotland Today*, which still contained the assertion that the day of the professional evangelist was past.[12] *Tell Scotland*'s core principles concealed and contained differences in methodology among its supporters. As it turned out, worries about DP's established practice would fade into insignificance when mass evangelism reinvented itself in 1955.

Tom Allan's position on this was, up to 1954, closer to that of George MacLeod than to DP, though not identical to either of the other two missionary leaders. Out of his reflections on DP's North Kelvinside Campaign had come his own focus: rebuilding the life of a traditional congregation by nurturing a smaller group as a dynamic missionary core.[13] The concept of the 'Congregational Group' in this sense and for this purpose was not original to Allan. It can be traced back to *Into All the World*, the 1946 report of the Joint Committee on Evangelism and the last word in the Kirk's thinking on mission while Allan was training for the ministry. The same concept had resurfaced in Nevile Davidson's Home Board pamphlet *The Parish Church*, part of the 'New Evangelism' series published in 1947. Bill Shannon's account of the Congregational Group Tom Allan had built at North Kelvinside shows what careful attention, reading and thought he had given since the 1947 campaign, as the original local team spawned house groups under lay leadership, which in turn provided leaders for evangelism within the community.[14] It was from his own hard-won experience that Allan now recommended the formation of congregational groups as the basis for *Tell Scotland*-inspired mission in the programmatic leaflets for 1954 and 1955 issued under the authority of the Movement: *The Agent of Mission: The Lay Group in Evangelism, its Significance and its Task* and *The Congregational Group in Action*. Indeed, in this latter he wrote that only the existence of a Congregational Group would allow any sort of local campaign to achieve results. Just such a thought may have been why he was reluctant to intervene in the Steering Group's discussions about the impact of DP's regional campaigns and schools.

Nevertheless evangelism by visitation was a technique that was advocated for *Tell Scotland* as, unlike any other mode of explicit outreach then in the churches' armoury, it relied upon the active involvement and witness of the ordinary Christian. D. P. Thomson was by now an acknowledged leader in Scotland for such methodology. Prickly, awkward, even wayward they might find D. P. Thomson, but the Home Board knew that they still needed him. A crunch between DP and the Board came in March 1954 when a decision had to be made as to whether or not to extend his appointment yet again. There were three issues to be settled. One was the relationship DP should have with the Church and Industry Committee and its Scottish Churches Industrial Order. To this was now added, what sort of relationship would DP's work, if it continued, have with *Tell Scotland*? There remained the question as to whether DP's position as Director of Work & Witness was compatible with holding a full-time Home Board post. Sir James F. Simpson, yet again on the Board's D. P. Thomson subcommittee, believed that it was no more compatible than his Wardenship at Lassodie had been. DP set out to meet the subcommittee on Wednesday 17 March, having begun his diary with the capitalised heading: 'THE FATEFUL DAY!!!!!!' In the event no decision was taken. The group left it to the Board's Vice-Convener, the chairman of *Tell Scotland*, Bill Smellie, to call on DP in person on 30 March at Crieff for frank and informal discussion, to which Tom Allan was summoned from Glasgow. DP recorded that 'an amicable understanding' was reached. Though, outside his carefully defined remit, DP was excluded from the more general executive authority entrusted to Tom Allan, he was well content to continue running Training Schools, 'whether on a congregational, parochial, or area basis' and using 'his own methods and techniques', even if under the *Tell Scotland* badge as his new appointment's terms and conditions instructed. His appointment was thus formally extended to 31 December 1958, technically for 5 years from the end of 1953.

Despite the difficulties and uncertainly about his post, DP was not, of course, idle. He held a Training School in Crieff itself over Christmas and New Year 1953-54, in support of the Crieff and District Ministers

Fraternal. He organised for Crieff a Christian Book Week at Easter 1954. Between January and April he was giving weekly lectures on aspects of evangelism at Glasgow's Bible Training Institute. He had held Report Meetings on Visitation Evangelism in Scotland's major cities: Edinburgh, Glasgow, Aberdeen and Dundee – he was disappointed that George MacLeod, among others, failed to attend. Attention was given to the development of Work & Witness: Bible Study groups were formed and a team provided for a BBC Scotland broadcast. He was part of the Church of Scotland delegation to the Assembly of the Presbyterian Church of Ireland in Belfast in June and, with Mary, took a few days' holiday in County Cavan in the Republic. 19-29 March, 2-15 April and 4-25 August 1954 saw three major efforts: the Nairn, Inverness and Caithness Training Schools, all of which required numerous time-taking visits to the north in preparation and long periods away from home.

Though the earlier two Schools were planned well in advance of any agreement about DP's appointment, the Training Schools at Nairn, Inverness and Caithness were extensively advertised as *Tell Scotland* Schools. Of the fifteen press-cuttings retained in DP's cuttings book relating to Nairn and Inverness, twelve all featured *Tell Scotland* as part of their headlines and told stories of success.[15] Success at Nairn was measured in terms of those attending: the final number of 50 in residence at Tarland House, the headquarters; the more than 500 that came to hear Tom Allan give an inspiring address on the aims of the Movement; the numbers who joined together for Bible Study; the packed congregation of 1,200 for the united 'Voice of the Pew' final service. Visitations took place in the Cawdor district, and also at Nairn Academy, following DP's constant emphasis on combining learning by hearing with learning by doing. Rt. Rev. D. McInnes, Bishop of Moray, Ross and Caithness, speaking on the opening night, emphasised the responsibility given to the laity by *Tell Scotland*. It was no stunt, he concluded, not something to be finished in a fortnight; its seed should mature for years to come. At the end of the School, Alex Gemmell, the Presbytery of Moray's *Tell Scotland* convener, endorsed DP's belief that many had gained new perspectives on their walk with Christ from their participation in the School. Indeed, so successful was the Nairn School, operating in a very limited area, that DP wondered what might be the reaction in the capital of the Highlands, in Inverness:

> Friday, 2nd April [1954] This is the fateful day of destiny. Rain, damp heavy clouds on the hills. In a few minutes we are due to set out – an hour at the most – for Inverness. The Advance Guard – 7 from St Colm's

> – was due last night. I have still to complete my packing. This is the greatest and most incalculable adventure on which I have ever embarked. Here anything may happen! We may do well: it may fizzle and crackle! The Highlands may go up in flames. The last is by no means impossible. I think there is something moving. Sunday night in the Free North may be decisive! Will the Wee Frees wait on? Will the Church of Scotland folks come? Will adversity bring the outsider? Will the country districts flood in? If all or any three of these happen not even the Free North will hold the vast crowd I will face!

Reaction at Inverness would actually be more appreciative than excited, though DP still concluded, 'It was a good and very worthwhile School.'

In terms of the overall *Tell Scotland* pattern, DP's 1954 Schools fell during the first phase [September 1953 - June 1954], of informing and motivating office-bearers; and that they did and something more, moving on towards the aims of the second phase [September 1954 - June 1955], the mobilising and training of the ordinary Christians of the congregations for missionary outreach. D. P. Thomson's aim was to present participants with both a broader and a deeper understanding of Christ's Church, so that they might the better find their part in its mission. Hence there were 14 nationalities among the participants at Inverness and a clear emphasis on the world-wide, multi-racial nature of Christianity. One lecturer, for example, was Miss Hiru Bose, Principal of the Duff School for Girls, Calcutta, speaking on 'Church and School in Modern India'; another was A. C. Craig, speaking on 'The World Church'. From the *Tell Scotland* Steering Panel, D. H. C. Read, Chaplain of Edinburgh University and a Chaplain to H.M. The Queen, spoken on questions he was regularly asked: 'Can a Christian be a Communist?' and 'Can I be a Christian without going to Church?' In essence, 'no' was his answer to both questions, which echoed similar discussions during the Strathmore and Fife Campaigns. Beyond the lectures, Bible study and worship, participants visited in the Inverness hospitals: Craig Dunain, Culduthel, Raigmore and the Royal Northern, as well as Inverness Royal Academy. DP preached at a number of churches and at a Parade Service at the Barracks of the Cameron Highlanders, and teams were sent to visit in the Merkinch area of the town and to congregations down Loch Ness: Drumnadrochit, Dores and Kiltarlity. Special services were held at the churches of the Inverness: Ness Bank and Inverness: Crown congregations of the Church of Scotland; at Inverness Baptist and Inverness Methodist Churches; at the Inverness: North congregation of the Free Church of Scotland, though the Free

Church as a denomination was not a participant in the *Tell Scotland* Movement.

A locally-staffed visitation of the whole town, with invitations to Easter Week services, was arranged to follow up the Nairn School, and after Inverness the elders of the Glenurquhart Church of Scotland began a first systematic visitation of their parish. During these Schools, however, those carrying out the visits and assignments were members of the teams of 50 or so in residence, who on the whole were not local Christians. This pattern was repeated in Caithness, with an even greater work-load for the 30-36 visitors and even less local participation, apart from attendance at events and services. As DP wrote in his Diary: 'The fellowship has been very good but we are not getting the local people in.' Besides special services in key churches in Wick and Thurso, Open Airs were held in Wick Market Square, at Watten Old Kirkyard and John O'Groats – the latter in (imagine it!) direct, vocal, competition with a Brethren congregation who declined to suspend their usual outreach there in favour of *Tell Scotland* – and at Latheron Old Bell Tower. Elsewhere in the county, church services were held at Bower – very well attended – and at Dunbeath; and at the Dunbar Hospital, Thurso, and Achvarasdal Eventide Home, Reay. Parties were sent out visiting in Latheron and Dunbeath and on a commando basis: hitchhiking, both to witness to their unsuspecting 'hitches', and to see where they might go and whom they would meet. DP himself lectured; and Edinburgh lawyer Fraser Maclennan, Tom Allan ['Tom Allan is with us – he has been a tower of strength'][16] and George Gunn, Edinburgh Presbytery's Mission Convener, were guest lecturers. All this was not entirely without result: four local speakers and a lay worship leader were recruited for the final Voice of the Pew service in Wick: Bridge Street. Overall the Caithness School followed the pattern DP had already experienced in Strathmore. In rural, small-town Scotland, crowds might well be attracted to special services and events, and there could be a deep sense of belonging to the church: but while the ministers might be progressive, there were also numbers who agreed with one 'old worthy' DP met on one of his preparatory visits to Caithness, 'He was very sceptical about *Tell Scotland* and all modern ways of approach.' True evangelism, for such folk, was via the preaching of the Word of God.

The sort of difficulty D. P. Thomson experienced advocating *Tell Scotland* in rural parishes was replicated across the country, and the Movement also faced other forms of resistance or misunderstanding. Some preferred to trust the normal ordinances of religion, disliking all stunts: these were the direct successors to those who similarly resisted the 'Forward Movement' of 1930. There was doubt expressed as to *exactly what* Scotland was to be *told*?[17] And besides, was not *showing* more convincing that *telling*? As 1954 went on, Tom Allan was more and more convinced that the church was not yet ready for the outreach planned by *Tell Scotland*.[18] Allan's *The Agent of Mission*, issued as the programmatic pamphlet for phase two, had insisted that evangelism had to find its place within a broad concept of mission. His ideal for phase two was building mission groups in each congregation, with three purposes: to be a training school for discipleship, to be a real Christian community sufficiently small that its members might enjoy togetherness, and to be a missionary agency. Service and evangelism, both individual and joint, were the expected outcomes. Urging the 'obligations of Christian discipleship – caring for the aged and infirm, the sick, the destitute; the involvement in the critical political issues of the times,' Allan recommended, as a partner to his pamphlet, James Maitland's Iona Community publication *Caring for People – the Church in the Parish*. As with much else of *Tell Scotland*, this was a radical, demanding agenda. 'Some fire has to be kindled before the *Tell Scotland* Movement itself becomes incandescent,' Allan wrote.[19] Particularly frustrating was the realisation that many ministers appeared to be unable to trust the laity in spiritual matters; others simply did not know how to enable the congregation's role in the church to become more than audience or social club.

D. P. Thomson and The All-Scotland Crusade of 1955

Across the questionably-developing momentum of this nascent grass-roots movement came Dr Billy Graham. The American evangelist led the Greater London Crusade in the Harringay Stadium for three months from March 1954, sponsored by the British Evangelical Alliance.[20] It was a campaign with an immense appeal that turned initial suspicion into appreciation of Graham's gracious personality and spiritual power. He even received a Royal invitation to preach for Queen Elizabeth in Windsor Chapel. His preaching was simple, Biblical and usually ended with an appeal for commitment, to come forward publicly – now – for counselling, using his own version of the old evangelical methodology. A conviction grew among groupings in Scotland associated with the Evangelical Alliance that Billy Graham should be invited to Scotland, and contacts were made with his Organisation. The Steering Panel were thus faced with a dilemma – Billy Graham could not now be ignored, so how was *Tell Scotland* to respond? Allan was quickly convinced that *Tell Scotland* should itself issue the invitation, believing that aloof, competitive or hostile attitudes would be immensely damaging and also that Graham's strengths could be invaluable to a Movement that he believed needed to catch fire if it was to achieve anything.

The pros and cons of this decision have been extensively debated; they were debated at the time.[21] Some became incandescent indeed, but with fury that *Tell Scotland* should sponsor such a very high profile old-style campaign, led by the archetypical outsider, the American independent, professional evangelist with only a small previous connection with Scotland and its churches. For sponsor it the Movement's Parent Committee did. Tom Allan's initial recommendation to the Steering Panel in March was referred to the Parent Committee of 3 May 1954. D. P. Thomson's 23rd volume of his Diaries contain his record of that debate, revealing that, by prior arrangement with Tom Allan, it was DP who formally moved that *Tell Scotland* invite Dr Billy Graham to Scotland:

> Tuesday, 4th May [1954] . . . The decisive day [*Monday 3 May*] proved quite dramatic . . . I reached Edinburgh . . . lunched with Tom Allan and over lunch we worked out a plan for the afternoon . . . At the meeting Tom led off, making some statements which clearly startled people. Letters of apology followed and critiques of George MacLeod's Memorandum, one very fine one from Charlie Duthie. Then came speeches against Billy, coming till I began to wonder if we would get a majority when it came to a vote. Then up got George Gunn and made a speech that seemed to begin quite against and ended all for. He was followed by Nevile Davidson and the Bishop of Edinburgh, both definitely for. With only 10 minutes left I got up moved and spoke to my motion. It was immediately seconded by the UF minister of Largs, and then Ralph Morton, who was sitting next me, moved a direct negative but got no seconder. Horace Walker pled for unanimity and the meeting agreed to send a deputation to London by air on Thursday – 4 people including Ralph and Tom.

Clearly the Movement was perplexed, but by Thomson's account Morton's straightforward proposed rejection found no seconder while there was significant ecumenical support for the invitation.

The 'Memorandum' presented in George MacLeod's absence is retained in the *Tell Scotland* folder of his archives.[22] His arguments against the invitation were both theological and practical. Was this the sort of initiative that would assist or hinder congregations as agents of mission? What sort of message was conveyed by glamorous events that seemed so much more electric than ordinary local ministry? If the methodology of an appeal to 'come forward' was acceptable, why wasn't it used by the Scottish churches – he might well have asked, why did D. P. Thomson choose not to use it? Was it the sort of campaign that, in fact, actually worked or had they rightly left this sort of thing behind? MacLeod referred to a recent free-standing campaign held in the Glasgow Odeon cinema and asserted that when its converts were followed up, it was found that most had lapsed: 'Have they not been left with the impression that they have closed with Christ but *nothing happens*?' MacLeod also challenged Billy Graham's consistent practice of speaking only on the individual's relationship with Christ and his refusal to discuss any of the 'big issues' of the day: was Dr Graham's Christ the Lord of History, George MacLeod asked, or was what he preached a form of escapism? He firmly believed that association with Billy Graham would divert *Tell Scotland* from its established path and create confusion as to its real purpose. Nevertheless on the motion of Charles Duthie the subsequent (14 May) meeting of the Parent Committee decided to issue the invitation: the die was cast.

George MacLeod was to remain consistent both in his support for *Tell Scotland* as a Movement and in his opposition to Billy Graham's methods. When the General Assembly of 1954 was asked to support the invitation extended by *Tell Scotland* he gave a passionate speech against the motion, and won massive applause but few votes. MacLeod later made it clear that his opposition had not been to Dr Graham personally. He also felt acutely the difficulty of opposing the ecumenical consensus, even questioning whether there was any element of personal jealousy in his hostility: 'a rationalisation of our envy'.[23] George further stressed that he did not reject the role of emotion in religion or the need to appeal for personal decision; indeed he wanted to see more opportunities for public display of personal commitment embedded in normal Church life, as the Iona Act of Belief was used at Iona Youth Camps.[24] MacLeod passionately believed that the church existed to challenge and to change the world in the name of Christ. He believed that the Christian faith showed itself to be real as it brought the mind of Christ to such issues as racial discrimination or a national defence strategy that relied on the nuclear bomb; in such grass-roots politics as poor housing. Equally, he argued the Faith showed itself to be irrelevant and hollow if Christians were not engaged with such issues. In the end he could not support the invitation and remain consistent to convictions he had held his whole ministry. By that stage, however, the Assembly was faced with only two possible courses. To support George MacLeod risked an immediate dissolution of the ecumenical enterprise of *Tell Scotland*; to support the invitation might or might not pose long-term risks but fell into line with what was being said by the rest of the protestant leadership of Scotland. Incidentally the 1954 Assembly was one at which MacLeod also failed in an attempt to persuade the Kirk to adopt his rejection of war as an instrument of policy, to join him in pacifism. D. P. Thomson wrote in his diary that he wished he could have been there – to vote with George.

If George MacLeod's opposition to Billy Graham was, perhaps, more in sorrow than in anger, others were more explosive. James Currie, minister at Glasgow: Pollock, for example, who had been a local 'Herald' for *Tell Scotland* in 1953, opposed the Crusade as promoting mass hysteria and was to continue into the future a vocal critic of mass evangelism.[25] Similar opposition to the Crusade was strong in the west of Scotland, where the Crusade's strongest supporters were also located. The evangelical Glasgow Christian Council, D. P. Thomson understood, was prepared to issue Graham with an invitation to the city if *Tell Scotland* turned down the opportunity. The 1955 Crusade was thus based primarily in Glasgow, at the Kelvin Hall: it naturally entirely swamped the preparations already made by the original *Tell Scotland* group in Glasgow for a programme directed less at proclamation and more towards service. Such was the backing that Billy Graham received from denominational central authorities that ministers in the west who distrusted, disliked or opposed his methods could not but be involved, for folk from their congregations were almost certain to be. Actual control of the Crusade was given to a new *ad hoc* body, the Sponsoring Council, with responsible to it an Executive convened by Tom Allan that acted in conjunction with Graham's own permanent Organisation and was not in practice answerable to any existing Scottish structure. For a not insignificant number of ministers, the Crusade was an elephant trampling heavily across their own gardens.

Why, then, did Tom Allan become a strong supporter, both of the All-Scotland Crusade and, indeed, of Dr Billy Graham? He acknowledged that he had not always been so. Indeed, on his first hearing of Billy Graham, in 1947 when Graham toured Scottish cities as a young man with Youth for Christ, Allan was distinctly put off by the flashy style – 'exaggerated drape suits of striking shades, exotically brilliant ties . . . a gold-plated trombone.'[26] On hearing Graham at Harringay, however, he was as impressed as the Archbishop of Canterbury by the Christ-centred, Biblical preaching, directed not so much to emotions as to the conscience and the will. In his September 1954 paper, 'The *Tell Scotland* Movement and Billy Graham: a discussion of the issues',[27] Tom Allan also argued that holding the Crusade in the context of the Movement would guard against an acknowledged danger of mass evangelism, that its loose connection with the main denominations left converts in the lurch. To the Crusade the Movement would lend its own momentum and training and local groups for prayer, enabling the two national campaigns to work not as rivals but in cooperation, so that any moved by the preaching to new commitment might seamlessly find a suitable fellowship for service and teaching. And, above all, the ability Graham had proven in London, to be a channel of spiritual blessing to the churches themselves, was exactly what the Scottish churches appeared to need if *Tell Scotland* was to achieve its potential in its forthcoming, outreach stage.[28]

In an attempt at mutual understanding Tom Allan attended the annual gathering of the Iona Community on Iona in June 1954. Ralph Morton reported on the overall event in the October 1954 edition of the Community's journal, *The Coracle*: the general conclusions were that the Crusade was likely to be disruptive of *Tell Scotland*'s focus on the missionary congregation as the agent of mission and that Billy Graham's methods were hazardous, not reflecting the full content of the Gospel or its implications for society.[29] While the Community was generally opposed to the All-Scotland Crusade, its leaders did not therefore withdraw from *Tell Scotland*, seeking from within the Movement to limit the dangers they perceived and to restore what they had understood to be *Tell Scotland's* original motivation; and some members did in fact participate in the Crusade. Evangelism remained on the Community's agenda after 1955,[30] though their direction of travel away from 'old' thinking and methods was confirmed by the events of 1954-55.

The All-Scotland Crusade began on Monday 21 March 1955 with the opening meeting in the Kelvin Hall. It concluded with a massive rally at the Hampden Park stadium on 30 April 1955. Special buses and trains were arranged to bring the interested into Glasgow. The *Forfar Dispatch*, for example, on 7 April carried a public notice on behalf of British Railways with details of their additional timetables to carry folk from Angus and the Mearns to Glasgow for the last week of the Crusade. The Church of Scotland Jedburgh & Kelso Presbytery's meeting in December 1954 noted the arrangements for similar trains from their area of the Borders. From all over Scotland people converged to hear Billy Graham. All the bookable seats in the 11,000 capacity Kelvin Hall were taken before the end of 1954 and some 15,000 filled both the Hall and its overflow accommodation six nights a week for six weeks. Tom Allan recorded that, in all, some

1,185,360 people attended meetings in connection with the Crusade and some 26,457 were known to have come forward for counselling about the faith.[31] The total population of Scotland at the time was just over five million.

D. P. Thomson's relationship to the All-Scotland Crusade was to be as ambivalent as his relationship to *Tell Scotland*. He was disappointed that, despite having moved the initial motion in favour of the Crusade, he was not invited to Glasgow for the first formal reception for Billy Graham:

> Tuesday, 15th March [1955] . . . I have not been asked to the Reception to Dr Billy Graham. Charlie Duthie and his wife are going. All three of my former assistants – Tom Allan, Bill Fitch and Bill Shannon – will be there, in their element and playing quite conspicuous parts, it may be. I wonder if any of them remember that the old chief had not been invited? Strange, that it should be so when I was responsible for moving the resolution that led to Dr Graham's invitation! Further reflection has made me think of my own inconsiderateness, on how many I must hurt by just such ways! That is, I think, what these experiences are meant to do for us!

Nevertheless DP did play a significant and public role in the Crusade. That the original concept of a Graham campaign in Glasgow developed into a genuine All-Scotland Crusade was in some measure due to him – at least he claimed responsibility in his later pamphlet, *Dr Billy Graham and the Pattern of Modern Evangelism*, for the essential idea of bringing the Kelvin Hall to the nation by a series of Relay Missions. From Harringay in 1954 Billy Graham's addresses had been transmitted by Post Office telephone land-line to additional centres, where audiences gathered to listen in. For Scotland, however, on Thomson's proposal, it was agreed that a national pattern of such Relays should be centrally arranged, each with their own missioner to speak in addition to Billy Graham to support the appeal, and with counsellors offered at each centre and not just at the Kelvin Hall. With Bill Shannon as Relay coordinator, the Glasgow Crusade therefore widened to link with local *Tell Scotland* committees across the land. There were to be 35 separate Relay Mission centres gathering some 217,700 people in all. In the northern archipelago of Orkney, for example, the local *Tell Scotland* committee organised its own Relay Mission in Kirkwall's Paterson Kirk, with the Rev. A. R. Thomson of Kirkwall: King Street Church of Scotland congregation as Missioner. Over 1,000 people filled the church every night for all six nights. One result of *Tell Scotland's* sponsorship of the All-Scotland Crusade was therefore to encourage its own local committees and others to engage in similar if smaller versions of mass evangelism, arranging their own rallies and evangelistic preaching. If *Tell*

Scotland offered the Crusade a national framework it would otherwise have lacked, the Crusade also influenced the thinking of many within *Tell Scotland*, restoring to preaching an authority and credibility that had been doubted.

Meanwhile, in Edinburgh, the local *Tell Scotland* committee had put D. P. Thomson in charge of the training of counsellors for its own Relays. With agreement from the Crusade he followed a pattern of his own, not that of the Graham Organisation. A school of seven weeks was organised, with each session including worship, group Bible Study, a lecture and opportunities for personal consultation. Over 1,000 came at some stage and by the end perhaps 700 (of which under 100 were ministers) had been individually authorised after a lengthy interviewing process. In Glasgow the attendance of some 5,000 at shorter training classes meant that vetting was an exercise in scrutinising questionnaires. Besides DP, Edinburgh's lecture programme featured the Principal of the Congregational College, Charles Duthie; Kenneth Warner the Bishop of Edinburgh; and George Gunn, then convener of the Church of Scotland's Committee on the Education of the Ministry. The capital's Relay Mission was, as far as possible, owned by the churches of Edinburgh. Relays took place in eight locations owned by Baptist, Congregational, Episcopal, Methodist and Presbyterian congregations, as well as in the city's municipal Usher Hall. Billy Graham also came to speak to students and staff of Edinburgh University and to preach at a major rally in the Tynecastle Football Stadium, attended by some 20,000 people. For this, DP had arranged for three nearby churches to be available as locations for counselling different age groups – the enquirers were paraded through the local streets from the stadium to the centres. On Saturday 30 April, DP recorded in his diary:

> Saturday, 30th April [1955] . . . All the week the interest in Edinburgh is growing and we have had well on for 5,000 most nights. 1,040 decisions have been reached in the Relays also, plus 920 at Tynecastle, making 1,960 in all. That may mean well over 2,000 before we finish in Edinburgh.

Tell Scotland and the All-Scotland Crusade were closely coordinated in Edinburgh. Besides the Training Classes for counsellors, on behalf of the local Committee Thomson had since August 1954 coordinated a series of visitation schools and campaigns in Edinburgh using the Youth Centre at Simpson House as a base. Craigmillar and Newcraighall, Fountainbridge, Tollcross and Lauriston all saw visitation-based missions. DP spoke on *Tell Scotland* to local groups in Restalrig, Morningside, Murrayfield, Lothian

Road, Blackhall, Tynecastle, Sighthill and Corstorphine. A Central Business Area Campaign was held which, beginning on March 22 1955, coincided with the All-Scotland Campaign: flats and pubs were visited, and teams coordinated by Rev. David W. Torrance as DP's Assistant fulfilled assignments to the staff of stores, shops and places of work. Such events prepared the ground by raising awareness and bringing together the teams of folk who provided the staffing needed both for the Crusade and for the post-Crusade Edinburgh-wide courses for instruction and after care which ran though May, and led to weekend Training Schools at Prestonpans, Dalkeith and Penicuik in June. A full-blown visitation campaign with the Abbeyhill Churches then followed in September and October. All of this, of course, was run on the D. P. Thomson pattern of gathering activists from a wide area as an experienced nucleus to which newcomers might be drawn. His experience with the Edinburgh Relay Missions of the All-Scotland Crusade considerably expanded his personal network of contacts, and they in turn supported his pattern of work for the next few years.

Enhancing the national impact of the Crusade were the local prayer groups organised by the *Tell Scotland* and other evangelistic networks.

#33: PREPARING FOR THE BILLY GRAHAM EDINBURGH RALLY, TYNECASTLE STADIUM 1955

Beyond all this Billy Graham himself and members of his team made themselves available during their time in Scotland to support occasional local events outside Glasgow. In addition to the main series in the Kelvin Hall, Billy Graham himself preached at what Tom Allan described as 'gigantic open-air rallies' in Aberdeen, Edinburgh and Inverness besides those in the Glasgow's Ibrox and Hampden Park sports grounds, and at also numerous special meetings – Allan's book *Crusade in Scotland - Billy Graham* named as examples the British Army's Redford Barracks, Glasgow's Barlinnie Prison and John Brown's shipyard. There was, of course, massive coverage in the British and Scottish daily and weekly papers, sometimes critical; and close support from the BBC, now via the new medium of television, with the Good Friday service in the Kelvin Hall and the final Hampden Park Rally being televised in full, in addition to other occasions when Dr Graham was invited to speak. Viewers were measured in millions, whether in their own homes or in churches where televisions had been set up and arrangements made to counsel those who came forward.

The response of the people of Scotland to the All-Scotland Crusade was thus overwhelmingly more than had been expected in advance, as Tom Allan admitted in *Crusade in Scotland*: 'We had under-estimated the hunger of the Scottish people to hear the Word of God.' Tom Allan's experience of the All-Scotland Crusade was to shape his future ministry. For Allan, who was based in Glasgow and at the heart of the work in the Kelvin Hall, it was the grace and power of Billy Graham's preaching that was the hallmark of the Crusade.

As a final codicil to the events of 1955, D. P. Thomson's personal if tenuous connection with Billy Graham raises one of those intriguing 'what might have beens' of history. Thomson was not shy of making his voice heard in the General Assembly – and by all accounts he had a very loud voice! At the Church of Scotland's General Assembly of 1955, with Billy Graham as a guest in the seats used by the Queen's representative, the Lord High Commissioner, DP moved a personal addition to the Deliverance on the Report of the Home Board, asking the Assembly to give thanks to God for what had been done through Billy Graham:

> The following morning on the HOME BOARD REPORT IN THE GENERAL ASSEMBLY OF THE CHURCH OF SCOTLAND I made my first speech in this year's Assembly. It took the form of an Addendum to the Deliverance giving thanks for what God had done through Billy Graham and for the work of the Counsellors and commending and urging training of the latter to the Church. I received a great ovation and the

Convener could do nothing but accept. Billy, who was in the Throne Gallery, was obviously moved and the following day he sent me this wire:

DR D. P. THOMPSON
HOME MISSION BOARD
GENERAL ASSEMBLY
CHURCH OF SCOTLAND
EDINBURGH

THANK YOU FROM THE BOTTOM OF MY HEART
FOR YOUR GREAT SPEECH YESTERDAY.
YOU WARMED MY HEART AND WE GIVE
GLORY TO GOD FOR YOUR FRIENDSHIP
BILLY GRAHAM.

That the friendship of the two evangelists was both real and tenuous was reflected in the telegram's warmth and in its inaccuracies: Thomson, of course, is not spelled with a 'p', nor had (at that stage) any doctorate been awarded to DP. Outside committee meetings, they had, in fact, only met once – an unscheduled *tête-à-tête* at Barnoak after the Crusade had ended but before Billy Graham left Scotland:

Tuesday, 10th May [1955] Billy Graham came last night! It was a very strange and moving experience all through – quite the most memorable hour we have spent in Barnoak. I had the hunch at 6 when Mary was out seeing Joan Murdoch off after her weekend with us to phone Gleneagles. They had mentioned and the papers had said that Billy was there and had been at Dunblane Cathedral on Sunday. Billy was there and I got him almost at once. He had been golfing at St Andrews with Jack Maclean and was leaving for London at midnight. He had his 'Hour of Decision' broadcast to prepare and an article 26,000,000 would read and other urgent matters – he didn't see how he could possibly come! Could I not dine with him? No, I said, I had no car – he could get over more easily than I could. I could sense that he felt the urge to come and he said that he would see if a car could be got and if it could he would come at once and dine later. If I didn't hear I would know he was coming. In three-quarters of an hour he was over and stayed for an hour and a half. He said he very much wanted to see me. I had felt when he had first said that at BBC House that he had meant it. We covered a great deal of ground – his future, the claims on him and the need for guarding against diffusion at the expense of depth, better integration and fellowship between the team and the locals, improved personal work and follow up, the danger of over emphasis on 'This is your last chance,' etc. Billy was deeply moved and profoundly impressed. He wished I could join the team and take

> charge of major strategy. He wanted me to come to Toronto and go through an entire campaign with them. Finally proposed that I should go into retreat with the team next December at Dawson Trotman's estate in California and help them rethink and replan their whole strategy. We had prayer together and they left – a never to be forgotten night.

The visit to California never materialised: DP's stipend was paid to make his services available to the Church *in* Scotland. But suppose D. P. Thomson had joined the Billy Graham Organisation?

Despite having moved the first formal proposal that Billy Graham should be invited to Scotland, Thomson was not uncritical of his methods, personally refusing to practise what he, disparaging, called *'raise your hand' evangelism*:

> Wednesday, 16th February [1955] . . . Yesterday I attended a meeting without parallel or precedent in the long history of the Christian Church . . . [in Glasgow at] . . . the YMCA Lyric Theatre for The All-Scotland Crusade Relay Missioners Conference at which there were about 40 present: Willie Still, Bill Shannon, A. J. Morrison, Gilbert Cameron, Ian Doyle, Forter Hall, Ralph Fairway, Jack, Ken Turnbull etc among them. Tom gave a masterly address at the morning session but he and I are far apart now in our thinking on many points, I can see! . . . We conferred from 11-12.30 and then lunched . . . Tom Allan has gone over to the 'raise your hand' school of evangelism. A big step down and back to my very great sorrow!

This description, *'Raise your hand' evangelism*, was of course shorthand for the practice of asking for a public response on the part of any whose hearts had been touched by an evangelistic address. Billy Graham actually asked, not for hands to be raised, but that enquirers come forward to the centre of his auditorium and stand publicly while others gathered, before going off for counselling. In his youth in the 1920s D. P. Thomson had followed a similar practice. Even then, DP had not used the extremes of blatant manipulation – he usually intimated that those who wished might stay behind, thus allowing the majority of the congregation their opportunity to leave. In his 1966 booklet, *Dr Billy Graham and the Pattern of Modern Evangelism*, Thomson gave five pages to explaining why, in his mature ministry, he did not use 'a reiterated appeal for a public response', an appeal that he had come to believe foreign to the long Scottish tradition. 'The Reformers knew nothing of it. The Covenanters knew nothing of it':

> Let us be quite clear about this – the history of 19 Christian centuries shows, beyond all shadow of doubt, that evangelism does not require for its effective prosecution the 'altar call', the reiterated appeal, the upraised

> hand, or the public coming forward. It is after, not before, a man has found Christ, or rather been found of Him, that he is called on to confess Him openly as Saviour and Lord.

DP had come to believe that, if the Holy Spirit was indeed moving in hearts and minds as a sermon was preached, special mechanisms – 'decision cards' for example – were not essential to 'harvest' the individuals concerned. He went on, 'If not necessary, is it wise?' and answered no. He wrote that as a parish minister he had met people who had responded under the sway of mass emotion and later regretted it:

> I know what a heartbreak this has been to me, and to so many of my clerical brethren. After my own experiences in the regular ministry I could never bring myself to use this method again on mission or campaign.

In 1957 DP thus refused to commit himself to making a 'public appeal' when invited to give the key address at an Evangelical Rally at Tranent Old Parish Church.

Billy Graham's Harringay Campaign had commended him to Tom Allan and many of the leaders of the British churches because, in fact, he spoke to the will rather than using the mass-emotional appeal that had been feared. D. P. Thomson still saw, besides the moving spectacle of the lines standing and coming forward, less impressive dramas:[32]

> I have also stood 'in the wings' where I could get a side view of the audience and felt and seen for myself the strong emotional tug to which so many were being subjected. One lad or girl in the bus party looking at the other, as much as to say, 'What about it? If you go, I will'; several half-rising, others following, and then still others not liking to be left behind. Afterwards in the counselling rooms it was sometimes only too obvious that many of those who had come forward just did not understand either what they were doing or why they did it. The results of this can be tragic.

Indeed, from his work with teenagers as part of the follow-up to the Crusade, DP had just a few days before the Barnoak 'summit' experienced the sort of mixed feelings that came from evangelism with a direct appeal for public decision:

> Tuesday, 3rd May [1955] . . . Yesterday I taxied straight from the station to GEORGE HERIOT'S SCHOOL where Andrew Graham met me . . . He is the only full-time School Chaplain in Scotland at a Day School – visits boys in hospital and everywhere. I think he could be just a little more evangelistically minded . . . I went into the School Chapel not knowing what I was going to speak on. I still didn't know when I faced 100 boys of classes IV, V & VI. Only a few minutes earlier had I learned

> the situation. The boys had been told at Ibrox that they were not going to go forward as I was coming to the school today. A few went in spite of that. They had been told that the meeting was for those who were at Ibrox – about 60 – 100 came! Andrew and I agreed that I would speak for 15 minutes then answer questions, then make a closing appeal – with silent prayer for decision. I spoke on Saul's Conversion. I felt I got there. Questions came steadily and first 'Was Dr Graham entitled to say to a boy of 17 that this was his last chance?' 'How old did I have to be to get converted?' etc. They kept me going. I finalised the appeal and then we bowed in silent prayer. Here I feel I failed. I should have given the choice then to wait at least – I didn't – it is a day that may never come again! I went away with very mixed feelings.

Some caution is needed when reading what Thomson wrote in 1966 in *Dr Billy Graham and the Pattern of Modern Evangelism*, as it reflects his interest in the technical details and nuances of evangelism and, perhaps, an element of retrospective disappointment. Preaching for decision, for conversion, he always believed to be important: it was pressurised, *reiterated* appeals, that he deprecated. During DP's preaching visit to Belfast in October 1955 he did, on occasion, use the traditional After Meeting methodology he regretted not suggesting at George Heriot's earlier in the year.

All in all, however, by 1955 DP no longer placed a demand for public response at the centre of evangelistic occasions and he was disappointed to learn that Tom Allan's growing cooperation with the Billy Graham Organisation had brought him to take a different point of view – 'a big step down and back' as Thomson saw it. It seems that when, finally, he had the opportunity to speak of these issues – the danger of over-emphasis on 'This is your last chance, etc' – with Billy Graham himself, the warmth between the two men overcame these differences of method. While he personally was determined to practise evangelism in ways he believed worthy of his Master, DP's essential loyalties meant he was committed to support Tom Allan and *Tell Scotland* in the All-Scotland Crusade, though in a restricted (if locally major) cameo role. He did not refuse to cooperate with those who took a different view from himself on the practicalities of evangelism. If he had gone to California, could he have resisted the pressure of the Graham Organisation? Would his views have influenced the future career of Billy Graham himself? DP's opinion in 1966 was that the momentum of the Organisation itself was too powerful and limited the Evangelist's freedom to alter course.

Tell Scotland continues – from Edinburgh to Sutherland

Tom Allan's recommendation that *Tell Scotland* bring in Billy Graham to rescue the Movement has sometimes been credited with achieving the exact opposite, its collapse. That the Movement never recovered from the Crusade is sometimes told as the story of the crisis of evangelism.[33] Complex situations rarely benefit from such simplifications, especially when underlying problems are ignored. George MacLeod had, after all, identified a crisis in the Kirk's outreach *before 1950*.[34] The 'new evangelism' faced real resistance before 1955, as DP had discovered in Strathmore. From the start *Tell Scotland* intended to challenge the 'conventional life of the Church'. Yet the Movement did not collapse after the Spring of 1955 and, indeed, it generated very considerable activity by groups of local congregations across Scotland between the autumn of 1955 and the spring of 1956. *Tell Scotland*, in fact, proved – for a time – sufficiently vigorous at a local level to mitigate the growing divisions on the doctrine and practice of evangelism among the ministry. Alongside a new emphasis on preaching, the years following the All-Scotland Crusade saw much laity-based initiative, including a number of ambitious D. P. Thomson campaigns. Beyond the Crusade, the Movement did not lack its successes.

Tell Scotland had always planned for its main, congregational, outreach to begin in the autumn of 1955 and in Tom Allan's mind a Crusade in the spring of '55 did not conflict with this. Rather, he hoped that with Billy Graham's help the necessary fire would be kindled. Assessment of what happened is made harder because what was planned locally was intended to be, indeed, local: though there were recommendations, there was no prescribed national timetable or method for the missions. The Editor of *The Scottish Congregationalist* complained in August 1955 that reliance on local initiative resulted in confusion. Some areas had already completed a house to house visitation: others showed no signs of starting. There was an inevitable contrast with the Crusade, with its focus on a single preacher, its professionally organised publicity and its tight national timetable. There was disappointment when Tom Allan resigned as Field Organiser to accept a call to a central Glasgow congregation. Yet, all in all, in the 12 months after the Crusade there was an unprecedented number of house to house missions conducted on an interdenominational basis all across Scotland.

The *Tell Scotland Bulletin* for winter 1955 reported examples of missions by visitation from Dumfries in the south to North Roe in the parish of Walls, Shetland and added 'In [Glasgow] Garrowhill a Mission of

Friendship organised by George F. MacLeod, Leader of the Iona Community, set *Tell Scotland* in motion.' Reports in the Church of Scotland's *Life & Work* for November 1955 listed some 15 locations where schemes were active. At the 1956 United Free Church General Assembly, their Moderator, David W. Roy, included a section on *Tell Scotland* in his keynote address, recognising the efforts made by UF congregations.[35] From this and other evidence in denominational records and magazines, it is clear that *Tell Scotland*, building on the Crusade's wave of enthusiasm, had succeeded in inspiring large numbers of congregations across Scotland to 'go out', mobilising their members to visit and share their faith.

In Edinburgh 23 local groups of churches planned the city-wide visitation that began in November 1955. By December the Evangelism Convener was able to report that over 60% of the homes in the city and its environs had been visited by lay members from all the cooperating denominations.

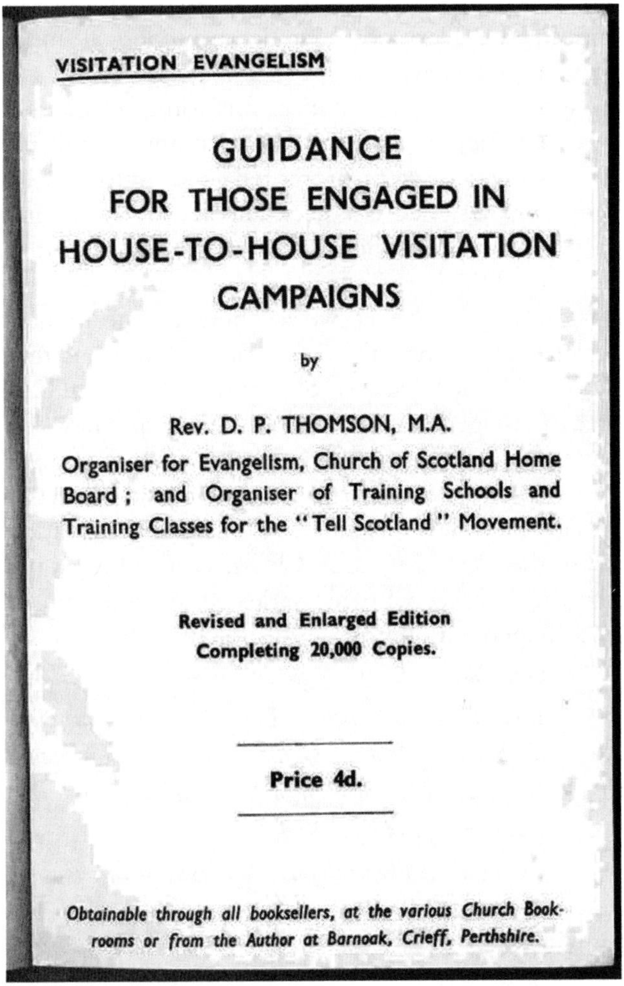

VISITATION EVANGELISM

GUIDANCE
FOR THOSE ENGAGED IN
HOUSE-TO-HOUSE VISITATION
CAMPAIGNS

by

Rev. D. P. THOMSON, M.A.
Organiser for Evangelism, Church of Scotland Home Board; and Organiser of Training Schools and Training Classes for the "Tell Scotland" Movement.

Revised and Enlarged Edition
Completing 20,000 Copies.

Price 4d.

Obtainable through all booksellers, at the various Church Book-rooms or from the Author at Barnoak, Crieff, Perthshire.

#34: COVER PAGE, *GUIDANCE FOR THOSE ENGAGED IN HOUSE TO HOUSE VISITATION CAMPAIGNS* 1955

Visible results were encouraging: the involvement of young people, the creation of house groups, increasing attendance and membership. One Church Extension congregation had tripled in size. Working on the presumption that any contacted in the spring during the Crusade would appear in statistics gathered at the end of 1955 while those contacted by the late 1955 visitations would appear in statistics for December 1956, the Clerk to the Presbytery noted in March 1957 an encouraging increase in the membership of the Church of Scotland in Edinburgh during 1956. 3,932 new members had joined by profession of faith. Large numbers of lapsed members had joined new congregations as local churches made contact and issued invitations. All this he attributed to *Tell Scotland* visiting. Indeed, the Clerk considered the numerical impact of *Tell Scotland* in Edinburgh to have been greater than that of the Crusade.

What did these visitation missions, conducted across the country, involve? They could, in fact, take a number of different forms – again, at its heart *Tell Scotland* promoted local initiative. There was the survey visitation, designed as a quick call on every house in the area to establish a map of the households to which congregations were or were not connected. This then formed the basis of slower and more thorough pastoral and evangelical work. There was the literature visitation, designed to take Bibles and other Christian publications round households – the National Bible Society of Scotland made special Gospel editions available free of charge. Invitation visitations brought news of church programmes and invitations to participate: this was a common method for Iona Missions. At its simplest, members of teams, in pairs, visited households to explain what *Tell Scotland* was about – to invite participation – for the visitors to share their experience of Christ. D. P. Thomson cornered a huge and growing market with his series of leaflets that offered guidance and encouragement on how all this might be tackled:

- *Guidance for those engaged in house-to-house visitation campaigns*
- *You are going out visiting? Let us tell you a little about it! By (1) Elders of the Kirk, (2) Women of the Guild, (3) The Young People*
- *We Saw the Church in Action! The Press and BBC report on those Visitation Campaigns 1947 to 1954*
- *Two by Two! The rank and file of the church report on what happened when they went out visiting*
- *Visitation Campaigns: an outline study for congregational groups and youth fellowships*

All five of these productions were available in 1955. 'What sales these books are having!' DP recorded in April. By November he was writing:

> Less than a fortnight ago I put through the third printing of *Two by Two* and *Guidance*. Both are nearly finished and next weekend at the latest we will have to print again. It is quite astonishing – I have never known anything like it since *Eric Liddell.*

Such demand for these pamphlets is in itself evidence of the success of *Tell Scotland* in promoting congregationally-based mission.

On the inside back cover of *Two by Two!*, Thomson printed what he described as 'A typical briefing for visitors':

> In going out you do not go alone – the Master Himself goes with you. That is His promise, and has been the experience – in quite unforgettable ways – of hundreds who have participated in this work. Remember that behind every closed door at which you knock or ring the bell, lies an unknown human situation, and one for which you yourself are quite unequal. Pause for a silent prayer on every doorstep, asking for the eye to see only what you are meant to see, and the ear to hear only what you are meant to hear, and for the right word to say and the right approach to make when the door does open.

Pray before you leave the church hall; pray on the doorstep – ask to come in. It was practical, realistic and spiritual advice, though based on the fact that it could then be assumed that each home did have a church connection, or at least that it was tactful to make that assumption. Thomson organised his visitors two by two. He preferred to match people who were different – older with younger; man with woman; people from different denominations; managers or professionals with working men or housewives. He tried to see that they were properly briefed, equipped with pencils and notebooks and such information as was already known from membership rolls about the households on their lists. Visitors were to be offered good support, spiritual and emotional via experienced leaders at the centre; tea and refreshments were on hand; there were prayers together before they all, finally, went home.

Two by Two! was compiled from extracts selected from the reports DP noted at the time and later received from members of Work & Witness, designed to show that even the hesitant and inexperienced, those without theological (or, indeed, only basic) education, women quite as well if not better than men, could find Christ with them in the homes they visited:

> Many a lonely person we met – I think of the maid waiting rather wistfully at the back door for a further talk, when her employer had monopolised

> the visitors; of the mother who had been three years in a town and whom no one had invited to a Church or Guild; of the shepherd far up a glen, who stayed two and a half miles from the last house on the road, and who was very much farther from the nearest Church; of the crofters in their secluded hamlet. These people were waiting for a message from the Church, reminding them of the Saviour's love and care.
>
> ***
>
> The welcome of the lonely old man who rarely received a visitor; of the crippled old woman who was unable to leave her room at the top of a tenement; the newly married couple who wanted their union enriched by the experience of spiritual fellowship; the little children who wanted to sing choruses in Sunday School; all these convinced us that our time had not been wasted.
>
> ***
>
> I learned much from my partner. She could make contacts where I could not. Her approach could break down barriers that I could not see. She was accepted where I was suspect. The Holy Spirit taught most of all, and time and time again we realised that He had prepared the way.
>
> ***
>
> One thing I shall always remember was the simple, natural, unaffected way in which the young people who were my partners witnessed for their Lord. To me that was most moving.

By the time the 1956 General Assembly of the Church of Scotland met, its Home Board was able to report: 'There is hardly a part of Scotland where there has been no evangelistic activity . . . The [*Tell Scotland*] Field Organiser has estimated that some 600 campaigns of house to house visitation have been carried through.'

D. P. Thomson had had responsibility for the training of counsellors for the Crusade in Edinburgh; he had run a series of post-Crusade follow-up and training events in conjunction with the city's *Tell Scotland* committee. His existing network of activists, organised in the Work & Witness Movement, was greatly increased by shared experience during the Crusade. Now came the idea from which his post Crusade campaigns flowed, recounted in his *The Sutherland Adventure: the* Tell Scotland *Campaign in the Presbytery of Tongue, August 9th to 29th*:

> Let us offer to our brethren in the north to take up a team of counsellors and converts during the summer holiday period, that we might share with those who lived so far from the centres of population something of

> what we ourselves had been experiencing and discovering. I was sitting by my fireside at home when that happy inspiration came.

The serendipity of this fireside meditation was the way it offered a solution not just to one but to two problems: on the one hand, an earlier request from Sutherland's ministers for action in their area; on the other, his desire to build on the fellowship the Graham Crusade had generated by finding new areas in which to deploy his people. Indeed, he wrote in *The Sutherland Adventure* that one major reason for his post-Crusade work was the need to offer a bridge between 'the crowded mass meeting and the ordinary church service'. Opponents of the Crusade had feared that a shadow would be cast on normal church life by the dazzling electricity of the Kelvin Hall. Thomson also saw this danger, and sought to find ways to channel new enthusiasm and commitment.

In August 1955 the 'Sutherland Adventure' therefore went ahead, under the name of the *Tell Scotland* Campaign in the Presbytery of Tongue. From this flowed campaigns in the Presbytery of Mull and around Ullapool in spring 1956, and the fantasy of a '*Tell Scotland* fleet sailing for Orkney and Shetland'. Following the pattern adopted in Sutherland for the summer of 1955, D. P. Thomson was to engage with what he described as the 'fringe areas' of Scotland for much of the next two years. In his *West Highland Adventure: The* Tell Scotland *Campaign in Mull and Iona, Coll and Tiree, Morvern and Ardnamurchan*, D. P. Thomson presented this whole series of campaigns as the solution to a problem: '. . . the man-power situation . . . in the Northern and Western Highlands and in the island groups off the Scottish Coast. There, parishes tend to be large; vacancies many, and ministerial resources less than in any other part of the country.'

Tell Scotland sought to reach the entire country, but what shape might it take in the Presbytery of Tongue, which covered a massive area of moor and mountain, twice the size of Fife but with a small population mainly located in crofting settlements strung out along the north and west coasts? As DP wrote, there was no town or secondary school in the entire area. Four of its eight Church of Scotland parishes were without ministers: additionally the Free Presbyterian Church had a sole Lay Missionary and the Free Church of Scotland but one minister in the area. 'Parishes . . . large; vacancies many' was a good description of the situation. The training school model used in Dunfermline, Inverness and Nairn was clearly inappropriate: no single centre existed from which to base a team and to which to gather volunteers. Instead, Thomson planned a simple three week visitation staffed entirely from the south, operating from different centres simultaneously and leading worship in the vacant churches.

The Church of Scotland Presbytery of Tongue approved his plans at its July meeting and the teams – 80 people in all – arrived for the August campaign. David W. Torrance was deputy leader. DP had recruited by circularising his contacts:

> The Team will comprise ministers, students, senior school pupils, members of the Work & Witness movement, and counsellors and converts from the Relay Mission in Edinburgh. The minimum period desirable is a week. There will be a leader at each centre and a hostess at each centre. Mrs Thomson and I will be at GHQ.
>
> Transport. We hope to take at least three vehicles north and to supplement these with local transport. You get to Sutherlandshire, if you are going, either (1) Walking, (2) Hitchhiking (not too difficult and great fun), (3) Cycling, pretty grim on the last stages; (4) Motoring. We will be only too glad to have what is left of your car; (5) By train to Lairg or Thurso and thence by bus; (6) By air to Wick, and thence by bus. In certain cases we may be able to meet you at Thurso or Lairg or Forsinard.
>
> What to Bring. Strong footwear and clothes for work over rough country; a stout heart, an open mind, an eager and willing spirit, a quiet determination and great hopefulness. The usual toilet requisites: towel, soap, toothbrush, sheets and pillowslip (or sleeping bag), etc.

Besides the supply, transport, accommodation and other such technical details hinted at in these instructions, other difficulties were foreseen. This was an area where the Free and Free Presbyterian Churches were strong, and these denominations were not part of the *Tell Scotland* coalition. In the congregations of these Churches and also of the Church of Scotland in the area, patterns of worship and theology remained much more traditional than had become common in the south. Yet more importantly, this was an area where Gaelic was still in common use at home and for worship. The ministers of the established church might issue an invitation, but would the people of Sutherland respond, DP wondered: 'Coming with all our inexperience and our inadequacies, with our crudities and our immaturities, with our Lowland outlook and our complete ignorance of the *language of Eden* [Gaelic], what sort of a reception could we hope for?'

The people of Sutherland were, of course, courteous and welcoming. Most homes had an existing congregational connection. The teams, working out of the empty manses at Scourie and Bettyhill, the Spiersesque mission church/ house in Strath Halladale, and Balnakeil House and Loch Loyal Lodge (lent by absentee landlords), often shared in short acts of worship during lengthy visits. At Scourie children were gathered for games and a cut-down seaside mission. The authorities made the team responsible for Chaplaincy at the RAF camp at Balnakeil. Besides homes, the hotels and shooting lodges of the area were also visited in an attempt to contact the many summer visitors – some of them men of immense wealth and power. An open air gathering was held in Strathnaver at the site of one of the notorious Sutherland Clearances. DP produced a booklet, *Tales of the Far North West*, containing colourful incidents from the church history of the area. By October the Presbytery of Tongue recorded that the mission: 'had been well received in the homes of the people. The services had drawn large congregations, and the ministers had been encouraged in their work.' A report by one of the lay leaders, David Maxwell Q.C., reprinted in *The Sutherland Adventure*, was later circulated by the Home Board to their contacts in all Presbyteries across Scotland. Maxwell emphasised the value of the visitation: 'The part of the work that counted for most, I feel, was the systematic visitation of the homes. It is amazing to discover how many lonely folk there are in the world, in the castle as well as on the croft.' And the sense of being one in Christ, despite the different ages and backgrounds of the people who comprised the teams, and despite their cultural differences from the homes they visited, was a lasting impression of the Sutherland Adventure and supported the conclusion that the enterprise had been successful.

#35: PART OF THE TEAM FOR THE 'SUTHERLAND ADVENTURE' 1955, COURTESY OF MRS MARSAILI MACKINNON, WHOSE FATHER FINLAY MACDONALD (LAY MISSIONARY AND LATER MINISTER) IS FIRST LEFT, AND DP 2ND LEFT.

Tell Scotland – The Mull, Loch Broom, Orkney and Shetland Campaigns

From this success, D. P. Thomson now sought to generalise, planning further similar, yet more ambitious expeditions to the fringes of Scotland. He gained a hearing at the September 1955 *Tell Scotland* Steering Panel and sought consent to what could be seen as a change of policy. Though *Tell Scotland* principles suggested that 'each area, if not actually each parish, should provide the necessary personnel for the carrying through of a Visitation Campaign within its own bounds,' his Tongue Campaign demonstrated (he argued) 'that there were areas in which the local forces, however well organised or trained, were quite inadequate to the task, and where the necessary ministerial leadership would not be available on the spot.' *Tell Scotland* wished to promote missions across the nation from autumn 1955; so, in these 'inadequate' areas, his teams would supply the need.[36] DP knew well that some in *Tell Scotland*'s leadership criticised his style of regional evangelism as evading the principle of local responsibility – even now the Steering Panel's support for this initiative was less clear-cut than he presented it – but if the Movement could embrace Billy Graham, then it certainly included D. P. Thomson.

The full stories of the campaigns organised by D. P. Thomson in the name of the *Tell Scotland* Movement in the Presbyteries of Mull, Orkney and Shetland, and in the Loch Broom area of the Presbytery of Ross, cannot be recalled here.[37] His booklets *West Highland Adventure* and *From Island to Island! Experiences and Adventures of the* Tell Scotland *Summer Campaign Team in Orkney*, both 1956, followed much the same pattern as *The Sutherland Adventure*. Something of the context of *Tell Scotland* was described; the recruitment of the teams, the pattern of the campaign, and the experiences of the teams were covered. A general impression of fruitful fellowship and spiritual blessing was conveyed. The size of these enterprises is clear – they were indeed ambitious, both in terms of the geography to be covered and the length of time they were planned to last. Sutherland had been a three week mission in August, but the Isle of Mull (with the islands of Coll and Tiree and the mainland peninsula of Ardnamurchan) lasted from 20 March to 5 May 1956. Ullapool / Loch Broom followed on from 13 May to 28 June and Orkney began on 1 July and lasted until 30 September 1956. The 1957 campaign in Shetland was even longer: from 30 May to 5 October.[38] Substantial teams were needed: for Mull, some 100, comprised largely of teachers and students, and with a good international component. Around 200 in all joined the Orkney expedition at different stages, including, again, an international element and a good number of ministers to offer pulpit supply for vacancies. A similar sized group was found for Shetland, with an enhanced number of senior pupils from schools in Edinburgh where the Crusade had made an impression. If Sutherland had been mainly supported by DP's Edinburgh contacts, the later and larger campaigns drew support from a wider area. After Orkney, reunion or report meetings were held at Edinburgh, Alyth, Airdrie and Montrose; after Shetland, at Edinburgh, Glasgow, Dundee and Cowdenbeath.

If the origins of these campaigns 'on the fringes' lay in part in D. P. Thomson's desire to further the spiritual experience of his Work & Witness and All-Scotland Crusade contacts, they also came out of local *Tell Scotland* initiatives. The Church of Scotland Presbytery of Mull had appointed a committee back in December 1954 'to study all the aspects of the *Tell Scotland* Campaign and to arrange evangelistic meetings in the Presbytery of Mull.' Little had apparently been achieved (at least nothing had surfaced in the minutes of the Presbytery) when it was agreed in January 1956 to receive a *Tell Scotland* team under D. P. Thomson. Similarly the local *Tell Scotland* committees in both Orkney and Shetland dated back to the earlier phases of the Movement: unlike Mull, both had ecumenical representation. Both had sponsored Relay Missions in 1955, and in Shetland an element of visitation had also been carried through following the Crusade.

There was some resistance to the Orkney expedition among its Church of Scotland ministers and the invitation to DP only passed the Presbytery after two contested votes. Some tended to resent the implication that their ministry was in any way inadequate. More widely, Orcadians asked whether their own churches were thought to be defective, that a major campaign from Scotland was thought necessary? A Stromness minister, Hector G. Ross, displaying a post-Crusade surfeit of evangelism, told DP that 'there ought to be no more campaigns of any kind for 20 years!' Visitation did not therefore take place in either Kirkwall or Stromness – and a proposed follow-up for Easter 1957 was vetoed when the majority of the elders of Kirkwall, Orkney's commercial and administrative centre, decided that such evangelism was not needed in their town. Thomson was disappointed that, at the end of the Shetland campaign during the month allocated to Lerwick, only limited numbers were attracted to the public meetings. The islands' professional and business classes thus displayed something of that reluctance to be involved that DP had met among the elders in the burghs of Strathmore and that Tom Allan had encountered in North Kelvinside back in 1947. And if DP was thought, perhaps, too enthusiastic among some Church of Scotland circles, he and *Tell Scotland* were condemned as unsound in theology by the Free Church Synod of Glenelg in advance of the Loch Broom mission of 1956. *The British Weekly* reported that the Synod had warned its members to beware of *Tell Scotland*'s activities, ruling that the campaign was an unwarranted intrusion by the Church of Scotland. Reverse mission by Loch Broom's Christians to the industrial central belt they thought would be more appropriate, and perhaps they were right in that! It was a different theology but perhaps the same resentment of southern interference.

#36: OPEN AIR RALLY AT THE ROUND CHURCH, ORPHIR, ORKNEY, 1956; DP, GOWNED, IN CENTRE, ACCOMPANIED BY THE SALVATION ARMY BAND

What, it may well be asked, do campaigns of this kind achieve? The Report of the Home Board to the 1957 General Assembly asked, rhetorically, this question about D. P. Thomson's visitation campaigns, and proceeded to offer several answers. His own primary answer was that, even if the response was limited in, say, Orkney, where there was already a high level of nominal church membership, '[The campaigns] have a profound and far-reaching effect on the lives of individual members of the teams.' He was concerned with training the laity to witness for Christ and – thinking only of the teams – this result could be demonstrated, as his booklets sought to show. This missionary outlook could diffuse into the wider church, as team members returned home carrying their experiences with them. And as to the areas visited, even if – as in these 'fringe' areas – most homes had existing church loyalties, it was hoped that meeting more vocal Church members and hearing their witness and that of the international teams would offer wider horizons and encourage a deepening of faith. Church membership in Orkney grew more in 1956 than in any other year of the decade 1949-1958, though that fact also suggests that the campaign failed to inaugurate any longer-term impetus.[39] It was an undoubted weakness of these campaigns to the fringes of Scotland that, for the most part, 'the fundamental *Tell Scotland* principle, which declares that the congregation must be the agent of Christ's mission in the area in which it finds itself' was deliberately sidestepped as all concerned colluded to leave mission largely in the hands of the incoming teams.[40] Nevertheless, thanks to D. P. Thomson's organisational skills and driving enthusiasm, most homes on almost every island within the Presbyteries of Mull, Orkney and Shetland were visited on behalf of *Tell Scotland* in 1956 and 1957, Stromness, Kirkwall and parts of Mainland Orkney being the main exceptions. Mull, Iona, Coll, Tiree; Erraid, Inchkenneth, Ulva; Papa Westray, North Ronaldsay, Gairsay, Flotta, Fara, the Pentland Skerries; Whalsay, Unst, Yell, Fair Isle and Foula – all these and more received DP's teams on behalf of *Tell Scotland.*

Tell Scotland – the Central Glasgow Churches Campaign and the Fading Years of the Movement

The *Tell Scotland* Movement faded with the 1950s. A restructuring took place in 1957, during which four Commissions were appointed to lead discussion of four key topics: Evangelism, the Bible, the Laity, and the Community. In 1960 these published, as interim reports, four pamphlets: respectively *The Lost Provinces, Truth in Action*, *The Layman at Work* and *Calling You In.* A series of national Kirk Week events were held, 1957-1964, for which the 'Kirchentag' assemblies in Germany were the inspiration. Conceived as motivational meetings for conversation, study and worship – precisely not as evangelistic rallies – Kirk Weeks in their own way sought to educate church people to take their faith to wherever they went on Monday mornings, into the whole of daily, and especially industrial, life. DP was involved in their preparatory discussions. To support Kirk Week, a member of the Iona Community, Colin Day, was appointed full time '*Tell Scotland* Secretary for the Laity' in 1958, organising the events, their 'Kirk Weekend' spin-offs and vocational 'Laity Workshops.' Under the chairmanship of Robert Mackie, who had returned to Scotland in 1956 from Geneva, the concept of the mission of the laity was thus broadened beyond the visitation campaign.

Besides Kirk Week, Tom Allan's successor as *Tell Scotland* Field Organiser, Ian MacTaggart, enabled numerous attempts at parish or area mission. Charles Duthie led *Tell Scotland* student teams that assisted such campaigns; at local levels *Tell Scotland* continued to generate interest and activity for several years after 1955-6. At a national level, however, the Movement found that running two separate wings – Kirk Week and parish mission – each with their own member of staff, did not enhance unity. In 1958 in his paper 'The Theology of Evangelism,' Duthie had to plead against factional strife.[41] A similar line had been taken by the Editor of *Life & Work* in July 1956, when he deprecated attacks not just on Tom Allan's policy but on his character. From the start somewhat outside *Tell Scotland*'s inner counsels, D. P. Thomson remained active in the field under *Tell Scotland*'s name: his influence on its affairs, however, if anything grew less as time went on.

The Central Glasgow Churches Campaign of 1958 was the last of the major *Tell Scotland* associated campaigns. With its training led by D. P. Thomson, the mission was centred on Tom Allan's new congregation, St George's Tron, in collaboration with a further three Churches of Scotland, one Methodist, two Baptist and two Congregational Churches. Following the 'three-fold' pattern of visits to the home, the place of work and where people gathered, the aim was to reach those living in the city centre parishes, those working there in offices during the day and, critically, the people of Glasgow-at-night. Something of the breadth of the vision of this campaign should be credited to DP: he recorded in his 28th Diary, 'Tom is clearly alarmed now at my ideas of what the Campaign may reach out to.' This probably also reflected some tension between himself and Tom Allan, for just as DP's style was to lead campaigns rather than just their training, Allan too led from the front.[42] Trying to lead from Crieff when Tom Allan was based in Glasgow was not without difficulty. On 23 January 1958 DP recorded: 'Letters from Purkiss & Tom Allan this morning that are a little disquieting. I feel far from happy about this whole Glasgow venture – very much happier about the Billy Graham Fellowship in Edinburgh.' Nevertheless DP remained officially the leader of the Campaign until January 1959 when Tom Allan took over, and a presentation was made to the older evangelist. A certain amount of restructuring of priorities and method followed: Tom Allan preferred to build relations with the management of local companies rather than follow DP's older method of 'entry by invasion'.[43]

By May 1958, however, it was already clear that the Campaign was making its mark in Central Glasgow as its church-hall headquarters remained open 24/7. A national conference of *Tell Scotland* local conveners met at Wiston Lodge and shared their experience:[44]

> It was clear that, as far as the church at large is concerned, *Tell Scotland* is not a success story. (In reporting, conveners were downright honest and pulled no punches.) . . . In the Central Glasgow Churches' Campaign, under D. P. Thomson, however, there had been a real measure of advance in that the Church did reach out to the 'submerged tenth'. Many of these came each night to the Church halls when they met with an organised and trained body of laymen and ministers who had already met them around coffee stalls etc. It made many of the campaigners very fully aware of the problems at the heart of a busy city and gave them a real sense of responsibility for their fellows.

Against a generally pessimistic review, the Central Glasgow Churches Campaign was thus picked out as outreach that was finally making contact with sections of the population normally beyond the orbit of the churches.

DP himself found the campaign an eye-opener:

> Friday, 18th April [1958] . . . [On 17 March 1958] the GLASGOW CENTRAL CHURCHES CAMPAIGN began. I have never been through anything like it. I broke down the first week and had to go home for two nights . . . Office and pub and other work followed the usual pattern – the feature of the Campaign was the coffee-stall work which went on night after night nearly all night and brought in a strange miscellaneous crowd of thieves, pickpockets, prostitutes, drunkards etc – the most moving and thought-provoking sight and experience of any Campaign I have ever been on. The way the ministers who came in from the country to help buckled to, and the way the young people of St George's Tron gave up their sleep to that work among thieves, prostitutes and social outcasts I will never forget.

The May edition of *Life & Work* gave a three-page, centre-spread editorial article by Glen Gibson on 'Glasgow – a tale of two cities' and asked 'Is the Church doing its job?':

> Glasgow by night has been a real shocker and an eye-opener to many good kirk folk. Not so much their visits to the public houses. The drink problem, bad as it is, is at least visible. It's the invisible sin that has shaken the kirk folk, and made them wonder what the Church has been doing

> for years. . . . Are church services, prayer meetings and traditional youth organisations all the church has to offer the people described in this article? What, in short, is the ministry of a city-centre church?'

What might be the 'ministry of a city-centre church' Tom Allan was to seek to answer. St George's Tron was to remain open daily as a place of quiet; mid-week lunch-hour services catered for day-time white-collar workers and, in collaboration with the central Church's Social Service Committee, a women's place of refuge was established for counselling and rehabilitation. He made himself personally, and with teams of volunteers, available to those in need. The state of down-and-outs in Glasgow in the 1950s takes imagination to recall, but Tom Allan had a gift of simplicity that communicated Christ's love to all kinds of people.

Tom Allan's short career, from 1947, was thus one of the most significant ministries of the post-war years: he shone in turn at seaside missions, North Kelvinside, *Tell Scotland*, the All-Scotland Crusade, and St George's Tron. He was a truly gifted preacher and broadcaster; a charismatic leader with a vision for the potential of ordinary Scots that combined both social and evangelical concerns; who (unlike DP) also contributed fruitfully in formal ecumenical, informal interdenominational and Church of Scotland agencies at all levels. Tragically, he was to have a heart attack while in the USA in 1962. Continuing weakness forced him to demit from St George's Tron and he died in 1966.

The Central Glasgow Churches Campaign was not, of course, DP's only commitment in 1958. He always multi-tasked. Following the end of the Shetland Campaign he was involved in the training for the St David's, Knightswood Campaign in October and November 1957 thus moving from an entire archipelago of islands to a single Glasgow parish, where the mission to a population of 12,000 (not far short of the total for Shetland!) was carried through without outside help. In Edinburgh he had had the inspiration for and, under the local *Tell Scotland* committee, the leadership of an All-Scotland Crusade Follow-Up Campaign that began in early 1958 to revisit those who had showed an interest three years before. A general Easter Training Weekend was held at Biggar in April, after which he had commitments in Ireland. During the summer and early autumn (besides his work in Glasgow) DP also led three Training Schools in Galloway, two based at Knock House, Portpatrick, and the third at Buittle, Kirkcudbrightshire. With a thoroughly-organised system of voluntary transport, these Schools had as good a local attendance as any DP had run. October 1958 saw him on one of his occasional tours of England: in the course of one day he addressed the Wolverhampton Free Church ministers, the Wolverhampton Anglican Evangelical Fellowship and the Presbytery of Birmingham. Mid-November saw him speaking at a succession of evening meetings in connection with the Stranraer Churches Campaign. It was not surprising that Tom Allan took over as Leader for the Central Glasgow Churches during the final weeks of campaign leading to Easter 1959.

By the end of the 1950s, despite all the nuances of his relationships to events and contemporaries, D. P. Thomson was recognised publicly as one of the key leaders in mission and evangelism in Scotland. 'Scottish Table Talk,' a column in the Scottish edition of the *British Weekly* [3 September 1959], placed him in the first rank with the Iona Community and the *Tell Scotland* Movement.[45] DP had travelled many miles since his wilderness time during the Second World War. His enthusiasm, his leadership, his vision for what the ordinary Christian might achieve, had won him a high place in the regard of many. The Rev. Peter M. Gordon, who in his younger days had taken part in the Orkney Expedition, wrote in October 2009:

> Looking back on my life it was great privilege to have met DP that summer [of 1956] . . . He was a dynamic personality who was able to motivate so many to come and share in campaigns both pre-war and post-war. How many people were led to faith and the service of Our Lord through his work as a supreme evangelist!

Gordon's judgment had not changed since January 1957, when he had amused and pleased DP by introducing him to a students' meeting as (with George MacLeod) one of 'the two greatest men in the Church of Scotland!' Unlike George, though, DP was never appointed Moderator of the General Assembly of his Church.*

---

* The nearest DP came to being considered as a possible Moderator was in October 1955: Thomson, The Diary of My Life part 26, 14-15: 'Friday 14 October 1955, 11.15 am . . . I ran into Hugh Watt ex-Moderator and ex-Principal of New College who asked if I knew who was going to be nominated on Tuesday for the Moderatorship. I said I didn't and he said he was the Convener of the Committee and for the first time he could recall no nominations had been notified. He thought George MacLeod and perhaps T. B. Stewart Thomson would be nominated. He liked even better my suggestion of George Gunn. Then he astonished me by turning to me and saying "Do you know who I would nominate?" "No" I said, "I don't." "D. P. Thomson," he said! I said, "You are a good joker." He said "I am not joking. I am absolutely serious." I know it could never be, I have not the slightest wish that it should ever be, but it was a revelation of how high I stand now in the estimation of some men of weight in the Church!'

As for *Tell Scotland*, it suffered from growing divisions similar to those described in *Life & Work* [July 1956] in the Church of Scotland: divisions between liberal and conservative on how to interpret the Bible; divisions on mass evangelism, divisions on the Iona Community's preference to accompany rather than to confront when making contact with the world.[46] No third Field Organiser could be appointed when MacTaggart left post in 1959, so a ministerial Panel of Missioners, 50+ strong, was recruited: these included George F. MacLeod, D. P. Thomson and David Orrock, formerly Tom Allan's Assistant at St George's Tron, besides – for example ministers James Philip and William Still; Ian Fraser, Prof. James Whyte and Robert C. Mackie. The Panel, too, were divided, as near-verbatim reports of their meetings during 1962 (retained in the *Tell Scotland* archives) clearly show. Opening the first conference of the Panel in January 1962, the convener, Dr A. J. Boyd said: 'There are at least one or two here today whose first reaction to our invitation was to say frankly *what is the good of setting up a conference of this kind – there is no hope of us coming to an agreement*.' The 'party spirit' Charlie Duthie deplored in 1958 was alive and well. For the meeting of Panel in September 1962, Dr Boyd produced a paper summarising their discussions over the year. His chosen central themes were: 'Do we know what the Gospel is?' and 'Do we know what Evangelism is?' Boyd valiantly attempted to bridge the differences and also acknowledged the divergences about conversion that remained: could discipleship begin without prior repentance? By the end of 1962 the Panel was no further forward towards agreeing any new central project. *Tell Scotland* was unable to sponsor the centrally-resourced National Mission that some advocated. The 'missioners' for the Scottish Churches had decided that the tactics of the 1950s were unrepeatable, and yet could agree little in their place. Differences in Christian doctrine had deepened the crisis in evangelism to the point when united action was impossible.[47]

The 'new evangelism' of the post-war era had run into the sands – a historic opportunity to prepare the Kirk for the post-modern era had been lost,[48] for, as division has a tendency to paralyse policy, no settled will took hold to implement any of the late 1950s or early 1960s visions for transforming the Church, whose conventional, minister-centred life and reticent laity proved enduringly resistant to all challenges to change. As one General Assembly Committee reported in 1953:[49] 'The message of Christianity, whether proclaimed in evangelism or explained in teaching, is sterile and bears no fruit when it is not spoken by a living, creative church.' The ordinary life of the churches had been seen as in itself a major barrier to missionary success even before *Tell Scotland* was born in 1952, and that it remained so lay behind the judgment of the local conveners in 1958, that the Movement was not, taken as a whole, a success story. And yet there had been successes.

Around 1960 the differences of opinion coalesced around their separate networks and were to an extent embodied in new residential centres that in their own ways attempted to continue the Movement's strategy of enabling the laity for mission. That disputes were now rooted in theology, however, reemphasised the role of the theologically trained, the ministers of Word and Sacrament. Together with much else in the UK of the 1960s, evangelism's note of authority was subverted. With its characterisation now ranged across a spectrum between those who specifically sought Holy Spirit-engendered conversion and those who advocated an entirely undogmatic life's quest, the theology and vocabulary of evangelism, and many of its traditional practices, were undermined. Those holding to a more conservative theology increasingly looked not so much to the witness of the un-ordained but to preaching, whether for decision or via the systematic Biblical teaching favoured by the Crieff Fraternal.

Visitation campaigns dropped out of favour on both sides of the theological divide. Even before there was any thought of Billy Graham coming to Scotland, DP had met opposition to his own methods of working. Often considered potentially embarrassing to participants and requiring high levels of congregational commitment, they had been enabled in the 1950s by the ecumenical consensus and high levels of energy generated first by his reputation and then by *Tell Scotland*. In the 1960s the consensus and the energy no longer existed. DP's visitation evangelism, George's Iona Missions, *Tell Scotland*'s outreach, the All-Scotland Crusade: all had had measures of success. The nation had responded to the churches' welcoming profile, but then a more inward-looking 'conventional life' reasserted itself and membership trends turned down.[50] *Tell Scotland* was the most sustained attempt since 1929 to blend the evangelical and territorial strengths of the UF and Established denominations in outgoing mission. Thereafter a routine focused inwardly on the ordinances of religion, on recruitment by nurture, proved incapable of resisting secular trends. The legacy of the UF Kirk was forgotten.

Out of the 1950s decade of evangelism there remained agreement on the need for better Christian education for the laity of the Church. Indeed, these years saw the creation of the first permanent Committee of the General Assembly with this remit: the Committee on Adult Christian

Education.[51] It was this trend that was to set D. P. Thomson the challenge of his final years of ministry.

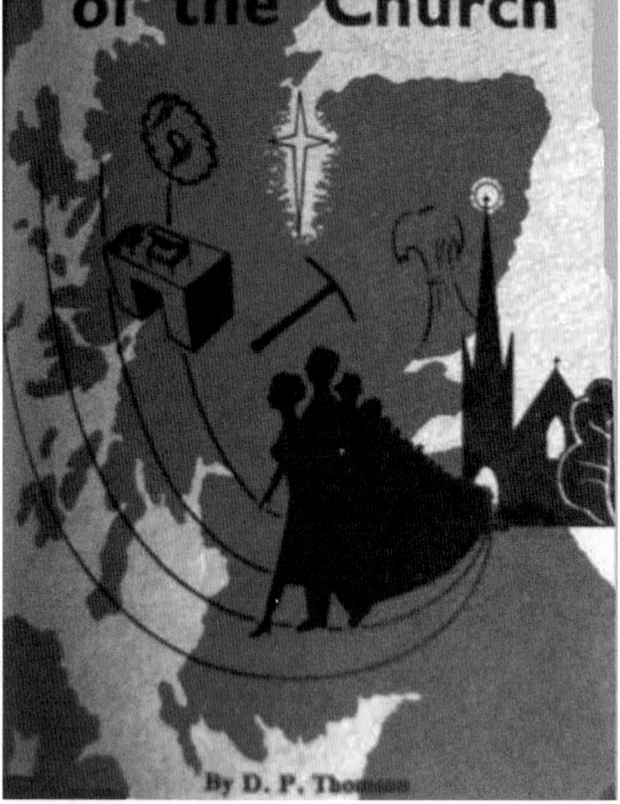

#37: COVER PAGE, *HARNESSING THE LAY FORCES OF THE CHURCH* 1958

THE FINAL YEARS, 1958-1974

> The General Assembly, on the occasion of the Rev. D. P. Thomson's retiral after twenty-four years as Evangelist in the service of the Home Board, acknowledge the unique service which he has rendered, and the fact that he has been one of the outstanding leaders of the Church in this generation.
>
> Deliverance of the 1966 General Assembly of the Church of Scotland, on the Report of the Home Board.

The final section of D. P. Thomson's ministry centred around his beloved St Ninian's Centre, Crieff: his final experiment in residential training for the laity, which opened in December 1958. While Warden of St Ninian's until retirement in 1966, and thereafter from his own home at Barnoak, he continued his 'ministry of the pen', producing a number of books and pamphlets. These years were more sedentary as both he himself and the wider church left in the past the regional visitation campaigns of the 1950s. His mind continued active, ready to explore new possibilities for mission, trying to understand his Lord's leading of the Church and trying to help others to find their vocation. During the 1960s he was honoured by both his University of Glasgow and the General Assembly. DP and Mary were to enjoy an old age supported by many friends.

Lay Training at St Ninian's, Crieff

There are always growing points and new possibilities in the life of the Church. *Tell Scotland* faded in the 1960s but a number of residential centres for the laity came into existence – St Ninian's, Crieff (opened 1958), Scottish Churches House, Dunblane (opened 1960) and Carberry Tower, East Lothian (opened 1962) – each in their own way taking up the Movement's theme of the missionary potential of the whole people of God. The first Wardens of these centres were men who had been leaders in different aspects of *Tell Scotland*: respectively D. P. Thomson, Ian Fraser and Colin Day.

Enthusiasm about residential lay training was growing in the Kirk of the later 1950s. Following the World Council of Churches at Evanston, USA (August 1954), the WCC Department on the Laity had sought to

#38: ST NINIAN'S CENTRE, CRIEFF, 1960S

follow up its emphasis on the mission of the whole church. In 1957 this Department focused attention on Europe's lay training centres, a movement that had begun with the Evangelical Academies of post-war West Germany, and published *Signs of Renewal: the Life of the Lay Institute in Europe*.[1] This booklet was reviewed in *Life & Work*, September 1957, as part of its coverage of the Aberdeen Kirk Week under the heading 'It is happening elsewhere'; the work of the Academies was described as new and exciting.[2] Just a few pages on from this plug came an article on the Iona Community's Community House, Glasgow, under the heading 'Scottish Layman's Centre'.[3] James Maitland, its Warden, insisted that a trained laity was more needed than ever and laid out his House's non-residential programmes in three areas of life: training for elders, Sunday School teachers etc; general courses on the interaction of a congregation with its parish; and politics and work. Meanwhile the Scottish Churches Ecumenical Committee and its related Association had been looking for a location for a House of their own since the WCC at Amsterdam in 1948.[4] By November 1957 *Life & Work* was able to report that the row of old houses in Cathedral Square,

Dunblane, was being considered as the location for Scotland's ecumenical Layman's Training Centre, again to focus on the connection between faith and daily life.[5] And, of course, on Iona itself, the Abbey and its reconstructed buildings functioned increasingly as a conference centre, if not one especially for the laity. D. P. Thomson, however, was to win the race to open 'Scotland's first permanent [residential] training centre for lay men and women'.[6]

In retrospect we see an inevitable connection between D. P. Thomson and the St Ninian's Centre, Crieff, to which so many look back with affection, but at the time he might have pursued other options. With his appointment from the Home Board due to end on 31 December 1958, DP was certainly looking to find the next stage of his ministry. During 1957 he had wondered about seeking a call to a further parish. His fundamental, life-long, interest was not so much the mode of promoting evangelism – student or seaside mission, residential centre, parish ministry or visitation campaign – but fulfilling the imperative that opportunities of outreach should be found. Since leaving St Ninian's Lassodie, DP had seen the potential of a number of the buildings he came across to be a church centre, but the rationale of his 1950s Training Schools had been to camp in a vacant manse or school or hall so that the training offered would be 'on the job'.

In 1958, however, various factors led DP to re-enter the field of residential centres. There was the location: the availability of a building so near to his own dear home at Barnoak, located in Crieff, a town well known to the Kirk's ministers who enjoyed subsidised holidays at the town's Hydropathic Hotel, then easily reachable by train, bus and car from most of central Scotland. The genesis of St Ninian's, Crieff, came on 29 January 1958 during a visit to DP of a delegation from the recently united congregation of Crieff: North and West. The former West Church building had become redundant and did he have any ideas as to how it might be retained in the service of the Church? There was also the opportunity: the arrow in his quiver called 'residential training' was once more in fashion within elements of the Kirk's leadership. DP could rarely resist putting his oar into the 'new and exciting'. The time was right in another way, too. He had now led major campaigns in most of Scotland – no more were in prospect to follow the Galloway summer campaigns, the September Training School, the Stranraer Churches Campaigns of November 1958. In any case he was feeling his age: even in the 1940s he had contemplated settling down to a more desk-based ministry. Finally the means were available, or could be put together.

Any residential Lay Training Centre needed both a suitable building and a client base. The West Church, Crieff, would need adaptation – kitchen, toilets, lecture and sleeping accommodation. Resources were, however, available to meet these requirements. On the one hand the Crieff: North & West congregation was a willing seller of their building for the nominal sum of £100; the Work & Witness Movement, on the other, was a willing supporter, a network with known fund-raising capacities: an existing structure for prayer, governance and vision-sharing. Moreover DP had supported the Crieff Ministers' Fraternal since his arrival at Barnoak, lending his support through pulpit supply and hospital services, an Easter Book Week and a Crieff visitation. He was thus able to establish a Committee of Management for St Ninian's that had representatives from the Presbytery of Auchterarder as well as from Work & Witness. The Home Board later nominated three members, including Tom Allan, and formally agreed first to DP's devoting time to offering courses and establishing the St Ninian's library; and then to a further appointment for him during which the Board's stipend responsibilities for their Evangelist would be curtailed, the balance coming from Work & Witness.

Meanwhile the necessary work on the fabric of the church was undertaken under the supervision of E. Forter Hall, a friend of DP's and formerly his assistant during the Strathmore Campaign. Hall had, with some success, taken a leaf out of George MacLeod's book and inaugurated in 1956 a scheme whereby craftsmen might offer a week or two of holiday to join teams repairing churches and manses in the Highlands and Islands – reports of this successful enterprise had been heard at Work & Witness meetings. Hall examined the West Church, Crieff, in February 1958 together with an architect, and by June DP was ready officially to launch his new project:

> Sunday, 8th June [1958] . . . Yesterday we launched **ST NINIAN'S CRIEFF:** A Residential Training Centre for Church Workers. The Board of Management met at the South Church Session House at 10.30 am . . . We devised the draft constitution and passed it, elected various folk and made T. B. Stewart Thomson the chairman. I lunched with the Work & Witness representatives.

By August a team had been assembled to whom DP could delegate the routine work of preparing the building while he attended to appointments in Galloway. Bob Jones, a campaigner since 1947 and a chartered accountant who helped with DP's accounts, recollects the result by the end of 1958:

> The original St Ninian's was a very Spartan place, even for those days. The side pews had been removed, and the side areas were partitioned into cubicles - you could hardly call them rooms. From memory the beds

> were old hospital beds. At either side of the vestibule a toilet and wash-basin were installed. The centre of the downstairs was retained as a worship area, with still the hard pews to sit on. Upstairs were the sitting and dining area and kitchen. DP ruled with an iron discipline, no horseplay, and definitely no fraternising with the opposite sex!

On 15 December 1958 this preparatory work concluded with a Service of Dedication and St Ninian's first full course was a Training Week, 2 - 9 January 1959, with a distinguished team of speakers:

> Friday, 9th January [1959] . . . a week that will be forever memorable – the New Year Training Week in Conference at St Ninian's Crieff. We have had over 30 living in and as many more attending. A very much smaller gathering than we had anticipated but in every way worthwhile. We have learned a lot! We had Charlie Duthie, Tom Allan, Willie Barclay and Ronnie Falconer among our speakers. We have learned a lot about St Ninian's – the heating, whatever it may cost, sufficed.

But what was the vision for St Ninian's, apart from maintaining the building of the West Church in the service of the church and providing DP with a final challenge before retirement? While on an English tour in October 1958 (during which DP secured promises of contributions to the St Ninian's library from a number of Christian publishers in London) he visited the William Temple Memorial College in Rugby, describing it in his diary as 'the nearest thing in England to what we hope to do at St Ninian's, Crieff'. Originally founded in 1947 as a Women's Theological College, by 1948 its governing body had been persuaded (in part by a limited market for its first purpose and in part by the post-war emphasis on the laity) to widen their ambitions:[7]

> The primary purpose of the College ought to be on educating the laity and especially those entering social, industrial and educational fields of service, and in providing basic training in Christianity and the Christian interpretation of life.

A move to new premises in Rugby was achieved in 1954, and by the time DP visited the College was home to at most 20 residential students, both women and men, undertaking a government-recognised one year course covering Christian doctrine, people in society, and the inter-relationship between faith and society. Many were teachers taking a sabbatical. A full collegiate discipline was followed and occasional Church of England ordinands and non-residential students for both internal and external examinations also came to study. An accepting ethos, academic credibility, and a concern to understand the outliving of the faith by the non-ordained in the contemporary world were at the heart of what was understood to be a Theological College for the laity.

Without the backing of a substantial Foundation and an archbishop's name, St Ninian's struggled to find such a medium-term educational niche as the College in Rugby achieved. DP's practical model at the start was, rather, his own short term Training Courses in evangelism. In December 1958's *Life & Work* he set out his prospectus. There would be day, weekend and week courses offered on 'every aspect of evangelism . . .':[8]

> . . . and for special classes such as Lay Readers, Bible Study Group leaders and workers in the new fields opening up to the laity in hospitals, prison, approved schools and institutions of various kinds. Courses of training will also be arranged on the meaning and implications of Christian discipleship today.

Beyond courses run by himself as Warden, DP was willing to host (with his collaboration) incoming groups that booked the premises for their own programmes; and he wanted to welcome for weekend breaks 'men and women whose minds are moving towards whole-time service for the Church at home or overseas' to give them a taste of Christian fellowship and outreach as part of a testing of their vocation. Whereas the College at Rugby had a broad theological syllabus, St Ninian's always had evangelism at its core: it embodied DP's belief that desk or group learning was best accompanied by practice in the field.

#39: MURAL FROM THE ST NINIAN'S CENTRE, CRIEFF

Both centres, however, sought by their residential basis to strengthen Christian faith through fellowship, and especially the fellowship of shared meals. Both had sleeping accommodation for 20 plus, DP at first supplemented this by using Crieff's church halls for overflow camping. If the Temple Memorial College, with its interest in industry, was based in the industrial heart of England, St Ninian's was intended to be a Work & Witness base for evangelism across central Scotland.

After the first general week-long course a number of specialist weekends followed. A Missionary Weekend was held 24-25 January – badly attended:

> . . . the local response was pitiful, as it was last weekend: THE MISSIONARY WEEKEND AT ST NINIAN'S CRIEFF where we had with us Willie Young (Pakistan) & Alec Urquhart (Calabar). They gave of their best to a handful – 16 at the most living in – a dozen others attending.

Next DP put a major effort into visiting local secondary and boarding schools, recruiting for the successive Senior Schoolboys and Senior Schoolgirls weekends, 30 January - 2 February and 6-9 February. Numbers from this age group had responded to Billy Graham and, especially from Crieff's own Morrison's Academy, had accompanied DP to both Orkney and Shetland. A Bible Study weekend followed 20-22 February and a Work & Witness weekend 27 February - 1 March. 'A very much smaller gathering than we had anticipated but in every way worthwhile' might sum up his reflections on all these courses, designed as inspirational rather than offering the vocationally-orientated syllabus of the William Temple Memorial College.

As it developed St Ninian's main clientele came to be congregationally-based groups, coming for a weekend course: Kirk Sessions, Youth Fellowships, Sunday School staff. Some 5,000 individuals visited during the first four years.[9] By 1965 a promotional booklet claimed:[10]

> Ample testimony has been borne from many sources throughout the past few years as to what such a weekend can achieve with careful planning, clear direction and an exhilarating if demanding programme, always geared into the local situation of those involved. Youth Fellowships appreciated immensely the facilities which Crieff provides. They would come in far greater numbers if space were available. The beauty and variety of the scenery, the accessibility of the Centre and of the countryside round about it, the freedom and the fellowship, the range and variety of training methods employed, the family atmosphere which pervades the place, and the daily discipline with its Morning Quiet Time, Bible Study Hour, Family Prayers and shared chores all make a very real appeal to them. Young people who come to St Ninian's in the summer months will find that the weekly programme embraces a great variety of outdoor activities.

> These include the visitation of camp and caravan sites, of beauty spots of historic interest and of country parishes in remoter areas where district visitation or survey work is carried out.

The description shows the extent to which DP's mobile School or Campaign headquarters of the 1950s were the model for St Ninian's: the joint fellowship and Bible Study; the practical out-door work; 'the family atmosphere'.[11] The pattern originated in DP's Student Campaigns of the 1920s when the teams camped in Church Halls. A similar experience had been enjoyed by the groups who came to Glassiebarns or Lassodie; and by the Seaside Mission teams. In a sense the content or syllabus studied was incidental, though something can be recaptured from his *100 Topics For Discussion: A Handbook For Study Circles, House Groups, Training Classes, Conferences And Training Schools*. DP believed that faith was best caught rather than taught. However, given his literary interests and his 'college' ambitions for St Ninian's, there was of course a library, some 12-15,000 books strong, and guests were encouraged to set time aside for study 'and are given guidance as to courses of reading they might pursue and books they might helpfully consult.' To the end of his life DP relished acquiring books both for his shelves and for resale for the funds, whether singly or whole libraries at a time. By 1966 he was able to boast that the library at St Ninian's was 'one of the finest collections in the world of the literature of Evangelism'.

The depth of the original vision for vocational training persisted. In 1962 the Board of Management appointed former Livingstonia missionary the Rev. Phil Petty as Sub-Warden and Theological Tutor and offered a Pre-Matriculation Course for young men leaving business or industry with a view to training for the ministry. This course was not continued after Petty was inducted to the North Church, Prestwick in April 1965. While it lasted, however, it was an invaluable experience to the men enrolled. Scott Carroll, for example, spent two years with DP before successfully qualifying for entry to Glasgow's Trinity College. Personal tuition in French and Greek was arranged for him; the other five in his year at Crieff also had their particular academic needs met, besides participation in missions and Sunday preaching and all the life of 'a true community'. Besides enabling access to university it was the best preparation for a divinity course that Scott could imagine. Later, when he was a Church of Scotland Reader, Scott's minister told him that if he had survived St Ninian's, he could preach anywhere!

St Ninian's had hoped by their appointment of a Theological Tutor to lure away from Glasgow's BTI those men being trained by the Home Board prior to appointment as Lay Missionaries. The Board, however, although it reluctantly agreed to help with the Sub-Warden's stipend, declined to send their Missionaries to Crieff for the main part of their training. Home Board Lay Missionaries, or Missionary candidates, nevertheless came to St Ninian's for assessment or *ad hoc* short courses. For example, Dennis and Stella Shepherd were appointed to the joint Home Board / Shetland Education Committee post on Papa Stour as, respectively, Missionary and Teacher. Dennis recounts:

> We went to St Ninian's Crieff on Easter Monday 1962, and after a most intensive course we were installed on Papa Stour in time to conduct a Whitsuntide service. I was the first candidate to go through this course, a guinea-pig. In hindsight I realise that the time factor must have set Dr D. P. Thomson a very difficult task, but the pressure of time was due to the necessity of complying with the legal requirements of the teaching post to which my wife was appointed. Therefore in the few short weeks between Easter and Pentecost Dr Thomson had to fit in Bible Study, the skills of preparing a sermon, lectures on arranging complete services, study times, tutorials and visits to let me observe the whole gamut of Church life. There were visits to Eventide Homes, work with the young, pastoral care, Sunday School classes. We met youth groups, elders' weekends, overseas missionaries. This, he achieved by splitting up the time, and splitting us up. Thus whilst my wife was visiting the sick, I was busy swotting or having a tutorial. Then it would be reversed, my wife preparing a draft talk or writing a précis while I went on house to house calls. We covered all the varied services of the church, met many people, interviewed and were interviewed. It was hectic, non-stop, demanding, exhausting, but I must give praise where it is due. In those short weeks I covered much ground, had the opportunity to see all facets of church work, took a trial service at Trinity Gask. We were taken by car to Perth, thence by train to Aberdeen and to Shetland aboard the *St Clair.* I was loaded with boxes of books generously given by Dr Thomson: concordances, books of reference and heaps of useful Sunday School aids. We arrived in Papa Stour from a small open boat feeling utterly exhausted.

Less fortunate was Lay Missionary James Urquhart who spent two weeks in Crieff immediately before his placement in Eday, Orkney: 'Prior to leaving for Orkney I was required to spend two weeks at St Ninian's, Crieff where the time was actually spent painting and decorating the new premises just purchased.'

Further courses – based on a series of residential weekends – were provided as a basis of training for the Readership within the Church of Scotland. After attendance at St Ninian's, 1958-9, Dr John Berkeley was accepted as a Reader by the Synod of Argyll in May 1960. The personal notes John retained from the course show that lectures had been given by Dr William Barclay for the New Testament and Prof. George Knight for the Old as well, of course, by DP himself. The book list contained authors like David H. C. Read and Prof. A. M. Hunter who, neither radically liberal in theology nor yet intransigently Calvinist, had a broad acceptance across the Scottish churches.[12] The course covered introductions to the Testaments; service and sermon construction; church history; some 40-plus 'pulpit themes for the Reformation year' (the 400th anniversary of the Reformation in Scotland, 1560-1960); several years' worth of material on Easter themes; the construction of children's addresses and hospital services; principles drawn from the lives of 'great preachers': R. W. Dale, J. H. Jowett, H. S. Coffin. DP offered his own assessment of the Kirk as it was in 1959: among a list of 19 points [!] was 'want of definiteness, directness and authority in sermon', 'emphasis on social and community service', 'place and worth of women', 'apostolate of laity', 'realisation of need for Christian witness at work', 'disappearance of Church discipline – border between church and world', 'growing emphasis on comfort, ease and speed – colour, glamour and variety – move with the times!' The list demonstrates DP's perception as well as his realisation that change is two-sided, with both positives and negatives. He sought to be both critical and optimistic. His Readership course was, naturally, both theoretical and practical: the students were attached to congregations for the weekend and their contributions to worship were thoroughly dissected on return to St Ninian's.

The ethos DP established for St Ninian's was that of the mission team. At the opening of Lassodie back in 1934 he had insisted on an egalitarian sharing of duties: 'the combination of a certain amount of manual and domestic work with prayer, meditation, discussion and fellowship' not only because this was useful and saved expense, but also because 'a finer fellowship will be fostered than is attained where the common distinction between guests and staff prevails.' The same combination of principle and pragmatism was built into St Ninian's, Crieff. The Centre began on a shoe-string and, as Willie Frame wrote in *Fire in His Bones*, not just the building but inevitably the living / working conditions were Spartan for the full-time staff. Rev. Ian Moir was appointed the first Deputy Warden on graduating from Christ's College, Aberdeen, having served with DP at the Knock House Training School in Galloway: in 1961 he took up a missionary appointment in South Africa. Ian recalls how, when visiting St Ninian's after one of its later renovations, he was struck that a formal Reception Desk was thought necessary. In the first years, people just walked in, calling 'Hullo!' DP believed in hospitality: an open house and an open door. Staff and guests sat down to meals and shared in family worship together. Thomas Caldwell remembers attending a weekend with a group from his congregation. After supper he asked when they were to meet 'the great man' – to be told that it had not been a caretaker but DP himself who, self-effacingly, had served the soup and brought round the tea. St Ninian's staff as it opened were his secretary Cathie Maver, and a voluntary housekeeper, besides DP, Mary and Ian Moir. 'Ladies with an interest in the work' assisted with cleaning and cooking on an occasional basis.

Miss Maver was to be DP's secretary for the whole 15 years of this latter period of his life. He had first met her and chosen her to speak in Voice of the Pew services in 1952 during the Strathmore Campaign. She was one of a select group he listed in March 1953 as potential recruits for Work & Witness, and since then she had been part of the teams in Caithness, Mull and Orkney and featured in Work & Witness broadcasts. In March 1959 DP noted in his diary that she 'is proving an excellent secretary'. He published a tribute to Cathie as 'my devoted secretary' in 1964 in the introduction to *Tomorrow's Ministers*. This was no more than she deserved, for living under DP's workaholic discipline while on a short campaign was one thing and coping with it as a way of life something else again. To be part of the St Ninian's team meant close Christian fellowship; it also meant long, unpredictable and irregular hours on duty. The weekly day off or even the annual holiday were unknown to D. P. Thomson's own routines.

With dedicated staff who shared DP's ethos and vision, St Ninian's proved to be a successful experiment, a place where (as Tom Burt told me he experienced as a sixth-former) faith was lived out, bringing challenge, offering wisdom. In all aspects of its life, DP sought to incarnate mission campaign principles:[13]

> No charges of any kind are made at St Ninian's, either for training or for accommodation. Those using the Centre, whether for longer or shorter periods, are asked to make such contribution as they can towards its upkeep, running expenses, and missionary work through the medium of the offering boxes. This principle has operated with great encouragement

> to the life and fellowship in the large-scale training schemes held up and down the country in recent years, out of the work of which St Ninian's originated. Interested individuals are asked to become Friends of St Ninian's . . .

A large neighbouring house, Beechknowe, was purchased following an Appeal for funds and adapted as an annex to the main Centre, with a lounge, dormitories and staff accommodation. Moreover in 1959 the Edinburgh: Fountainhall Road Church was acquired by the Work & Witness Movement as its headquarters, opening in 1960 as 'St Ninian's, Edinburgh' – a further Conference and Training Centre, supported by the Edinburgh and District Churches on an ecumenical basis. Elsie Fraser, who had been part of the Shetland and Galloway teams, was appointed Warden. In time St Ninian's, Edinburgh, proved one Centre too many, however, and Work & Witness concentrated its resources at Crieff. To Crieff for decades many came for refreshment and challenge, inspiration and fellowship.

#40: THE WARDEN, 1961

Publications and The Research Unit

In 1962 the University of Glasgow awarded D. P. Thomson their honorary Doctorate in Divinity, the D.D., in recognition of his distinguished services to the Church. This was a possibility he had dreamed about in his Dunfermline days:

> Friday, 14th August [1931] . . . out for a country walk . . . Had many dreams by the way and assessed my worldly ambition:
>
> The D.D. of Glasgow
>
> The Moderatorship of the General Assembly
>
> The Freedom of Dunfermline. It's not quite outwith the range of possibility, should I stay here.

He had delighted in the achievements of his brother Dr Robert Thomson and his sister Dr Christine Thomson, and had regretted that the University of St Andrews had not thought fit to offer his solicitor father an honorary doctorate in law. A member of a very literary and academic family, DP valued Glasgow's recognition even though it came somewhat late in his career. He valued, too, the accolade offered by the Church of Scotland when, at the General Assembly of 1966, the year he retired, the Moderator of the General Assembly moved the vote of thanks 'to resounding and prolonged applause'. But, of course, DP did not 'retire' in 1966, though he now finally left the staff of the Home Board in receipt of a pension and a new Warden, Bill Shannon, was appointed for St Ninian's. From Barnoak, where he appointed himself Director of 'The Research Unit', DP continued a series of publications that contributed to debates in the church as well as bringing to fruition some long-researched topics. Between 1958 and 1974 some 35 books and pamphlets were published from Crieff under his name.

Some of these were long over-due. *David Inglis Cowan* had been requested by Margaret Cowan, David's widow, soon after his death, a decade before. DP had in fact done most of the research and even written most of his text before the Strathmore Campaign and all that followed deprived him of the necessary time for final reflection. *Scotland's Greatest Athlete: The Eric Liddell Story* and *Eric H. Liddell: Athlete & Missionary* were detailed versions of the 1945 pamphlet, *Eric Liddell: the Making of an Athlete and the Training of a Missionary*: two editions of the same biography, described by Prof. Willie Barclay as 'a joy and an inspiration to read'. *When Christ Calls: Evangelistic Addresses* was a follow-up to 1937's *Men Christ Wants: Evangelistic Addresses.* For his sources for *New Testament Christianity: 60 Short Studies* DP

#41: DP AND MARY AT THE DOOR OF BARNOAK

ranged beyond sermons back to exercises written in his college days, but the 'studies' were still independently conceived. He left no systematic account of his faith of any length, though he did arrange to publish a transcript of a BBC Scotland biographical interview, *Why I Believe / Tom Allan, James S. Stewart and D. P. Thomson, discussing personal Christian belief with Ian Pitt-Watson on B.B.C. Scottish Television, 1962-3*. Another pamphlet deriving from a BBC broadcast was *What Christ Means To Me / An open-air service of Christian witness / Held at Macrosty Park, Crieff on . . . 2nd August 1959*. His final study of regional Church history was *It happened in Iona*, while *The Epistle to the Romans chapters 12 to 16: A Question Course for Preachers, Teachers, Bible Students and Bible Study Groups* (1965) was the last of his series of Bible studies via the 'question course' approach. Materials for a 'History of the House Church in Scotland' and 'An Evangelist Looks Back' retained in the D. P. Thomson Archive never achieved published form.

D. P. Thomson, more than most of his generation, recognised the part that Christian women play in the church. One group of his life-time's publications reflects this interest, beginning with *Women In The Pulpit / Sermons And Addresses By Representative Women Preachers*, which he edited in 1944 as a companion to *The Scottish Pulpit / Sermons By Representative Scottish*

Preachers (1937) and *Professor As Preacher / Sermons By Scottish Theological Professors* (1939). *Women In The Pulpit* was not a financial success, despite selling out during 1944. Three biographies had followed: *Scotland's First Deaconess - Lady Grisell Baillie of Mellerstain and Dryburgh* and *Sweet Singer of Melrose: the Story of Elizabeth Clephane*, both in 1946, with *Janet Melville of Aberdeen - and Her Famous Boys' Class* in 1947. This was material rescued from DP's projected 'Women of the Scottish Church' to which he gave much attention while at Cambuslang. Other Christian women of note found places in his regional booklets on Church history and two (Janet Colquhoun and Annie H. Small) featured in his *Scottish Devotional Treasury* (1955). A higher proportion of space had been given to the testimony of women in *The Voice of the Pew: What Christ and His Church Mean to Me*, just as DP had offered them a place in the campaign services from which this booklet derived. 'Justice has never been done to the part played by women in the life and work of the Scottish Church' DP wrote at the beginning of his longer book *Lady Glenorchy and Her Churches*, aware that his own study of the topic had yet to be published. A further pamphlet-sized instalment had surfaced in 1960 for the 400th anniversary of the Reformation in Scotland: *Women of the Scottish Reformation; their Contribution to the Protestant Cause*. Perhaps with *Women of the Scottish Reformation* DP was also seeking to balance his other booklet of 1960, *Through Sixteen Centuries: The Story of the Scottish Church from Earliest Times to the Present Day*, in which the sole female featured was St Margaret. *Through Sixteen Centuries* was, however, based on the text of his lantern-lecture series 'The Romance of the Scottish Church', first written in honour of, and at the time of, the 1929 Union. In his introduction to *Through Sixteen Centuries* DP admitted that 'my own perspective has altered considerably' (in unspecified ways) between first writing and publication. Indeed, by the 1940s (at the latest) his lantern lectures contained slides on 'Women who blazed the trail', 'Women of the Celtic Church', 'Women of the Covenant', 'Women of the Disruption' and 'Women Hymn Writers of Scotland'.

Out of the work of St Ninian's came booklets of greater topicality. *The Minister's Wife: Her Life, Work & Problems* arose from a conference held in May 1964, requested by a number of (male) ministry-candidates to cover 'what the duties and responsibilities of a minister's wife really were to-day, and where preparation for these could be obtained.' Attending the conference were a number of wives and fiancées of divinity students, men still to be inducted to their first charge, and some five existing ministers' wives, come to offer advice. A further 40 or so had sent in written submissions and these formed the basis of the booklet. The ethos of middle-class families during the 1950s and early 1960s was that men went out to work and wives kept the house: this was reflected in the vast bulk of the contributions to the booklet, as, indeed, it was in DP's relationship to Mary, who on marriage had ceased her employment. Though there was one enthusiastic page from a working teacher, who believed her outside interests kept her 'mind in top gear' and her personal assurance at a high level 'for I have the confidence of doing a worthwhile job', the article DP chose as a conclusion took the traditional line. Being a minister's wife was in itself a worthwhile calling, if unpaid. Similar thoughts and a similar conference lay behind *The Elder's Wife: her place in the life and work of the Church,* published in 1973.

Yet, just as during the 1930s DP had appreciated the independent spiritual gifts of women while also looking for a bride who would willingly be a minister's wife, in the 1960s he explored – with the Church of Scotland discussions of the time – the admission of women to both the Eldership and the ordained Ministry of Word and Sacrament. *Tomorrow's Ministers: Who are they? What are they thinking? What shall we say to them?*, published in 1964, came out of DP's research for the series of weekends he led for boys and young men thinking of full-time Christian service. He invited written contributions on a number of topics from such ministry candidates, and printed a selection of their views on the ordination of women, whether to the eldership or the ministry. 'No! Both are expressly forbidden in Scripture' one replied; 'If they have a call, why not? What else matters?' another. In fact the Church of Scotland was to admit, on the same terms as men, women as elders in 1966 and as ministers in 1968. DP issued his pamphlet *Women as Elders: The Verdict of Experience* in April 1965, a month ahead of the General Assembly's discussion of the issue. He had researched the experiences of the Presbyterian Church of England and the United Free Church of Scotland, both of which admitted women elders, the former for over 50 years and the latter since 1930. Also in 1965 DP produced *Women Ministers in Scotland: Personal Records of Experience and Discovery*, which contained six personal reflections from serving ministers of Scottish UF and Congregational Churches, one of whom (Rev. Vera Kenmure M.A. B.D.) had been ordained over 36 years. In none of these three booklets did DP offer, unequivocally, his own opinion. In the interests of impartial research he printed both sides of an issue. Yet though the 'Questions for Discussion Groups' at the end of *Women Ministers* were open-ended, ['Is this primarily a theological or a practical issue?'] in the

Introduction he at least showed the way he was minded. For if, as for some, the issue was settled by appeal to decisive Scriptural texts, why listen to experience at all? He was willing to state that his correspondents had made 'vital' contributions to the life of the churches in Scotland; that 'the experience they had gained and the discoveries they had made' should be listened to. While at Cambuslang: Trinity he had supported, in his Presbytery of Hamilton, the cause of the eligibility of women for the eldership.

In the end there is no doubt that D. P. Thomson welcomed the decisions of the Church of Scotland to offer ordination to both the eldership and the ministry to women. DP continued work on his magnum opus, *Women of the Scottish Church* and his literary executor, Ian Doyle, arranged for its posthumous publication in 1975, the book containing an up-to-date final chapter recounting the history of the debates in the Kirk on ordination since overtures by Presbyteries of the United Free Church to their Assembly in 1926. DP offered a very favourable account of the appearance at the bar of the 1931 General Assembly of the Church of Scotland of the Dowager Marchioness of Aberdeen and Temair, Ishbel Lady Aberdeen, after royalty he thought the best known Scotswoman of her day, to argue that in the Christian Church all were one in Christ Jesus and that as no distinction fell between male and female, all ought to be eligible for ordination. Men had debated the issues from Assembly to Assembly more or less his whole career in the ministry, but DP had been on the side of the reformers since his upbringing in the United Free Church.

Indeed there is a sense that, like Gladstone, D. P. Thomson became more radical in his old age. In 1969 he published *The Radical Reappraisal Report: Churches Under The Spotlight, A New Approach To Congregational And Parish Life*, and discussed the experience of 'Focus Weeks' that he had led for six congregations during the previous two years. Whereas during the regional visitation campaigns he had worked with people gathered from all over the country, once he settled in at St Ninian's he dealt more intensively with groups from single congregations, coming to re-examine their corporate life. From 1967 DP offered himself as a visiting consultant, drawing on his St Ninian's experience to enable congregations to reappraise their life and structures. He made a point of listening to *all*, attempting to think outside the normal organisational frameworks. Towards the end of *The Radical Reappraisal Report*, Thomson wrote:

> What provision, then, is made in the average church to-day – of whatever denomination – for the men and women in the pews to voice what they

> think and feel about the hours of worship, the form and length of the service, the choice of the hymns, the nature and content of the prayers, or the length, relevance and language of the sermon? What attempt is made to find out how far the real needs of both young and old are being catered for? Is the answer not just: None at all? . . . Take the Sunday School, the Bible Classes, the Uniformed Youth Organisations, as we know them in our churches to-day. What opportunity is given to those for whom they are designed to cater – or to their parents – to say what they really think and feel about them? . . . Again, for all practical purposes, the answer is: None!

The most revolutionary aspect to the booklet was its democratic emphasis – his insistence that everyone had a right to be heard. Here he was truly radical, tackling the entire system of control by elders, unelected, holding office for life in self-perpetuating Kirk Sessions:

> Take the Courts and Committees of the Church. Has the membership not a right to express its mind and have the young people not a right to express theirs – and both of them to be listened to; as to whether the prevailing system in, say, the Church of Scotland, where the Kirk Session – the governing body in the congregation – is virtually a closed corporation, a self-perpetuating body, is really democratic, or Christian, or in any way relevant to congregational life and work as it is and should be to-day?

In his enabling of congregational reappraisal, the work that resulted in *The Radical Reappraisal Report*, DP was tackling issues still at the heart of the life of the Kirk.

Such questions had been asked earlier when in 1960 *Tell Scotland* published *The Lost Provinces*, written by its Commission on Evangelism. The pamphlet had called for a radical re-assessment of the current patterns of church life. They clearly had had purely social dancing and badminton clubs in their sights: for what, actually, was purpose of the church? What counted as building it up? Was it merely about bringing in new members? Was a conversion experience essential? What relationship did conversion have to baptism, or to confirmation – to the Church of Scotland practice of joining the church as a communicant member and having one's name added to the roll? And more fundamental yet, was Church of Scotland practice in any major area of its life actually conducive to outreach? Were the social organisations actually the only – or even the main – problem? If the purpose of the Church was mission, was it fit for purpose at all?

Why was it, DP was asking in his retirement, that so often those brought in by either mass or visitation evangelism had found they could not fit in?

That no-one listened to them? Why was it that, if a congregation had through a Stewardship Campaign gathered a list of volunteers offering time and abilities, too often they had no real use for them? Why were his Work & Witness members so under-used in their own congregations? Why, in fact, were the longer-term results of his own campaigns less than he had hoped? His reappraisal technique was devised to bypass the normal system of congregational government in order to allow everybody their say – to allow all to know that they had a voice in the Church:

> For the ordinary man or woman in the pew, for the older boy or girl, or the teenager taking part, it can mean the realisation for the first time that they really belong, that they count, that they have their place within the life of the fellowship, that they have something worthwhile to say, something of value to communicate; that what they have to say will be listened to, will be heeded, will be given its place in the whole context of the ongoing life and thought of the church; will even have repercussions on its policy and its planning. That means much; it may mean very much indeed. It may hold for the individual also a very real emancipation – a breaking free from the feeling of not mattering, of frustration, of non-ability to participate in any really meaningful way, except as a passive recipient of what is offered by the church to which he or she belongs.

The taster on the back cover of *The Radical Reappraisal Report* thus asked: 'Mass Evangelisation, Parish Visitation, Stewardship Campaign – we have had them all! What next? Should it be the Radical Reappraisal for which Dr Thomson pleads so eloquently in these pages? Might this perhaps be the first of our priorities?' It was somewhat late in his career, but as he took up the Commission on Evangelism's plea for 'radical reappraisal', DP was tackling some of the institutional barriers to the mission of the laity. His vision (though from a different theological perspective) was now not wholly remote from T. Ralph Morton's thoroughly democratic *God's Frozen People* (1964), that sought to de-construct ecclesiastical structures. Even DP's *The Beadle: Yesterday and Today* (1971) was based on an attempt to listen (as usual via questionnaires and conferences) to the views and experience of another under-valued group of Christian workers, the Church Officer.

A further four volumes – two books and two pamphlets – among DP's publications in his latter years may be described as part of his final attempt to contribute to the Kirk's thinking on evangelism – to contribute from his experience to a vital debate. We have seen that in 1955 DP held firm to his belief that '*raise your hand' evangelism* was not for him, while also affirming the possibility of conversion through the moving of God's Spirit. He had made efforts to follow up some at least of those who had attended All-Scotland Crusade counselling, and had found the experience disappointing. In *Dr Billy Graham and the Pattern of Modern Evangelism* (1966) DP tried to assess the way he had practised evangelism since the Second War as against the mode offered by the Graham Organisation, arguing that:

> History knows only two ways in which the man outside the Church can be reached, and every evangelistic technique and strategy is a variation of one or other of these.

Either you appoint a place and time and try to persuade people to come in; or else you go out

> . . . to them where they are, at home, at work, and at leisure, talk to them in the setting in which they are at home, and with which they are familiar, and find that you have the opportunity of evangelising the environment as well as the man. You see him as he is, and you know just what he is up against when it comes to trying to live the Christian life in these surroundings.

And of course DP concluded, 'Of these two types there is no question as to which is the more effective so far as the point of contact is concerned.' He accepted the argument made by others in 1955 and 1956, that organising 'the bus party or cavalcade going to Harringay or to the Kelvin Hall, to Wembley or to Earl's Court' could be simply an easy way out, avoiding the much harder task of enabling the daily work and witness of the membership of the Church. His own style of campaigning, dependent on volunteers, based in local areas, tackling places of work and leisure as well as homes, enduring often for a lengthy period of time, he believed more effective, more efficient and more flexible, and moreover done

> . . . with the least possible interruption to the ordinary activities of the participating churches, with the organisation and administration centred in their buildings, and at a minimum of cost compared with a Billy Graham Crusade. You have not had to turn the spotlight too obtrusively on any one man, and you have brought the challenge of mission – as the ongoing activity of the Church – directly and inescapably to every congregation in the area. This is something that no large-scale Crusade can achieve (however impressive its set-up, however rich and varied its personnel, however far-reaching its plans).

When DP was to write in *A Fraction of His Image*, the memorial tribute to Tom Allan, that he and Tom 'differed considerably' 'in our judgment of certain significant movements in the church life of our day', this evaluation of a Thomson as against a Graham campaign was what was in mind. Their differences, however, 'never dimmed our friendship or marred our fellowship'.

Aspects of Evangelism drew on material DP had written over his long career, from the *Handbooks of Evangelism* of 1924 as well as from the books and pamphlets that came after the Second War. It represented the core of his thought, and contained powerful advocacy of his own ideal of orthodox evangelism:

> Evangelism is more than the mere proclamation of evangelical truth. It is the winning of individual men and women for Jesus Christ, with all that means in the reshaping of outlook and character. While fully alive to social values, it proceeds on the assumption that the key to the mass is the man, that social redemption can only be attained through the regeneration of individual men and women, and that for this regeneration only the Gospel of Christ is adequate . . . Evangelism demands directness of appeal. It presupposes the possibility of immediate and far-reaching results in the field of human life and character. Its one valid note is ever the note of authority, an authority based on reason and revelation and born of corporate and personal experience. Evangelistic preaching is at once direct and personal, urgent and compelling, simple and clear, calculated to enlist reason and judgment on its side, and at the same time to arouse the conscience and to awaken a responsible chord in the heart. Such preaching constitutes a legitimate demand of every age, and forms the adequate response to the need of every individual. The evangelist can speak with authority and power only when he uses the language of his own day, communicates his message in the light of current conceptions, and appeals to the dominant aspirations of his own time. The great evangelists of every age have dealt with Christian truth in such a way as to make God intensely real to the men and women of their own generation. The timeliness of their appeal was no less striking than the genuineness of the experience which gave it birth. The evangelism of to-day will fail of its purpose unless it comes to men with a message at once fresh and compelling, instinct with spiritual power and beauty, embracing the eternal truths of the Christian Gospel, and applying them with spiritual insight to the immediate problems of the hour. What we need to-day, and need supremely, is a daring application of the mind and teaching of Christ to the whole field of contemporary life.

Evangelism for D. P. Thomson was enabled by a communication of revealed Christian truth that included but was not confined to doctrinal teaching. He sought to convey an appeal that was personally and socially relevant; and he recognised four methods or media by which that appeal could be conveyed. These were the spoken word, whether preached or gossiped; the written or printed word 'the Bible or book I lend . . . the letter I write to a friend'; the pictorial or dramatised word; and the 'embodied word':

> The embodied word may be the beauty and strength, the sheer Christlikeness, of some one life lived out before the eyes of those who become aware of its significance and of its challenge; or it may be the strength and variety of the corporate life of a group, revealing a fellowship with undertones and overtones so compelling that those brought into intimate contact with it feel a growing urge 'to belong', combined with a growing willingness to pay whatever price may be demanded for that privilege. Again, speaking as an evangelist of more than 50 years' experience, I have no hesitation in saying which of these four media I have found to be the most potent, and which in my judgment comes nearest both to the record and to the experience of the New Testament. It is not the spoken or the written word. It is not the pictorialised or dramatised word. It is the embodied word. It is, in point of fact, that for which the Apostle Paul pleaded so eloquently, the incarnate word, the 'living epistle known and read of all men'. No word speaks as that does.

Thomson's pamphlet *New Testament Conversions*, based on Bible-studies used in training the Edinburgh Relay Mission counsellors, thus looked to the example of Jesus, who had used no single formula, who had led the people he met by different roads: 'Along his own path He would lead each of them to that life of faith and obedience in which salvation and satisfaction alike are found.'

In DP's emphasis on the personal and on the journey, points of contrast from the Crieff Fraternal may be seen, as well as points of contact with Dr Ian Fraser, first Warden of Scottish Churches House, Dunblane, from March 1960. Two books, both by Fraser, tell the story of the House. *Ecumenical Adventure: a Dunblane Initiative* describes the range of concerns – cultural, social, national, theological – by which the House pursued its vision. His earlier *People Journeying: a Source Book of Scottish Churches House* contained rather more polemical material. In that book he defined the House and its programme as evangelistic, because for Fraser true evangelism was journeying in company and in community; it involved mutual listening, holding the entire experience open to God for His Spirit to work as He chose. Holding a licence to preach – or ministerial or lay status – was entirely irrelevant. And if this was evangelism, then it was clear what was not: pressurised, conversion-seeking mass evangelism. Their emphasis on experience and 'the incarnate Word' made both DP and Ian Fraser, more so than Tom Allan post-1955, early exemplars of the post-modern paradigm of mission.[14] At root, however, Thomson's approach was an older, liberally-conceived, evangelism, that sought to make effective contact in order to win individuals to Christ and His Church within a framework of thought doctrinally orthodox.

If there had in the past been a separation between the ordinary routine of parish life and special evangelism, the mature DP sought to bring the two together: the call to evangelism was, certainly, a call to the whole church, but it came first and with force to the ministry. He advocated using all the opportunities of parish life to present Christ simply and directly, enabling personal response – the pulpit, the sacraments, the organisations, pre-wedding instruction, 'the great hours of home and family life, and the times of sorrow, of suffering and of setback.' In *First Communion* he pursued this theme by publishing, with comments, the results of a questionnaire survey of local practice whereby new members entered the Church of Scotland. DP called for time to be given for preliminary interviews with each candidate before the course began; time to allow the participation of elders and representations of organisations, for the non-ministerial voice and experience to be heard; time to follow up the service of admission; time for discussion, for 'two-way traffic', so that not just formal instruction was given but real communication and listening between teacher and class. He was also disturbed that so many of his correspondents saw the function of communicants' classes as evangelistic: for if a minister was really doing his job as an evangelist, should not candidates for admission be coming forward in response to his wider ministry? 'Is the class not primarily intended to harvest the fruit of his ministry?' To DP, an evangelistic outlook should pervade the whole life of Christ's Church.

The Church in the Open Air had also been foreshadowed. It derived, in part, from DP's course of lectures delivered at Glasgow's BTI, though its format of a representative photograph for each topic, with accompanying text, must have meant that much went unsaid:

> In these pages an attempt is made, in what I realise to be a quite inadequate way, to show how moving and varied a thing is the service which our own Church seeks to render out where the sun is shining and the winds are blowing, and where men can still be reached with the Gospel.

Seaside Missions, Christian Highway, soap-boxes at street corners, special services for May Day and Easter mornings, historical commemorations, Remembrance Day services at War Memorials: these and more DP listed as ways in which the Kirk might make contact with folk in the world, connecting with a sense of occasion, or through shared interest or by simply grabbing passing curiosity. DP certainly defined himself as an open-air evangelist and it is perhaps a pity that *The Church in the Open Air* barely scratched the surface of what these possibilities meant to him. Rev. Stewart Frizzell remembers when, as a young man returning from Summer Mission, DP met the team off the train in Glasgow. He assembled them in the station, and then pointed his umbrella skywards. They looked up – a curious crowd gathered, also looking up; and then DP, taking the Ascension as a text and the angels' question – 'Why stand ye gazing up into heaven?' – reminded all present that Christ would come again! 'This same Jesus, which is taken up from you into heaven, shall so come in like manner as ye have seen him go into heaven.' *Church in the Open Air*, *Dr Billy Graham*, *Aspects of Evangelism* and *First Communion* all bear re-reading and consideration for the principles incorporated, despite their many time-bound examples from DP's own experience and *First Communion*'s survey-based content. He advocated a holistic practice and his thought was not confined to one special area of the Church's work.

Looking Back

We have arrived at the place from which we must look back on the life and work of Rev. David Patrick Thomson, M.A., D.D. , Evangelist of the Church of Scotland, sometime Warden of the St Ninian's Centre, Crieff. The question 'Would I have wanted to meet him?' the reader must answer for himself! D. P. Thomson was not universally liked in his own day: 'DP is marvellous for a weekend, but hardly anyone can stand him for more than four days!' one of Frame's sources said.[15] But what did he achieve? What was his legacy? It is very tempting to plagiarise DP himself. In 1957 he contemplated writing a biography of one of his Christian heroes, John Wesley, whose motto 'The world as my parish' had been one of his own long-held ambitions:

> 27th September [1957] . . . I was reading there John S. Simon *John Wesley And the Methodist Societies* in which I am nearing page 100. I am minded to prepare two books, one on 'John Wesley: a Study,' the other on 'John Wesley: Open Air Preacher.' In the first I would have: Wesley: The Son / The Brother / The Husband / The Open Air Preacher / The Personal Worker / The Man of Prayer / The Student of the Word / The Friend / The Leader / The Founder of Methodism / The Colleague / The Man / The Reader / The Publisher / The Theologian / The Christian / The

> Traveller / The Guest – and so on! I am not aware that any one has so far attempted to work in that field. Add: The Hymn Writer / The Controversialist / The Letter Writer / The Amateur Physician / The Citizen / The Social Reformer.

It is easy to see how many of these categories fit DP himself so well – Son – Brother – Husband – Open Air Preacher – Personal Worker – Reader – Publisher. Hopefully some idea of DP in these aspects of his life has already been conveyed.

If 'The Man of Prayer' and 'The Student of the Word' have, perhaps, not been highlighted, this is because DP's relationship to his Master was very personal. Small incidents throughout his diaries and the overall thrust of his publications reveal his day-to-day dependence on the guidance, inspiration and love of Jesus Christ, by his Word and Spirit. Perhaps the clearest instruction on these matters was given in his *Beginning the Christian Life* – the following extracts come from his introduction to the pamphlet:

> You have trusted Jesus Christ as your Saviour. You have asked him to take your life into his care and keeping. You must renew that trust, with an ever deepening sense of its meaning and value, in the light of each new morning, before the day's work begins. Then, hour by hour and moment by moment, you must trust him, whatever experiences life may bring, whatever situations or temptations it may confront you with . . .
>
> If you are to be a worthy follower of Jesus Christ you must aim high. Be content with nothing less than the best as your ideal for character and your service. Go steadily forward, seeking every day a fuller knowledge and a deeper experience of Christ, and a closer approximation to his mind and will. In the Christian life there is no standing still . . .
>
> You must begin and end every day with prayer – prayer for yourself and prayer for others – prayer that has in it a place for thanksgiving, a place for confession, and a place for adoration. You must cultivate the habit of lifting up your heart to God in prayer whenever temptation meets you, whenever opportunity confronts you, or where the burdens of life tend to weigh you down, as sooner or later they will . . .
>
> You must set yourself to learn the joy of Christian Fellowship . . .
>
> Every day, however crowded, you must make time for the study of the Bible. You will discover it to be more and more a source of instruction and inspiration as you advance in the Christian life . . .

These were principles that D. P. Thomson had sought to follow in his own life.

In his *New Testament Christianity* DP published a study entitled 'Can the dead really speak?' based on Hebrews 11:4. He asserted:

> Long after we are gone these lives of ours will speak. They will speak in the most unexpected ways and in the most unexpected places. It is a thought calculated at once to sober and to challenge . . . Of what will these lives of yours and mine speak? To what interests and values will they bear witness? In what lives and to what effect, will the influence of our lives live on?

As I have met those who had known DP in life, as I never knew him, I often asked: Why was DP described (by Prof. T. F. Torrance) as 'one of the most loved men in Scotland?' It was striking that much the same answer came back – because he lived his life in an open and candid way, and because his was an enabling ministry. He genuinely wanted the best for those he met, and somehow he managed to enable women and men to attempt and to achieve more than they had expected. Perhaps the sense of this was (and is) most strongly felt by women who came across him: too little was expected of women in the Scotland and the Kirk of the 1950s and 60s. By all accounts he could be dictatorial.[16] Brief phone calls were common during the campaigns of the 1950s, demanding that he be met at some railway station or hotel, with all involved expected to share his sense of enthusiasm and urgency. Elsie Moir remembers the unexpected instruction just before DP departed from some public meeting: 'Speak till I come back!' He was dogmatic about arrangements, knowing what he wanted done and by whom. Not everyone could stand his lifelong 'Officer in Command' manner, which perhaps grated most with other ministers, equally used in their parishes to having their own way.[17] One of the early lay leaders in Strathmore had to withdraw from the campaign to protect his wife's nerves, shattered by DP:[18] 'Long contact with me gets on her nerves and she couldn't sleep.' DP's loud – stentorian – voice and pointing hand could intimidate, but yet it is remembered that unlike other church leaders (to 'right' and 'left') of his generation, he did not try to squeeze those he met into one mould. That testimony was given to Willie Frame in 1974 and I have heard the same 35 years later.

The teaching of DP's advanced years was so often done by instigating discussion: the influence of those months of enthusiasm for the Oxford Group in 1931 stayed with him. Bible Study, whether on campaign or at St Ninian's, was not a matter of detailed exposition but of opening up a passage by asking questions.[19] At a time when divisions on the doctrine of Scripture – whether it was infallible or inerrant or whether sections were scientifically, historically or theologically wrong – were increasing and increasingly bitter, DP did not seek to proselytise for his view: his *Pocket*

Guide for Personal Workers asked counsellors to respect the fact that 'the one to whom we find ourselves speaking may be under a ministry based on a different view of inspiration to our own.' His essential theological position has been discussed. While certainly evangelical, he did not lobby for the self-proclaimed conservative evangelical position that Tom Allan came to accept, with specific doctrinal points held to be essential.[20] Once again it is worth repeating that for D. P. Thomson [*When Christ Calls*] 'It is not *what* I believe that matters in the end of the day; it is in *Whom* I have put my trust; it is to *Whom* I have committed my life.' It was surely because DP's own faith centred round a Person that he was able to allow those close to him space to find their own way and their own relationship with Jesus Christ.

Another way of restating this central aspect of DP's life and faith is to recall his early and lasting stress on an ecumenical approach to Christian work. All his organisations – GSEU, FMF, FiE, Work & Witness – were based on a shared willingness to serve rather than on doctrinal statements. As DP began his ordained ministry in Dunfermline he knew that his first task was, within his own sphere, to implement the Union of his United Free Church with the Established Church. He remained convinced of the benefits of this Union and was also an enthusiastic learner from the experience of other Christian denominations through his life, whether from his voracious and extensive reading of Church history or from his repeated tours of parishes, centres, colleges and church leaders in England and Ireland. He was always willing to engage with the new, whether the Oxford Group or the Iona Community or the reappraisal movement. From his youth he (like his parents) was committed to the world church – remember his boyhood ambitions, the International Meetings held on campaigns, the welcome St Ninian's gave to missionaries. DP closed his final volume of explicit autobiography, *Personal Encounters*, with an account of a conference held at St Ninian's in 1962 by representatives of the Student Christian Movement branch at St Andrews University, on the theme of 'The Pattern of Our Common Worship', led by the Church of Scotland, Anglican and Roman Catholic Chaplains to the University. Congregationalist students were also part of the group. It was a gathering that, as DP said, would have been unthinkable even five years earlier. He was pleased to facilitate it, typically overstating its historical significance 400 years after the Reformation. He ended his autobiography with an equally typical and heart-felt plea:

> I am convinced that we have to understand one another better, and that, as far as our convictions will allow, we must be ready to pray and to work with one another.

The title *Personal Encounters* was no accident. DP's lifelong emphasis on the personal shines through his career. He gave personal time to the young people of Gillespie and to the young servicemen and servicewomen of Cambuslang: Trinity. He was an inveterate correspondent, keeping in touch with colleagues from his student days, or with 'his bairns', those who came to Christ through his ministry, and those who joined his teams. Rev. Bill Watt still retains the telegram he received on the day of his wedding, 'Warmest good wishes from your fellow campaigners – Thomson' (24 November 1956). DP's belief in the role of personality in evangelism was confirmed by his reading on D. L. Moody; and when looking back on his own career DP saw the importance of two-way interaction of people. Hence his choice, for autobiography, to concentrate on people he had met:

> Life brings to all of us throughout the years encounters with men and with movements which ultimately stand out as meaningful in our experience because of what they did for us. It is by these, to a very large extent, that thought, character and service are alike shaped. Here I have tried to recapture some of these, and to assess, as best I can, something of their significance.

During after-campaign assessments and at St Ninian's courses, DP placed emphasis on 'two-way traffic', on what might be learnt by all sides involved, whether those officially in charge or those junior in status. His friends were thus struck by his humility, his preparedness to learn from others. Scott Carroll remembers that there was 'a loving charity in his theology', a mark of his care for those he met.

A generosity of spirit that set his face against bitterness was also part of DP's own personality. We have seen DP put aside disappointment that projected invitations to New Zealand, Canada and California came to nothing, and turn to the next task his Master had for him. On that most personal of levels, we have seen how he tackled, so soon after their marriage, the news that Mary would be unable to conceive. We have seen how he had to live with his rejection by the Home Board's Convener, John White – yet DP gave White a chapter in *Personal Encounters*, describing him as 'the great man'. Similarly DP, aware that they shared much in common, tried to avoid any personal animosity developing from his differences of policy with George MacLeod – a difficult task when their younger associates were less particular, and when George appeared to have gained a stature in the Church that eluded DP.

All people have limitations. When he was at his busiest in the mid-1950s DP accepted that his influence was as a practitioner, not a policy-maker: 'As I am feeling the strain of the work and have no say in the shaping of policy it might be best that I should go.' He seldom attempted to meddle in church politics, the business of the remits and memberships of central committees, the management of factions to drive through policy, on 26 September 1956 writing in his diary 'How hateful church politics are!' DP's dictatorial style actually disqualified him from much of ordinary presbyterian business. He had good friends but few ministerial allies and even his friends could find his intensity off-putting. His vision of how the Church might be therefore took root in individuals and not (St Ninian's apart) in the institutions of the Kirk, to its loss. His ministry was no means a straight or easy road and, the only remaining son of a financially challenged father, sometimes struggling with debt and/or illness, carrying for decades some of the burden of his sister Dr Christine's illness, in maturity he had little to rely on apart from his Lord and his Mary.

D. P. Thomson was, as Ian Doyle wrote, a complex man with contradictory elements about him. As I have read his diaries I have been amazed at the way he seemed, in retrospect, to waste time writing diary entries. On 9 November 1950 Mary accused him of having 'Diary-itis' and DP's willingness to use time to write up his diary early on a Sunday morning, in advance of determining what, in a few hours time, he was to preach, would not be my own priority! He used 'The Diary of My Life' for many purposes: practical, spiritual, even psychological. Keeping account of expenses was an enduring nightmare for him – he was still trying to complete his accounts for the Strathmore Campaign in October 1954, almost a year after it had closed. Bob Jones was never able to sign off St Ninian's accounts for any of the seven years 1959-1966. By DP's diary's narrative of where he had been and when, and where he bought meals, some sort of check was kept on receipts. Similarly, writing the diaries was a way of keeping track during a maelstrom of engagements: of what had happened and what was to come next. An emotional man, DP also used his diaries to face fears and express strong feelings that perhaps could not be expressed in any other way. Having honestly written what he felt, he could then move on. His very frequent references to ill-health, his illnesses and possible impending death are probably best understood in this way – no-one aware of his work-rate could ever accuse him of hypochondria!

Occasional tiffs with Mary – one occasion comes to mind when she outraged his scruples by 'borrowing' the Home Board's shooting brake for a private outing – were recorded and the anger, having been expressed, was put aside. In DP's youth, when his diary habit began, both home and foreign missionaries were often required by their Societies to keep diaries in order to be accountable and that their work might be transparent. John Wesley, his enduring exemplar, had of course kept a Journal. Behind the practicality of 'The Diary of My Life' and DP's compulsion to record seemingly trivial details was this sense of being accountable to his Master. The Diary was kept, ultimately, for the God who gave DP the days and hours and years, and commissioned him in His service:

> Wednesday, 28th March [1945] . . . Now I close Volume 13 of my Diary, with profoundly thankfulness to God for all He has bestowed upon me and enabled me to do for His Cause — especially for our happy and beautiful home, and for the dear little wife He has given to me — so constant and true, so patient and understanding, so loving and tender, so ready to bear and forbear.

What was DP's legacy? Willie Frame cited an obituary that identified his greatest memorial as St Ninian's, Crieff, and indeed the Centre – transferred to the ownership of the Church of Scotland – thrived under DP's successors, Bill Shannon and Peter Bisset, albeit DP disliked aspects of its modernisation. Its programmes and staff (and former staff) developed the vision for the mission of the laity via, for example, the programme 'Developing the Missionary Parish' of the 1980s / 1990s; Brian Burden's 'contract' style of focussing on congregational mission; Ian Moir's enabling of Urban Priority congregational life. An echo may be perceived in the 'Church without Walls' movement associated with another former Director at St Ninian's, Peter Neilson. During the 1990s, however, capital resources were not secured to update the accommodation to the hotel standard increasingly demanded by a prosperous society: and that society also placed less value on evangelism, especially via the non-ordained. The Church lost something of its vision for the mission of the laity and also and therefore for the St Ninian's Centre. In spite of high levels of protest from those whose spiritual lives had benefited from St Ninian's, the General Assembly of 2001 agreed it should be closed.[21]

In 2009 the Church of Scotland remembered the 75th anniversary of the work of Summer Mission, as counted from 1934, as DP's own (somewhat self-focused) leaflet *The Church on the Sands: the Summer Seaside*

Work of the Church of Scotland suggested. D. P. Thomson's foundational place in this work, still [2010] continuing under the name of iMPACT!, was duly honoured. An article in *Life & Work*, August 2009, paid its respects to DP's name as the one who established this programme in the life of the united Church of Scotland: 'He simply asked two questions: Where are the people and How can the Church engage with them?' Yet as we have seen, even when appointed as Evangelist in the 1930s and Seaside Missions Organiser in the early 1940s, DP was not a Children's Evangelist. On his Jamaica tour he took Jack Malloch with him to be the children's specialist. DP would not have thought that 'the people' were primarily on the beaches except for the terms of his appointments. He wanted to engage with Scots in the open air, on the streets as well as on the beaches, and in their homes, and at their work. Given that in both decades he sought after a relatively short time to move on from seaside missions, it is a touch ironic that this segment of the Church's life is the one that now primarily recalls his name. Of course both Mary and DP retained an affection for the work and kept prayerful contact as far as his campaigns permitted. As Warden of St Ninian's he delighted in supplying participants from a variety of courses to lead at Summer Missions. He would, I think, be surprised that this now seems to be regarded as his enduring legacy.

DP was very conscious of the flow of church history. 'Never in the history of . . .' was a favourite way of beginning a crowd-pulling speech. Yet while he would have been pleased to have had the time to research and publish an authoritative work on some aspect of the Church's history, something that would last, he never did achieve this. As Ian Doyle comments, DP's writing, in the end, was subordinate to his calling as an evangelist. DP would want his life assessed not in terms of institutional or tangible legacies for the future, but in terms of faithfulness in his own time, the legacy of people he had introduced to Christ or assisted to find their vocation. He was given a vision for enabling the ordinary Christian for the evangelistic work of the Church: a new vision for a new time. He gave his heart and soul, his total energies, to incarnating this vision: to finding out through experiments what it might mean and how it might be done: how the Scottish churches might indeed 'Go to the people', as he had urged in 1922.[22] The visitation evangelism campaigns of the 1950s and their accompanying publications – more so even than the work of St Ninian's – were indeed unique in the history of the Church for their scope, for the numbers to whom they brought the Gospel of Jesus Christ, for their reliance on the non-ordained. In our more private age, without a supportive media,[23] within a society determined not to be offended and a church uncertain of its message and still more focused on its ordained ministry, their methodology has ceased to appeal. Even in his own time, DP's impact was greatest on his regulars and had less lasting effect among the generality of the Kirk's laity than he had hoped. 'Mr Thomson', according to Ian MacTaggart, dealt with 'the spearhead, the vanguard': but 'the vast body of troops' were still disengaged; 'nor do they (most of them) hope to be engaged.'[24] In his campaigning years DP also, perhaps conveniently, overestimated the impact his returning teams were allowed to have within their own congregations. Yet through his preaching, campaigns, networks, publications and broadcasts D. P. Thomson did indeed make contact; he did on behalf of Christ *go to the people* of Scotland. That is surely how he would want to be remembered.

Beyond DP's primary vision, two other results from his ministry may be identified. Besides seeking to widen the horizons of service for countless women and men he also sought to encourage young men more particularly into the ministry of Word and Sacrament. William Watt, recalling DP in 2009, wrote:

> To see DP at work, to hear his voice, to come under his magnetic charm and understanding was inspirational. In our contacts with DP in the 1950's there were many, probably hundreds, who decided to enter the full-time ministry or become Elders, Sunday school teachers, church workers. In our team at Lochinver one young man decided that he wanted to be a medical missionary. This is the lasting value to the Church, that ordinary people, like myself, decided to dedicate their lives to further the Gospel and the results although astounding will probably never be calculated.

Many young men that encountered him came in time to have their own significant ministries: his assistants of the immediate post war years, Ian Doyle and Bill Shannon have been mentioned already.

Bill Temple, too, may be recalled. He was eleven years younger than DP and, being licensed in 1932 and ordained to Peterhead: East in 1934, was a first-generation minister of the united Church of Scotland. His ability was recognised early when he was one of the select dozen ministers set apart as evangelists by the General Assembly in 1938. During the Second War he was a leading member of FiE and moved from his second charge of Glasgow: Rutherford to the traditionally evangelical pulpit of Edinburgh: Barclay. No other of DP's friends had then obtained such a level of national recognition and, if Temple's name is not now remembered among the post-war leaders of the Church of Scotland, this is because he accepted a call in 1948 to the presbyterian charge of Wellington: St John's in New Zealand. There he had a happy and fruitful ministry – and there he introduced the name and methods of one D. P. Thomson both to St John's and to the 'New Life Movement' of parish missions and church extension in post-war New Zealand:[25]

> Bill Temple had been warmed to his task by the renowned Scottish evangelist, David Patrick Thomson. In 1935, two years after Temple's ordination to the ministry, Thomson had laid Christ's case on the line: 'No ifs and buts or apologies,' I can hear 6-foot-4 DP saying, with the quiet intensity and challenging look, that made my heart burn, 'Brother, the Master is come, and calleth for thee,' Temple recalled. With this adult challenge and commitment, Bill Temple absorbed two trademarks of evangelical style he was to make his own, one personal and the other Presbyterian. On the personal level, Temple absorbed the D. P. Thomson strategy that evangelism needed planning. Let there be a situation of need, a goal to be accomplished, and within that possibility, set out the challenge . . . On the Presbyterian plane, Temple had absorbed a key Reformation teaching that church and individual alike must not only be reformed but continue in an ever-ongoing process of continual reformation. On this foundation, Temple avoided the fashion of many an 'evangelist' who belittles everything before the Great Call and all that has been achieved by older folk and former generations. Bill Temple loved the Kirk, and indeed the church universal.

'To preach a clear and relevant message that invited and indeed expected a definite response,' to plan wisely, to love the Kirk and the Church catholic or universal: these were indeed key features of D. P. Thomson. And further, if DP sought to recognise and promote the ministry of women in the kirk, so too did Temple dedicate a window in St John's 'to the Glory of God, and in loving remembrance of the faithful women who through 100 years have worshipped and served in this Church.'

As to DP's influence among the wider ministry, Prof. Stanley Wood conducted a survey of Church Extension ministers for his 1996 doctoral thesis for Aberdeen University, and his research chronicles (anonymously) a number who were happy to acknowledge their experience with DP.[26] Indeed, Wood concluded that, after the Iona Community, DP was *the* major influence on Church Extension ministers, both in terms of their ministerial formation and in terms of their evangelistic practice. Given that the Community's own focus was very much on Church Extension and that the movement was (to his regret) somewhat peripheral to DP's own work, this result is the more striking. Through his 1920s student evangelism, his Seaside Mission work before and after the Second War, through the campaigns of the 1950s and his St Ninian's Centre in the 1960s, D. P. Thomson was a very significant influence on several generations of Church of Scotland ministers. When, at the General Assembly of 1966, the motion was introduced to acknowledge his 'unique service', those present responded with 'resounding and prolonged applause', confirming the praise of the Home Board report:

> Retirement of the Rev. D. P. Thomson, D.D.
>
> Dr. Thomson is due to retire on 17th May from his post as an Evangelist of the Home Board after an association of over thirty years, interrupted by a spell of work in a Cambuslang parish during the Second World War. Dr. Thomson's energy, opportunism, and dedication to his work have made him almost a legendary figure in the Church. Many ministers now serving the Church, and a host of its ordinary members, would gladly acknowledge what they owe to DP for first directing their lives into the way of Christ. He has also been an outstanding pioneer of many new forms of evangelism, and the books which he has written on evangelistic method have been studied in centres all over the world, and have been an inspiration to many to follow his example. As preacher and lecturer his services have been in constant demand, and during the last eight years he has built up a remarkable Centre at St Ninian's, Crieff, where many have found spiritual guidance, refreshment, and stimulus. No one who has worked with DP could fail to be influenced by his unflagging zest for new enterprise, his wide-ranging interest in the life of both Church and nation, his immense capacity for work, and his burning zeal in the cause of Christ. The Church in our day owes him an inestimable debt.

What is the value to today's church of remembering D. P. Thomson? Over the course of this book we have traced the vigorous and varied efforts made by DP – along with the generation of the 1929 Union and the Recall to Religion, the Baillie Commission, George MacLeod, Ralph Morton, Charles Duthie, Tom Allan, and others – to find ways to implement the vision that 'the proper agent for evangelism is nothing less than the whole body of the faithful.' We have seen how four decades of their quest for a 'new evangelism' finally ran into the sands, away from the mainstream of church life. The growth of what Duthie called 'party spirit' meant that even the successes that were achieved have been too often discounted. That there was a long decade of Church growth during the post-war period should be recognised: perhaps the principles underpinning its outreach may still resonate? Consciousness of the primary evangelistic role of the laity subsided as disputes questioned the very meaning of the word 'evangelism'. We live in the aftermath of the crisis of evangelism of the 1950s and 1960s, in a very different society, yet making contact with Scotland's people is more critical than ever.

The issues on which DP focused are still issues the church faces. He would want us to find new ways to convey the personal challenge to follow Christ alone. Beyond that, he gave priority to investment (in the broadest sense of that concept), not only in mission by Word and Sacrament but also by the whole people of God. He – very early – recognised the need, not just for ministries that maintain a structure but that have a thorough theological and practical education for mission. He knew the benefits that can come from crossing parish boundaries and from inter-church interaction: the sowing of ideas, the fresh modelling, the new voices to hear. D. P. Thomson knew Christ's Church must engage with the whole of life: his 'three-fold simultaneous approach' to home, work and leisure may have been a somewhat sledgehammer technique but the vision, surely, was correct. We still need the enthusiasm, the sense of urgency, the vitality, the innovative zest that DP brought to recommending outreach as the primary calling of Christ's Church:

> It is the first business of the believing community to make Jesus Christ known in the fulness of his Saviourhood and in the wonder of His power, to ring out the invitation and challenge of His Gospel, and to summon men and women by persistent and impassioned appeal, not merely to embrace His ideals, but to enter His fellowship and to give themselves in glad abandon to His service.
>
> *Aspects of Evangelism*

****

Mrs D. P. Thomson, née Mary Rothnie, 'Nanka' to her wider family, died suddenly on 6 March 1974, aged 70, and David Patrick Thomson ten days afterwards. Dr Christina Jane Thomson followed them in 1978, the last of the close-knit family from 1 Hyndford Terrace, Dundee. DP came to the end of life sustained by streams of visitors to his beloved Barnoak, by the friendship and prayers of countless people. He had faithfully passed on the gospel of Christ to those coming after him. The generation that knew DP is itself now passing, but as Ian Doyle wrote:

> Those who remember him in his prime will never forget the commanding figure, the stentorian voice proclaiming Christ, the outstretched hand that challenged so many in the name of Christ.

Even if the Scotland and the Scottish Kirk that he served so loyally have, in so many ways, changed, D. P. Thomson's inspiring passion and catholic faithfulness, his determination to adventure in his Master's service, and his grass-roots evangelism, are worth recalling.

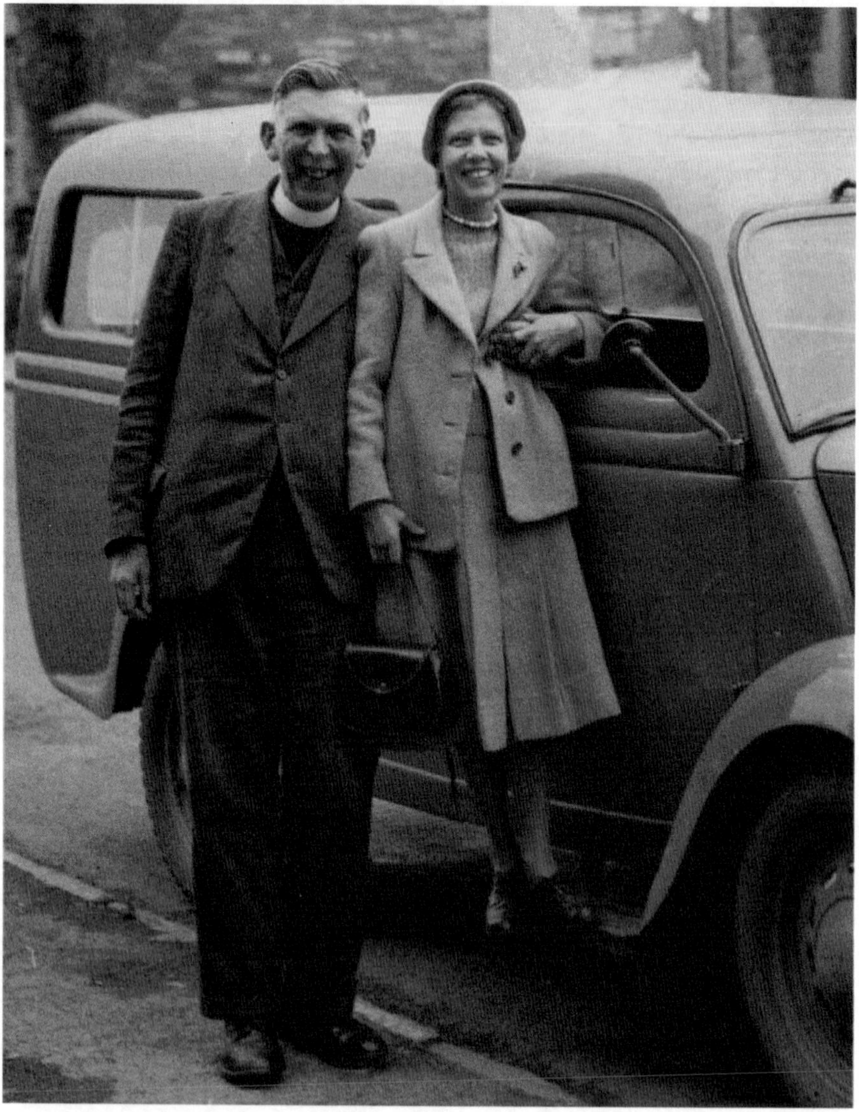

#42: DP and Mary on campaign

ENDNOTES

Introduction

1 Frame, *Fire in His Bones* (a 48 page booklet c.1974) and Doyle, *D. P. Thomson*, Edinburgh 1983, a 6 page pamphlet republishing 'An Introductory Memoir by Dr Ian B. Doyle' in D. P. Thomson, *Women of the Scottish Church*, private posthumous publication 1975, 7-11.

2 Doyle, 'Introductory Memoir', 11.

3 Highet, *The Scottish Churches: a review of their state 400 years after the Reformation*, 70.

4 Storrar identifies the 1950s as a time of transition between the modern and the post-modern world: Storrar, 'A tale of two paradigms: mission in Scotland from 1946' in Anderson, Wright *et al*, *Death or Glory*, 54-69.

Chapter 1: Evangelist in Training I

1 Barclay, *Mary,* 23-32.

2 Green, *Fact Stranger Than Fiction*, 249-250. My source for this reference was the electronic edition made available by the Library of the University of North Carolina at Chapel Hill, to whom thanks are due.

3 The D. P. Thomson Archive includes a typescript 'History of the Thomson family 1790-1965' prepared by Russell Currie.

4 Storrar, 'A tale of two paradigms: mission in Scotland from 1946' in *Death or Glory*, 55-56.

5 Simpson, *The Life of Principal Rainy* vol. I, 409.

6 Longfield, *The Presbyterian Controversy*, 117; 133-136.

7 See also Thomson, *The Road to Dunfermline*, inside back cover.

8 I have concealed the identity of the girl concerned.

9 Thomson, *Personal Encounters*, 12.

Chapter 2: Evangelist in Training II

1 Dunnett, *The Church in Changing Scotland*, 138.

2 Vincent, *C.T. Studd and Priscilla* offers a documented if devotional biography of the Studds. See also: Grubb, *C.T. Studd: Cricketer and Pioneer.*

3 Pollock, *The Cambridge Seven*, 94-97, 100-104.

4 Grubb (ed.), *J.D. Drysdale, Prophet of Holiness*, 92.

5 Bebbington, *Evangelicalism in Modern Britain*, 195-6.

6 McIntyre, *Christ the Crucified*, 14-17.

7 'Renwick Church' / 'Christian Life and Work in Glasgow' in *The Record of the Home and Foreign Mission Work of the United Free Church of Scotland,* March 1924, 106.

8 Information courtesy of the St Andrews University Library and Dr Marie Robinson.

9 In these extracts I have concealed the identity of the people concerned.

10 *The Dundee Directory* shows James Thomson's home address as Torwood, 18 Duntrune Terrace, West Ferry, Dundee from volume 1925-26 through to 1927-28. There was no entry for him in the *Directory* after 1927-28. The D. P. Thomson Archive contains an album of family photographs which include a number of family groups at Torwood, which was (relative to 1 Hyndford Terrace) a more modest semi-detached stone-built villa.

11 Home Mission and Church Extension Committee, 'Report for 1927' in *Reports to the General Assembly of the United Free Church of Scotland*, section VI, 3-5, 15, and especially 'Paper on Evangelism,' 17-20 and 'Presbytery Reports,' 46-50.

12 Home Mission and Church Extension Committee, 'Report for 1928' in *Reports to the General Assembly of the United Free Church of Scotland*, section VI, 3.

13 Brown, *The Death of Christian Britain*, 128-9.

Chapter 3: Evangelist in Training III

1 Bebbington, *Evangelicalism in Modern Britain*, 2-3 and in detail 5-17.

2 Cheyne, *Transforming of the Kirk*, 82-83.

3 Thomson, *The Road to Dunfermline*, 32.

4 D. P. Thomson, 'A Student's Impressions' in *The Record of the Home and Foreign Mission Work of the United Free Church of Scotland*, February 1922, number 254, 43-44.

5 This openness to theological approach, this refusal to deny Christian fellowship because of differences of opinion, was one that imbued much United Free Church thinking. Rev. James Black, 'Fundamentalism in Edinburgh – a remarkable circular' in *The Record of the Home and Foreign Mission Work of the United Free Church of Scotland*, September 1925, 395-7: 'We have had enough of such unchristian policy in the history of the Church. It is this wretched, negative and unchurching conduct which has been the curse of aggressive fundamentalism across the seas.'

6 *Ecumenical Studies: Evangelism in Scotland*, 29.

7 Thomson, Diary of My Life part 6, 190: Saturday 15 October [1921].

8 Longfield, *The Presbyterian Controversy*, 72-79; 100-103; 125-127; 128-130; 147-153.

9 Longfield, *The Presbyterian Controversy*, 83-84 citing a letter from Edinburgh written by Rev. H. S. Coffin in 1897.

10 Bebbington, 'The persecution of George Jackson: a British Fundamentalist Controversy,' in Sheils (ed.), *Persecution and Toleration*, 421-433.

11 Riesen, *Professor A. C. Cheyne,* 63-65 for a recent discussion of liberal evangelicism.

12 Coffin, *The Portraits of Jesus Christ in the New Testament*, 26.

13 Longfield, *The Presbyterian Controversy*, 87-99.

14 Bebbington, *Evangelicalism in Modern Britain,* 222-223.

15 Clow, *The Cross in Christian Experience.*

16 Johnson, *Contending for the Faith,* 71-75; Barclay, *Evangelicalism in Britain*, 18.

17 Johnson, *Contending for the Faith,* Appendix 2, 359.

18 Cheyne, *Transforming of the Kirk*, 85.

19 Blackie, 'Robert Mackie' in N. Blackie (ed.) *A Time for Trumpets*, 53-64.

20 These letters are held at the Centre for the Study of Christianity in the Non-Western World, New College, Edinburgh: CSCNNW, box T. Ralph Morton, 1/3, file 1-4.

21 Begbie, *Life Changers,* 94-97.

22 A. S. Loudon Hamilton, 'Description of The First Century Christian Fellowship' in *The Messenger* (the Journal of the International Union Mission, New York) vol. 2, no. 6, New York June 1923. Thanks are due to Susie Wolfe, Archivist, and the Director of Communications, Calvary Episcopal Church, 315 Shady Avenue, Pittsburgh PA, USA, who made materials available from the Research Collection of Dick B.

23 For example, Brown, *The Oxford Group Movement: Is it of God or Satan*, 42-45, 46-48.

24 Thomson, 'Introduction' in *Evangelism in the Modern World*, 11.

Chapter 4: Parish Minister and Evangelist I

1 Murray, *Freedom to Reform*, 11 and passim.

2 NCL, The John White Papers box 54, paper (n.d.) beginning 'It is said that we have entered on a new age'.

3 Thomson, *The Church in the Open Air,* inside back cover.

4 I was delighted to be given, in 2009, by Rev. David J. Torrance, some of the remains of DP's lantern slide collection, rescued when St Ninian's was closed. Although the lecture notes did not accompany the slides, sufficient numbers of these survive to allow for DP's approach to his subjects to be deduced. Larger collections of slides are held in the D. P. Thomson Archive.

5 The references from *The Dunfermline Press* that follow in this and subsequent paragraphs all come from a book of press-cuttings that DP maintained and that now forms part of the D. P. Thomson Archive.

6 Ferguson, *George MacLeod*, 55-64.

7 'Church News: The Old Testament: Its Dangers for the Child: Blood-Thirsty Stories' in *The Scotsman*, Wednesday 18 October 1933, 14.

8 'The Old Testament and the Sunday School' in *The Scotsman*, Friday 20 October 1933, 11.

9 'Points of View: Letters from Readers / An Attack on the Old Testament' in *The Scotsman,* Saturday 21 October 1933, 15; and *ibid.*, Monday 23 October 1933, 13; and 'The Old Testament: Dr James Kelly on Its Use in Education' *ibid.*, 16.

10 Brown, *The Social History of Religion in Scotland since 1730*, 233-239.

11 So, too, had American evangelist Charles Finney. Drummond, *Charles Grandison Finney*, 113.

12 D. P. Thomson, 'Can England teach Scotland? / The Impressions and Discoveries of a Band of Pilgrims' in *Life & Work* September 1931, 355.

13 'Churches take the gloves off / Stirling's United Drive against Materialism / Fighting Parsons Billet like Soldiers' in *The Stirling Observer*, 17 February 1931, 5.

14 D. P. Thomson, 'The Stirling Campaign: some impressions and reflections' in *The Scots Observer* no. 231, vol. 5, 5 March 1931, 6.

15 Allen, 'The Groups in Oxford' in Crossman (ed), *Oxford and the Groups*, 12-13.

16 Rowlands, *The Oxford Group - a First Century Christian Fellowship,* 14-15.

17 D. P. Thomson, 'Letters to the Editor: Our Readers' Views / Stirling Campaign' in *The Scots Observer: the Churches Weekly*, no. 233, vol. 5: 17 March 1931, 10.

18 A. S. Loudon Hamilton, 'Some Basic Principles of Christian Work' contained in *Letter 4* (August 1928) of the First Century Christian Fellowship. Thanks are due to Susie Wolfe, Archivist, and the Director of Communications, Calvary Episcopal Church, 315 Shady Avenue, Pittsburgh PA, USA, who made this material available from the Research Collection of Dick B.

19 'Church of Scotland / Stirling and District Office-Bearers' Union / Life-Changing Religion' in *The Stirling Observer*, 31 March 1931, 12.

20 Bebbington, 'The Oxford Group' in *Voluntary Religion*, 502.

21 Anon., 'The Group Movement: Is it the key to the longed-for Revival of Religion?' in *Life & Work* November 1932, 442-44; see also George S. Gunn, 'Religious Movements of Today, II: The Oxford Group' in *Life & Work* May 1936, 182-84.

22 Thomson, The Diary of My Life part 8, 2: 'Tuesday 17th July [1923] Here we are at Montrose – well started on our Campaign and there is much to chronicle . . . Splendid retreat – Rossie Farm School – perfect weather – we played football and cricket and bathed – all but me. We had a very profitable discussion on Open Air work and an even more inspiring one on personal dealing.' Cf: *The Call to the Church*, 34: 'The so-called *Oxford Groups* are an attempt to find a satisfaction for this spirit of fellowship and many testify to the benefits they have received.'

23 Frame, *Fire in His Bones*, 11.

24 D. P. Thomson, 'Glassiebarns - Craigluscar, by Dunfermline / A Retreat and Conference Centre for Experiments in Group Fellowship' in *Life & Work* July 1931, 304. Also, D. P. Thomson, 'That Cottage at Craigluscar! / A Year's Experiments in Group Fellowship' in *Life & Work* August 1932, 309-10.

25 Mackenzie, *Preaching the Eternities*, 65.

26 Thomson, The Diary of My Life part 9, 132: 'Thursday 16 April [1931] Phoned Ham at 10.40. Pitcorthlie had brought him – God! Through personal contact with Bob Mackie, and along lines which carried him further away from OG and SSCM methods than ever. So be it."The Varieties of Religious Experience" was William James' happy phrase.'

27 D. P. Thomson Archive, press cuttings book: A.C.McN-C, 'Two books of interest' in *The Strathearn Herald*, 17 November 1951, 2: a review of *The Road to Dunfermline*; Small, *No Uncertain Sound*, Edinburgh 1963, 117.

28 *Daily Light on the Daily Path: a Devotional Textbook for Every Day of the Year, in the Very Words of Scripture, prepared by Jonathan Bagster and Other Members of His Family.* New York, The American Tract Society, *c.* 1875.

29 D. P. Thomson Archive, press cuttings book: D. P. Thomson, 'New Experimental Centre in West Fife', undated cutting from an unnamed magazine.

30 D. P. Thomson, 'A College Contrast / Anglo-Catholic Monastery and Quaker Settlement', in *Life & Work* November 1931, 454-456.

Chapter 5: Acceptance and Rejection

1 Editorial, 'Our views on the Forward Movement', in *The Scots Observer: the Churches Weekly*, no. 215, vol. 5: 6 November 1930, 9.

2 'Letters to the Editor: Our Readers' Views / The Forward Movement', letter subscribed 'Inquirer' in *The Scots Observer: the Churches Weekly*, no. 237, vol. 5: 16 April 1931, 10.

3 Editorial, 'Scotland needs a Preacher', in *The Scots Observer: the Churches Weekly*, no. 253, vol. 5: 30 July 1931, 8.

4 Rev. John McConnachie D.D., 'New Theology needed for the Forward Movement / 1. Theology Yesterday and Today in Scotland,' in *The Scots Observer: the Churches Weekly*, no. 250, vol. 5: 9 July 1931, 9.

5 Rev. J. W. Stevenson, 'The Church Must Tell Scotland / Bridgeton has raised the flag for the Forward Movement,' in *The Scots Observer: the Churches Weekly,* no. 237, vol. 5: 16 April 1931, 16.

6 'The Responsibility of a National Church: The Care of the People,' *The Call to the Church*, 37. The *Call's* statistics derived from those gathered by the Scottish Churches Council in 1927: NLS, MacLeod of Fuinary and Iona Community, acc.

9084.204, Report of the Scottish Churches Council, May 1927 (2nd annual report) '. . . approximately 1,107,000 non-church-going adults, of whom the vast majority are protestant'.

7 This phrase referred to the Scots-Irish and to the Kirk's continuing campaign against the immigration from Ireland of many of the Roman Catholic faith. Lynch, *Scotland: A New History*, 438.

8 Butler, 'Scripture Union' in *DSCHT*, 763.

9 Dunnett, *The Church in Changing Scotland*, 156-161.

10 Dunnett, *The Church in Changing Scotland*, 162-63.

11 Dunnett, *The Church in Changing Scotland*, 164.

12 In his *The Church on the Sands*, 2, DP dated the beginning of the Kirk's Summer Seaside work from 1934. This was true only of activities organised *centrally* by the *post-Union* Kirk: two significant qualifications, and somewhat self-serving.

13 'What Children think of Mr Grieve's services' in *The Record of the Home and Foreign Mission Work of the United Free Church of Scotland*, September 1922, number 261, 290-91. This article was based on a month of Seaside Mission at Saltcoats during 1922.

14 'King's Park v. Queen of the South / "Observer" Cartoonist's Impressions' in *The Stirling Observer* 24 February 1931, 12; and accompanying photograph, 'Ministers at Forthbank Park'.

15 For a fine account of the mission at North Berwick: Rev. J. G. Grant Fleming, 'North Berwick Seaside Mission' in *Life & Work* October 1934, 410-412.

16 'Through the Camera / Glimpses of the Church's Life and Work / Some Summer Activities' in *Life & Work*, September 1937, 352-53.

17 D. P. Thomson, 'Stood out as a Leader' in A. Macdonald (ed.) *A Fraction of His Image*, 28.

18 Sir James F. Simpson, Kt., 'The Church in the Open / Seaside Services at Ayr, Prestwick, and Troon' in *Life & Work* October 1936, 388-89.

19 'Evangelistic Campaigns / Summer Seaside Missions' in *The Scotsman*, 26 April 1937, 12. I. Mackenzie, 'Archie Craig' in N. Blackie (ed.), *A Time for Trumpets*, 29-38.

20 'Church News / Seaside Missions / Church Enterprise in Scotland / August Programme / Younger Ministers and Students' in *The Scotsman*, 3 August 1936, 10.

21 Charles E. Kirsch, 'The International Team of the Church of Scotland Seaside Mission' in *Life & Work* October 1938, 422-23.

22 'Edinburgh Students at St Ninian's, Lassodie' in *The Scotsman,* 22 June 1935, 20.

23 Doyle, 'Introductory Memoir', 8.

24 J[ohn] H[all], 'Home Mission Work: Evangelism the duty of the church' in *Life & Work* February 1933, 72-3.

25 Rev. John Hall, 'Religious Movements of Today: VII: The Revival of Evangelism' in *Life & Work* November 1936, 421-22.

26 Rev. John Hall, 'Another King' in *Life & Work* December 1938, 497.

27 R. J. Drummond, 'God's Call to the People of Scotland: A Summons to His Church' in *Life & Work* April 1937, 137-138.

28 Dunnett, *The Church in Changing Scotland*, 16-17.

29 *Ibid.,* 17-18.

30 Ferguson, *George MacLeod*, xv for George's genealogy, and *ibid.*, 3-16.

31 Rev. George F. MacLeod, 'The Churchless Million: I - The Advantages of the Parish System' in *Life & Work* January 1936, 5-7; 'The Churchless Million: II - An experiment in the application of the Parish System' *ibid.* February 1936, 51-53; 'The Churchless Million: III - Suggested adaptation of the Parish System' *ibid.* March 1936, 94-97.

32 *Ecumenical Studies: Evangelism in Scotland*, Geneva, 31.

33 Ferguson, *George MacLeod*, 152-55.

34 'New Cambuslang Minister' and 'New Warden for St Ninian's, Lassodie' in *The Scotsman*, 1 and 17 February 1939, pages 8 and 7 respectively.

Chapter 6: Parish Minister and Evangelist II

1 Doyle, 'Introductory Memoir', 8.

2 Bardgett, 'Secession, Disruption and Reunion, 1790-1929', in *Two Millennia of Church and Community in Orkney*, 101-128.

3 An edited volume of his own sermons, *Men Christ Wants,* also initially published by Marshall, Morgan and Scott in 1937, was sufficiently successful to merit a reprint in 1952 in abridged form by the Glasgow publisher Pickering & Inglis, attracting international interest.

4 NLS, MacLeod of Fuinary and Iona Community, acc. 9084.194; 9084.59, 9084.60.

5 NLS, MacLeod of Fuinary and Iona Community, acc. 9084.203 and 347. See also G. F. MacLeod, 'Parish Missions in Scotland' in *Coracle: The Journal Of The Iona Community*, no.17 (November 1949), 11-12; W. C. V. Smith, 'Iona Works In Glasgow: An Assessment of Four Years of Parish Mission in St. Margaret's, Polmadie, Glasgow, By its Minister' in *Coracle* no. 17 (November 1949), 17-19.

6 He did not deny the experience was possible. D. P. Thomson, The Diary of My Life part 26: 'Friday 23 February 1956 . . . We went on to Ardnamurchan Point & the Lighthouse, where I found the Keeper to be a convert, disciple and professed admirer of George MacLeod, [who] . . . led him from darkness to light and from futility to Christ.'

7 NLS, MacLeod of Fuinary and Iona Community, acc. 9084.194, leaflet 'Addressed to the Household of the Faith in Garrowhill.'

8 NLS, MacLeod of Fuinary and Iona Community, acc. 9084.59, letter from W. A. Smellie to George MacLeod, 11 July 1941.

9 NLS, MacLeod of Fuinary and Iona Community, acc. 9084.268, document entitled: 'The Iona Community: Names of those who attended the two conferences, 12th to 26th August 1941.'

10 The D. P. Thomson Archive, Minute Book of the Church of Scotland Fellowship in Evangelism, 1, Monday 23rd March 1942 at 11.30am.

11 In *The Church on the Sands*, 2-3, DP stated 'The outbreak of war in 1939 almost brought this work to a standstill . . . In 1946, after an interval of seven years, a fresh start was made.' This was a misleading simplification. What ceased in 1939 and restarted in 1946 was the *central direction* of seaside missions.

Chapter 7: The New Evangelism

1 Baillie, *Invitation to Pilgrimage*, 106.

2 'Report of the Commission for the Interpretation of the God's Will in the Present Crisis,' *GA 1941,* 705-718; citation, 707. Reporting annually between 1941 and 1945, the Commission's findings were published by the SCM Press under the titles *God's Will for our Time*, *The Church Faces the Future*, and *Home, Community and Church*; and finally, edited, as a single book, *God's Will for Church and Nation.*

3 'Report of the Committee on Survey of the Parochial System,' *GA 1946*, 636 for these three quotations, summarising and recommending Presbytery responses.

4 'Preaching apart from Public Worship' in 'Report of the Commission for the Interpretation of the God's Will in the Present Crisis,' *GA 1943,* 454-55; citation, 454.

5 The Joint Committee on Evangelism, *Into All The World: A Statement on Evangelism*, 13.

6 These were: (1) V. C. Alexander, *What the Church Expects of the Church Member;* (2) E. T. Vernon, *The Practical Witness of a Christian*; (3) Prof. J. G. Riddell, *Your Parish Needs You*; (4) Nevile Davidson, *The Parish Church.*

7 Morton, *Evangelism in Scotland Today*: a shorter pamphlet preceded by the booklet, *Ecumenical Studies: Evangelism in Scotland.*

8 D. Baillie, 'The Place of The Iona Community' in *Coracle* issue 19: January 1951, 8-11. *Emphasis* added.

9 Morton, *Missionary Principles for the Home Front*, 1.

10 G. F. MacLeod, 'A Message Of Friendship: An Account of the Principles of a Parish Mission' in *The Coracle: the Journal of the Iona Community*, combined issues 20 & 21, July 1951, 11.

11 Morton, *Missionary Principles for the Home Front*, 10. Cf T. Allan, 'The Road

Ahead' in T. Allan (ed.), *Crusade in Scotland ... Billy Graham*, 120-123.

12 NLS, Acc. 9084, MacLeod of Fuinary and Iona Community, 640, Minutes of the Experimental Parishes Committee, 16/6/1947 – 12/1/1950: Meeting held in Community House 18 December 1947.

13 Allan (ed.), *Crusade in Scotland ... Billy Graham*, 122.

14 Highet, *The Scottish Churches*, 72-73.

15 Still, *Dying to Live*, 114-119.

16 'Throughout Our Churches' column in *Stedfast,* March 1956, 15.

17 NAS, CH2/121/64, Presbytery of Edinburgh Minutes 1950-1952 (6 November 1951), 367: 'Reference from Edinburgh Churches' Committee – Proposed Evangelistic Campaign.'

18 J. Highet, 'The Churches' in *The Third Statistical Account of Scotland: The City of Glasgow*, 738.

19 NLS, Acc. 9084, MacLeod of Fuinary and Iona Community, 197, pamphlet: 'Glasgow for Christ: GCC – 1950 - On Congregational and Commando Lines, Bulletin no 2, February 1950.'

20 NLS, Acc. 9084, MacLeod of Fuinary and Iona Community, 347, folder 'Glasgow Churches' Campaign': paper marked '1950, Crieff.' All the citations in this paragraph are from this paper.

21 Highet, 'The Churches' in *Glasgow*, 738.

22 Falconer, *Message, Media, Mission*, 85-6.

23 The Tom Allan Archive contains a press-cutting of the 1952 published schedule with Action Points.

24 Dinwiddie, *Religion by Radio*, 102.

25 Highet, *The Scottish Churches*, 70.

26 NLS, MacLeod of Fuinary and Iona Community, acc. 9084.203, bundle of papers headed: 'Committee on Relations of Home Board to Iona Community,' paper 'Panel Relationship to the Home Board, December 1946.' These suggestions were never put into effect, but the paper shows George MacLeod's appreciation of DP's position as 1946 moved to 1947. At the October 2007 meeting of the Scottish Church History Society I heard it suggested that George personally supported DP's recall to work with the Home Board.

27 Ferguson, *George MacLeod,* 109-110, 131, 194.

28 Personal communication from Margaret R. Brehaut, née Lovell, September 2008.

29 Cited Ferguson, *George MacLeod*, 195.

30 T. R. Morton, 'The House Church: The Next Step? Or A First Step?' in *Coracle* (issue 28, March 1956), 1-8.

31 *Ecumenical Studies: Evangelism in Scotland*, 16.

Chapter 8: D. P. Thomson, Evangelist

1 Allan (ed.), *Crusade in Scotland . . . Billy Graham*, 120.

2 Barclay, *Evangelicalism in Britain*, 13.

3 Thomson, *Men Christ Wants*, 101-2: section 'Your eternal destiny depends on what you do with Christ.' See also: R. Law, as substantially abridged by D. P. Thomson, *Death and the Life Beyond*, 7, where the discussion, based on the resurrection of Christ, dealt with the spiritual body and the heavenly world, life and society beyond death and, refusing to use the word 'hell,' spoke briefly of death without Christ as 'a curse – the uttermost of all curses; an evil – the sum of all evils – a penalty and a doom – the sum and end of all penalty and all doom.'

4 See especially the section 'Of what will we wish to speak?' with its list of 20 points of doctrine, with supporting texts.

5 Barclay, *Evangelicalism in Britain*, 11-12.

6 See the discussion in N. T. Wright, *Evangelical Anglican Identity: the connection between Bible, Gospel and Church*, Latimer Studies 8, Oxford 1980, though related to specific issues within the Church of England.

7 *The Forfar Dispatch*, volume 1953-1956, Thursday 8 October 1953, 2.

Chapter 9: Family Matters and Paisley Mid-Century

1 D. P. Thomson Archive, press cuttings: book 'Mid-Century Campaign in Paisley / Area no. 4 / Programme of Events for the guidance of Holy Trinity Members.'

2 Thomson, *We Saw the Church in Action* (1954); *Harnessing the Lay Forces of the Church* (1958) and *Aspects of Evangelism* (1968).

3 D. P. Thomson Archive, press cuttings book: a column or letter printed as 'The Study Chimney Corner' and addressed 'My Dear Women Friends;' presumably from a parish newsletter or Supplement to *Life & Work*.

4 D. P. Thomson Archive, press cuttings book: Letter by Rev. Sydney C. Still, *St James's Church, Paisley: Quarterly Review, no. 327, December-March 1950-51.*

5 *Ecumenical Studies: Evangelism in Scotland*, 35.

6 *Ecumenical Studies: Evangelism in Scotland*, 34.

7 NAS: CH3/1487/11, Orr Square Church of Scotland Kirk Session Minutes 1936-1968, unpaged, 19 March to 10 December 1950.

8 D. P. Thomson Archive, press cuttings book: Rev. Stanley Andrews, 'Adventure in Evangelism, Paisley Churches Mid-Century Campaign' marked 'Christian World, 10 /5/ 51.'

Chapter 10: The West Fife, Kirkcaldy and Strathmore Campaigns

1 Bardgett, *Devoted Service Rendered*, 155-162.

2 Dunnett, *The Church in Changing Scotland*, 124.

3 'Report of the Commission on Communism,' *GA 1951,* 649-650.

4 D. P. Thomson Archive, 'Dunfermline Training School' in press-cutting book 41. Reconstructed from articles entitled 'Threat to Church by Communism' in *Evening Times* 8 August 1951, and 'Minister says: Too Many Playing at Religion' in *Cowdenbeath Advertiser & Kelty News,* 8 August 1951.

5 D. P. Thomson Archive, pamphlet retained in book of press-cuttings: *The Second Dunfermline Summer Training School - Programme Handbook.*

6 'A Word about the Author' in Frame, *Fire in His Bones*, 47.

7 D. P. Thomson Archive, press-cutting book: 'Local Churches Campaign Arouses Tremendous Interest' in the *Cowdenbeath Advertiser & Kelty News*, 7 December 1951.

8 D. P. Thomson Archive, press-cutting book: Tom Allan, 'Scottish Commentary: Evangelism in West Fife' in *The British Weekly* 27 December 1951.

9 *Ecumenical Studies: Evangelism in Scotland*, 22.

10 Tom Allan, 'Scottish Commentary: Evangelism in West Fife,' *op. cit.* citing 'Mr Thomson's own words.'

11 D. P. Thomson Archive, press-cutting book, contains a number of un-attributed cuttings related to the 'Heckling Meeting.'

12 *Ecumenical Studies: Evangelism in Scotland*, 33-34.

13 Montrose Library, *Montrose Review and Angus & Kincardineshire Advertiser*. For early coverage of the Campaign: 'Recall to the Church / Montrose Evangelistic Campaign / Visits to Homes, Factories and Clubs,' 17 April 1952, 5; 'Montrose Evangelical Campaign / Volunteer workers called for,' 24 April 1952, 5; 'Good start to Evangelical Campaign / 100 voluntary helpers from Montrose,' 15 May 1952, 5; 'Round the Town / Back to the Church!' 29 May 1952, 4. For the induction of Rev. A. Fraser: 'Welcome to new minister of St John's / Importance of well-filled pulpit, pews and plate,' 5 June 1952, 4. For the debate on Christianity: column 'Readers Views' in 12 June 1952, 7; 19 June 1952, 7; 26 June 1952, 7; 3 July 1952, 7; 10 July 1952, 7.

14 Montrose Library, 'Readers Views / A Heathen Replies' in *Montrose Review and Angus & Kincardineshire Advertiser*, 2 October 1952, 7.

15 Montrose Library, 'Readers Views / Campaigners There' in *Montrose Review and Angus & Kincardineshire Advertiser*, 9 October 1952, 7.

16 Montrose Library, 'Readers Views / Questions Unanswered' in *Montrose Review and Angus & Kincardineshire Advertiser*, 9 October 1952, 7.

17 Thomson, *We Saw the Church in Action!*, 48-50, citing 'Campaign brings Record Church Attendances / 3,800 Worshippers on Sunday' in *Montrose Review and Angus & Kincardineshire Advertiser*, 30 October 1952, 5.

18 'Round the Town / Back to Church' in *Montrose Review and Angus & Kincardineshire Advertiser*, 30 October 1952, 4.

19 *Ecumenical Studies: Evangelism in Scotland*, 32-33.

20 'Campaign brings Record Church Attendances / 3,800 Worshippers on Sunday' in *Montrose Review and Angus & Kincardineshire Advertiser*, 30 October 1952, 5.

21 The Tom Allan Archive, ms Minutebook of United Christian Witness, 24: 27 October 1951.

22 *Ecumenical Studies: Evangelism in Scotland*, 45.

23 Bisset, *The Kirk and her Scotland*, 9.

Chapter 11: D. P. Thomson and *Tell Scotland* – Movement and Crusade

1 The Tom Allan Archive contains an envelope of sheets of music with this text.

2 1950 was seen as the Church of Scotland's coming of age, 21 years after the Union. 'Coming of age of Church of Scotland' in *The Scotsman*, 1 June 1950, 5.

3 F. D. Bardgett, '*Tell Scotland*: Failure and Success' in *RSCHS* 2008, 105-154.

4 Dinwiddie, *Religion by Radio*, 102.

5 Small, *Growing Together*, 55-56, 59.

6 CSCNWW, Tell Scotland Minutes 1952-1962, Notes of the Steering Panel (9 September 1953), 1-2.

7 NLS, Acc. 9084, MacLeod of Fuinary and Iona Community, 347, folder 'Glasgow Churches' Campaign': paper marked '1950, Crieff.' Compare, Allan, *The Face of My Parish*, (1984), 98-117.

8 T. C. Berg, 'Proclaiming Together?' in *Religion and American Culture*, vol. 5, no 1 (winter 1995), 52; Coalter, 'Presbyterian Evangelism, a case of parallel allegiances diverging' in *The Diversity of Discipleship*, 41-46; Wood, *Like a Mighty Army*, 25-35; S. Thomson, *Church Standing Tall*, 42-47.

9 Storrar to my mind over-emphasises Allan's originality, though not his leadership, as a missionary thinker. Storrar, 'A tale of two paradigms: mission in Scotland from 1946' in *Death or Glory*, 60-65.

10 Forsyth, Edinburgh (2010) dissertation, 'To *rescue the fallen*: the sources, content and context of the missiology of Tom Allan (1916-1965)' is an able and illuminating discussion of Allan's missiology in the light of the recently available Tom Allan Archive and other contemporary resources.

11 Falconer, *The Kilt Under My Cassock*, 76-77.

12 Morton, *Evangelism in Scotland Today*, 8; cited Shannon, *Tom Allan in a Nutshell*, 10.

13 See editorial, *The British Weekly (Scottish edition)*, 30 October 1952, 1-3 and then articles in *ibid.* 6, 13, 20 and 27 November 1952; 11, 18 and 25 December 1952 and 1, 8, 15 and 22 January 1953. These articles were re-edited and republished as Allan, *The Face of My Parish*.

14 Shannon, *Tom Allan in a Nutshell*, 6-7.

15 The D. P. Thomson Archive, Press-cuttings book, 60-67. This collection of press-cuttings was the basis of the chapter 'Along the Moray Firth' in Thomson, *We Saw the Church in Action!*, 56-64.

16 Presumably the occasion when Allan had to catch a train to Wick! Ferguson, *George MacLeod*, 271-2.

17 Ian Doyle's 'Tell Scotland' chorus/hymn, with which this chapter is headed, sought to answer just this question.

18 *Rev. Tom Allan in conversation with Rev Henry B. Meikle,* recording held at William Smith Morton Library.

19 Allan, *Agent of Mission*, 21.

20 Colquhoun, *Harringay Story: The London Crusade 1954.*

21 Ferguson, *George MacLeod*, 270-276.

22 NLS Acc. 9084, MacLeod of Fuinary and Iona Community: folder 254, *Tell Scotland* Campaign 1953-9; paper 'Should Billy Graham *Tell Scotland*?'

23 NLS Acc. 9084, MacLeod of Fuinary and Iona Community: folder 533, Billy Graham 1955; article 'Billy Graham' in *Ariel,* June 1955, 19-23.

24 George F. MacLeod, 'An aid to personal commitment: the Iona Act of Belief' in *Life & Work* January 1956, 9-10 and as an Iona Community Publishing Department pamphlet, Glasgow (no date).

25 Coffey, *God's Conman*, 67, 75, 109-110; Colin Craig, 'More than Singing Choruses' in *The British Weekly (Scottish edition)* 21 June 1956, 10 and subsequent exchanges with Currie, *ibid.* 28 June 1956, 10; 5 July 1956, 10; 12 July 1956, 10.

26 The Tom Allan Archive, box 1, collection of articles from *Rally* magazine: T. Allan, 'Evangelism in the United States' in *Rally* September 1956, 4.

27 The Tom Allan Archive, box 1, collection of articles from *Rally* magazine: printed leaflet, T. Allan, 'The *Tell Scotland* Movement and Billy Graham: a discussion of the issues.'

28 In his context in the United States, Graham was for a time a bridge between the mainline denominations and the smaller more fundamentalist evangelical groups. Berg, 'Proclaiming Together?' 54.

29 Editorial by T. R. Morton, 'Iona 1954' in *Coracle*, no 25, October 1954, 3.

30 NLS Acc. 9084, MacLeod of Fuinary and Iona Community: folder 340, Meetings Files: Minutes and Reports of Community Meetings and Related Papers 1942-85: 'Minute of Meeting of the Executive of the Iona Community held in Community House, Glasgow on Thursday 4 October 1957.' James Maitland convened the Community's Working Group on Evangelism, one of four such groups, the others being Political, Liturgical and Divine Healing.

31 T. Allan, 'Scotland hears Billy Graham' in Allan (ed.), *Crusade in Scotland - Billy Graham*, 8.

32 Thomson, *Dr Billy Graham and the Pattern of Modern Evangelism,* 18.

33 F. D. Bardgett, '*Tell Scotland*: Failure and Success' in *RSCHS* 2008, 105-154.

34 NLS, Acc. 9084, MacLeod of Fuinary and Iona Community, 347, folder 'Glasgow Churches' Campaign': paper marked '1950, Crieff.'

35 'Address by the Moderator Rev David W. Roy' in *Stedfast* July 1956, 2, in the section – 'Our work and witness / *Tell Scotland*.'

36 Thomson, *West Highland Adventure*, 1; cf, CSCNWW, Tell Scotland file, Minutes of Meeting of Tell Scotland Steering Panel held on Tuesday 13th September 1955.

37 For the Orkney story: F. D. Bardgett, 'D. P. Thomson and the Orkney Expedition - a *Tell Scotland* case study' in RSCHS (2010, 185-228).

38 DP's introduction to the Shetland Campaign was printed in '*Tell Scotland* Campaign in Shetland' in *The Shetland Times*, Lerwick, 31 May 1957, 3. Much of the story of this campaign was recounted by *The Shetland Times* as the campaign progressed.

39 The Orkney Archives: OCR 4/29, Presbytery of Orkney Minutes 1949-61, annual reports of Persons and Agencies, as minuted pp.26, 47, 66, 89, 124, 154, 189, 220, 247, 275.

40 C. Craig, "An answer to an unanswered question" in *The British Weekly (Scottish edition)* 14 June 1956, 10. See F. D. Bardgett, 'D. P. Thomson and the Orkney Expedition - a *Tell Scotland* case study' in RSCHS (2010, 210-26).

41 F. D. Bardgett, *Tell Scotland*: Failure and Success' in *RSCHS* 2008, 145-146.

42 Those disappointed by Allan's departure from *Tell Scotland* could place a negative interpretation on his drive to lead. Thomson, The Diary of My Life part 26: 93-94, 'Wednesday 8 February 1956 . . . Yesterday . . . I was met by Ian MacTaggart and we repaired to Wendy's where we spent a full hour. ... He said Tom Allan was his biggest headache and was depressed by both his egocentricism and his inconsistency — there are, Ronnie Falconer had told him, 2 Tom Allans. There are at least 4 D. P. Thomsons!'

43 The Tom Allan Archives retain a copy of the minute of Executive Committee of the Glasgow Central Churches Campaign, 4 December 1958.

44 CSCNWW, Paper, 'Notes on Wiston Lodge Conference of *Tell Scotland* Conveners, May 7th - 9th, 1958'.

45 'Scottish Table Talk / Architects of Mission' in *The British Weekly,* 3 September 1959, 3.

46 Editorial, 'Let's Stop The Sniping' in *Life & Work* July 1956, 165.

47 Ferguson, *George MacLeod,* 327-330.

48 Storrar, 'A tale of two paradigms' in *Death or Glory*, 54-60 & 65-69.

49 'Report of the [*ad hoc*] Committee on Adult Religious Education,' *GA* 1953, 556.

50 Sissons, *The Social Significance of Church Membership in the Burgh of Falkirk*, 107-09 has much to suggest about the failure of evangelism in the era of *Tell Scotland.*

51 A spin-off from the Commission on Communism, the Church of Scotland General Assembly's *ad hoc* Committee on Adult Religious Education (its first secretary, T. Ralph Morton) reported in 1953 and 1954; a Commission on Adult Christian Education began reporting in 1955: *GA 1953*, 553; *GA 1954*, 567; *GA 1955*, 599.

Chapter 12: The Final Years

1 World Council of Churches, Department on the Laity, *Signs of Renewal: the life of the lay institute in Europe*, Geneva 1957.

2 'It is happening elsewhere' in *Life & Work* September 1957, 216.

3 'J.M.', 'Scottish Laymen's Centre: Community House, Glasgow' in *Life & Work* September 1957, 228.

4 Fraser, *Ecumenical Adventure: a Dunblane Initiative*, 2.

5 'Dunblane: a place of training?' in *Life & Work* November 1957, 269.

6 'Scots Laymen will train here' in *Life & Work* December 1958, 300.

7 Keiser, Christian Engagement with the Secular World, 47.

8 'Scots Laymen will train here' in *Life & Work* December 1958, 300.

9 So DP claimed in *21 Topics for Discussion Groups*, inside front cover; and 'from 61 different countries,' too.

10 *Life and Work at St Ninian's, Crieff*, 6-7.

11 D. P. Thomson Archive, leaflet *St Ninian's Training Centre, Crieff.*

12 Among the reference books recommended were Read's *The Christian Faith* [1955] and Hunter's *Introducing the New Testament* [1945 & 1957].

13 D. P. Thomson Archive, leaflet *St Ninian's Training Centre, Crieff.*

14 Storrar, 'A Tale of Two Paradigms' in *Death or Glory*, 59.

15 Frame, *Fire in His Bones*, 30.

16 Is it fair to say that there was something Churchillian about DP's character? Both shared a sense of personal destiny and an intense, workaholic association with a cause, though (unlike Winston's) DP's earlier self-belief was subverted in maturity by his Christian faith. Both, also, could be described as in some ways childlike, and both inspired a similar loyalty even from those they bullied. See Holmes, *In the footsteps of Churchill* under index for 'character'.

17 Doyle, 'Introductory Memoir' in *Women of the Scottish Church*, 11.

18 Thomson, The Diary of My Life part 21, Sunday 4 October 1953.

19 Six of these carefully prepared courses were published: *New Testament Conversions; Epistle to the Philippians; Parables of Jesus; The Ten Commandments. A question course for Preachers, Teachers, Bible Students and Bible Study Groups; The Gospel of St John; The Epistle to the Romans chapters 12 to 16.*

20 Happy to describe himself as a conservative evangelical, Allan explained what he meant by this definition in an interview [with Kenneth Bagnell, printed 15 March 1962, an off-cut retained in the Tom Allan Archives from an unattributed magazine]: 'It means I stand by certain great fundamentals – the deity of Christ, the substitutionary atonement, the physical resurrection of Christ, the personal return of Our Lord. As Christ came in Bethlehem, he will come again. I don't know how, but he will come again.' 'And I believe,' he said, 'in the virgin birth, though I don't insist that it is one of the fundamentals. And I believe finally in the authority of the Word of God.'

21 In the interests of transparency I should add that, as an executive of the then Board of National Mission, I was intimately involved in clerking one of the reviews that led to this decision, a complex of events the stress of which hastened my early retirement.

22 D. P. Thomson, 'A Student's Impressions' in *The Record of the Home and Foreign Mission Work of the United Free Church of Scotland*, February 1922, number 254, 43-44. See section 'The Glasgow Students Evangelistic Union' in chapter 'Evangelist In Training: III - With The Students, 1922-1928' above.

23 Thomson, *We Saw the Church in Action*, inside front cover: 'To the daily and weekly press of Scotland, national as well as provincial, and to those who represent the Church in the British Broadcasting Corporation north of the Tweed, I wish to pay ungrudging tribute. But for the interest, friendliness and helpfulness shown us – by proprietor, editor, reporter and representative – *it would have been impossible for us to have carried through what we did*. In no other country, I believe, would cooperation on the same scale or of the same quality have been available. This is one of the many happy things we who serve the church in Scotland are privileged to enjoy, even in these dark and difficult days.' *Emphasis added.* And he thought 1954 was a 'dark and difficult' time!

24 CSCNWW, I. MacTaggart, 'Reflections on Lay Initiative in the Church' in file: Department of Mission, minutes 1-10 and Papers re *Tell Scotland* leading to Dept. of Mission 1959-67. F. D. Bardgett, 'D. P. Thomson and the Orkney Expedition – a *Tell Scotland* case study' in RSCHS 2010, 222-3.

25 S. Thomson, *Church Standing Tall*, 50.

26 Wood, 'Leadership Profile of Church Extension Ministers in the Church of Scotland 1945-1965.' See appendix II nos. 1102, 1129, 1137 for particular examples of the general point.

Bibliographical Note

1 Thomson, *Dr Billy Graham and the Pattern of Modern Evangelism*, inside front cover.

2 Doyle, 'Introductory Memoir', 11.

3 A collection of press-cuttings is retained in the D. P. Thomson Archive.

4 Frame, *Fire in His Bones*, 39, singles out the historical pamphlets for praise.

D. P. THOMSON – A BIBLIOGRAPHICAL NOTE

In 1966,[1] D. P. Thomson claimed that his 'publications number over 100, and their circulation has passed the million mark.' The list below supports this claim, though it includes books and pamphlets edited and/or published by DP as well as those written entirely by him, and also collections of previously-published pamphlets rebound in hard covers with nothing additional beyond a new title. I have been unable to verify *The Great Alternative*, a tract mentioned in his Sixth Diary, 22nd October 1921, as being accepted for publication. I have not included in this Bibliography the many articles DP wrote that were published by magazines like *Life & Work* or to the daily and weekly press.

In his 'Introductory Memoir' to DP, Ian Doyle wrote:[2]

> His written work was perhaps less effective than it would have been had he not been his own publisher. The topics he sometimes chose and the style he developed would have benefited from the criticisms of a helpful publisher. Instead of producing so many pamphlets and leaflets he might have concentrated on a major study that his experience could well have provided. But these booklets were produced as aids, very effective aids, to evangelistic work he was doing at the time. This pragmatic approach was very typical of DP.

In fact DP did, on occasion, publish through recognised companies – Marshall, Morgan & Scott; Pickering & Inglis – and a few of his books obtained international sales. His own early publishing enterprise, Thomson & Cowan, won critical recognition for the *Handbooks of Modern Evangelism*.[3] The shortage of paper during the Second World War was among other factors that saw the end of DP's Lassodie Press. Thereafter, as Ian Doyle wrote, although he had been busy for some time on what he hoped would be his 'magnum opus', *Women of the Scottish Church*, the priority DP gave to active evangelism meant that many of his projected titles were either delayed or came to nothing.

DP's most successful pamphlets were associated with the key period of 1954-6: those on visitation evangelism, written for the All-Scotland Crusade and *Tell Scotland*.[4] 'What sales these books are having!' DP recorded in June 1955. By October he was writing:

> Less than a fortnight ago I put through the third printing of 'Two by Two' and 'Guidance.' Both are nearly finished and next weekend at the latest we will have to print again. It is quite astonishing – I have never known anything like it since 'Eric Liddell.'

That extract from his Diary also serves as a reminder of DP's three biographical publications about Eric Liddell, the Scottish Olympic gold-medallist and missionary to China. The 4th edition of the 1946 pamphlet *Eric Liddell: The Making of an Athlete and the Training of a Missionary*, brought its printing total to 55,000. DP's literary executors (a Board of the Church of Scotland), exploiting the success of the 1981 film *Chariots of Fire,* were able to sell to Hollywood the film and other rights to *Eric Liddell*'s successors, a full-length paperback (1970) and hardback (1971) – the contract was a tribute that would have delighted DP!

D. P. Thomson: *The Diary of My Life* (manuscripts)

Part 1	16/3/13	to	31/7/14
2	31/7/14		26/6/15
3	1/8/15		24/11/15
4	9/2/16		25/5/19
5	30/5/19		12/11/20
6	13/11/20		6/3/22
7	13/3/22		7/7/23
8	7/7/23		7/6/24
GAP			
9	16/8/30		15/8/31
GAP			
10	3/1/41		22/6/43
[11 missing]			
12	17/12/43		2/9/44
13	6/9/44		28/3/45
14	1/4/45		3/3/46
[15 missing]			
16	28/4/47		18/1/48
17	22/1/48		10/6/50
18	13/6/50		19/4/51
19	20/4/51		28/7/52
20	30/7/52		29/3/53
21	30/3/53		13/11/53

22	15/11/53	12/2/54
23	12/2/54	5/9/54
24	7/9/54	27/3/55
25	9/4/55	27/9/55
26	28/9/55	12/5/56
27	13/5/56	25/2/57
28	27/2/57	12/3/59

D. P. Thomson: List of Printed Publications

This list does not record the order within each year that items were published. Because DP very often self-published, he regularly omitted the publication data now standard.

----

* 'Two University Men' (ed.), *Evangelism in the Modern World / The Handbooks of Modern Evangelism*, Thomson & Cowan: Glasgow, London and New York 1924. Includes, by the Editors, 'Introduction'.

* 'Two University Men' (ed.), *Modern Evangelistic Movements / The Handbooks of Modern Evangelism*, Thomson & Cowan: Glasgow, London and New York 1924. Includes, by the Editors, 'Introduction'.

* 'Two University Men' (ed.), *Winning the Children for Christ / The Handbooks of Modern Evangelism*, Thomson & Cowan: Glasgow, London and New York 1924. Includes: by D. P. Thomson: 'The case for evangelistic meetings for children' and 'The conduct of Children's meetings'; by 'One of the Editors', 'The fruits of evangelistic work among children'; and, by 'The Editors', 'Introduction'.

* 'Two University Men' (ed.), *The Modern Evangelistic Address / The Handbooks of Modern Evangelism*, Thomson & Cowan: Glasgow, London and New York 1924. Includes, by 'The Editors', 'Introduction'.

---

* **Note**: By 1937 *Men Christ Wants* attributed *The Handbooks of Modern Evangelism* to D. P. Thomson 'in collaboration with R. W. M. Thomson, *Two University Men*.'

D. P. Thomson (ed.), *The Scottish Pulpit / Sermons by representative Scottish preachers*, Thomson & Cowan: Glasgow, London and New York 1924.

D. P. Thomson (ed., with James Kelly and Carey Bonner), *The Sunday School in the Modern World,* Thomson & Cowan: Glasgow, London and New York 1924.

Hubert L. Simpson and D. P. Thomson (ed.), *United Free Church Sermons*, Thomson & Cowan: Glasgow, London and New York 1924. Includes 'Foreword' by D. S. Cairns.

Newton H. Marshall, *Conversion or The New Birth*, 1909 and republished Thomson & Cowan: Glasgow, London and New York 1924

David C. Mitchell, *The Nonsense of Neutrality and other sermons from a city pulpit,* Thomson & Cowan, Glasgow, London and New York 1924

James Sommerville Smith, *Miller of Ruchill: the story of a great achievement*, Thomson & Cowan, Glasgow, London and New York 1925; with, by D. P. Thomson, an 'Introductory Chapter'.

D. P. Thomson (ed., assisted by Daniel Patterson and others), *Scottish Churches' Handbook*, Lassodie Press, Dunfermline / Edinburgh / London 1933.

Alexander Hetherwick, *The Romance of Blantyre: How Livingstone's Dream came True*, Lassodie Press, Dunfermline, ?after 1933.

William McMillan, *The worship of the Scottish reformed church, 1550-1638*, Lassodie Press, Dunfermline, ?after 1933.

D. P. Thomson (ed.), *How I found Christ. Personal narratives of conversion*, Marshall, Morgan & Scott, London 1937.

D. P. Thomson, *Men Christ Wants. Evangelistic Addresses,* Marshall, Morgan & Scott, London 1937; various international editions, some in translation, followed; also reprinted, Pickering & Inglis, Glasgow 1952.

D. P. Thomson (ed.), *Scottish pulpit / sermons by representative Scottish preachers*, Lassodie Press, Dunfermline & London 1937.

D. P. Thomson (ed.), *Professor as preacher / sermons by Scottish theological professors*, Lassodie Press, Dunfermline & London 1939.

D. P. Thomson (ed.), *Women in the pulpit. Sermons and addresses by representative women preachers,* Lassodie Press, Dunfermline & London 1944.

D. P. Thomson, *Two Scotsmen See Jamaica; An Account Of A Three Months' Missionary And Travel Tour In The 'Isle Of Beauty And Romance' In The Winter Of 1937-8, In The Form Of Letters To A Correspondent At Home*, published as bound typed sheets, Cambuslang 1945, for the Cambuslang: Trinity Service Personnel Committee.

D. P. Thomson (ed.), *Letters To The Manse From Members And Adherent Of Trinity Church, Cambuslang, On Service With The Navy, The Army, The Air Forces, The WMS The ATS, The WAAF, The Mercantile Marine, The Land Army And The Nursing Services 1939-1945*, a duplicated and stapled typescript c.1945, published by the Service Personnel Committee of Trinity Church, Cambuslang, on behalf of its funds.

D. P. Thomson, *Eric Liddell: The Making Of An Athlete And The Training Of A Missionary*, for the Eric Liddell Memorial Committee, Glasgow 1945.

D. P. Thomson, *Alexander Waugh: An Earlston Grammar School Boy*, Galashiels, for the Melrose Presbytery Campaign Fund 1946; rebound in *Border Booklets.*

D. P. Thomson, *James Guthrie: The Covenanting Minister Of Lauder And Stirling*, Galashiels, for the Melrose Presbytery Campaign Fund 1946; rebound in *Ministers and Ministers' Wives* and in *Border Booklets.*

D. P. Thomson, *Lad From Torwoodlee, – The Romantic Story Of Principal John Lee Of Edinburgh University*, for the Melrose Presbytery Campaign Fund 1946; rebound in *Ministers and Ministers' Wives* and in *Border Booklets.*

D. P. Thomson, *Scotland's First Deaconess – Lady Grisell Baillie Of Mellerstain And Dryburgh*, for the Melrose Presbytery Campaign Fund 1946; rebound in *Border Booklets.*

D. P. Thomson, *Sweet Singer Of Melrose: The Story Of Elizabeth Clephane And Her Famous Hymn,* for the Melrose Presbytery Campaign Fund 1946; rebound in *Border Booklets.*

D. P. Thomson, *Those Ministers Of Galashiels!* for the Melrose Presbytery Campaign Fund 1946; rebound in *Ministers and Ministers' Wives* and in *Border Booklets.*

D. P. Thomson, *George Wishart: The Man Who Roused Scotland*, Edinburgh 1946 at the request of the Wishart Quarter-Centenary Committee; rebound in *From Caithness to Kintyre.*

D. P. Thomson MA (ed. and abridged), *Death and the Life Beyond – what the New Testament Teaches by Robert Law DD*, Glasgow 1947, for the Editor; with profits allocated to the Eric Liddell Memorial Fund.

D. P. Thomson, *Janet Melville Of Aberdeen – And Her Famous Boys' Class*, Edinburgh 1947.

D. P. Thomson, *Labrador To Savage Island. Stories Of The Ships Of Christ. Maritime Missionary Adventure Throughout The World / With . . . Illustrations By Robert Marshall,* Pickering & Inglis, London 1947.

D. P. Thomson, *Visitation Evangelism Or Tackling The Parochial Problem: A Report On The North Kelvinside (Glasgow) Experiment,* Glasgow 1947.

D. P. Thomson, *Goodwin Sands To Solomon Islands. More Stories Of The Ships Of Christ. Maritime Missionary Adventure Throughout The World / With . . . Illustrations By Robert Marshall*, Pickering & Inglis, London 1948.

D. P. Thomson, *The Church On The Sands; The Summer Seaside Work Of The Church Of Scotland,* Glasgow 1948 (2nd edition, revised).

D. P. Thomson, *The New Evangelism [I] Beginning With The Ministry*, Crieff c.1950; rebound in *Aids to Evangelism* and incorporated in *Aspects of Evangelism.*

D. P. Thomson, *The New Evangelism [II] Incarnational Evangelism,* Crieff c.1950; rebound in *Aids to Evangelism* and incorporated in *Aspects of Evangelism.*

D. P. Thomson, *The Road To Dunfermline : The Story Of A Thirty-Five Years' Quest. Pt.1, An Evangelist In Training, 1916-1933*, Crieff 1952.

D. P. Thomson, *Border Booklets*, Crieff 1952; a rebinding of *James Guthrie, Alexander Waugh, Those ministers of Galashiels, The lad from Torwoodlee, The Sweet Singer of Melrose, Scotland's First Deaconess.*

D. P. Thomson, *Born In Kirkcaldy. A First Series Of Short Biographical Sketches Of Famous Natives Of The Town And District,* Kirkcaldy 1952.

D. P. Thomson, *Raith And Kirkcaldy: A Second Series Of Short Biographical Studies Of Famous Natives Of The Town And District,* Kirkcaldy 1952.

D. P. Thomson, *By The Water Of Leith. The Life Of A North Edinburgh Parish*, Edinburgh 1952.

D. P. Thomson *It Happened In Kintyre*, Glasgow 1952; rebound in *From Caithness to Kintyre.*

D. P. Thomson, *Kintyre Through The Centuries,* Glasgow 1952; rebound in *From Caithness to Kintyre.*

D. P. Thomson, *Men Christ Wants. Evangelistic Addresses,* Pickering & Inglis, Glasgow 1952; reprinting of 1937 edition.

D. P. Thomson, *On The Slopes Of The Sidlaws – On Some Of The Ministers Of The District,* Crieff 1953; rebound in *From Caithness to Kintyre.*

D. P. Thomson, *They Came From Caithness. A Gallery Of Northern Notables, Being Pen Portraits Of Famous Caithnessians,* Crieff 1954; rebound in *From Caithness to Kintyre.*

D. P. Thomson (ed.), *The Voice of the Pew: What Christ and His Church Mean to Me: A Work and Witness Symposium By A Doctor And A Shop Assistant, A Clerk And A Mathematics Master*, Crieff 1954; rebound in *Aids to Evangelism.*

D. P. Thomson (ed.), *We saw the church in action! The Press and BBC report on those visitation campaigns 1947 to 1954*, Crieff 1954/55; rebound in *Visitation Evangelism in Scotland.*

D. P. Thomson, *Guidance For Those Engaged In House-To-House Visitation Campaigns,* Crieff 1955; rebound in *Visitation Evangelism in Scotland* and in *Aids to Evangelism.*

D. P. Thomson (prepared by), *New Testament Conversions. A Question Course Handbook For Preachers, Teachers, Personal Workers and Counsellors, And Bible Study Groups*, Crieff 1955; rebound in *Aids to Evangelism.*

D. P. Thomson (ed.), *Scottish Devotional Treasury. 1st series. Arranged in the form of a month's daily devotional readings from the great Scottish preachers and writers*, Crieff 1955.

D. P. Thomson, *Tales Of The Far North-West. A Sutherlandshire Miscellany. Stories Of The Church In Sutherland.* Crieff 1955; rebound in *From Caithness to Kintyre.*

D. P. Thomson (ed.), *Two by two! The rank and file of the church report on what happened when they went out visiting*, Crieff 1955; rebound in *Visitation Evangelism in Scotland.*

D. P. Thomson (ed.), *You are going out visiting? Let us tell you a little about it! By (1) Elders of the Kirk, (2) Women of the Guild, (3) The Young People*; Crieff 1955; rebound in *Visitation Evangelism in Scotland.*

D. P. Thomson, *The Road Ahead: A Word To Those Who Are Beginning The Christian Life*, Crieff 1955; republished in *Personal Work for Christ* and *Aspects of Evangelism.*

D. P. Thomson, *A Pocket Guide For Personal Workers And Counsellors Engaged In After Meeting And Enquiry Room Work,* Crieff 1955, 1958, 1962 ('completing 18,000 copies'); republished in *Personal Work for Christ* and *Aspects of Evangelism.*

D. P. Thomson, *Visitation Campaigns: a study guide for congregational groups and youth fellowships*, Crieff c.1955.

D. P. Thomson, *Beginning The Christian Life: A First Month's Daily Bible Reading From The New Testament For The Young Disciple,* Crieff 1955 & The Research Unit Crieff 1967; rebound in *Aids to Evangelism.*

D. P. Thomson, *The Sutherland Adventure. The 'Tell Scotland' Campaign In The Presbytery Of Tongue, August 1955 / With Contributions By David Maxwell . . . And Other Members Of The Team,* Crieff 1956; rebound in *Visitation Evangelism in Scotland.*

D. P. Thomson, *West Highland Adventure. The 'Tell Scotland' Campaign In Mull And Iona, Coll And Tiree, Morvern And Ardnamurchan, Spring, 1956, Etc,* Crieff 1956.

D. P. Thomson, *Visitation Evangelism In Scotland,* Crieff 1956; being a rebinding of *Guidance For Those Engaged In House-To-House Visitation Campaigns*, *You Are Going Out Visiting?*, *Two By Two*, *We Saw The Church In Action*, *The Sutherland Adventure*, and *West Highland Adventure.* My copy contains the ms inscription: 'To Tom Allan – friend and colleague – with whom the first so far-reaching venture in this new medium was made. DPT, August 1956.'

D. P. Thomson, *Aids To Evangelism*, Crieff 1956; being a rebinding of *Beginning With The Ministry*, *The Way Of The Incarnation*, *Men Christ Wants*, *New Testament Conversions*, *Beginning The Christian Life*, *The Voice Of The Pew*, and *Guidance For Those Engaged In House-To-House Visitation.*

D. P. Thomson (prepared by), *Epistle To The Philippians. A Four Week Question Course For 'Tell Scotland' Training Schools And Campaigns And For Preachers, Teachers, Bible Students And Bible Study Groups*, Crieff 1956.

D. P. Thomson, *Iona To Ardnamurchan By Mull, Coll, And Tiree. A Pilgrimage Through The Centuries,* Crieff 1956.

D. P. Thomson, *From Caithness To Kintyre: Historical And Geographical Studies,* prob. Crieff 1956; being a rebinding of *They Came From Caithness*, *Tales Of The Far North-West*, *George Wishart*, *On The Slopes Of The Sidlaws*, *It Happened In Kintyre*, and *Kintyre Through The Centuries.*

D. P. Thomson, *Orkney Through The Centuries. Lights And Shadows Of The Church's Life In The Northern Isles,* Crieff 1956; rebound in *Orkney to Iona.*

D. P. Thomson, *From Island To Island! Experiences And Adventures Of The 'Tell Scotland' Summer Campaign Team In Orkney. July To September, 1956 . . . With Map And Illustrations,* Crieff 1956.

D. P. Thomson (prepared by), *The Parables Of Jesus. A Question Course For Preachers, Teachers, Bible Students And Bible Study Groups*, Crieff 1956.

D. P. Thomson, *Harnessing The Lay Forces Of The Church. Experiences, Adventures And Discoveries In The Work Of Visitation Evangelism In Scotland, 1946-57*, Crieff 1958.

D. P. Thomson, *Visitation Evangelism In Scotland*, prob. Crieff after 1958; a rebinding of *We Saw The Church In Action*, *The Sutherland Adventure*, *West Highland Adventure*, *From Island To Island!* and *Harnessing The Lay Forces Of The Church.*

D. P. Thomson, *What Christ Means To Me. An Open-Air Service Of Christian Witness. Held At Macrosty Park, Crieff On . . . 2nd August 1959 . . . With . . . D. P. Thomson And Others,* St Ninian's Crieff 1959.

D. P. Thomson, *Through Sixteen Centuries: The Story Of The Scottish Church From Earliest Times To The Present Day,* St Ninian's, Crieff 1960.

D. P. Thomson, *Women Of The Scottish Reformation; Their Contribution To The Protestant Cause*, St Ninian's Crieff 1960.

D. P. Thomson, *It Happened In Iona: Forgotten Chapters In The History Of Scotland's Sacred Isle*, St Ninian's Crieff after 1956; rebound in *Orkney to Iona.*

Members and Friends of Work and Witness, *Answered Prayer*, The Book Department St Ninian's, Crieff after 1960.

D. P. Thomson, *David Inglis Cowan: Man And Minister, 1892-1950,* St Ninian's Crieff 1961.

D. P. Thomson (prepared by), *The Gospel of St. John. A Leaflet for the use of Bible Study Groups,* St Ninian's Crieff c. 1962.

D. P. Thomson (prepared by), *The Ten Commandments: A Question Course For Preachers, Teachers, Bible Students And Bible Study Groups,* St Ninian's Crieff 1962.

D. P. Thomson, *21 Topics for Discussion Groups*, St Ninian's Crieff, 1962.

D. P. Thomson (ed.), *Why I believe / Tom Allan, James S. Stewart and D. P. Thomson, discussing personal Christian belief with Ian Pitt-Watson on B.B.C. Scottish Television, 1962-3,* St Ninian's Crieff 1963; rebound in *Ministers and Ministers' Wives.*

D. P. Thomson (ed.), *Tomorrow's Ministers: Who are they? What are they thinking? What shall we say to them?,* St Ninian's Crieff 1963; rebound in *Ministers and Ministers' Wives.*

D. P. Thomson (ed.), *The Minister's Wife: Her Live, Work & Problems,* St Ninian's Crieff 1964; rebound in *Ministers and Ministers' Wives.*

[D. P. Thomson], *Life And Work At St Ninian's Crieff,* St Ninian's Crieff 1965.

D. P. Thomson, *The Church In The Open Air,* St Ninian's Crieff 1965.

D. P. Thomson (prepared by), *The Epistle to the Romans chapters 12 to 16; a question course for preachers, teachers, Bible students and Bible Study Groups*, St Ninian's Crieff 1965.

D. P. Thomson (ed.), *Women as Elders: The Verdict of Experience*, St Ninian's Crieff 1965.

D. P. Thomson (ed.), *Women Ministers in Scotland: Personal Records of Experience and Discovery,* St Ninian's Crieff 1965.

D. P. Thomson, *Dr Billy Graham And The Pattern Of Modern Evangelism*, St Ninian's Crieff 1966.

D. P. Thomson, *Lady Glenorchy And Her Churches,* The Research Unit, Crieff 1967.

D. P. Thomson, *Personal Encounters: Reminiscences Of 70 Years,* The Research Unit, Crieff 1967.

D. P. Thomson, *Aspects Of Evangelism*, The Research Unit, Crieff 1968; includes material from *A Pocket Guide for Personal Workers* and *The Road Ahead*; and borrows from DP's writing back to *Evangelism in the Modern World.*

D. P. Thomson, *Personal Work For Christ*, The Research Unit, Crieff 1968; republishing material from *Aspects of Evangelism.*

D. P. Thomson, *When Christ Calls. Evangelistic Addresses,* The Research Unit, Crieff 1968.

D. P. Thomson, *The Radical Reappraisal Report: Churches Under The Spotlight: A New Approach To Congregational And Parish Life,* The Research Unit, Crieff 1969.

D. P. Thomson (ed.), *First Communion: The Preparation And Admission Of New Communicants; Report And Comment By 120 Ministers Of The Church Of Scotland,* The Research Unit, Crieff 1969.

D. P. Thomson (ed.), *100 Topics For Discussion: A Handbook For Study Circles, House Groups, Training Classes, Conferences And Training Schools,* The Research Unit, Crieff 1970.

D. P. Thomson, *Scotland's Greatest Athlete: The Eric Liddell Story,* The Research Unit, Crieff (paperback) 1970.

D. P. Thomson, *Eric H. Liddell: Athlete & Missionary,* The Research Unit, Crieff 1971; hardback version of *Scotland's Greatest Athlete.*

D. P. Thomson, *The Beadle Yesterday And Today*, The Research Unit, Crieff 1971.

D. P. Thomson, *New Testament Christianity: 60 Short Studies,* The Research Unit, Crieff 1971.

D. P. Thomson, *Ministers And Ministers' Wives*, [Crieff c.1972]; rebinding of *James Guthrie, Those Ministers of Galashiels!, The Lad from Torwoodlee, Why I Believe, Tomorrow's Ministers, The Minister's Wife.*

D. P. Thomson, *Orkney To Iona: Studies In Regional Scottish Church History*, [Crieff c.1972]; rebinding of *George Wishart, Women of the Reformation, Orkney through the Centuries, It happened in Iona.*

D. P. Thomson (ed.), *The Elder's Wife: her place in the life and work of the Church*, The Research Unit, Crieff 1973.

D. P. Thomson, *Women Of The Scottish Church,* for the D. P. Thomson Estate 1975; posthumously with an 'Introductory Memoir' by Ian B. Doyle.

Other members of D. P. Thomson's family – list of printed publications

James Thomson, *Practical Handbook For Justices Of The Peace In Scotland,* Edinburgh & Glasgow 1920.

James Pringle Thomson, *Alexander Henderson, The Covenanter*, Edinburgh & London 1912.

James Pringle Thomson, *The Scottish Covenanters 1637-1688,* London 1914.

James Pringle Thomson, *The Jacobite Rebellions 1689-1746,* London 1914.

Christine Jane Thomson, *Still-Birth And Neo-Natal Death In India: A Preliminary Enquiry*, New Delhi & London 1931; sponsored by the Lady Irwin Research Fund, The Countess of Dufferin's Fund Council.

SOURCES

Private collections

The D. P. Thomson Archive, c/o the Church of Scotland Council on Mission and Discipleship, The Church of Scotland Offices, 121 George Street, Edinburgh.

Minutes of the Church of Scotland Committee on Home Mission, c/o the Church of Scotland Council on Mission and Discipleship, The Church of Scotland Offices, 121 George Street, Edinburgh.

Minutes of the Church of Scotland Home Board, c/o the Church of Scotland Council on Mission and Discipleship, The Church of Scotland Offices, 121 George Street, Edinburgh.

Public collections

MacLeod of Fuinary and Iona Community National Library of Scotland, acc. 9084.

The Tom Allan Archive New College Library, University of Edinburgh.

The John White Papers New College Library, University of Edinburgh.

T. Ralph Morton Papers The Centre for the Study of Christianity in the Non-Western World [CSCNWW], New College, University of Edinburgh.

The Tell Scotland Archive Deposited by Action of Churches Together in Scotland at the Centre for the Study of Christianity in the Non-Western World [CSCNWW], New College, University of Edinburgh.

Minutes of Church of Scotland Presbyteries and Kirk Sessions

were examined at the National Archives of Scotland, Edinburgh, with the exception of those from Orkney and Shetland, held by the respective local authorities in the Orkney Archive, Kirkwall, and the Shetland Archive, Lerwick.

SOME SECONDARY SOURCES

Reference

The Church of Scotland: Reports to the General Assembly, Edinburgh. Annual series published by the Church of Scotland.

The Church of Scotland Year-Book, Edinburgh. Annual series published by the Church of Scotland.

Dictionary of Scottish Church History and Theology, ed. N. M. de S. Cameron *et al.*, Edinburgh, 1993.

The Dundee Directory. Annual series, published in Dundee and consulted at the Dundee Archives, the Dundee Central Library.

Fasti Ecclesiae Scoticanae, ed. Hew Scott *et al.*, vols. 1-11, 1915-2000.

The Fasti of the United Free Church of Scotland 1900-1929, ed. John A. Lamb, 2 volumes, Edinburgh 1956,

Reports to the General Assembly of the United Free Church of Scotland, Edinburgh. Annual series published by the United Free Church of Scotland.

Scottish Life and Society: Religion, ed. C. MacLean and K. Veitch, Edinburgh 2006 as volume 12 of *A Compendium of Scottish Ethnology*.

Magazines

The Congregational News Review, Church of Scotland North Kelvinside Parish (courtesy of Rev. Bill and Mrs Betsy Shannon)

Coracle: The Journal of The Iona Community

Life & Work: the Record of the Church of Scotland

The Monthly Record of the Home and Foreign Mission Work of the United Free Church of Scotland

The Scottish Baptist Magazine

The Scottish Churchman

The Scottish Congregationalist

Stedfast: The Record of the United Free Church of Scotland

Newspapers (weekly)

The British Weekly (Scottish edition)

The Cambuslang Advertiser

Dundee Advertiser

The Dundee Courier and Argus

Dunfermline Press and West Fife Advertiser

The Forfar Dispatch

The Glasgow Herald

Kirriemuir Free Press and Angus Advertiser

The Montrose Review and Angus & Kincardineshire Advertiser

The Oban Times & West Highland Times

The Orcadian

The Orkney Herald

The Scots Observer: the Churches Weekly

The Scotsman

The Shetland Times

The Stirling Observer

Books and theses

Allan, Tom, (ed.), *Crusade in Scotland . . . Billy Graham*, London 1955.

Allan, Tom, *The Face of My Parish*, London 1954 / Glasgow 1984.

Allan, Tom & Meikle, Henry B., 'Tell Scotland Movement', recorded at Aberdeen 31 October 1954; held at William Smith Morton Library, Union-PSCE, Richmond, Virginia USA.

Allen, G.F., 'The Groups in Oxford' in Crossman, R.H.S., (ed.), *Oxford and the Groups: the influence of the Groups considered*, Oxford 1934.

Anderson, D., Wright, D. *et al*, *Death or Glory: studies honouring the contribution of Dr Geoffrey Grogan to the Church / The Church's mission in Scotland's changing society*, Fearn & Edinburgh 2001.

Baillie, John, *Invitation to Pilgrimage*, London 1942.

Barbour, R., *J. S. Stewart in a Nutshell*, Edinburgh 2000.

Barclay, J. B., *Mary: A Biographical Memoir*, Edinburgh 2004, limited circulation.

Barclay, O., *Evangelicalism in Britain 1935-1995, a personal sketch*, Leicester 1997.

Bardgett, F. D., 'D. P. Thomson and the Orkney Expedition – a *Tell Scotland* case study' in Records of the Scottish Church History Society 2010.

Bardgett, F. D., *Devoted Service Rendered: the Lay Missionaries of the Church of Scotland*, Edinburgh 2002.

Bardgett, F. D., 'Missions and Missionaries: Home' in *Scottish Life and Society: Religion.*

Bardgett, F. D., 'Tell Scotland: Failure and Success' in Records of the Scottish Church History Society 2008.

Bardgett, F. D., *Two Millennia of Church and Community in Orkney*, Durham etc 2000.

Bebbington, D. W., *Evangelicalism in Modern Britain: a history from the 1730s to the 1980s*, London & New York 1989.

Bebbington, D. W., 'The persecution of George Jackson: a British Fundamentalist Controversy', in W. J. Sheils (ed.), *Persecution and Toleration*, Oxford 1984.

Bebbington, D. W., 'The Oxford Group Movement between the wars', in Sheils and Wood (eds.), *Voluntary Religion: Papers read at the 1985 Summer and 1986 Winter Meetings of the Ecclesiastical History Society*, Oxford 1986.

Begbie, H., *Life Changers: Narratives of a Recent Movement in the Spirit of Personal Religion*, London 1923.

Berg, Thomas C., 'Proclaiming Together? Convergence and Divergence in Mainline and Evangelical Evangelism, 1945-1967' in *Religion and American Culture*, vol. 5, no 1 (winter 1995).

Bisset, P., *The Kirk and her Scotland*, Edinburgh 1986.

Blackie, Nansie, (ed.), *A Time for Trumpets*, Edinburgh 2005.

Brown, C. G., *The Death of Christian Britain*, London & New York 2001.

Brown, C. G., *The Social History of Religion in Scotland since 1730*, London and New York 1987.

Brown, J. C., *The Oxford Group Movement: Is it of God or Satan*, London, Glasgow and Edinburgh 1932.

Brown, John E., *A Time to Serve: a collection of Sunday Sermons*, Edinburgh 1994.

Cheyne, A. C., *Studies in Scottish Church History*, Edinburgh 1999.

Cheyne, A. C., *The Transforming of the Kirk*, Edinburgh 1983.

Church of Scotland, *The Call to the Church: the Book of the Forward Movement of the Church of Scotland,* Edinburgh 1931.

Church of Scotland / Commission for the Interpretation of God's Will in the Present Crisis, *God's Will for our Time*, London 1942.

Church of Scotland / Commission for the Interpretation of God's Will in the Present Crisis, *The Church Faces the Future*, London 1943.

Church of Scotland / Commission for the Interpretation of God's Will in the Present Crisis, *Home, Community and Church*, London 1944.

Church of Scotland / Commission for the Interpretation of God's Will in the Present Crisis, *God's Will for Church and Nation*, London 1946.

Church of Scotland / Home Board / Alexander, V. C., *What the Church Expects of the Church member*, *'New Evangelism series'*, Edinburgh 1947.

Church of Scotland / Home Board / Davidson, N., *The Parish Church*, *'New Evangelism series'*, Edinburgh 1947.

Church of Scotland / Home Board / Riddell, J. G., *Your Parish Needs You*, *'New Evangelism series'*, Edinburgh 1947.

Church of Scotland / Home Board / Vernon, E. T., *The Practical Witness of a Christian*, *'New Evangelism series'*, Edinburgh 1947.

Church of Scotland / Joint Committee on Evangelism, *Into All The World: A Statement on Evangelism*, Glasgow 1946.

Church of Scotland / Sissons, P. L., *The Social Significance of Church Membership in the Burgh of Falkirk*, Edinburgh 1973.

Clow, W. M., *The Cross in Christian Experience*, London 1908.

Coalter, M. J. (ed. *et al.*), *The Diversity of Discipleship: The Presbyterians and Twentieth-Century Christian Witness*, Kentucky 1991.

Coffey, William, *God's Conman: the life and work of the Reverend James Currie*, Moffat 1988.

Coffin, H. S., *The Portraits of Jesus Christ in the New Testament*, New York 1926.

Colquhoun, F., *Harringay Story: The official record of the Billy Graham Greater London Crusade 1954*, London 1955.

Denney, James, *Studies in Theology: lectures delivered in Chicago Theological Seminary*, London 1894.

Dinwiddie, Melville, *Religion by Radio: its place in British broadcasting*, London 1968.

Drummond, L. A., *Charles Grandison Finney and the Birth of Modern Evangelism*, London 1982.

Dunnett, A. H., *The Church in Changing Scotland*, London [1934].

Duthie, Charles, *Outline of Christian Belief*, London 1968.

Falconer, R., *Message, Media, Mission: the Baird Lectures 1975*, Edinburgh 1977.

Falconer, R., *The Kilt Under My Cassock*, Edinburgh 1978.

Ferguson, Ronald, *George MacLeod: Founder of the Iona Community*, London 1990.

Forsyth, Alexander C., 'To *Rescue The Fallen*: The Sources, Content and Context of the Missiology of Tom Allan (1916-1965)', M.Th. dissertation for Edinburgh University, 2010.

Frame, W. H., *Fire in His Bones: a short biography of D. P. Thomson, Church of Scotland Evangelist,* Dunfermline after 1974.

Fraser, I. M., *Ecumenical Adventure: a Dunblane Initiative*, Action of Churches Together in Scotland 2003.

Fraser, I. M., *People Journeying: a Source Book of Scottish Churches House*, Dunblane 1969, limited loose-leaf publication.

Green, John P., *Fact Stranger Than Fiction: Seventy-Five Years of a Busy Life with Reminiscences of Many Great and Good Men and Women*, Cleveland, Ohio, U.S.A. 1920.

Grubb, N., *C.T. Studd: Cricketer and Pioneer*, London, 16th ed. 1951.

Grubb, N., (ed.), *J.D. Drysdale, Prophet of Holiness*, London 1955.

Harvie, C., *No Gods and Precious Few Heroes: Scotland since 1940*, Edinburgh 1993.

Highet, J., 'The Churches' in Cunnison, J. and Gilfillan, J.B.S., (eds.), *The Third Statistical Account of Scotland: The City of Glasgow*, Glasgow 1958.

Highet, J., *The Churches in Scotland Today*, Glasgow 1950.

Highet, J., *The Scottish Churches: a review of their state 400 years after the Reformation*, London 1960.

Holmes, R., *In the Footsteps of Churchill*, London 2005.

Johnson, D., *Contending for the Faith: a History of the Evangelical Movement in the Universities and Colleges*, Leicester 1979.

Kernahan, A. Earl, *Visitation Evangelism: its methods and results*, New York / Chicago / London / Edinburgh 1925.

Keiser, Jack, *Christian Engagement with the Secular World: the William Temple Foundation and its Origins and History with a Postscript 1990*, The William Temple Foundation Ltd 1990, limited circulation.

Lean, Garth, *Frank Buchman – A Life (The Life of Frank Buchman, a Small Town American who awakened the Conscience of the World),* London 1985.

Longfield, B. J., *The Presbyterian Controversy: Fundamentalists, Modernists & Moderates*, New York & Oxford 1991.

Lynch, M., *Scotland: A New History*, London 1991.

Maitland, J., *Caring for People – the Church in the Parish*, Glasgow 1954.
Maitland, J., *New Beginnings – breaking through into unity: early years in Livingston's ecumenical parish*, Edinburgh 1998.
Macdonald, A., (ed.) *A Fraction of His Image* published for the Magazine Committee of St George's Tron Church, Glasgow after 1964.
McIntyre, David M., *Christ the Crucified*, London 1935.
Mackenzie, Hamish C., *Preaching the Eternities (The Warrack Lectures)*, Edinburgh 1963.
MacLeod, George F., *Are Not the Churchless Million Partly the Church's Fault?*, Edinburgh 1936.
MacLeod, George F: 'Modern Evangelism with particular reference to Scotland', recording made at Union Seminary, 2 January 1955; held at William Smith Morton Library, Union-PSCE, Richmond, Virginia USA.
MacLeod, George F., *Only One Way Left*, Glasgow 1956.
MacLeod, George F., *We shall Re-build: the work of the Iona Community on mainland and on island*, Glasgow 1944.
McLuskey, F., *The Cloud and the Fire: His Path for Me*, Durham 1993.
Morton, T. Ralph, *Evangelism in Scotland Today*, Tell Scotland 1953.
Morton, T. Ralph, *The Household of Faith*, Glasgow 1951.
Morton, T. Ralph, *The Iona Community: personal impressions of the early years*, Edinburgh 1977.
Morton, T. Ralph, *Missionary Principles for the Home Front*, Glasgow 1944.
Morton, T. Ralph & Gibbs, M., *God's Frozen People*, London 1964.
Murray, D., *Freedom to Reform: the 'Articles Declaratory' of the Church of Scotland 1921*, Edinburgh 1993.
Pollock, John, *The Cambridge Seven: centenary edition 1885-1985*, Basingstoke 1985.
Riesen, Richard A., *Professor A. C. Cheyne: An Appreciation*, Edinburgh 2006.
Rowlands, F. W., *The Oxford Group – a First Century Christian Fellowship*, London [1932].
Shannon, Bill, *Tom Allan in a Nutshell*, Handsel Press 2000.
Simpson, P. Carnegie, *The Life of Principal Rainy* vol. I, London 1909.
Small, M., *Growing Together: the Ecumenical Movement in Scotland 1924-1964*, Dunblane 1964, limited publication.
Small, R. Leonard, *No Uncertain Sound*, Edinburgh 1963.
Stewart, J. S., *A Faith to Proclaim*, London 1953.

Still, William, *Dying to Live*, Fearn 1991.

Tell Scotland / Allan, Tom, *The Agent of Mission: The Lay Group in Evangelism, its Significance and its Task*, Tell Scotland 1954.

Tell Scotland / Allan, Tom, *The Congregational Group in Action,* Tell Scotland Glasgow 1955.

Tell Scotland / Commission on the Bible (Gunn, G. S.), *Truth in Action*, The Scottish Churches Tell Scotland Movement 1960.

Tell Scotland / Commission on the Community (Fraser, I. M.), *Calling You In*, The Scottish Churches Tell Scotland Movement 1960.

Tell Scotland / Commission on Evangelism (Macdonald, M. E.), *The Lost Provinces*, The Scottish Churches Tell Scotland Movement 1960.

Tell Scotland / Commission on the Laity (Dinwiddie, M.), *The Layman at Work,* The Scottish Churches Tell Scotland Movement 1960.

Tell Scotland / Stewart J. S., *The Missionary Church*, Tell Scotland c.1953.

Tell Scotland / *Strategy for Mission*, Tell Scotland c.1953.

Templeton, E., *God's February: a life of Archie Craig 1886-1985*, London 1991.

Thomson, Scott, *Church Standing Tall: a people's history of St John's in the City 1853-2003,* Wellington Aotearoa New Zealand 2003.

Vincent, Eileen, *C.T. Studd and Priscilla: United to Fight for Jesus*, Bromley 1988.

Weatherhead, J. L., *The Constitution and Laws of the Church of Scotland*, Edinburgh 1997.

Wood, H. Stanley, 'Leadership Profile of Church Extension Ministers in the Church of Scotland 1945-1965', Ph.D. thesis for Aberdeen University 1996, restricted publication.

Wood, M.A.P., *Like a Mighty Army*, London 1955.

World Council of Churches, Secretariat for Evangelism, *Ecumenical Studies, Evangelism in Scotland*, Geneva 1954.

Wright, D. & Gray, A. (eds.), *Local Church Evangelism, Patterns and Approaches*, Edinburgh 1987.

D. P. Thomson Analytical Index

Select Index